SELECTIVE PERSECUTION

The Legalization of AMERICAN FASCISM

SIMONE GOLD, MD, JD

FOREWORD BY DENNIS PRAGER

Skyhorse Publishing

Skyhorse Publishing books may be purchased in bulk at special discounts for sales promotion, corporate gifts, fund-raising, or educational purposes. Special editions can also be created to specifications. For details, contact the Special Sales Department, Skyhorse Publishing, 307 West 36th Street, 11th Floor, New York, NY 10018 or info@skyhorsepublishing.com

Visit our website at www.skyhorsepublishing.com.
Please follow our publisher Tony Lyons on Instagram @tonylyonsisuncertain.

10 9 8 7 6 5 4 3 2 1

Library of Congress Cataloging-in-Publication Data is available on file.

Hardcover ISBN: 978-1-5107-8432-1
eBook ISBN: 978-1-5107-8433-8

Cover design by David Ter-Avanesyan

Printed in the United States of America

This book is dedicated to the Ordinary American.
For you are the repository of freedom.

Contents

Foreword
by Dennis Prager

In every generation, our society has had to decide whether it will stand for its foundational principles or abandon them out of fear, ideology, or mere convenience. This book is about such a moment in America's history.

The United States was founded on an extraordinary moral premise: that every human being possesses inherent rights granted by God. Chief among these rights is equal treatment under the law. Without this, freedom cannot exist. When justice is applied selectively, based on a person's race, wealth, beliefs, affiliations, or political leanings, freedom erodes.

The greatness of a nation is not determined by its economic strength or military might. It is determined by its commitment to justice and freedom—the ideals enshrined in America's founding documents. Periodically these principles come under siege. This book chronicles such a moment: specifically, the selective persecution of January 6 defendants.

Regardless of how one views the actions of those involved, the response by the federal government exposed a far graver danger: the weaponization of the justice system against citizens based on their beliefs. This is the very definition of selective justice, and it marks a profound departure from the ideals upon which America was founded.

Consider the facts: Militarized SWAT teams arrested nonviolent offenders, and judges imprisoned those who were either convicted of or pled guilty to nonviolent misdemeanors, including those with no prior criminal record. The conviction rate was as absolute as the show trials of dictatorships, as was gratuitous cruelty—some of those imprisoned were put into solitary confinement for months for no legitimate reason. These are the hallmarks of a police state.

Beyond the courtroom, defendants faced a cascade of extrajudicial punishments. They were barred from flying, labeled as terrorists, had their bank accounts closed, were fired by their employers, ostracized by their communities, and subjected by the media to relentless humiliation. As a result, more than a few killed themselves.

Sadly, many Americans accepted or even celebrated these injustices—because they were being applied to "the other side." This is not only a profound moral failing, it is extremely dangerous. The principle of equal justice under the law cannot be a partisan issue. To abandon it for political gain would set a precedent that will eventually come for everyone, regardless of their politics.

It is easy to rationalize injustice when it targets those we dislike or disagree with. Once a society accepts selective justice, it is only a matter of time before the machinery of repression expands to include others. America's Founders understood this. They knew that government power must be constrained or both liberty and justice end.

In my view, Dr. Simone Gold, the author of *Selective Persecution: The Legalization of American Fascism* is one of the most courageous and principled voices for truth and justice. As a physician, attorney, and advocate, she works tirelessly to save lives, defend individual rights, and expose institutional corruption. As readers will see, her experience as a January 6 defendant is a perfect example of selective prosecution. Her story should be a wake-up call to all Americans who want to preserve America as a free country. This story, and that of more than a thousand others, demonstrates how quickly a free country can become a police state. Ronald Reagan was right: We are always but one generation away from losing our freedom.

Dr. Gold was subjected to a terrifying arrest—her door broken open with a battering ram, a dozen FBI swat officers swarming and shouting orders, red laser dots from weapons trained on her body—was sentenced to sixty days in a maximum-security federal penitentiary and, once there, subjected to solitary confinement. This is the type of arrest and punishment normally meted out to the most violent criminals. Yet, all Dr. Gold was guilty of was "entering and remaining in a restricted building." She engaged in no violence whatsoever.

Moreover, prior to January 6, 2021, Dr. Gold had no criminal record of any kind. She was, in fact, an exemplary citizen. She had spent her career taking care of patients in emergency rooms. The most that could be said about her behavior on January 6 is that she possibly committed a minor infraction—left-wing demonstrators who illegally entered congressional offices in November 2018 protesting the nomination of Brett Kavanaugh to the Supreme Court were issued tickets with nominal fines. Dr. Gold presents further evidence of America's drift toward a police state. She offers proof of US prosecutors lying and DC judges so ignorant and so biased as to require impeachment. Finally, she was subjected to public humiliation as a tool of state-sanctioned retribution.

Like Dr. Gold, the overwhelming majority of January 6 protestors were present to exercise their constitutional right to assemble and protest. The USA has a robust history of political protest, which sometimes spills over into civil disobedience, and it is rare in the post-Civil Rights era for the police to make arrests. In contrast to the violent "summer of love" protests six months prior to January 6 carried out across the country in the wake of the death of George Floyd, no January 6 protestors had guns. In fact, not one J6 protestor took any actions toward insurrection, which is why not a single one was charged with insurrection.

Yet more than 1,500 American J6 protestors were attacked (in some cases physically; in all cases, legally) by their own government. What do I mean by attacked? On January 6, Capitol Hill Police opened fire with rubber bullets and tear gas on people peacefully milling about below the Capitol long before there was any disturbance by the crowd—in fact, before President Trump finished his speech at the Ellipse forty-five minutes walking distance away. In carrying out the FBI's arrests, heavily armed SWAT teams stormed their homes in the dead of night. Law-abiding citizens were handcuffed, shackled, and perp walked in front of their terrified children and shocked neighbors. Many were held in solitary confinement for months. Show trials occurred in Washington, DC, the most reliably left-wing jurisdiction in the country, predictably resulting in a 100 percent conviction rate. Judges publicly made biased statements about defendants appearing before them and issued rulings they had never made in their entire careers—such as denying bond hearings and holding the accused in indefinite pretrial detention. The media apparatus defamed and mocked these people so viciously that, as noted, several defendants killed themselves. Our legal and media system was weaponized against individuals who held the "wrong" opinions. Such practices are more than un-American; they are the practices of a police state.

For decades, I have warned that freedom is not the natural state of humanity. Most people do not yearn to be free; they yearn to be taken care of. Freedom must be nurtured, fought for, and defended, or it will be lost. The treatment of these defendants reveals how easily institutions meant to protect liberty can be turned into instruments of repression when ideology replaces morality.

Justice must be blind, or it ceases to be justice. Power must be restrained, or it becomes tyranny. And liberty must be defended, or it will vanish.

Indeed, it almost did.

One of the lessons of life I have come to is that virtually all good is accomplished by outliers. Simone Gold is one such example. The world is better because she is in it.

Preface

Power tends to corrupt and absolute power corrupts absolutely.
—Lord Acton to Bishop Creighton, 1887

While this book is my story, I tell it for a purpose bigger than me. When 2020 arrived, I stood at a very specific intersection. I had been a highly trained board-certified emergency physician for more than twenty years, and I was legally trained as an attorney. I was living in a very progressive (i.e., backward) city, and I had worked for many years at a poor, inner-city hospital that the CDC mistreated during the Ebola scare. As the daughter of a Holocaust survivor, I grew up knowing the most meaningful thing I could do with my life was help others. I was a typical private citizen, working hard and raising two children. I had good friends and family, meaningful work, and a pristine reputation. Life was good. And then I came face to face with large-scale evil, although I did not know how large at the time.

During COVID, I saw hospital executives craft policies that killed their own patients, especially Medicare patients. I saw doctors and nurses become cold and uncaring about their patients. I saw governors promulgate edicts that sentenced hundreds of thousands of nursing home patients to death. I saw public health officials lie to the public. I learned that the origin and destination of "public health" is fascism. I saw many federal government health agencies, including the CDC, NIH, FDA, HHS, and CMS, set policies that killed and harmed many millions of people. And the biggest threat I saw was the media parroting these lies instead of having journalistic curiosity.

I experienced severe censorship by Big Tech including Facebook, YouTube, Instagram, TikTok, LinkedIn, Twitter (pre-Elon), as well as severe defamation by all media including *The New York Times*, CNN, Huffington Post, *The Intercept*, ABC, MSNBC, the Associated Press, and the BBC. I am one of the most censored and defamed people in the country. Many federal government agencies, including the FBI, DOJ, BOP, DHS, and TSA, were weaponized specifically against me. I was also targeted by Congress and various state government agencies, including the California Medical Board and New York Bar. Chapter by chapter my story reveals the anarcho-tyranny that underlies our American lives. What I have gone through could not have happened unless multiple socio-political-cultural institutions had failed.

My story reveals the fascist infrastructure that is the scaffolding to American life. During my lifetime, America has become fascist-corporatist on the outside and socialist on the inside. This is roughly parallel to China, which has long been communist on the outside and fascist on the inside. Although fascism, communism, and tyranny proselytize different beliefs, from the perspective of an average citizen, it does not matter which structure exists. If too much power rests in one authority, it's a dictatorship, or nearly. So I simply call it fascist.

From COVID policies, wherein a whole nation followed the most obviously foolish edicts of government bureaucrats of the executive branch; to J6 prosecutions, wherein a whole bench of judges followed the most obviously biased edicts of weaponized government bureaucrats of the Executive Branch; to media propaganda, where almost every news outlet repeated the same slogans given to them by a handful of bureaucrats; we are seeing whole swaths of the population and entire agencies follow the edicts of a tiny ruling class.

Each chapter of this book describes something I directly experienced, and the details of each experience demonstrate the tyrannical environment swirling around us. I share my story so you will see what I have seen. Once you have seen it, you will feel an urgency to push it back. While you will vacillate between feeling incredulous to feeling furious, you will not feel pessimistic—you will feel empowered. There is so much opportunity to reclaim our freedom! Although it is under severe attack, our Constitution still lives. And my story is not depressing—it's astonishing.

I have done my best to provide proof of everything I say in this book. I have attached links and references throughout,* and many documents and links can be found as appendices at my website.** For instance, there is a video compiled from the government's closed-circuit TV so you can watch my entire time in the Capitol. You can see me giving my speech in the Rotunda. What happened to me following this speech was so methodically punishing, it could not have happened unless the *infrastructure* for fascism was already in place throughout our nation. While this book is a story I have lived, it is also a historical reference—and these references are part of *your* history as well.

Everything about our Constitution is genius—but the most genius of all is that political power is not vested in a single person or entity. Decentralized decision-making allows for independence, innovation, and better decision-making. On paper, we have a Constitutional Republic that guarantees us freedom from government tyranny, so to lose our freedom requires citizens' cooperation. That is exactly what is happening. How? Using censorship and propaganda, tyrants exploit the intrinsic human fear of being a victim of social ridicule to control people. This is known as cancel culture. Avoiding being "canceled" has become *the* top priority for Americans. That's very unfortunate. Because while enduring cancel culture is unpleasant, it is far preferable to temporarily walk through the fire than to be permanently engulfed by the flames.

Everyone must understand that what happens is the best possible outcome given the circumstances. I did *not* watch silently when other doctors lied to patients. I did *not* stay silent when Anthony Fauci and his posse killed millions. I did *not* do nothing when my enemies blackmailed me to try to destroy me. My soul and my integrity are intact, and I am stronger than ever.

---

* E-readers can click on the hyperlinked words. All readers, including print readers, can find the URLs listed in the endnotes at the back of book.

** Readers will find this notation in parentheses (see DrGoldReferences) throughout the book indicating appendices that can be read at my website. https://drgold.vercel.app/book/resources/

All the persecution I endured required the compliance of ordinary Americans. Sometimes this complacency is out of ignorance (censorship or propaganda), but more often you have not done what you should have done because of the fear of being canceled. It is for that reason I'm going to show you all the nastiness I endured—precisely so you can understand that *anyone* can survive being victimized by even very dark forces. You must not let fear of gossip, in modern times known as cancel culture, stop you from doing what must be done. Self-censorship contributes to the selective persecution of people like me, and that is moving us closer to fascism.

I write this book to demonstrate that American Fascism is occurring without the passion of a Mussolini or Hitler or Stalin or Pol Pot. American Fascism will not be obvious, like China's Xi Jinping removing his own term limits. It will appear more subtly in our nation, specifically through our "public health" institutions, like the former CDC director admitting his lethal scam to the world and never being punished, while a truth-teller like me is severely punished. Americans are obediently allowing ourselves to be shepherded into a world of doublespeak, groupthink, cancel culture, silence, and subservience. The external tools of our oppression are already in place: centralized power, digital currency, evaporating middle class, and government reliance for necessities. And the number one reason we are allowing this is that we don't want to be canceled: socially, culturally, or economically.

Human freedom for a very diverse citizenry can only be accomplished with a Constitutional Republic that guarantees inalienable rights to *all* people. If this is to be more than mere words on a paper, Americans must insist that all people are treated equally under the law. Every American must stand up for every other American's inalienable right to be treated equally, so collectively we can stop tyrants from using these tools to oppress us. I am living proof that you can do this—both effectively and joyfully.

This book will help you recognize the fascist infrastructure that already exists in America—and empower you to actively reject it when you are called upon to advance a tyrannical goal.

Welcome to my world. Buckle up.

Introduction

In 2020, I decided to sidestep the media and organize doctors and social media influencers to meet in Washington, DC, for a White Coat Summit. This was an entire day of physicians educating, lecturing, speaking on topics such as masks, lockdowns, schools, children, the healthy elderly, the frail elderly, early treatment, and Africa models. In the middle of the education day, we walked over to the Supreme Court steps and held a press conference. In eight hours, we had 20 million views, becoming the most rapidly viral video of all time.

Between seven and eight ET that night, all the big tech companies deplatformed us within one hour of each other. All these different companies, ostensibly competitors, acted as a single entity. Our 20 million views just stopped—we were suddenly off Instagram, Facebook, YouTube, Twitter, even LinkedIn, Squarespace, everywhere. And then within hours, I was attacked by everyone, and I mean everyone. There wasn't *anyone* sizable who didn't slander me. I was a quack, a lunatic, fringe, right wing, conspiracy theorist, evil, you name it. And my personal life trajectory changed overnight.

The day before, strangers applauded my heroism. The day after, I was mocked.

The day before, I ran the COVID ward in two hospitals. The day after, I was fired.

The day before, I had a pristine reputation. The day after, I did not.

You cannot find a negative word printed about me until that date. Now you search my name in any browser and lies about me abound. The defamation intensified into outright persecution after January 6. (Here's a nifty trick. When doing a Google search, if you want a more accurate result, include "before:2020" at the beginning of your search. Presto—the disinformation disappears.)

Over the years many people have asked me how I emotionally coped with the massive attacks on my character.* It certainly helped to stay laser focused on more important objectives. But my faith also protected me. Let me share a story, which I learned in my childhood.

In a small town in Eastern Europe lived a man who gossiped. He knew it was wrong, but it was too tempting. One day he shared a story about a businessman who eventually went to the rabbi of the town and complained that he was ruined. His good name and his reputation were gone with the wind. The rabbi decided to summon the gossipy man.

When the man heard from the rabbi how devastated his neighbor was, he felt remorse. "What can I do to make it undone?" he sobbed. "I will do anything you say!" The rabbi said: "Bring me a feather pillow from your house." The man was mystified, but he did as instructed. The rabbi opened the window and handed him a knife. "Cut it open."

The man cut the pillow. A cloud of feathers came out. They landed on the chairs, on the bookcase, and on the clock. They floated over the table and into the teacups, on the rabbi and on the man with the knife, and most of them flew out of the window in a big swirling, whirling trail. The rabbi waited ten minutes. Then he ordered the man: "Now bring me back all the feathers, and stuff them back in your pillow. All of them, mind you. Not one may be missing."

The man stared at the rabbi. "That is impossible. The feathers in the room I might get, but the ones that flew out of the window are gone. Rabbi, I can't do that, you know it."

"Yes," said the rabbi and nodded gravely, "that is how it is: Once a rumor, a gossipy story, a 'secret,' whether true or false, leaves your mouth,

---

* https://www.youtube.com/watch?v=98vOV1QBQEY.

you do not know where it ends up. It flies on the wings of the wind, and you can never get it back."

When I faced massive defamation, it helped that I already knew that, although it was unfair, there was very little I could do to change it. Armed with that foreknowledge, I made the practical and emotionally healthy choice not to focus on it.

I was a victim of cancel culture. That is the modern version of severe defamation. I had been both digitally assassinated—my website was canceled—and persona non grata with many people, including my employers who fired me. I had had the audacity to not follow tyrannical orders about what to think, say, or do. I acted as though I was a citizen who is free to speak the truth.

George Orwell famously observed that "freedom is the freedom to say two plus two make four." Why did he not say "freedom is the freedom to say two plus two make *five?*" Because tyrants don't care about people who speak falsely. False words don't gain traction like true words do. Only Truth could have gotten 20 million views in eight hours. That I was so censored and so persecuted is proof positive that there are extremely vested interests in keeping the truth hidden.

I knew the medical truth because of my training, my education, my experience, and I was uniquely able to save lives by speaking of what I knew. So of course I spoke up. Even if I had known the defamation and persecution that was going to befall me, I would make the same choice. This is why I write this book: to encourage *you* to recognize the moments in your life when you should speak up no matter the cost. You can get through persecution. But you will not emerge intact when you silence yourself.

Because there was so much urgency, because people's parents, grandparents, and siblings were in jeopardy, I felt compelled to keep speaking publicly. Prior to 2020, I had lived my whole life as a private citizen. But I am a doctor. My knowledge could save people's lives. My words needed to be heard.

Since I was censored on social media, I spoke in person everywhere I could. I spoke in churches, in restaurants, before state legislatures. I spoke at civic meetings, I spoke to community groups, I spoke at rallies. I always spoke of what I knew from my education, training, and experience. There are no speeches by me on politics, elections, election fraud, the 2020 election. I spoke on medical freedom, on the true medical facts, and about every person's inalienable right to make their own medical choices. And so of course I accepted an invitation to speak at the Capitol on January 6 because there would be a large audience.

I personally was not there for any reason other than to save lives. I realize this may seem irrational to others. But that is *my* story. I was one of twenty scheduled speakers, including various congressmen who were all canceled at the last moment, and so I started to speak from where I was—at the top of the Capitol steps. That is why I was in our nation's capital on January 6, 2021.This is when the words against me turned from mockery and contempt to aggressive persecution. That is where this story begins.

CHAPTER ONE

Practicing Cruelty

The ultimate tragedy is not the oppression and cruelty by the bad people but the silence over that by the good people.

—Martin Luther King Jr.

To this day, I can still feel the razor-sharp bite of the cold. For something as neutral as the weather, it seemed decidedly vicious. Then again, early in the morning on the fateful day of January 6, 2021, warmth wasn't really on my mind. This was a big day with an enormous opportunity, and I believed the stakes couldn't be higher. That turned out to be right . . . for a completely unexpected reason.

I was filled with the anticipation of addressing an enormous groundswell of citizens dedicated to free speech and American liberty. I had a prominent speaking position in the afternoon rally expected to bring hundreds of thousands of people right into the heart of our beautiful and historic capital city: Washington, DC.

Key lines of my speech were running through my head, distracting me even as I returned a polite "Good morning!" from fellow excited Americans riding down the hotel elevator. A dash through the lobby's coffee bar on the way out the door was the last bit of comfort we would experience until returning to the hotel that evening as my security guard and I made our way into the streets. We were heading into a storm unrelated to the frigid temperatures, one that would remain unseen to us until after we had passed completely through it . . . our lives never to be the same again.

* * *

Early in the "pandemic" most of us realized that something had changed. I don't mean the virus. There are always new strains. I mean the reactions–of the media, of health officials, and of hospital management. For me, it was the normalization of unethical behavior by doctors and nurses due to the implementation and enforcement of immoral hospital policies. In 2020, "Frailty–thy name is woman . . ." became "Cruelty–thy name is hospital."

In the spring of that infamous year, I watched as one of my charge nurses was boxed in. Heather, an incredibly talented and professional nurse, was calm, cool, and collected while handling trauma victims, overdoses, heart attacks, strokes, and anything else you can imagine. I never saw her break down until the day during lockdown when one of her elderly patients had a fatal stroke in the ER. Death is a routine reality of hospitals; this would not bring Heather to tears. No, on this day, Heather was forced by her boss, the hospital leadership, to tell the woman's husband and two adult children that they could not see their wife and mother in her final moments. Her husband of fifty-two years wouldn't be allowed into the hospital room, not even in a hazmat suit. Dozens of staff and other corona patients could walk freely in that ward, but not the family of a dying woman.

The elderly woman soon passed away, cut off from her loved ones . . . and this hardened nurse sat in a corner and cried.

What does it do to a nurse, to a doctor, to a hospital system, to a nation, when compassionate professionals are forced by their employer to be cruel? There are only two choices when your boss makes such a demand: comply or quit. With their own families to support, most did not quit, and so hospitals overwhelmingly turned into institutions of inhumanity, practically overnight.

I had never in my entire career seen doctors and nurses literally practicing cruelty. This represented a paradigm shift in our medical system. Heather's tears stemmed from the cavalier cruelty of a useless policy. She knew that if the ER was seeing all patients (we were), if the staff was walking around normally (we were), then there was no public safety reason why a husband could not be at the bedside of his dying wife. *Obviously.*

In 2020 and 2021, the conventional healthcare system pushed out those doctors and nurses who simply could not abide casual and needless cruelty. Compassion and common sense simply evaporated.

I was working as the attending emergency physician in two hospitals when COVID came to America: a Native American Tribal hospital and an extremely busy community hospital. The work was always challenging but never contentious. I was not remotely controversial. I was highly respected and liked, even loved, by nearly everyone. In twenty-five years, I never had a professional complaint, and I never had a medical malpractice suit. Every day I took care of critically ill patients (heart attack, stroke, hip fracture, drug overdose, laceration, major trauma, minor trauma, miscarriage, pneumonia, influenza, kidney failure, foreign bodies inappropriately placed in the human body . . . literally anything you can imagine) with my decades of education and experience. I was the person in charge. Then came COVID.

For me, nothing changed. I continued to try to find the best way to treat my patients.[1] But medical care radically changed. Public health officials suddenly made proclamations about how to treat patients, forcing a one-size-fits-all strategy throughout the nation that was often completely inappropriate and even dangerous to individual patients' needs. As an ER doctor, I'm used to dealing in reality, not what I might wish reality to be. But in 2020, the "system" switched from playing on #TeamReality to playing on #TeamLunacy.

How You Treat Your Mother

I have been defamed in many ways. Some of the more subtle forms of defamation were that I did not treat COVID patients or that I did not take COVID seriously or that I did not think it existed. Nothing could be further from the truth. I treated many COVID patients throughout 2020.

While CDC officials sat in their offices, far away from the patients I was seeing in the ER, I listened to my patients' histories and put my stethoscope, blood pressure cuff, and otoscope to use, measuring vital signs while looking into ears, noses, and throats.[2] As usual, I took test results, including COVID results, into consideration. As usual, I looked at the whole picture of the patient sitting before me. A patient with a clear chest X-ray and normal breathing, but showing signs of a stroke, would be treated for a potential stroke in my ER, regardless of a positive or negative COVID test. Using this industry standard and common-sense approach in the COVID era, however, made me an outlier. A noncompliant miscreant. A "dangerous doctor." Yet, not a single patient I treated for COVID died from the disease.[3]

Obviously, treatment for stroke is very different from treatment for respiratory failure, but the nonstop updates and discussions about coronavirus forced every emergency department to focus almost exclusively on COVID.

But That's Not How I Would Treat My Own Mother If She Came to My ER!

I never treated a patient differently than I would my own mother—I wasn't going to start treating them differently during a pandemic. For nearly everyone else, however, no other diagnosis mattered during 2020. It was COVID or bust. *Did* the patient have COVID, *could* the patient have COVID, could the patient *get* COVID, did the patient have a *family* member with COVID, did the patient have a person to stay with *if* she did have COVID? Conversations with admitting physicians were the same. The patient has a broken hip, but did you check to see if the patient had COVID? Your patient has a stroke, but maybe it's COVID. I won't take care of this patient with a GI bleed unless you're sure it's not COVID. I don't think this patient should be admitted because they have COVID, and I don't think this patient should be admitted because it's *not* COVID. It was total insanity.

Medical Revolution

What was happening in America's emergency rooms was nothing less than *revolutionary*—unprecedented, formulaic protocols for treating viruses and senseless checklists leading to inhumane treatment of suffering and vulnerable humans. Patients were ventilated and given risky, experimental drugs if they had a positive COVID result, but received neither if their test was negative, even if their symptoms were the same or worse. This was #TeamLunacy: treating all patients the same, treating a (flawed) test instead of the patient, and continuing to use harmful treatments long after we knew they were harmful. I recognized that treating any individual person with inhumanity or cruelty was a paradigm shift in America. When the individual ceases to matter that is #TeamCommunism.

As the general rule goes for *revolutions*, things do change but typically not for the better. Doctors and nurses complied as hospitals instituted cruel protocols such as separating patients from loved ones, even though it caused only harm and brought no benefit.

This practiced cruelty was in addition to the deadly treatments that hospitals were *financially incentivized* to use. A hospital was eligible for a bonus of thousands of dollars for each COVID patient, but only if the hospital used the frequently harmful drug remdesivir, while simultaneously *blocking* the use of FDA-approved ivermectin (IVM) and hydroxychloroquine (HCQ). Think about that.

Remdesivir was reincarnated from its previous life as a failed Ebola treatment after its use for that deadly virus was terminated due to its extraordinarily high death rates caused by severe damage to the kidneys and liver. Meaning, even with a highly lethal virus such as the original Ebola scare, remdesivir was banned, but our government recommended its use with the overwhelmingly nonlethal SARS-CoV-2 virus. Simultaneously, our government aggressively opposed the use of cheap, safe drugs such as IVM and HCQ that showed real results in reducing illness and mortality risk.

That's worse than #TeamLunacy.

That's #GovernmentManslaughter.

In fact, many so-called COVID patients were in the ER for unrelated reasons, and the test they were all forced to take often resulted in a "false positive," meaning they had a positive test result even though their lungs had little if any live COVID virus particles—certainly not enough to cause respiratory distress. How can such a faulty and dangerous practice occur in modern hospitals?

Well, it's always been known that COVID test results depend on how many times the test is *cycled*. A positive test cycled too many times could mean the patient truly did have live contagious virus, *or* it could mean the test captured dead viral particles that are not infectious, *or* it could mean there was no virus at all. Unfortunately for patients, but so widespread it could not be an accident, *all* labs in the United States cycled the test too highly to be accurate. The number of amplification cycles is the Ct value, and virtually all labs used a Ct value ≥ 35. Multiple studies have indicated that Ct values above 30 very rarely produce positive virus cultures.[4]

There is no debate about this. The testing scam was publicized by independent doctors on social media so often that even Tony Fauci, the nation's most famous nonpracticing doctor and top health official for far too long, was forced to publicly admit this (his words are cheap as he never changed the actual policy). Fauci said, "If you get a cycle threshold of 35 or more . . . the chances of it being replication-confident are minuscule . . . So, I think if somebody does come in with 37, 38, even 36, you got to say, you know, it's just dead nucleotides, period."[5]

An instant workaround, requiring no complicated changes, would have been simply noting the *cycle threshold* on the lab slip, which would have given doctors the opportunity to correlate the test result to the patient's symptoms and make a determination as to its relevance. But the cycle threshold was treated as a classified national security secret—even the doctors were never told the cycle threshold used by the lab![6] We doctors were told to treat all positive tests the same, which was ludicrous and unprecedented in medicine. Using wildly inflated numbers (90 percent of people with positive tests carried barely any virus), elite power brokers created massive disinformation campaigns all across the world. It was, in fact, both dangerous and cruel.

As *The New York Times* reported in August 2020 with the headline "Your Coronavirus Test is Positive. Maybe It Shouldn't Be":

> The PCR test amplifies genetic matter from the virus in cycles . . . the number of amplification cycles needed to find the virus, called the cycle threshold, is never included in the results sent to doctors and coronavirus patients, although it could tell them how infectious the patients are . . . Most tests set the limit at 40 . . . this

> means that you are positive for the coronavirus if the test process required up to 40 cycles to detect the virus . . . Tests with thresholds so high may detect not just live virus but also . . . leftovers . . . akin to finding a hair in a room long after a person has left . . . A more reasonable cutoff would be 30 to 35 . . . 30, or even less. Those changes would mean the amount of genetic material in a patient's sample would have to be 100-fold to 1,000-fold that of the current standard for the test to return a positive result . . . The CDC's own calculations suggest that it is extremely difficult to detect any live virus in a sample above a threshold of 33 cycles.[7]

Prescribing Hope over Fear

Adding to these jarring changes in hospital care were distancing protocols that kept patients isolated from their families and erased the human touch of hospital staff smiling at them, showing their faces, and giving them encouragement and reassurance. For those who haven't seen a patient treated by doctors and nurses in hazmat suits, it's difficult to describe the emotional toll it takes on a patient, especially when combined with (highly inaccurate) dire descriptions of the virus's lethality replayed all day and all night across television and social media. This all combined to create extreme fear among patients—and fear should never be part of a treatment protocol for any patient, not even those showing up after a serious car accident or heart attack.

I always aimed to provide hope to all my patients, and there were many things that provided hope for patients with the coronavirus; they just weren't part of the national monolithic COVID protocol. Things like hydroxychloroquine (HCQ) and ivermectin, both included on the World Health Organization's List of Essential Medicines, were providers of hope for patients. HCQ is a commonly prescribed medication with 500 million doses dispensed annually in the United States for arthritis and lupus and even more outside of America to prevent malaria. Ivermectin won the Nobel Prize in (human) Medicine in 2015,[8] but the glib media of the pandemic mocked it as "horse paste." Both medications have an incredible safety profile with the Food and Drug Administration. For comparison's sake, consider that both of those prescription medicines are *much* safer than over-the-counter Tylenol, whose toxicity starts at approximately 12 grams—only twenty-four standard 500 mg tablets. In fact, Tylenol toxicity is the number one reason for liver transplants in the US, but there is no panic or fear over Costco selling countless 1,000-capsule bottles.

Early in 2020, studies appeared showing HCQ's effectiveness in blocking SARS-CoV-2 from replicating. It does this by allowing zinc to enter the body's cells, after which the zinc itself interferes with the virus's attempts to spread. That's why, like other doctors treating COVID with HCQ, I also had my patients take zinc. In addition to actually fighting the virus, this simple treatment brought *hope* to my patients. Later, the evidence accumulated: an avalanche of studies and reports have shown that ivermectin and hydroxychloroquine are unquestionably lifesaving remedies for coronaviruses.[9]

Another even more fundamental approach to treatment for COVID was simply ignored by the government, public health officials, and the media. Altering a patient's diet to stabilize their blood sugar level within a narrow range has an enormous impact on the severity of COVID. It is criminal that this was not the national strategy. While reducing excess weight is always the best long-term approach to improving health, swiftly lowering a patient's glucose through immediate dietary change was critical in treating COVID—and the medical journals, media doctors, and government officials simply refused to talk about it.

Vitamin D received the same silent treatment. We knew quite early that patients with low vitamin D levels were hyper-represented among COVID ICU patients. Low vitamin D levels are common among black Americans; and again, the medical journals, media doctors, and government officials simply refused to talk about it. Instead, they fabricated a racist etiology as the reason for the heightened severity in black people. The evidence was overwhelming that the observed racial differences were due to non-racial individual factors such as diabetes, obesity, and vitamin D levels and non-racial social factors such as crowded living and working environments.

The pressure to ignore real science and blindly follow senseless protocols continued increasing with media sensationalism and propaganda, and the bureaucratic chokehold of state medical licensing boards tightened around hospitals and physicians. Pressure can be resisted if a person has an internal North Star, but resistance comes with consequences.

Moral Compass

The stench could no longer be ignored. When junk science denying the safety and effectiveness of early treatment started to be labeled as legitimate research by the CDC, NIH, FDA, and state health departments; when the government financially incentivized hospitals to comply with death protocols, with payments for each ventilated COVID patient; when hospital administrators around the nation forced their doctors (knowingly or not) to deny early treatment to patients; I knew the system was rotten to the core. This was not ordinary corruption. In American healthcare, ordinary corruption looks like excessive use or inflated prices. No, this was entirely different.

For the first time in my career, putting the patient first became a hard conflict between the hospital and the doctor. There was a complete severance between what was good for the patient and what was good for the corporate employer (hospitals, insurance companies, etc.) and downstream employees. How disgraceful it was for most doctors to follow unethical orders. Then again, most other Americans did the same, prioritizing employment over ethics.

I refused to do so. I kept advocating for patients. I organized a thousand physicians to coauthor a letter to the president, challenging the nationwide lockdown in May 2020 (see DrGoldReferences Appendix 1).[10] I prescribed early treatment when indicated, and I wrote a thirty-page white paper explaining its safety and effectiveness. Persistent censorship of nearly all my activities, and of any other voices challenging the cult-like narrative of the global bureaucracy, became the impetus for me to form America's Frontline Doctors (AFLDS), a 501(c)(3) nonprofit uniting ethical and diverse physicians from around the nation.[11] We launched with a "White Coat Summit" on July 27, 2020, in Washington, DC, with a full day of truthful medical analysis and accurate scientific education, and an explosive press conference on the steps of the Supreme Court.[12] Against the full weight of unprecedented global propaganda, we decided to bypass government officials and legacy media, presenting the truth directly to the people. We brought them real science and real hope.

Storming the Frontlines

The White Coat Summit was wildly successful, becoming the most-viewed video in the world that day with over 20 million views in just a few hours, and the most viral video of all time (for its short duration) before being systematically purged by the entire Internet ecosystem, including Facebook, Twitter, YouTube, Google, Instagram, LinkedIn, and so on.[13] Censorship to the point of almost complete erasure was disconcerting enough, but then it was followed by a slew of hit pieces from major media channels, and I was left unable to point people to the very video for which I was being attacked. A nerve was touched, and a paralyzed nation starving for the oxygen of truth and hope took an enormous collective gasp, jump-starting the national heartbeat back into rhythm. The response from the public, both in America and worldwide, was staggering.

America's Frontline Doctors was completely overwhelmed with a deluge of requests for access to early treatment resources and uncorrupted data and with scores of medical professionals reaching out, newly empowered to reclaim their courage in questioning the establishment propaganda.[14] Within hours, the AFLDS.org website was deleted by Squarespace, the hosting service I had used in my hasty beginnings. I had to scramble to relaunch AFLDS right as thousands of inquiries came pouring in from every corner of the globe. This early stage "cancellation" was only a preface to the escalating digital assaults and other attacks that soon engulfed not only AFLDS, but also me as an individual.

Now blocked from reaching the public effectively through media, I began speaking in person to groups of all sizes. Church by church, synagogue by synagogue, conference by conference, I used whatever channels were available to share the message of early treatment, the dangers of masks and lockdowns, and, later, the insanity of experimental injections, especially for children and pregnant women.

The corporate bureaucracy and mainstream media were portraying me as a "dissident" within the medical profession, but that label was misleadingly complicated. The truth was, I just wanted to help people. As doctors have done throughout history, I read, watched, learned, and applied what I found to helping patients. This was the same as I had always done throughout my career. I may be a more prominent "dissident," but there are thousands of us who steadfastly insist on using our own independent thinking and experience. Consider Dr. Cameron Kyle-Sidell of New York's Maimonides Medical Center.

Dr. Kyle-Sidell was an ER physician who was considered so skilled that he led an intensive care unit for the sickest coronavirus patients at Maimonides. He treated a woman who walked into his unit unassisted and speaking coherently, which led the doctor to doubt she needed intubation.

> The hospital's protocols called for placing her on a ventilator except she didn't seem ill enough to warrant it. She should have been gasping for breath and possibly comatose, yet she was fully cognizant, talking to Kyle-Sidell and other caregivers, with no complaints of shortness of breath.[15]

Following protocol, the doctor anesthetized and ventilated the patient at a high-pressure setting. Shortly after, she died. So the doctor came home, still in his scrubs, and recorded a video for other doctors, warning that New York City was ten days ahead of the rest of the country in terms of the pandemic, and hospitals outside New York needed to learn from the mistake made there:

> A hundred thousand Americans might be put on a ventilator and yet . . . the patients I'm seeing in front of me, the lungs I'm trying to improve, have led me to believe that COVID-19 is not [acute respiratory distress syndrome (ARDS)] and that we are operating under a medical paradigm that is untrue.
>
> In short, I believe we are treating the wrong disease and I fear that this misguided treatment will lead to a tremendous amount of harm to a great number of people in a very short time.[16]

Kyle-Sidell's prophetic concern was a simple one: the cure must never be worse than the ailment.

> This method being widely adopted at this very moment in every hospital in the country which aims to increase pressure on the lungs in order to open them up is actually doing more harm than good and that the pressure we are providing . . . we may be providing to lungs . . . that cannot take it, and that the ARDS that we are seeing, that the whole world is seeing, may be nothing more than lung injury caused by the ventilator.[17]

The doctor's video, which went viral, "ruffled feathers," and his administrators put him on *vacation* at the height of the pandemic. Still unwilling to follow national protocol in the coronavirus ward, Dr. Kyle-Sidell, having shown signs of being a "dissident," was returned to the ER, but prevented from treating coronavirus patients, and the controversy surrounding his video faded.

Running into the Storm

The controversy surrounding my own situation did just the opposite, exploding as reactions to the White Coat Summit reached every corner of the country and much of the world, including the directors of my two hospitals, both of whom promptly fired me.[18] Being removed from a hospital department, for some, might mark the end of a chapter of dissidence. For me, it marked the beginning.

I hit the ground running, writing my first book, *I Do Not Consent: My Fight Against Medical Cancel Culture,* documenting the HCQ scandal, the censoring of my medical views, and the relentless cancellation of me as an individual.[19] I brought my personal experience to a wider audience, letting those outside the health profession know about my first confirmed COVID patient in April 2020, who improved dramatically after I treated her with HCQ + zinc. I led the same audience through the ensuing mask controversy, arriving at my new status as the most censored person on earth just three months later. I don't claim that title lightly. A video posted by a social media user in good standing with Big Tech could be removed in less than a minute, sometimes instantaneously, if *yours truly* appeared in any part of the clip.

As my book went to press, I took the battle for alternative treatment to the next level. I filed a citizen petition with the FDA, with the support of fellow physicians, to make HCQ over-the-counter so patients in America could obtain the lifesaving medication that is easily available without a doctor all over the world (see DrGoldReferences Appendix 2).[20] To this day (more than three years later at the time of this writing) the FDA has not made a determination on the petition. And yes, I pestered them.

With each new hit piece, I remained confident that the truth would eventually prevail and I'd be vindicated. For some length of time, however, an opposite plan was being formed to cast a net for the entanglement of dissidents . . . not necessarily me and not necessarily medical freedom dissidents specifically, but dissidents just the same.

A *trap* was being set.

CHAPTER TWO

January 6

Those who want to kill me set their traps, those who would harm me talk of my ruin; all day long they scheme and lie.

—Psalms 38:12

On January 5, 2021, I gave a speech on medical and Constitutional freedom at the Freedom Plaza in Washington, DC, just a mile from the Capitol Building. I saw my message as a nonpartisan issue; everyone should value such medical and Constitutional freedom, right? So despite being in DC and despite a massive protest about the presidential election set to start the next day, I only briefly acknowledged this political topic in my introduction in order to turn the focus *away* from candidates or political races and toward my topics of medical choice and personal courage.

I was also invited to speak, alongside congresspeople and conservative activists, at the January 6, 2021 (J6) "March to Save America/Wild Protest" rally supporting President Trump. They had obtained government-approved permits for the protest and the speeches, including the one I was scheduled to give.

With Big Tech instantly purging my videos on social media, I accepted nearly every speaking invitation I received, including this one, as my primary means to get the message out. People were dying amid the COVID propaganda; this was urgent to me. My speech at the Capitol was to be the same nonpolitical speech I had given the day before at Freedom Plaza, a summary of a longer speech I had delivered two days prior at a large

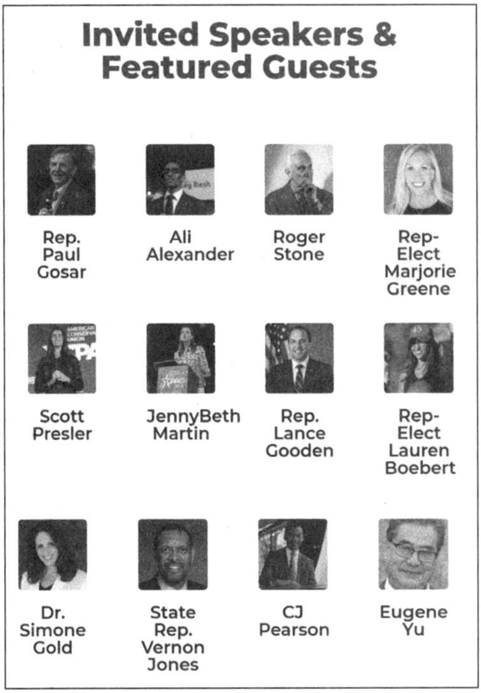

church. Constitutionally protected health freedom, our inalienable right to medical care of our own choosing and the pursuit of our own lives, transparency in determining public policy, and preventing medical discrimination were my specific topics.

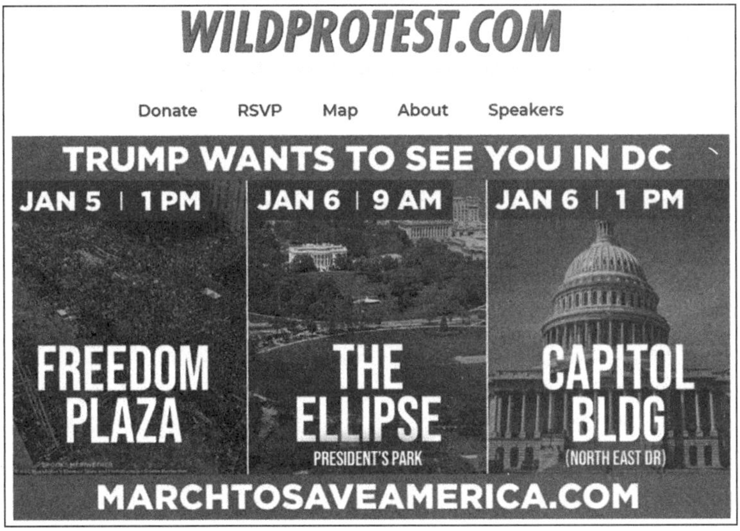

We began early in the morning on a frigid day, with temperatures far below freezing and a windchill that punished any exposed skin. Two America's Frontline Doctors (AFLDS) workers were with me, the social media director, and John Strand, the creative director. John, a model and musician who was also a licensed security guard, was serving as my security guard that day. He joined me as we gradually made our way from the downtown district through enormous throngs of people to the VIP section at the Ellipse, where we joined several congresspeople, Rudy Giuliani, and other well-known figures as President Trump addressed the "Women For America First" rally.

With Trump's speech taking longer[1] than expected, John and I left with two dozen others around one p.m. in order to reach the location for my scheduled afternoon speech. Our group was linked hand to hand, forming a human chain to prevent anyone from getting separated or trampled. The crowd was the largest I had ever seen. Unbeknownst to me, or to the President, a portion of the protestors had left the Ellipse, and some had overrun a police barrier on the west side of the Capitol about a mile away.

With regard to the crowd size, in my estimation as an eyewitness over the course of an eight-hour day, the total crowd citywide easily exceeded a million people. I base my estimation on two direct observations. First, it took more than a full hour to walk from the Ellipse to the Capitol, which would normally take me 30–40 minutes. It took that long because, virtually the entire way, the streets were more crowded than a New York subway car at rush hour. The whole area was densely packed, and it was slow going.

The second observation indicating the crowd exceeded a million people was that the extreme population density extended for virtually the entire distance. One square mile packed with people can contain 26 million people. So estimating one million attendees, allowing for the buildings and structures, seems like a very low number. I think it was closer to 1.5 million. It was incredibly dishonest for the media to report "10–30 thousand" protestors. Minimizing the crowd size is not a small lie. It was disinformation propaganda. It was definitely not a mistake. A crowd size of one million is immediately and obviously different than one of ten thousand.

Unaware of the breach, we continued along Constitution Avenue, slowed by the extremely dense crowd. Just after 2 p.m. we presented ourselves at the permitted location, and we were informed that the entire afternoon rally had been canceled, without any explanation as to why or what anyone was expected to do instead.

By then, we were standing outside the Capitol Building on the northeast side, across from the Supreme Court. Many people have since seen videos of protestors aggressively scaling walls and scaffolding on the west side. This was entirely invisible as we arrived on the east side, where we were completely disconnected from the chaos developing on the opposite side of the enormous Capitol building.

On our side, we saw a peaceful crowd that looked more like a megachurch gathering or a large sporting event rather than a protest.

Even as the numbers grew, we did not witness any breaking down of barriers or overrunning of law enforcement. In fact, we had no idea such barriers even existed, as not only is the plaza commonly open to the general public, but we also knew that government-approved permits had been arranged for the speeches that day. There were no visible barriers whatsoever when we were there, at approximately 2 p.m. and onward.

We did notice about six police officers stationed across the wide steps near the large ceremonial entrance commonly referred to as "The Columbus Doors." The doors were closed, as they almost always are. They are only opened for rare processional entries by dignitaries, and we had no reason to think anyone had any notion of entering the building that day.

As we stood by the edge of the east plaza in confusion, we hoped to gain more information about the sudden changes in the event planning. The still-growing crowd began shifting toward the steps, rapidly filling the entire area and adjacent balconies, waving flags and other symbols of patriotism and political expression. I listened as some in the crowd broke out in a spontaneous rendition of the African American spiritual "Kumbaya," with the calming refrain, "Someone's praying, Lord, kumbaya." Various chants, prayers, and songs echoed throughout the plaza.

When I realized that the crowd was moving in the direction of the steps and away from the grass nearby, I knew I had to try to gain their attention along the north edge. I was hoping to reach a visible vantage point at the balcony on the right-hand side of the steps in order to deliver my speech to a crowd that I believed was excited to hear it.

I turned briefly to John and simply said, "I have to go speak"—and then walked straight into the trap disguised as a large waiting audience.

Paved with Good Intentions

I found out later that all I describe here was captured on the closed circuit TV (CCTV) monitoring the area, meaning there is video proof of all that I write here. The video footage can be found at my codefendant's website, JohnStrand.com.[2] As I joined the crowd, those closest to the front directed the mass of people toward the bronze Columbus Doors and their flanking balconies. Upon reaching the top of the steps with John, I could see that the size of the crowd was quickly expanding, making it impossible to go back down the steps. I saw a police officer and asked him if I could begin speaking. He merely shrugged his shoulders. I understood his gesture as meaning, "Why not?" I started my speech. Due to the size of the crowd, the noise level was totally unmanageable. Nobody could hear me, and I quickly gave up.

It took just minutes of the crowd pushing in from behind for us to arrive at the right-hand corner of the doorway, where I came within an arm's length of one of the few police officers I could see in that densely packed area. He wore a helmet and tactical glasses, standing stationary in front of the right-side door, trapped by the same crowd as I was.

I tried to move toward a balcony area, but the growing crowd behind me was accelerating, creating a funnel effect that forced John and me closer toward the central doors, where he guided me toward the wall to minimize my exposure to the crowd. Caught in the large crowd, we huddled against an outside wall, which was the safest spot. The dense throng of people still growing in size was moving ever forward toward those enormous bronze doors. I suddenly noticed that they had inexplicably opened, revealing another set of large metal doors with small glass windows set back a few feet inside the door frame. To this day, the government has never explained why and how these enormous, presumably locked outer doors that each weigh 20,000 pounds were opened, something that never could have been accomplished by protestors if those doors had been locked. When closed and bolted, they are as solid as the stone walls that surround them.

Those enormous bronze doors, created in the mid-nineteenth century, have old-fashioned surface-bolt magnetic locks that are impossible to open from the outside. They can only be opened by someone sliding the bolts open from the inside. These bronze doors weigh ten tons apiece and mysteriously swung open at the critical moment, as the crowd was pressed up against them. So who unlocked the doors? When were they unlocked? And why? In retrospect, this appears to have been a trap.

Still pressed against the wall with the crowd continuing to build and press in from behind us, a sharp explosion suddenly shattered the air. I sucked in my breath, instinctively bracing for a strike. The crowd panicked as chemical irritants filled the air and the people realized they were under attack . . . by the police.

Pandemonium broke out. People suddenly felt the genuine fear of attack and injury. John was especially concerned about my risk of being trampled. We were further alarmed when we saw a young man use a tool of some sort to break the glass window of the doors. In the whole day, this was the only example of vandalism or violence that I personally witnessed.

At this point, one of the few police officers nearby looked faint in the densely packed crowd. He moved a few steps past me and then fainted and fell to the ground. Immediately, he was surrounded by people chanting, "Get him up! Get him up! Get him up!" I couldn't reach him myself, but saw that others had pulled him back up to his feet and made sure he was safely able to stand. This entire episode (fainting and regaining upright stature) was perhaps ten to fifteen seconds total. The crowd was large, but it was not hostile.

We were packed together like an energetic mosh pit pushing toward a stage. There was just nowhere left to go. Suddenly, the giant doors in front of us swung wide–opened from the inside!

People surged through the entrance, seeing it as an escape valve from the mounting pressure behind them. John and I were driven forward by the momentum, forced ahead to avoid being trampled. We stumbled through the doorway, quickly continuing forward to seek safety away from the turmoil at the entrance.

Forty-Eight Life-Changing Minutes

Once inside, we realized there were already many other people (likely hundreds) in the building, including a few police and building employees. There was no clear direction or organization from any of them. We saw only a general flow of people mainly walking between the red velvet ropes that led through the main public hallways. We didn't see any vandalism or violence, only people observing their beautiful surroundings, many taking videos and selfies as they might on a guided tour. We neither saw any signage giving instruction, nor did we hear any officer tell the crowd, "This is a restricted area," or "Please leave." It was both surreal and disorienting, like an eerie flashback to a high school field trip.

There was obviously no way to exit through the east doors we had just been pushed through. With the enormous crowd still bottlenecked outside, we walked calmly through the main public hallways, trying to get our bearings and determine where a safe exit might be. We instinctively avoided doors or passageways that appeared private or unintended for the general public.

After several attempts to skirt the denser crowds and find an exit route, we again became surrounded and pushed through an entry way past Statuary Hall, where we became trapped in a vestibule with closed doors ahead. We had no idea if this was a public or private chamber or a hallway toward an exit.

Eventually, one or two police officers entered the vestibule and spoke to some of the people near the closed doors, but we could not hear their exchange above all the voices and shouting. After a few minutes, we perceived the officer directing the crowd to turn back and leave. So, as space was made to move safely, we followed those directions and turned back toward Statuary Hall.

By now, we had realized that we were trapped in the central areas of the Capitol Building until the crowds blocking the exits dissipated. I also realized that after the afternoon's strange and unexpected developments, there would be no further opportunity to deliver my speech. Again, I told John to film me giving my speech while we waited for a safe exit to become available.

As I began speaking, a few police officers appeared to be directing people around me. Suddenly, in midsentence, one of them turned and pushed me toward the Rotunda. Startled, I tried to explain that I was a doctor and scheduled speaker, but they insisted that I leave the area, so I turned and left as they directed.

Upon reentering the Rotunda area, we found it even more crowded than before. Still unable to leave, and thinking that the large group of people waiting there would likely benefit from having something to keep them occupied, I once again resumed my speech. Bystanders began to pay attention but struggled to see and hear me due to the large crowd now gathered in the echoing chamber.

Somebody in the crowd then handed us a megaphone. I carefully gained some height by standing on the pedestal of a statue against a wall and gave my speech. A large section of people in the area moved toward me to listen, and in fact it began to help settle down the crowd.

After completing my five-minute speech and taking some questions, we simply waited for direction against a Rotunda wall. A few minutes later, a different police officer made his way over to John and informed him that the exit was now accessible and the crowd was calm enough to exit safely, so we should leave through the east doors as soon as possible. We thanked him and immediately went in that direction. There were still many people pouring in as others were trying to leave, so we very slowly shuffled in the crowd for twenty-one minutes until we were able to exit the building.

That was my entire journey inside the Capitol on January 6: Forty-eight minutes, all captured by the CCTV cameras. My forty-eight minutes included twenty-five minutes attempting to leave and twenty-three minutes walking in public areas or giving two brief speeches on the Constitution and medical freedom. This was described later as a restricted space, despite any indication of such status, and only a handful of police officers positioned to direct a crowd that had been anticipated to reach hundreds of thousands in total. All this occurred just a short distance from the government-approved venue of a preplanned event. None of the protestors we witnessed entered private offices, committed vandalism, stole items, or in most cases, even walked beyond the velvet ropes.

A Tale of Two Protests

As we emerged from the Capitol, we saw that the crowd was even larger than when we had been pushed inside, with many different groups formed in numerous areas as people discussed the events of the day, some still singing songs and waving flags. It was about 3:30 p.m. and the energy had returned to the moderate buzz of a post-concert crowd. Some people, including John, remained, enthusiastically applauding and thanking various police officers as they slowly exited the emptying building.

The mood was a mix of emotions, with protesters continuing to field political concerns, but buoyed by a shared sense of patriotism. We spoke with others on the steps and exchanged our "Capitol tour" stories, commenting on the overwhelming positivity of most attendees and agreeing to remain committed to peaceful activism. After some additional friendly conversation with bystanders, John warned me that dusk was approaching. He was concerned about troublemakers potentially instigating violence, so we left.

Upon returning to my hotel, I heard that there had been some noticeable violence and vandalism on the western side of the Capitol. It seemed, however, entirely unrelated to what I had personally seen and experienced on the east side. This was my third speech in two cities in over four days, and I spent a quiet night in the hotel, not suspecting that I, or any other innocuous bystanders, had done anything controversial, much less criminal. I remained in DC for several days.

The following evening, I went out for dinner with friends who were very upset to hear that I had been inside the Capitol. Having watched hours of (highly selective) media coverage, they warned me that the protest had turned into, as they put it, "a really big deal." I agreed that maybe it was serious if someone had committed violence, but what of the vast majority of nonviolent protesters caught up in the crowd? America has a long and passionate tradition of protests as a legitimate expression of political dissent. Six months earlier was the violent "summer of love" with "mostly peaceful protests" of burning buildings with no arrests.

With the benefit of hindsight and a bird's-eye view provided by endless video surveillance, it became clear to the nation that there were individual persons who had gotten out of hand. Any bad actors in the crowd who may have come with the intent to act violently certainly needed to be held accountable. I am a lawyer as well as a doctor, and I take the rule of law seriously. But, from the very beginning, the media did *not* focus on the few individuals who engaged in criminal activity, but rather the media came together in a massive coordinated campaign of deceit, using omission bias and selective editing to paint an extreme and inaccurate picture of the entire crowd.

I also saw that by any fair standard, the events of J6 paled in comparison to the destructive violence of the numerous "social justice" riots during "the summer of love" a year prior. These violent events were both excused and defended by both Kamala Harris and the mainstream media.[3] They claimed that this highly destructive lawlessness—including deadly attacks on police and extensive damage to federal buildings and small, often minority-owned businesses—was fully justified.

This claim was further evidenced by Harris's personal support, as she bailed "summer of love" protesters out of jail and watched as most of their criminal *misdemeanor* charges were swiftly dropped. In contrast, the Trump-supporting voters' sincere concerns about election integrity were dismissed as an irrational conspiracy theory—now an obvious reality with the revelations of the subsequent Twitter files, the Laptop from Hell, and 2,000 Mules. The J6ers were tarred and feathered en masse as "domestic terrorists" intent on planning and executing a violent "insurrection." Then, they were all hunted and prosecuted with extreme and totally unprecedented aggression.

The massive sledgehammer that came down upon anyone who questioned the 2020 election result is itself revealing. Tyrants care about suppressing truth, not lies, because truth is inherently powerful. The numbers in real time, and in retrospect, support massive fraud. For our entire national history (except one obviously fraudulent 1876 election that led to the Compromise of 1877), voter turnout in an American presidential election is typically 50%–60%. The highest voter turnout was 63 percent in the wildly popular Kennedy versus Nixon race in 1960. In 1984, when Ronald Reagan swept the entire nation, voter turnout was 53 percent. In the 1990s, Bill Clinton's races had 49%–55% voter turnout. In 2008, the highly popular and "change" President Obama resulted in an extremely high 62 percent voter turnout for a total of about 130 million voters. Four years later, Obama only turned out 58 percent of voters. In 2016, President Trump received the same 58 percent of the vote. But in 2020, Biden supposedly caused the highest turnout in American history at 67 percent, massively exceeding the very popular Presidents Kennedy, Reagan, and Obama. Biden supporters claimed that more than 30 million voters showed up for Biden than Obama. It begs credulity.

Very upset that these facts were being ignored, more than one million Americans showed up in person to protest what appeared to be massive election fraud. Normally such people would be considered the best type of American: citizens concerned enough for their nation to inconvenience themselves. Instead, these people were demonized like terrorists, and that double standard is an existential threat to our nation. I was personally shocked to find that many intelligent people I knew and respected were so easily convinced to abandon the constitutional protections of public demonstrations over political ideology.

It was my friends' concerns, however, that proved most prescient—not because the J6 rally-turned-riot was unusually violent or destructive, but because it was dishonestly framed and delivered to the country. What might have been a First Amendment-sanctioned event gone sideways was portrayed as a historic terrorist attack inflicted by domestic "extremists" trying to overthrow the government.

This was as intentional as it was incorrect.

CHAPTER THREE

Dirty Cops

The only power any government has is the power to crack down on criminals. Well, when there aren't enough criminals, one makes them. One declares so many things to be a crime that it becomes impossible for men to live without breaking laws.

—Ayn Rand, writer and philosopher, after escaping near starvation in the Soviet Union

Despots rarely do their own dirty work; it is the perpetually predictable symptom of weaponizing law enforcement against their political opposition that indicates the birthing of a new tyranny.

Less than twenty-four hours after I delivered my speech inside the Capitol, federal authorities made a 180-degree turn from the way they had previously handled protests on federal property. Past patterns of dispersing protestors and arresting only the key violent agitators were suddenly abandoned. *HuffPost* reported that "they're working to hunt down the [participants], most of whom were allowed to leave without being arrested."[1] *Allowed to leave* . . . because they were nonviolent with no apparent criminal intent. In other words, these people were engaging in what was normal American behavior until criminality itself was redefined on January 7, 2021.

Federal Bureau of Insurrection

In response to January 6, the government did not settle for arresting only those who chose to act violently. They certainly didn't drop any charges, even against those guilty only of being caught in the ensuing chaos. Suspicions about the true origin of that chaos quickly arose when it emerged that there were government agents dispersed throughout the crowd, some of whom did indeed act as agents provocateurs to stimulate violence, something that was subsequently admitted in court documents by a federal prosecutor.[2] Even more alarming were numerous instances of video evidence capturing instigators clearly committing violent acts who were easily identifiable and yet never charged at all. Such tactics have been used many times in the FBI's controversial history.

In fact, it came to light that many members of the conspiracy to kidnap Michigan Governor Gretchen Whitmer turned out to be FBI plants who premeditated and incited the scheme. Furthermore, the director of the FBI field office in Michigan overseeing that Whitmer "Fednapping Hoax," Steven D'Antuono, was later promoted to be the director of the bureau's DC field office . . . just in time to "prepare" for the upcoming January 6th event.[3] Yes, read these sentences twice. The same fellow who oversaw the FBI field office that was responsible for a massive hoax in a single state now was in charge of a similar (but larger) scenario at the federal level.

On January 5, veterans of conservative rallies noticed a person later identified as Ray Epps, a suspected federal agent, calling for aggressive behavior the next day, specifically saying people should "go inside the Capitol tomorrow," implying that this was permitted. Astute observers at the time alerted fellow protestors and can be seen in videos yelling, "FED, FED, FED," as Epps speaks.[4] Later, witness transcripts from the congressional January 6 Select Committee revealed that Epps had written in a text message that he "was in the front," and he "orchestrated it."[5] There is still no official explanation of his role, and he was, strangely, never charged despite an initial presence on the FBI's Most Wanted List for Capitol violence.[6]

Eventually, after about two-and-a-half years of circumstantial evidence swirling around Epps being an FBI informant, Epps was finally charged with a single misdemeanor and received twelve months' probation—an incredibly light sentence in comparison to other J6 defendants who received years in prison.

Attorney General Merrick, who is the mob boss, refused to answer a question from Congressman Thomas Massie about whether there were "Federal Agents present on 1/6 and whether they agitated [others] to go into the Capitol."[7] *Revolver News*, however, did report on FBI operatives among the protestors. *The Epoch Times* also reported on further government involvement, showing disturbing evidence of multiple police officers agitating a crowd with explicit use-of-force violations, which were meticulously detailed by a law enforcement protocol expert.[8] This is shocking factual evidence of government malfeasance and stark proof of their criminal culpability, and yet it evaporates in the truth vacuum of media propaganda.

Congressman Massie described the behavior of suspected federal agent provocateur Ray Epps saying, "As far as we can determine, the individual who was saying he'll probably go to jail, he'll probably be arrested, but they need to go into the Capitol the next day, is then directing people into the Capitol the next day."[9] Epps worked aggressively to provoke protestors into entering restricted spaces, and his behavior was clearly documented on video footage.

Congressman Clay Higgins raised the probability of there being hundreds of FBI informants in the Capitol and surrounding areas that day. Many criminal defense attorneys have said the same thing—that there were at least dozens of FBI informants. Even in 2021, *The New York Times* reported that there was at least one FBI informant. But not a single FBI informant has been charged.

The element of government culpability was later raised again during a J6 trial by US District Judge Trevor McFadden, who acquitted defendant Matthew Martin of all four counts, including the "Entering and Remaining" charge.[10] The judge said it was reasonable for the protester to believe that outnumbered police officers allowed him and others to enter the Capitol through the Rotunda doors, with video showing two officers standing near those doors and allowing people to enter as Martin approached.

With every passing hour after the actual events of J6 had concluded, the heated rhetoric and extreme bias of the public portrayal of those events only clashed harder with my personal observations and my attorney instincts about the rational explanation for the various factors involved. Something smelled absolutely rotten, and it turned out to be just the first ripple of a cesspool that plunged much deeper than I ever imagined.

American Witch Hunt

More pronouncements quickly followed. Acting Attorney General Jeffrey Rosen promised that the protestors would "face the full consequences of their actions under the law,"[11] while FBI Director Christopher Wray said the agency had already "deployed its full investigative resources to pursue" them. When he added, "we will hold accountable those who participated in yesterday's siege of the Capitol,"[12] I never imagined that he was referring to the tens or hundreds of thousands of nonviolent protesters embroiled in the ensuing chaos. Why pursue protesters who didn't besiege anyone and who peacefully complied when clearly told to leave a space they neither entered by force nor understood to be legally restricted?

FBI officials added that:

> Hundreds of federal officers are poring over video footage and social media . . . and will also be using cell phone warrants to determine who, exactly, breached the Capitol and what they did.[13]

Of course, one would (logically) assume that the FBI wants to know what *else* they might have done besides entering a building. If they did nothing else, why would the government waste time and taxpayer resources in arresting them?

With this mindset, it didn't even strike me as serious when I received a text with an FBI Most Wanted poster, which included photos of me and John standing inside the Capitol.[14] The text came in while I was sitting in a DC restaurant with friends, telling them how different my experience was from what they had seen on TV. My initial reaction was, "Okay, which fake news outlet photoshopped me into that poster?"

Even when I was assured the picture was legitimate, it didn't register as anything more than a mistake. I thought, *Perhaps, in their mad dash to create flyers of people who might have vandalized property or assaulted officers, they included my photo. Surely they'll realize that I didn't do anything like that. If necessary, they'll contact me, and I'll confirm I had no connection to anyone engaged in criminality.*

I realized I wasn't exactly anonymous by this point—they'd be able to find me if they wanted to—but I couldn't comprehend that I was being targeted. *No,* I thought, *the government can't be going after people walking between the velvet ropes.* I didn't even think about lawyering up. In fact, the FBI tweet of the wanted poster was itself reassuring, going out of the way to point out that they only wanted the public, "to help identify individuals who *actively instigated violence* on January 6."[15] Okay, so definitely not me.

Near the beginning of the lockdown, an anonymous Twitter account suddenly appeared in my comments, bearing the picture of a young woman with the username Toxic Wooden Woman (Toxic) and claiming to be a fellow resident of Southern California. Of course it could be anyone, perhaps even a PR firm hired by some pharma company who felt my criticisms of the medical industry's recent failures were raising too many eyebrows.

One thing it wasn't was a bot. There was at least one real person attempting to attack everything I did or said in specific detail. Within hours of the FBI poster going up with my picture, Toxic put out a professional video montage identifying John and me by name, while playing footage of us in the Capitol between clips from other unrelated public events. The video is still pinned to the top of Toxic's profile to this day. This is how I learned about sad, empty people who choose to make a complete stranger their entire life's focus. Creepy and hateful attacks were nothing new, and Toxic had clearly been obsessed with me long before (and after) J6. Still, so confident of my innocence that I remained relatively unconcerned, I continued my East Coast speaking tour as scheduled. I traveled to Florida for a final engagement on January 8, a speaking event for Jewish medical freedom activists, and then headed home to California.

On January 11, I received a call from the *Washington Post.*

"Is that in fact you in the picture from the Capitol?"

"Yes, it was me."

I answered innocently, still not sensing any need to guard my responses. *WaPo* ran a story the next day including a link to Toxic, but they did allow some of my voice to be heard:

> "I can certainly speak to the place that I was, and it most emphatically was not a riot," the California resident said in a phone interview Monday. "Where I was [throughout the day], was incredibly peaceful."
>
> Gold confirmed that she went inside the Capitol, saying she followed a crowd and assumed that it was legal to do so.
>
> Gold said she was worried that photos of her inside the Capitol would distract from her advocacy work with America's Frontline Doctors. [For that reason,] "I do regret being there," Gold said."[16]

The qualifying portions of the comment were omitted from the *WaPo* report. Even so, it still seemed far-fetched to think that the FBI would ask me to report directly to them. I was there for a scheduled speaking event, which in itself I did not regret. I had no plausible connection to any nefarious plans or activities, which I would immediately condemn. If the FBI were to call, I would go in without hesitation and tell them what I saw. I didn't feel the need to hire a criminal attorney. I didn't even ask any lawyer friends to be on standby.

The FBI never called.

Living Room Assault

Twelve days after my speech in the Capitol, I was working with John in the living room of my apartment. We were on a Monday morning conference call with several other colleagues, when suddenly the quiet neighborhood was shattered by the loudest, most aggressive pounding imaginable on the front door. I then heard, *"FBI, FBI, open the door! Open the door!"* screamed at a terrifying volume.

I immediately decided that some sort of criminal was using a ruse to gain entry. My brain could not conceive that it was actually the FBI at the door. I froze, unable to even call out a request for identification. Within seconds, my front door was shattered with a battering ram. Yes, a battering ram, with twenty FBI and other law enforcement agents waiting behind it. I was maybe six feet from the door when it crashed open, and heavily armed agents rushed in with military assault rifles pointed at us, red laser sight dots appearing on our chests. The agents screamed, *"Face the wall! Face the wall! Face the wall!"*

At a time when police departments are cutting back on forced entries to avoid dangerous situations where potentially armed homeowners may think they're under criminal attack, we were crushed by a SWAT team assault meant for a dangerous drug cartel.[17]

I was a public figure. The government had my name and address, and they already had the visual evidence they would use to charge me with trespass at the Capitol. They even had my phone number. For contrast, serial rapist Harvey Weinstein received a phone call with a request to come to the local precinct to surrender and face charges.[18] But that wouldn't do here. These agents weren't reacting to victim complaints and making an arrest as the culmination of an investigation. They were politicized storm troopers making an arrest where there was no victim and no evidence of a violent crime, only an entry into a restricted space. They were sending a message.

Meaning, the video wasn't enough. *WaPo* already reported that I believed the Capitol to be open to the public. Was the arrest made to "capture me"? Was the violent SWAT team ordered to prevent a "dangerous criminal" from escaping or being violent? How far we have fallen from the Fourth Amendment.

Many months later, I looked up the justifications for using a SWAT team and learned there are extensive common sense rules and guidelines about when a SWAT team is to be considered.[19] There is a scoring system using cumulative points to determine if deploying a SWAT team is appropriate. For example, if the defendant has a violent criminal history, is charged with a particularly violent crime, is known to have many weapons, has been incarcerated in the past, is a member of a violent gang, etc. Being a full-time employed doctor and lawyer and mom with no criminal history, no charge of violence, no drug or gang connection . . . there was no basis whatsoever for a SWAT team arrest.

Here is a list of scenarios when a SWAT team might be called:[20]

> Most SWAT teams in the United States claim a list of their common "duties and responsibilities," which are included in, but not limited to, the situations outlined below. It is important to note that based on the number of things listed that rarely if ever occur, the list might be more accurately described as the things for which the team has taken responsibility to plan, prepare, train, and equip.
>
> - Terrorist incidents
> - Hostage rescue
> - Barricaded suspect/subject incidents
> - High-risk warrant service
> - Interaction with dangerous, mentally ill subjects

- Dignitary escort/protection
- High-risk prisoner security/transport
- High-risk narcotics operations independent of warrant service, including officer safety/security during drug buys; buy/bust operations; vehicle assault/arrest scenarios; and high-risk surveillance of drug fields, labs, and suspects
- General high-risk surveillance (armed robbery stakeouts, etc.)

Sending out SWAT teams inappropriately has many downstream harms. Consider first the enormous expense, second the diverting of resources away from serious crimes, third the extreme risk of causing a deadly result, and fourth the intimidation of law-abiding citizenry.

It turns out, scenes like this were taking place all over the country. The FBI had mustered all of its considerable resources for a nationwide manhunt to find and arrest people they chose to label as "insurrectionists," regardless of their actual role in the events of J6. How did the Bureau source hundreds of agents for this task? *USA Today* provided the details:

> . . . agents in all but one of the FBI's 56 field offices have been drafted to track down those who participated . . . Investigators who typically work cases involving the trafficking of drugs, child pornography and [prostitution] have taken tip calls from rioters' angry ex-wives, former girlfriends and employers. They've mined tens of thousands of photos and videos. They followed trails rioters left on social media . . .[21]

And here they were in my living room. Unable to process the idea that a SWAT team could be in my house for any reason other than saving me from some grave threat, I instinctively took a step toward them to inquire. They shrieked at top volume, *"Face the wall! Face the wall! Face the wall!"*—fortunately, without shooting.

I realize now that forces far above the individual FBI officers have set up scenarios specifically so unsuspecting officers might kill ordinary

Americans the DOJ deems irritating. In my case, I was only about three feet away from several officers who had their fingers on the triggers of massive assault rifles with red laser sight beams visible on my chest. I could see sweat on one officer's upper lip. As I was confused and stunned, I took one step forward. Had he shot me dead, it would have been spun in the news as an insurrectionist resisting arrest, but the officers themselves most likely would have been permanently traumatized by the incident, never able to accept the evil they had perpetrated.[22]

No decent officer would have wanted to kill a person like me, but one almost did. Only after shooting me dead, he would have discovered I was a physician dedicated to saving lives, a civil rights activist, and a mother. But because he was told by his superiors that I was dangerous and sent on a violent SWAT team arrest, he had a massive amount of adrenaline coursing through his veins, and he almost shot me dead. So the officers are also pawns in this game, and I believe many ordinary officers are finally beginning to see this. *Ordinary Americans must stop following unethical orders.*

After these twenty heavily armed FBI and other officers broke down my door and aimed their massive assault rifles directly at my chest, they handcuffed and shackled me. The following pictures are not from my arrest but approximate half the size of the force deployed to arrest me.[23]

I thank God my two children were not at home. I don't know how they would have been affected by this violent assault, but even I, with far more life experience, was severely traumatized. In the weeks that followed, every inch of that room brought back vivid images of uniformed government thugs. I eventually fled California entirely for the free state of Florida.

Common Cruelty

The agents had questions.

"Where's your phone?"

"On the counter."

"What's the password?"

What would you do? Honestly, you have to be in that situation to understand the pressure to comply. It's difficult to imagine yourself looking them in the eye and saying, "I'm not talking without my lawyer present."

I told them the code. After all, I had no crimes to hide. I was then handcuffed and shackled at the ankles, perp walked through the streets, and shuffled to the backseat of a government vehicle to sit there awkwardly with arms pinned behind my back for hours while they searched my home.

"May I take cash for a cab home? Eventually you're going to release me."

"No."

"My phone?"

"No. And take off your shoes."

"Take off my shoes?"

"Yes."

"May I make a call to let someone know . . . ?"

"No."

No Miranda explanation, and no questioning. They knew I was nonviolent with no criminal record. They were looking for something else. Something more interesting than mere potential trespassing.

What I found most unsettling was the bureaucratic control of an operation that was dialed in by an invisible director thousands of miles away, using ordinary field agents to act violently against ordinary citizens. Some of these agents appeared to understand their actions were outrageous. They avoided eye contact, and quite a few seemed uncomfortable and embarrassed. And yet, they continued to carry out their orders with robotic efficiency. These foot soldiers had become the hands of evil, failing to refuse illegitimate pressure to weaponize the government against its own people. *Again, ordinary Americans must stop following unethical orders.*

These officers reminded me exactly of the nurses in the hospitals who cruelly—but ever so politely—refused to let loved ones see their family because "It's against hospital policy." These officers practiced their version of the same casual cruelty by bashing in the door and almost shooting a peaceful American citizen—but as politely as possible. The American public is witnessing a terrible shift in what is acceptable American behavior. These agents surely did not enter law enforcement to intimidate ordinary citizens, and yet they gave no resistance to this corruption of their positions.

Aggressive tactics are understandable when the FBI follows an internally consistent protocol. A violent target known to be truly dangerous requires aggressive measures, perhaps including a SWAT team arrest and the seizure and removal of any weapons. But such tactics had *never been used against nonviolent suspects.* Now, my eyes were being opened to the sordid evolution of this storied American institution, the FBI, now authorizing harsh and deadly force against thousands of citizens *who the government knows are nonviolent.* Their selective persecution was unmistakable in its duality. They were violent storm troopers when they invaded my home yet, at the same time, minor bureaucrats who, per their checklist, left my firearm unlocked and open in plain view, awaiting my return after my eventual release.

In the meantime, I went to jail, which included handcuffs and shackles, a total body cavity search, and an orange prison jumpsuit. You can bet that I smirked for the mug shot.

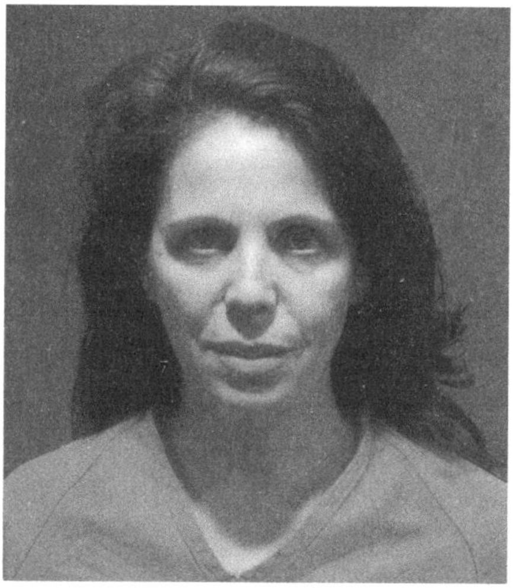

I was arrested on MLK Day (the irony is not lost) when processing was suspended at the LA Metropolitan Detention Center. The agents drove me all the way down to Santa Ana City Jail, leaving me in an eight-by-ten-foot cell with only a steel bench and toilet. About ten hours after the initial arrest, I still had not talked to anyone. Finally, around 9:00 p.m., a guard called me into her office to explain, and I mentioned I had never been provided with any information or a phone call. She took pity on me and placed me in a cell with a phone that accepted collect calls.

This was terrific news—a phone!

But who has anyone's phone number memorized these days?! Friendly tip: If you plan to attend a protest, commit a few numbers to memory. I at least remembered my son's.

It was now almost twelve hours since I had been "disappeared," and I prayed he would answer the call. It was a jolt when I heard the recorded robo-message he was hearing:

"This is the Santa Ana Jail. Do you accept a collect call from Simone Gold?"

In my entire life, never had the thought crossed my mind that any family member of mine would ever call any other family member from jail. Hearing my son listen to this message was one of the most surreal moments I've ever experienced in my life.

It served to highlight a sobering realization: If we don't stop this weaponizing of government institutions into tools of selective persecution, any American from a disfavored class will, quite literally, be subject to arrest and imprisonment at any moment. You should internalize this.

My minor son kept a very cool head as I briefly related the bizarre circumstances I was now dealing with. At least the outside world finally knew where I was. After a sleepless night under fluorescent lights, the government transferred me to LA MDC jail, where the saga continued.

Eventually, I was informed that I was set for an initial appearance—on Zoom, of course, because of "COVID." Even my court-appointed public defender was just another face on the Zoom call. I couldn't consult with him as lawyers and defendants are supposed to do.

I listened at the arraignment as the government rattled off five separate charges. Despite having a law degree, I was left as disoriented as any other

J6 defendant who had simply walked through the velvet ropes. Picketing and demonstrating? Disorderly conduct? Obstruction of an official proceeding? I hadn't been anywhere near an official proceeding.

Imagine being swept in as part of a crowd of thousands, wandering around aimlessly, giving a speech, calmly leaving when officials asked . . . and then having twenty Rambo-esque heavily armed SWAT team officers break down your door two weeks later to arrest you on multiple charges, including a felony.

Oh, but it gets worse.

CHAPTER FOUR

Guilty Until Proven Guilty

If, in the opinion of the people, the distribution or modification of the constitutional powers be in any particular wrong, let it be corrected by an amendment in the way which the Constitution designates. But let there be no change by ***usurpation****; for though this, in one instance, may be the instrument of good, it is the customary weapon by which free governments are destroyed.*

—George Washington [Emphasis added]

While behind bars, I had my initial (Zoom) appearance in court. This became a demonstration of how quickly a citizen could lose their civil liberties without any basis in law or fact, and without going through any process, let alone the process due to every citizen.

The judge, appearing in one of the Zoom frames, began listing my release conditions, which somehow included being monitored for drug use. What? Turns out, some unnamed bureaucrat had capriciously checked a box for drug testing on the government arrest forms. As infuriating as this was, I still didn't realize the foreshadowing it represented. Eventually, I was told I could leave.

"Where's my phone, laptop . . . my property?"

"Your lawyer can contact the FBI about that."

"How am I supposed to get home?"

"You can call someone."

"I don't have a phone. I don't have any cash."

"You should have planned for that."

"I did. You all refused."

That was the conversation I had with the officer who released me from the LA Metropolitan Detention Center. It was a foreshadowing of everything to come with the Bureau of Prison (BOP). My work as an ER doctor had given me a lot of experience with people showing up in an emergency situation empty-handed, expecting "the system" to figure out the solution. So when I was being arrested, I *anticipated* what I would need upon release: phone or cash. I specifically tried to avoid a future problem by taking cash with me, but those FBI agents refused, and I was then reprimanded by the next officers in line for not being prepared. This is the BOP from top to bottom.

After that conversation, the officer took off my handcuffs, walked me down a flight of stairs, and opened an outside side door to a downtown Los Angeles street with no shoes, no cash, and no phone. Thank you to the Good Samaritan who let me use his phone to call my son, who called an Uber, whose driver found me. But while I made it home, none of my work or personal equipment was going to be returned any time soon—not a single item.

I had recently launched America's Frontline Doctors (AFLDS),[1] a non-profit organization providing unbiased and uncensored medical information to the public. The organization did not yet have a solid infrastructure and was in need of my constant involvement. Meanwhile, AFLDS.org was exploding with visitor volume and demand for information and alternative health options.

The daily COVID "case" count (see Chapter 1) was dominating every news outlet; health officials were repeating the same scripted nonsense on all the networks 24/7; and the nation was pleading for real information and asking questions such as: *What can I do for preventive care? Are masks harmful to children? What should I do if my kids test positive? Should I get the vaccine? Should I get the vaccine if I'm pregnant? What about if I'm planning to get pregnant?* We were receiving a deluge of urgent questions to answer, not to mention the legal division I was building to handle lawsuits on behalf of those harmed by various unconstitutional government mandates.

After my arrest, things shifted. The front door of my apartment had been destroyed by officers primed to take down a hardened criminal. The world was less stable, built on quicksand. But the demands of my young nonprofit were unchanged. Work continued, and though I plunged back in, my pace was halved by the loss of my phone and computer and being locked out of social accounts due to lack of phone and ability to authenticate my accounts.

Thanks to the FBI, I would have to re-create everything. It would be more than a year before I saw my equipment again. In the meantime, I was in great need of information that should have been at my fingertips, such as the sources of specific data and materials, meeting notes, strategic conversations, and more. I had to do all of this with only a few dedicated volunteers, forging ahead with my fledgling grassroots crew as we developed a new website and technology infrastructure, responded to endless requests for early treatment, released an independent news resource, and continued to speak and share publicly.

I also had to comply with pretrial "release from custody" rules including: weekly phone calls to "report my status," which I constantly stressed about missing absent-mindedly; a requirement to submit a detailed request in advance of any travel outside my home district; and restrictions on visiting Washington, DC. This punishment would last for eighteen months before my charges were adjudicated. All the while, the government blocked me from access to commercial flights. By this time, I was in constant demand for speaking engagements across the country, so travel restrictions were the best punishment for someone the government was (and still is) trying to silence.

My initial shock turned to anger, because it was clear to me that this had nothing to do with an alleged trespass and everything to do with a plan to instill fear and intimidation. I was being taught to fear continuing my work challenging the government's propaganda, and others were being taught to fear exercising their First Amendment rights.[2]

Even so, for the first year, I really believed that justice would be served. I believed that government prosecutors would eventually chastise the federal agents for arresting me as though I were a violent gang leader and summarily close the case. Even if somehow the prosecutors themselves were derelict, surely no judge would condone such harassment of a private citizen, regardless of political views.

So I was eager to move my case along, asking my attorney to set my next hearing as soon as possible so I could plead innocent, get an early trial date, and put an end to the madness. This was, after all, my Sixth Amendment right: "The accused shall enjoy the right to a speedy and public trial, by an impartial jury."[3]

For unstated reasons, though, the government balked at going to trial. Month after month, at numerous continuance hearings, the prosecutors told the judge they weren't ready, weren't ready, weren't ready, weren't ready, weren't ready, weren't ready, weren't ready, and my lawyer advised me to agree to the delay and relinquish my constitutional right to get this over with. I acquiesced each time. It wasn't as if they could be assembling a stronger case—there existed no evidence of criminality, and they immediately had the exculpatory video of my entire experience in the Capitol. I tried to peacefully give a speech outside; I was then pushed inside; I then casually wandered through only public hallways seeking proper direction; and I peacefully gave my speech while waiting for a safe exit. That's all they would find, because that's all that happened. They also wouldn't find any evidence that I knew the area was officially restricted because I didn't and there were no barriers in place.

As time wore on, I grew more frustrated with the baseless restrictions on my freedoms. The government could have made a digital copy of everything on all of my devices within hours (and surely had). Yet they refused to return my property. The government initially put me on a terrorist watch list that prevented me from boarding any flights. This was "modified" to something almost worse: SSSS. An "S-quad" designation for "Selective Secondary Security Screening," TSA ex-cathedra bureau-speak for *permissible severe harassment* from start to finish at every airport. The process consumed an entire day with no guarantee of ever even making the scheduled flight and included TSA glee when I inevitably missed it. James O'Keefe was put on the SSSS list as well. It's obvious that even "ordinary" federal agencies such as the TSA have been weaponized against civilians.

This process included the most invasive inspection of both my body and property imaginable. Not once per flight, but two or three times, I would be subjected to a full body rubdown in public view of the entire plane's passengers—now alarmed that some dangerous suspect was sharing their flight, which was both humiliating and infuriating. Every inch of every surface of every item in my luggage was meticulously swabbed. The swabs were then inserted into obtuse machinery for the predictable reports of absolutely nothing. Each instance wasted hours of time—my time—my most precious and limited resource. I was beginning to recognize the telltale pattern of *casual cruelty* in practice: a process conceived by a powerful overlord, initiated by a mindless bureaucrat, and executed by an ordinary citizen. A previously atypical and relatively unknown experience in America, *casual cruelty* is expanding as punitive treatment for anyone deemed noncompliant by the state.

Presumption of Punishment

The same constitutional amendment that provides for a speedy trial also mandates that a defendant shall "have the assistance of counsel for his defense."[4] Not only was I prevented from having the benefit of an attorney at my side during my initial appearance by Zoom (who likely would have refuted the drug screening I was cattle-herded into doing), but I continued to be blocked from in-person consultations even after my pretrial release from prison.

For some eighteen months, COVID lockdowns around the nation prevented me from meeting with my attorney face-to-face. We needed to collaborate on obtaining witness statements, evidence of the government's involvement and malfeasance, evidence that the area I was in was not marked restricted, and numerous other details. The hardest part to accomplish long-distance was to demonstrate my specific location without being able to meet together. For a year we struggled to even speak a common language about the layout of the Capitol Building. I was like nearly 100 percent of Americans who could not possibly know exactly where I was in the Capitol Building. I could have very easily walked the specific route with them, but that was not permitted.

The extra judicial punishments continued to mount. Pressure and attacks came from all directions. I was attacked as a private citizen. I was attacked as a physician. I was attacked as an attorney. My child was targeted. My coworkers were targeted. My hospital colleagues were targeted.

In March 2021, I attempted to open accounts for my nonprofit operations with four different lower-profile banks, bringing them my perfect credit score of 850. Three closed my accounts with no explanation, and the fourth advised me not to open an account. During a Tucker Carlson interview, I mentioned this fact, and he asked me to name the banks. Here are the shameful banks that engaged in cancel culture: One AZ Credit Union, Foothills Bank AZ, Nevada State Bank, and East-West Bank of Beverly Hills (the last one turned me down verbally in person).

Blocked from commercial flights, I still had to travel constantly for my speaking engagements. Occasionally, a chartered flight was donated by patriotic supporters. On one of those trips I received a serious scare, in some ways more concerning than the SWAT team arrest. I always suspected the most likely way to discredit me was to frame me, a medical doctor, for a narcotics crime. While refueling at a tiny airstrip in a rural town in Colorado, I, two passengers, and our pilot were suddenly surrounded by six men in street clothes claiming to be Department of Homeland Security agents, accompanied by a K9. One of the men had his dog suddenly leap up the stairwell into our plane, without warning or permission, claiming he had a positive narcotics hit. My stomach sank. This was the very trap I had imagined. I protested and chased their dog down the steps, while the men argued they had a legal right to their "search." (They did *not*—another lie).

The men demanded we deboard the plane, which I adamantly refused. I knew if I exited, one or more of them would plant drugs, and I would have no recourse. It was a standoff: me and six agents. There was no foreseeable way out. While the two passengers were videotaping everything, I began furiously dialing every lawyer I knew. The pilot of the plane, a thirty-five-year retired employee of the nation's largest commercial airline, was totally bewildered and told the supposed agents that he believed he was witnessing a political hit.

After a forty-five-minute standoff, the incident concluded when my son had the idea to call a "local man in blue" to watch the search. What a brilliant idea: The odds that the feds and state coordinated with a local cop were much lower. We called 911, and the local police provided a uniformed officer to witness the search by these self-proclaimed DHS agents who refused to give their names or leave any business cards. Later, when we tried to track down an official report of this incident, it seemed not to exist. While there were four of us on the plane who experienced this, and we have plenty of photos and video evidence, apparently there is no official paperwork related to this incident.

Pueblo Memorial Airport
April 20, 2021 at 7:46:05 PM · 4,770 of 8,831
Edit

Pueblo Memorial Airport
April 20, 2021 at 7:46:19 PM · 4,773 of 8,831
Edit
flower

Next, the New York Bar and the California Medical Board (CMB) sent me threatening letters. Keep in mind that attorneys who are convicted of a DUI have less administrative hassle. Years later, the New York Bar case is still pending at the time of this publication. Doctors accused of sexually assaulting their patients receive far less attention than this. By state law, the CMB has authority *only* over the practice of medicine. When they started investigating me for *free speech,* they were engaging in *usurpation.* The CMB is *not* empowered to delve into this area. Virtually every administrative attorney I contacted told me "it wasn't possible" to threaten me for free speech. Except, of course, it was, as the theoretical impossible became my practical reality.

Stripping Citizens of Their Livelihood

I graduated medical school at age twenty-three and was the youngest graduating doctor in the nation at that time. I have been a licensed physician since 1990. I spent most of my career in the most challenging emergency department environments. I typically chose low-paying, inner-city, high impact hospitals, and I was considered an excellent emergency physician by my peers. In all those years, I never had negative professional evaluations or experiences, even though emergency medicine is an especially litigious field. That means I have never had a patient complaint, professional complaint, board complaint, or medical malpractice litigation. Having such a pristine reputation was uncommon. This is not unsubstantiated boasting. I had been held in such high regard for so many years that many physicians gave sworn testimony to this fact (see DrGoldReferences Appendix 3).[5] I am humbled and appreciate their courage.

Suddenly, starting on July 27, 2020, the date of the original White Coat Summit, I was being called a quack by the leftist media. As annoying as it was (mainly to me it was humorous), how could anyone take criticism that only started after I publicly denounced the government narrative seriously? There is nothing negative printed about me prior to 2020. (As noted earlier in this book: When doing a Google search, if you want a more accurate result, include "before:2020" at the beginning of your search. Presto—the disinformation disappears!)

Then, on December 22, 2021, I received a letter from the CMB accusing me of "misinformation." Here's the part where the fascism can be seen. As a physician, attorney, and ordinary American citizen, if you had asked me prior to receiving this letter what the state medical board did, I would have said that they investigated patient or hospital complaints about a doctor. It turns out . . . not so much. Legislatively, the CMB is tasked with "protecting the public health," but, in reality, tiny bureaucrats have taken excessive power to themselves far beyond any normal understanding of the phrase. In my case, it turned out there were exactly zero patient complaints. The CMB allegations against me consisted of a random person complaining to the CMB that, "Dr. Gold misleads and lies about Hydroxyxhloroquin [*sic*], Ivermectin, contagious COVID, masks, and vaccine." The following picture is a copy of the letter I received:

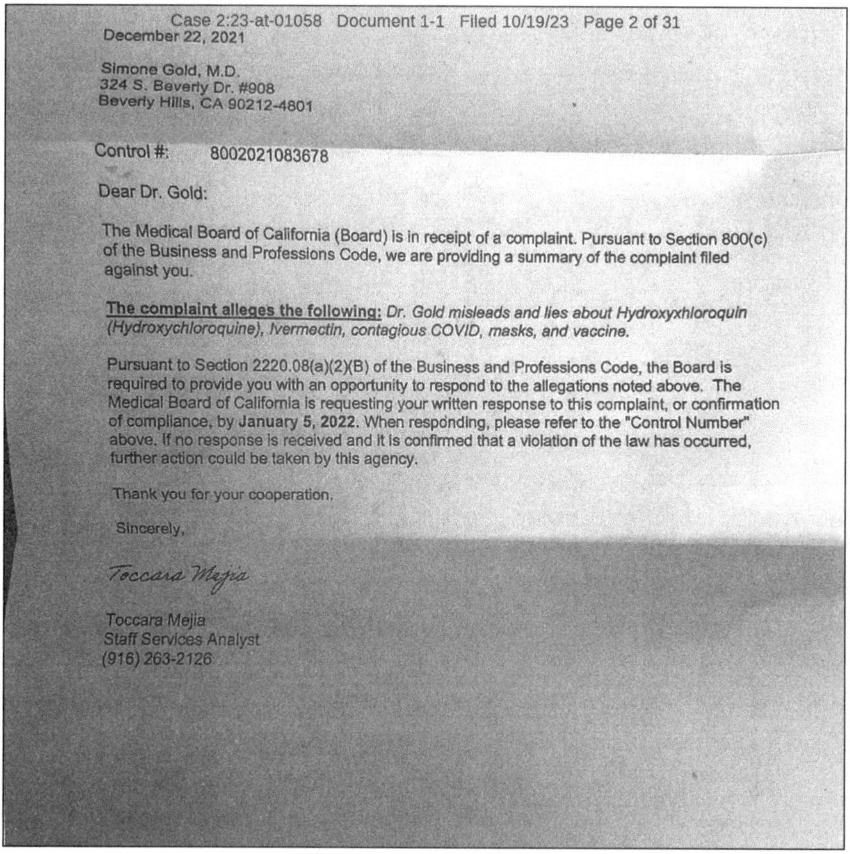

Case 2:23-at-01058 Document 1-1 Filed 10/19/23 Page 2 of 31

December 22, 2021

Simone Gold, M.D.
324 S. Beverly Dr. #908
Beverly Hills, CA 90212-4801

Control #: 8002021083678

Dear Dr. Gold:

The Medical Board of California (Board) is in receipt of a complaint. Pursuant to Section 800(c) of the Business and Professions Code, we are providing a summary of the complaint filed against you.

The complaint alleges the following: *Dr. Gold misleads and lies about Hydroxyxhloroquin (Hydroxychloroquine), Ivermectin, contagious COVID, masks, and vaccine.*

Pursuant to Section 2220.08(a)(2)(B) of the Business and Professions Code, the Board is required to provide you with an opportunity to respond to the allegations noted above. The Medical Board of California is requesting your written response to this complaint, or confirmation of compliance, by **January 5, 2022**. When responding, please refer to the "Control Number" above. If no response is received and it is confirmed that a violation of the law has occurred, further action could be taken by this agency.

Thank you for your cooperation.

Sincerely,

Toccara Mejia

Toccara Mejia
Staff Services Analyst
(916) 263-2126

Seriously. *A random person with no connection to me at all.* Not a patient, not a coworker, not an office manager. Not a family member, not a billing company, not a hospital executive. A random person who heard my words and *disagreed* with me was all the authority the California Medical Board believed it needed to threaten my livelihood. Usurp much?

Physicians are already extremely regulated. The rules and regulations with which I must comply to have a physician's license are extensive. In addition to all the (obvious) educational requirements, the amount of paperwork to receive a physician license is voluminous and presently takes about five to six months to complete. (It used to take less than one month.) Once physicians receive their licenses, they must pay a biannual fee of nearly $1,200 and fulfill extensive continuing medical education requirements. In my father's day, the state licensing fee was nominal. The modern exorbitant fees are supposedly to "protect the public" by investigating physicians. But instead of protecting the public, the California Medical Board has become a beast that requires feeding.

To retain my physician's license, I had to respond to the board allegations. In a revealing comparison, at the exact same time the CMB was persecuting me for speaking words they did not like, the *Los Angeles Times* reported extensively on the California Medical Board and the failure of its president, Kristina Lawson, to stop physician-predators from sexually abusing patients.[6] Instead of protecting patients, the CMB was undeniably more interested in punishing physicians who exercised the First Amendment than performing their actual job—protecting patients.

I was very familiar with Kristina Lawson's failures. I publicly called for her to resign over misusing her position and authority as president of the CMB to persecute individual physicians. When I did this, Ms. Lawson used social media to accuse me of stalking and harassing her and to thank Governor Newsom for her position (see DrGoldReferences Appendix 4).[7] Her non sequitur response sent the perfectly coded message of her political reliability to California's chief bureaucratic overlord. Shortly following my public criticism of her, it was *her* agency that targeted me. Such a result would be predictable in a fascist environment. At the time I criticized her, I thought we still had free speech. I did not realize we were as fascist as we are. Then, Kristina Lawson went even further. She abused her position of power and wrote directly to my J6 judge and falsely stated that I had stalked and harassed her and advised him to punish me harshly. Pre-pandemic it would be impossible to make this up (see DrGoldReferences Appendix 5).[8]

I was certain the CMB had overstepped its authority. No government agency can legally suppress anyone's free speech, and the CMB's accusation literally said that I spoke words some unidentified persons did not like. So when the CMB attempted to intimidate me into taking a "deal," I refused. Instead, I went the distance. Two years after receiving their first letter, I battled the CMB in court.

In addition, it appears that the California State Legislature was so determined to take my medical license away specifically that they attempted to also create a brand-new process just to stop *me*. In addition to attacking my free speech, which legally is a losing argument, they spent considerable effort in creating a new basis to attack me. Quite literally, the California State Legislature attempted to change the law to prevent people like me from speaking freely to patients. They referenced me by name multiple times in their committee hearings as they labored to find every possible avenue to cancel physicians who dared to exercise the First Amendment right to free speech:[9]

> Despite what would appear to be repeated conduct perpetrated by Dr. Gold involving the dissemination of false information regarding COVID-19, Dr. Gold's license remains active with the MBC and there appears to be no record of any disciplinary action taken against her. Given the air of legitimacy she sustains from her status as a licensed physician, Dr. Gold likely serves as an illustrative example of the type of behavior that the author of this bill seeks to unequivocally establish as constituting unprofessional conduct for physicians in California.
>
> Regardless of whether similar authority is already available to the MBC through other enforceable provisions in the Medical Practice Act, it is understandable that the author desires to make this authority explicit and confirm that doctors licensed in California who

> disseminate misinformation or disinformation should be held fully accountable.

Persons who need a state license to earn a living generally just comply with the government. "Needing" a state license is a social construct most of the time. Why does a hairdresser "need" a license? And if she has a California license and then moves to Wyoming, why should she need another state license? Whether you think this is good or bad for the public (my opinion is that it is a financial windfall for the government and enables it to exert control over its citizens), you cannot deny that the intent or side effect is compliance by a citizen who then needs to retain a state license to pay their bills. If state agencies can threaten license holders *based upon their speech,* nearly everyone who holds a state license will be silenced from controversial speech. A state license is a precarious permit subject to the most irrational regulatory appetite for control.

The risk and expense of fighting the government is so enormous to the licensee it can bankrupt a person or family or business. So if you are a license-holder such as a physician or hairdresser or restaurant owner, you are vulnerable to government extortion forcing you to comply. This is exactly what happened in 2020: Business owners who wanted to remain open had their business licenses threatened if they did not close. This was the control exerted over "nonessential" businesses. The government did not threaten Walmart or strip clubs. But the neighborhood hardware store, hairdresser, and church did have their business licenses threatened if they remained open during the COVID lockdowns.

Some brave American business owners (Tony Roman[10] of Basilico's in Huntington Beach, California, and Alfie Oakes[11] of Seed to Table in Naples, Florida)[12] refused to close. State agencies punished businesses who did not comply by calling the cops, who then took various actions including chaining the businesses, stripping their licenses, or assessing enormous financial penalties on them. I took on this fight, not to save my own livelihood, but because it was a stand against **usurpation** and a stand for free speech. Even now, I urge ordinary, local police officers to stand with the average citizen and not comply with agencies that take unauthorized power.

Ultimately, I prevailed against the California Medical Board.[13] They spent two years attempting to revoke my physician's license and failed. This is a huge victory for free speech. The CMB's final order after a three-day hearing was that I be publicly reprimanded and take an ethics course.[14] This requirement was ironic because everything I did was to save lives, while the CMB was literally killing people by withholding access to life-saving medications.

Similar to Joseph Heller's Captain Yossarian's catch-22 predicament,[15] during COVID in California, a physician was forced to violate the oath she was required to take to obtain this license. My catch-22: I could harm a COVID patient by withholding effective treatment and be safe from any accusation of violating my oath, which I had sworn I would never violate. My Jewish heritage was helpful. I well knew there was an upside-down time when it was *illegal* ("unethical") to save Anne Frank and *legal* to kill her. That's where the California Medical Board is right now.

State medical boards' powers are statutorily limited, but they must be judicially restrained to stay within those limits. The citizens of California are much worse off with an unrestrained CMB that engages in usurpation: "The act of taking control of something without the right to, especially of a position of power."[16] Similar boards across the nation have successfully revoked the medical licenses of freedom physicians who should never have had to endure a threat to their livelihood by a weaponized state medical board. While I am pleased that I was vindicated,[17] California law gives me the right to challenge the CMB's ruling in court, and I am pursuing that right to hold the board accountable for their unchecked abuse of power.

California attempted usurpation in the form of its prosecutor, Christine Rhee. Ms. Rhee was a capable attorney, but her own behavior should have alarmed her. She spent a full day asking me about my political beliefs and thoughts. She spent another full day trying to prosecute me for my actions on January 6, 2021, a job she was not capable of doing because *she was not the prosecutor for that criminal case and therefore did not possess the requisite facts.* She made a mess of it, confusing details because she did not know the facts about the day. It is alarming that she allowed herself to be used in this way. Her behavior is a warning for all of us to not comply with micro-tyranny in our daily lives. Here are some examples of Ms. Rhee's political questions to me:

> *Do you recall posting a tweet or a post on X, quote, "fraudulent political persecutions of all J6 detainees must end," end quote? . . . And so my question to you is the content of this post that the fraudulent political persecutions of all J6 detainees must end. Is that your personal belief? . . . Do you often post your opinions on Twitter or what it's now called X?*

My attorneys objected to every single question about my thoughts and political speech as constitutionally protected and irrelevant to the California Medical Board, but each time the judge overruled their objections. (Eventually, a full year later, I won on appeal on these issues.)

If I were in her position (and as an MD-JD with a pristine record, if I wanted her job, I could have had it), I would never query a witness about her political beliefs, opinions, or thoughts. And I would never attempt to prosecute a misdemeanor trespass as there is obviously no connection to the California Medical Board. Perhaps such deviation from freedom dovetails with her personal opinions. Or perhaps she does not mind being a mere cog in a bureaucratic wheel, getting her biweekly paycheck. Whatever her motivation, she failed to follow the law, and she violated her oath to defend the Constitution.

Because the CMB was so clearly focused on punishing the *content* of my speech (wholly impermissible by law), I sued the CMB and Lawson in federal court for damages under 42 U.S.C. 1983 and 1988 on the grounds that their entire proceeding against me was illegal due to being unconstitutional. That case is proceeding as of the time of this writing.

Congressional Persecution

So as to not miss an opportunity to flex its bureaucratic muscle—or risk leaving a gap unfilled in the new comprehensive government overreach schema—I was directly targeted by Congress. On October 29, 2021, I received an alarming seven-page letter from the "Select Subcommittee on the Coronavirus Crisis" accusing me of disinformation and harming the public (see DrGoldReferences Appendix 6).[18] Dealing with their harassment took fourteen months and cost tens of thousands of dollars in attorney fees. On December 14, 2022, even this dishonest cohort ended up conceding defeat after wasting untold amounts of taxpayer dollars. It is worth recognizing that this attack brought the entire institutional weight of Congress to bear against a single private citizen—something that is, as I learned in law school, prohibited. They were coming awfully close to something called a "bill of attainder," which is essentially declaring a person guilty of a crime without a trial—a standard practice for the monarch in English common law but prohibited by the US Constitution's Article 1 §10.[19] A threat by Congress to subpoena a private citizen over "disinformation" seems like a direct violation of the First Amendment. As is clear to all by now, this perilous situation is incapable of fixing itself.

Reading the actual congressional letter was quite disturbing (see DrGoldReferences Appendix 6), I was accustomed to being defamed and misrepresented, but the lack of factual material and abject absurdity of the letter was truly a shock. The entire basis for Congress's inquiry into me stemmed from a false and malicious story in a disreputable publication. There was no other so-called evidence. They made their "misinformation" accusation without so much as a single reference to anything I myself ever wrote or said! It was incredibly sad to realize how lazy and irresponsible Congressmen James Clyburn, Maxine Waters, Carolyn Maloney, Nydia Velazquez, Bill Foster, Jamie Raskin, and Raja Krishnamoorthi were. Remember, this was an accusation against me with the implicit threat of government power, and yet there wasn't even an attempt to quote me directly. They used only quotes from antagonistic tabloids.

I witnessed this lazy "groupthink" over and over again. Both the Medical Board of California and Congress levied a "disinformation" charge, but couldn't be bothered to listen to any of my speeches or read any of my writings to know what information I was actually sharing. Everything they "quoted" was lifted from partisan articles of what people *said* I said. The incompetence, laziness, and outright malice was startling.

The Harassment Awards

The award for "outstanding efforts in the harassment category" goes to the California Medical Board. If I am not Public Enemy #1 to the CMB, I feel sorry for whoever is. I later discovered that the California Medical Board had even created its own designated "January 6th Committee" for the State of California, some three thousand miles away from the scene of January 6. One of my attorneys sardonically commented, "You mean the Dr. Simone Gold Committee." I doubt they had any other California physician involved in their J6 dragnet! The fact that this board was creating entirely new mechanisms to attack an individual licensee is a deeply troubling sign. State medical boards already have scores of regulations to manage doctors accused or convicted of crimes, and this is a legitimate purpose and part of a well-ordered society. They did not need a new process just for me. Clue to bureaucrats: If you find yourself creating new rules to target a specific person . . . you're a tyrant in training.

But the award for "most outrageous behavior by a government agency" belongs to the FBI-Los Angeles branch, which informed the Florida Department of Health in writing that I had been charged with *treason*—while correctly listing the statute of the *trespass* charge—18 USC §1752 (see DrGoldReferences Appendix 7).[20] This could not have been an unintentional error, seeing as they inputted the correct number, which would have been automatically correlated to the written description of the statute. Confusing *trespass* with *treason* is quite the bureaucratic typo, but defamation did not apply to the FBI. My lawyers protested the FBI printing a defamatory document intentionally and falsely accusing me of treason, but the "process" for protesting the FBI is an administrative "wait for six months" until you can even complain.

Don't forget, while all this was occurring, I was still (supposedly) presumed innocent. This was all prior to a trial or adjudication! The DOJ was more intent on using the entire bureaucratic state to crush me immediately than to humor me with a nuisance like holding a fair trial. The DOJ even published to the Internet an exhaustive list of every charge against each J6 defendant, regardless of adjudication, even if the charges were later dropped. This is akin to being listed on a public sex offender registry before a conviction, a process of smearing a person with the stigma of, in some cases, multiple felonies that are later dropped. Of course, this list was frequently the very first listing on a Google search of any given J6 defendant's name: a vicious and permanent "scarlet letter." Unjustified drug testing and travel restrictions, seized property and disrupted business operations, outright physical harassment, public defamation, personal humiliation, psychological trauma, and bureaucratic bullying: this was death by a thousand persecution paper cuts.

Suddenly, those old warnings about "anti-terrorism" laws eventually being used against people the government finds inconvenient didn't sound so conspiratorial. When I wrote to the Department of Homeland Security to request a reversal of my absurd inclusion on the terrorist list, they robotically responded but said nothing helpful (see DrGoldReferences Appendix 8).[21]

> DHS TRIP can neither confirm nor deny any information about you which may be within federal watchlists.

Leave it to the government to use the maximum amount of bureaucratese to say absolutely nothing. Eventually, they targeted other people I knew, including my minor son and a person who worked for me. All three of us had to litigate with the TSA.

Banks and businesses don't care for clients on terrorist suspect lists, I learned. Despite a longstanding pristine record, several banks began dropping or denying me services. Seemingly from all corners, I was attacked, blocked, or impeded from advancing my work and life. Eventually, I discovered that the source of this persecution could be traced directly to the Biden White House.

"The Buck Stops Here" (Truman 1945) Has Become "Censorship Starts Here" (Biden 2023)

Murthy v Missouri, formerly known as *Missouri v Biden*, has been called the most important First Amendment case to come before the United States Supreme Court in decades. Judge Terry A. Doughty, who ruled on this case, said the following:

> This case is about the Free Speech Clause in the First Amendment to the United States Constitution. The explosion of social-media platforms has resulted in unique free speech issues—this is especially true in light of the COVID-19 pandemic. If the allegations made by Plaintiffs are true, the present case arguably involves the most massive attack against free speech in United States' history. In their attempts to suppress alleged disinformation, the Federal Government, and particularly the Defendants named here, are alleged to have blatantly ignored the First Amendment's right to free speech.[22]

Missouri v Biden was filed on May 5, 2022, by the attorneys general of two states, Missouri and Louisiana,[23] against many government plaintiffs to combat the relentless social media censorship of disfavored viewpoints by government actors which is a clear violation of the First Amendment.

> [1] Plaintiffs consist of the State of Missouri, the State of Louisiana, Dr. Aaron Kheriaty ("Kheriaty"), Dr. Martin Kulldorff ("Kulldorff"), Jim Hoft ("Hoft"), Dr. Jayanta Bhattacharya ("Bhattacharya"), and Jill Hines ("Hines").
>
> [2] Defendants consist of President Joseph R Biden ("President Biden"), Jr, Karine Jean-Pierre ("Jean-Pierre"), Vivek H Murthy ("Murthy"), Xavier Becerra ("Becerra"), Dept of Health & Human Services ("HHS"), Dr. Hugh Auchincloss ("Auchincloss"), National Institute of Allergy & Infectious Diseases ("NIAID"), Centers for Disease Control & Prevention ("CDC"), Alejandro Mayorkas ("Mayorkas"), Dept of Homeland Security ("DHS"), Jen Easterly ("Easterly"), Cybersecurity & Infrastructure Security Agency ("CISA"), Carol Crawford ("Crawford"), United States Census Bureau ("Census Bureau"), U. S. Dept of Commerce ("Commerce"), Robert Silvers ("Silvers"), Samantha Vinograd ("Vinograd"), Ali Zaidi ("Zaidi"), Rob Flaherty ("Flaherty"), Dori Salcido ("Salcido"), Stuart F. Delery ("Delery"), Aisha Shah ("Shah"), Sarah Beran ("Beran"), Mina Hsiang ("Hsiang"), U. S. Dept of Justice ("DOJ"), Federal Bureau of Investigation ("FBI"), Laura Dehmlow ("Dehmlow"), Elvis M. Chan ("Chan"), Jay Dempsey ("Dempsey"), Kate Galatas ("Galatas"), Katharine Dealy ("Dealy"), Yolanda Byrd ("Byrd"), Christy Choi ("Choi"), Ashley Morse ("Morse"), Joshua Peck ("Peck"), Kym Wyman ("Wyman"), Lauren Protentis ("Protentis"), Geoffrey Hale ("Hale"), Allison Snell ("Snell"), Brian Scully ("Scully"), Jennifer Shopkorn ("Shopkorn"), U. S. Food & Drug Administration ("FDA"), Erica Jefferson ("Jefferson"), Michael Murray ("Murray"), Brad Kimberly ("Kimberly"), U. S. Dept of State ("State"), Leah Bray ("Bray"), Alexis Frisbie ("Frisbie"), Daniel Kimmage ("Kimmage"), U. S. Dept of Treasury ("Treasury"), Wally Adeyemo ("Adeyemo"), U. S. Election Assistance Commission ("EAC"), Steven Frid ("Frid"), and Kristen Muthig ("Muthig").

These numerous government actors justified their coordinated censorship by claiming that they were combatting "misinformation, disinformation, and malinformation." However, these government bureaucrats knew or should have known that "misinformation, disinformation, and malinformation" are all protected categories of free speech, excluding certain well-known exceptions such as threat of imminent harm. This is very basic First Amendment law.

The attorneys general conducted extensive discovery and depositions for over a year, deposing many high-profile government actors such as NIAID Director Anthony Fauci, CDC Division Director Carol Crawford, Surgeon General Vivek Murthy, and many employees of the FBI, CDC, NIH, FDA, HHS, DHS, Surgeon General, White House, CISA, the Census Bureau, Department of Commerce, and others. Through this discovery, the attorneys general uncovered countless examples of government employees threatening, coercing, and demanding that Twitter, Facebook, Instagram, YouTube, etc. either delete social media posts with which they disagreed or delete the social media user's account entirely.

Appropriately issued on July 4 (2023), Judge Doughty, the trial judge, handed down a stunning 155-page opinion,[24] well worth reading, that identified hundreds of examples of this illegal government censorship in action. There are innumerable emails, phone calls, and meetings between the government and the media companies wherein the government threatened the companies if they did not remove specific posts or deplatform certain individuals. The volume of the evidence is overwhelming. Judge Doughty issued a preliminary injunction prohibiting such unconstitutional censorship.

Judge Doughty noted that these government censorship efforts were directed to suppress speech about major issues of our time, summarized as follows: the Hunter Biden laptop story prior to the election; the lab-leak theory of COVID-19's origin; the efficiency of masks and COVID-19 lockdowns; the efficiency of COVID-19 vaccines; election integrity in the 2020 presidential election; the security of voting by mail; negative posts about the economy; negative posts about President Biden; and parody content about Defendants.[25]

AFLDS was mentioned among the long list of the government actor defendants in this case. The names of the other suppressed victims, including me, is shocking. I found myself in illustrious company. Major American voices were silenced. The court document listed the following on pages 85–86:

i. Jill Hines and Health Freedom of Louisiana;
ii. One America News;

iii. Breitbart News;
iv. Alex Berenson;
v. Tucker Carlson;
vi. Fox News;
vii. Candace Owens;
viii. The Daily Wire;
ix. Robert F. Kennedy Jr.;
x. Dr. Simone Gold and America's Frontline Doctors; and
xi. Dr. Joyce Mercula[26]

Furthermore, the court document discussed AFLDS and the controversies surrounding the various COVID treatments in detail:

> When America's Frontline Doctors held a press conference criticizing the Government's response to the COVID-19 pandemic and spouting the benefits of hydroxychloroquine in treating the coronavirus, Dr. Fauci made statements on *Good Morning America* and on *Andrea Mitchell Reports* that hydroxychloroquine is not effective in treating the coronavirus. Social-media platforms censored the America's Frontline Doctors videos. Facebook, Twitter, and YouTube removed the video. Dr. Fauci does not deny that he or his staff at NIAID may have communicated with social-media platforms, but he does not specifically recall it.[27]

These egregious violations of the constitutional rights of AFLDS (and of my truthful and accurate medical free speech) by government bureaucrats are very dangerous to our Constitution and very dangerous to everyone's health and well-being in general.

Even false information is protected free speech, excluding only the well-recognized exceptions to free speech such as "clear and present danger." But here, the government censored lifesaving, truthful, and accurate medical facts, depriving millions of people of information that they could have used in formulating personal informed consent. "Informed consent" must be *informed* to qualify as *consent.* Informed consent can never be coerced, nor distorted by censored and incomplete information.

America's Frontline Doctors and I filed an *amicus curiae*[28] in the Fifth Circuit[29] supporting the trial court, and we also filed an *amicus curiae*[30] brief in the Supreme Court on February 9, 2024, arguing for affirmance of the orders of the lower courts. Many other states and organizations filed amici briefs in the Supreme Court supporting Missouri, Louisiana, the private plaintiffs, and the lower courts as well. The case was argued on March 18, 2024. As this book goes to press, the decision is expected soon.

Since *Murthy v Missouri* is a pretrial appeal of the preliminary injunction, the case may arrive at the United States Supreme Court yet again after the trial. So the current case is round one of this battle to protect free speech.

In defending free speech by granting the preliminary injunction, Judge Terry Doughty perfectly quoted George Washington and Benjamin Franklin:

> *For if men are to be precluded from offering their sentiments on a matter which may involve the most serious and alarming consequences that can invite the consideration of mankind, reason is of no use to us; the freedom of speech may be taken away, and dumb and silent we may be led, like sheep, to the slaughter.*
>
> —George Washington, March 15, 1783

> *Whoever would overthrow the liberty of a nation must begin by subduing the free acts of speech.*
>
> —Benjamin Franklin, Letters of Silence Dogwood[31]

Despite these attacks, I continued to press ahead, keeping my focus on the efforts of America's Frontline Doctors to provide accurate science and uncensored medical resources and to fight exhausting uphill legal battles to defend civil liberties. Only by refusing to be defeated and remaining steadily engaged in the struggle, one day at a time, am I able to successfully navigate this targeted persecution.

CHAPTER FIVE

Doctor, Lawyer, Warrior

When you find yourself going through hell . . . keep going.
—Attributed to Winston Churchill

What do you do when you're in the government's crosshairs? Keep moving. As public health officials changed their strategies from spreading fearmongering propaganda to unleashing government coercion through attempting to mandate everyone take an experimental shot, I adjusted accordingly.

When I was only twenty-three years old, I had an abstract reason for going to law school after having already finished medical school. I've joked that it was a rebellion against my father, a highly dedicated physician and associate professor of medicine. I had a hazy ambition to fix our nation's healthcare system. The drive to acquire a law degree while my friends at medical school were all scrambling for hospital residency programs had an immeasurable impact on my life's trajectory. After medical school, I attended Stanford University Law School and then studied intensely to pass the bar examination during my first months of medical residency training in emergency medicine. Yes. Seriously.

The knowledge, experience, and credentials I acquired throughout my medical career and legal training gave me a great deal of authority in opposing the government's claim to having a monopoly on "science," something that would have aided many doctors and citizens in their fight for truth. The knowledge of those who began to realize that the government was exaggerating the infectious danger of COVID-19 while downplaying the harms of experimental injections was useless without the ability to freely speak and act upon it.

As governments brazenly mandated masks and vaccines, enforced lockdowns, closed down gyms and houses of worship, and created senseless restrictions on early treatment options, they severely eroded the constitutional freedoms of the American people to make personal life and healthcare choices. Only a combined effort to share accurate medical and legal information and defend the right of all free people to act on that information could provide a viable solution to the growing threat against our God-given liberties. Thus, the battle lines were clearly drawn.

A Play Call for Panic

Early on, I wrote a research-driven white paper on the safety and effectiveness of early treatments (see DrGoldReferences Appendix A).[1] It was soon followed by our White Coat Summit,[2] which gathered independent physicians at the Supreme Court. Combined with the publicity around my citizen petition (see DrGoldReferences Appendix 2)[3] to make the safe, effective medication hydroxychloroquine (HCQ) available over-the-counter, we succeeded in raising awareness of alternative approaches to coronavirus infections. By the spring of 2021, two months after my arrest and initial jail stint, thousands of emails were pouring in daily to the AFLDS website with requests for early treatment.

Tragically, just when people needed it the most, the "medical deep state" made a deeply sinister move. There is a "ping-pong" quality to what happened. Hydroxychloroquine has been FDA approved for seventy years and is one of the safest medications on the planet; it is on the WHO's List of Essential Medications that all nations should have. It is over-the-counter in the majority of the world. In the United States, more than 500,000 prescriptions are written for it annually, mainly for lupus and rheumatoid arthritis patients. All or most physicians are familiar with this noncontroversial and benign medication.

All over the world, many doctors were already using hydroxychloroquine for early treatment for COVID, and the research was pouring in that it was effective. It had been definitively proven to be safe for decades by the government's own FAERS (FDA Adverse Events Reporting System) database, which records adverse medication side effects. Suddenly, the FDA *falsely* claimed HCQ was "unlikely to be effective in treating COVID [while carrying a danger of] potential serious side effects."[4] With a straight face, FDA officials had to simultaneously include, on that very same notice, a statement to calm the fears of the millions of patients who take HCQ daily for years and decades! The FDA stated that HCQ had "been prescribed for years to help patients with [malaria and other] debilitating, or even deadly, diseases, and FDA has determined that those drugs are safe and effective when used for these diseases."[5]

In other words, doctors could go ahead and continue prescribing HCQ daily for years if the patient has rheumatoid arthritis or lupus, and they could prescribe it for short-term use if the patient planned to travel to Africa, but they could *not* prescribe it for other persons (e.g., those in contact with COVID-positive persons) because the side effects of using it for five or ten days could be "serious." Notice the sleight of hand: conflating *efficacy* with *safety*. The lunacy was obvious to an unbiased reader. The tragedy is that the lunacy was widely accepted without hesitation.

Similarly, the FDA stated—with no legitimate evidence—that "off-label" drugs can be "highly dangerous" if given as a COVID treatment. In fact, prescribing off-label is so routine that 20%–30% of medicines are prescribed off-label.[6] The FDA took down this link in 2024 following a lawsuit by a frontline doctor.

The FDA mocked ivermectin as horse medicine even though it won the Nobel Prize in Medicine in 2015.[7] The FDA suggested that the drug ivermectin poses a great danger because overdosing on ivermectin had, in fact, led to hospitalizations when . . . wait for it . . . people indeed took *lethal* amounts.

All this time, similar medications were freely available across the world without a doctor, without a prescription, for pennies, at the local grocery store in the vitamins section, where they belong. All across the world, government workers went door to door with "doggy bags" handing out hydroxychloroquine and vitamin D. Costa Rica, Honduras, Brazil, El Salvador, Guatemala, India—this picture is from an ordinary Indonesian market on July 16, 2020. In the United States of America and Western Europe, on the other hand, the medical deep state was actively manipulating information and threatening doctors and pharmacists to withhold safe medicine from people with legitimate need of it.

Unlike the FDA, I allowed people to consider taking appropriate doses of HCQ, and I posted the actual statistics on early treatment in the AFLDS.org library. For HCQ,[8] we noted that:

> With over 70 years of proven safety, the W.H.O. considers hydroxychloroquine one of the "most efficacious, safe and cost-effective medicines" on the market. When used as part of the "Zelenko Protocol" [including zinc], developed by Dr. Vladmir Zelenko, COVID hospitalizations were reduced by 84 percent in high-risk patients. Countries that used HCQ during the "first wave" experienced significantly better recovery outcomes.[9]

Unfortunately, just as off-label usage of HCQ was exploding, several studies were released proclaiming the drug to be ineffective and even dangerous by testing it only on patients already hospitalized, using *lethal* doses, and omitting zinc. Yes, you read that correctly. The Medical Industrial Complex (MIC)[10] explicitly set up "studies" to produce and publish HCQ failure. Several of those studies were withdrawn within weeks for relying on unverifiable data, described as a "shocking example of research misconduct,"[11] a huge humiliation to the previously esteemed medical journals that recklessly published the faulty reports. Suddenly, decades of extremely safe usage—billions of doses given across the world for many ailments—was "invalidated" by demonstrably fraudulent "studies" exploited by a panicked bureaucracy desperate to maintain control.

In contrast, during the pandemic, the AFLDS.org website provided accurate information about safe, early treatment options:

> When used prophylactically in patients [ivermectin] was 83 percent effective; as an early treatment it was 63 percent effective; and when used as a later stage treatment it was 42 percent effective.

Eighty-three percent effective. Nonetheless, the FDA warnings discouraging the use of these treatments meant that both doctors and pharmacists providing these well-known medications, both listed on the WHO Model List of Essential Medicines,[12] could suffer financial liability or threatened revocation of their licenses if a doctor prescribed these medications. That is a grave threat.

In April 2020, all licensed physicians and nurse practitioners and physician assistants in California and most of the other states were warned by their state medical boards that they could lose their licenses if they prescribed hydroxychloroquine . . . for COVID. You read that right: Doctors could continue to prescribe hydroxychloroquine for anything else, *just not COVID.* That was a total acknowledgment that the drug is safe. Usurping a doctor's authority had never happened in the past, but in 2020 the government unleashed tiny bureaucrats (who were practicing medicine without a license) to micromanage individual doctor-patient decisions. Until

2020, nobody had ever interfered with the individual physician determining the best course for their specific patient.

In my two-year legal battle with the Medical Board of California, they insisted on interrogating me to learn exactly how many early treatment prescriptions I had written. I know many other doctors with pristine reputations who suffered the same insulting and reputationally damaging treatment from state medical boards.

Most doctors predictably acted based on their fear of negative consequences to themselves. Following protocol is, of course, the legal way out of liability, regardless of patient outcome. A cancer patient died right after treatment started? No liability. The patient took the chemotherapy according to NIH protocol.[13] Anxious and/or depressed teenager killed herself after being medicated? Again, follow the protocol[14] and there can't be malpractice in a legal sense. So doctors studiously ducked behind these government protocols, and by the time of my arrest, it is estimated[15] that nearly a million lives[16] worldwide were lost due to a lack of access to early treatment.[17] In fact, it is now widely accepted that more than 75 percent of deaths were entirely avoidable. By threatening the doctors, inexpensive and generic medications that we use every day, such as asthma inhalers, became unobtainable to COVID patients.

I mean #GovernmentManslaughter quite literally.

With the Executive Branch of government wildly out of control and not responding to my citizen petition about HCQ over-the-counter availability, I now had a critical mandate: legal action to protect civil liberties (see DrGoldReferences Appendix 2).[18]

Dr. Brian Tyson,[19] an AFLDS affiliate physician who evaluated over 17,000 patients and treated more than 1,900 COVID-positive cases with only one hospitalization and zero deaths, suddenly had his ivermectin prescriptions refused by the local CVS. The pharmacy had invented a new rule that allowed the pharmacist to override a treating physician's "off-label use."

Dr. Tyson had an attorney's letter sent, explaining the legality of such "off-label" use, and the subsequent illegality of a pharmacist's unlicensed and negligent practice of medicine in violation of the civil rights of Dr. Tyson's patients.[20] Dr. Tyson's pushback quickly brought an end to the dangerous chain pharmacy interference. The publication of his letter also provided support for other doctors facing noncompliant pharmacies. The law is indisputably clear that pharmacists are not allowed to interfere with a physician's clinical decision-making. Yet such interference was ubiquitous and then normalized over the course of the lockdowns. In fact, to protect patient privacy, pharmacists have been prohibited for decades from even asking the patient's diagnosis, another rule that was flagrantly violated during this time.

Protect the Children

A letter, however, is sometimes not enough. In May 2021, as public health officials were preparing to extend the Emergency Use Authorization for mRNA injections to minor children, AFLDS lawyers filed an emergency request asking a federal court to issue a restraining order to prevent the CDC from such an authorization.[21] This came at significant financial cost that required strenuous fund-raising efforts. It is difficult to imagine the enormity of the legal and operational expenses involved with such complex litigation efforts, aimed against a fearsome federal bureaucracy, but children are truly priceless.[22] In our preface to the eighty-page lawsuit, AFLDS declared:

> Kids are one third of our population, and one hundred percent of our future. Kids are never the experiment. **Protect the Children.**[23]

Pointing to the science, we noted that children:

> . . . are a population for whom serious illness and mortality from COVID-19 represent a zero percent (0 percent) risk statistically, but who face substantial risks from these experimental injections.[24]

Tragically, the "substantial risks" warning has been proven to be well founded.[25] Steve Kirsch, an entrepreneur with no fear of employer retaliation since inventing the optical mouse, wrote:

> The "safe and effective" narrative is falling apart - Here is my list of over 50 leading indicators that the momentum is moving in our favor.[26]

If anything, our lawsuit was too mild. We charged that: "It is unethical even to advocate for COVID-19 vaccine administration to persons under the age of 50."[27] One of the fifty indicators listed by Kirsch was, "UK data showing that the vaccines kill more people than they help even for those over 60."[28]

The science behind our claims, like the law, was clearly in our favor. The judge, however, didn't see it that way—the case requesting injunctive relief remained pending over a year later,[29] while Emergency Use Authorization was extended to infants. Ultimately, the majority of children were injected. This judicial indecision was typical for coronavirus-related lawsuits. Judges across the nation seemed paralyzed. The facts were presented clearly, and the data were overwhelming. The problem was, recognition of such information would have required the judges to believe the Executive Branch (CDC, FDA, NIH) was susceptible to corruption. Most judges were unwilling to even consider such a conclusion. When faced with the total incompatibility between what they were reading and what they were feeling, they generally delayed until the issue was no longer relevant.

Abdication of judicial responsibility had also become the American way of life. Forty-plus years ago, in a clumsy analysis, the Supreme Court had created a legal principle known as the "Chevron doctrine," which required judges to favor Executive Branch agencies (such as the CDC, NIH, FDA, etc.). This allowed agencies to say and do outrageous things. When judges were faced with an agency vs. a medical civil liberties group such as AFLDS (for example), they believed they were legally required to give deference to the agency.

A well-educated teenager would have known that judges who defer to non-elected bureaucrats in the Executive Branch have not complied with their oath to the Constitution, which requires the Judicial Branch to *judge* the Executive Branch. But for more than forty years this is what judges have been doing—until June 2024, in *Loper Bright Enterprises*, when SCOTUS reversed this erroneous doctrine and held that it is unconstitutional for judges to defer to Executive Branch agencies. But AFLDS litigated these cases while the courts were still acting unconstitutionally under *Chevron*.

Despite these legal hurdles, new data on the dangers of the injections were being revealed almost daily, often from the release of Pfizer's own records. This made it increasingly difficult for the government to discredit our suit, and it most likely played a role in the FDA delaying the emergency authorization for younger groups. Which was my goal.

My goal was to delay, delay, delay unnecessarily administering the shot to children, as the truth always wins in the end. As I knew these shots were not effective, I knew the world would eventually know this truth, too, and that the judicial paralysis would become irrelevant. Every delay saved lives. By the time teenagers were approved to receive the shot, parental interest had plummeted due to expanding awareness of the dangers involved in taking mRNA injections. By the time infants and toddlers were approved to receive the shot, the public was in outright rebellion against public health officials. In New York, less than 1 percent of kids four and younger have been fully "inoculated." Most parents are saying no. Less than 10 percent of parents are complying with official government recommendations for ongoing shots.

Going on the Offense

Keeping the pressure turned up and working its new legal department at a frenetic pace, AFLDS laid out a list of legal priorities and followed the #ProtectTheChildren lawsuit with a new action just three months later.[30] In August 2021, we made the effort to block another of the most dangerous actions in the government's medical overreach: the mandating of injections for the very soldiers whose health and fitness keep us alive.

A bit of legal research revealed that a similar mandate was previously thrust upon the members of our military, only to be determined illegal by a federal court. In 1998, the Department of Defense (DoD) began a forced mass inoculation program for healthy soldiers and civilian employees of the department. They were injected with anthrax vaccine adsorbed (AVA) as a preventive measure against battlefield anthrax inhalation.[31] It took five years, and an extremely determined Colonel Tom "Buzz" Rempfer,[32] but the mandate was ultimately overturned by a judge who was clearly unimpressed with the government's position:

> The AVA product insert, which originally stated that the adverse reaction rate to the vaccine was 0.2 percent, was recently revised to reflect an adverse reaction rate between 5.0 percent and 35.0 percent. At least six deaths have been linked to the vaccine and the vaccine's pregnancy use risk has been upgraded from a Category C risk (risk cannot be ruled out) to a Category D risk (positive evidence of risk) . . .
>
> The women and men of our armed forces put their lives on the line every day to preserve and safeguard the freedoms that all Americans cherish and enjoy. Absent an informed consent or presidential waiver, the United States cannot demand that members of the armed forces also serve as guinea pigs for experimental drugs.[33]

Citing this very case, as well as death statistics following mRNA injections and demonstrating flaws in the safety studies conducted, AFLDS assisted an Emergency Temporary Restraining Order preventing the forced injection of military personnel.[34] Unlike the anthrax case, the coronavirus injections were granted Emergency Use Authorization. Thus, to ensure a meritorious claim, the suit was limited to employees who had already acquired natural immunity through prior infection. Since natural immunity exempts military personnel from inoculation programs, it should have been an easy win. Army Regulation 40-562 makes the case itself:

> General examples of medical exemptions include the following . . . Evidence of immunity based on serologic tests, documented infection, or similar circumstances.[35]

Throughout this litigation period, I stayed in touch with the courageous colonel who went before me, a man to whom we all owe a debt of gratitude. Nonetheless, in the same fashion as our prior lawsuit, this judge punted on granting relief, claiming that the lawsuit was premature since the DoD had not yet made a final decision on the plaintiffs' requests for exemptions.[36] Bizarrely, this meant that the DoD could control the lawsuit outcome by simply not ruling on the exemption requests of the named plaintiffs. Yet again, lunacy seemed to be the order of the day.

Positive momentum was generated, though, as the DoD retreated and argued only that the case was premature, rather than a full defense of the forced injections. Soon after, a different judge ordered a nationwide injunction against mandated shots for civilian employees of the federal government.[37] The DoD not only stopped coercing civilian employees to take the shots, but it also allowed soldiers who declined the shots to continue serving if they played along with the bureaucratic hamster wheel of weekly COVID tests.[38]

A sliver of sanity seemed to be returning. Never had there been a situation where civilian adults were forced to take shots. Never. Nonstop propaganda had left people susceptible to rationalizing compliance. The court decision invalidating federal injection mandates helped people to wake up and realize, "that's right; medication without consent is not legal."

A Case of Real Collusion

Not satisfied with merely blocking the government from forcing medical treatment on nonconsenting adults, we set our sights on Kaiser Permanente,[39] one of the nation's largest healthcare organizations. The company had threatened each of its 217,000 employees with termination by December 2021 if they refused the COVID shot, including remote workers and those with natural immunity. More than four thousand Kaiser employees contacted America's Frontline Doctors. We filed for an injunction against this draconian private sector mandate in October 2021, ahead of the target termination date.[40]

I published a video explaining that we were not only exposing Kaiser as a rogue private employer coercing its employees to accept unwanted gene therapies, but showing that the company was acting as an arm of the federal government with connections so substantial they could not legitimately claim independence.[41] The judge blithely dismissed our case claim without even recognizing any of the extensive evidence we submitted.[42] We know this because the judge returned his terse ruling within only a few hours of our filing, which meant he didn't even read through the detailed pleadings.

One piece of evidence for this collusion was that the government's vaccine commissar simultaneously served as Kaiser's chief health officer. Another was that out of the nine healthcare organizations comprising the CDC's Vaccine Safety Datalink (VSD),[43] five were Kaiser and three others were Kaiser-affiliates. In other words, the government outsourced to Kaiser what it couldn't constitutionally do on its own. The coordination between Kaiser and the government was a flagrant example of collusion.

In a decision that has aged quite poorly per CDC data and CDC directors' admissions, the judge made findings that must feel tremendously embarrassing. He said he found Kaiser's "evidence" that the mRNA shots would be effective was based on "strong empirical evidence." He would be much less embarrassed in 2025 if he had done his job, which was to read the overwhelming and substantial proofs provided by AFLDS experts. It is such a shame so many judges are so lazy. All this judge had to do was read what was handed to him.

It is rulings like this (and others in this book) that cause me to wonder about the overall intellect level of so many judges. This judge quoted precedent vaccine cases, all of which included the prevention of the transmission of a disease to others. But this ruling on November 18, 2021, came more than three months since the CDC director herself had publicly stated the shots did not stop transmission! Once the director publicly acknowledged these shots did not stop transmission, the judge needed to protect the average citizen. And this ruling was more than two months after the Harvard School of Public Health published a very large study with the title "Increases in COVID-19 are unrelated to levels of vaccination across 68 countries and 2947 counties in the United States."[44]

Despite the CDC director and the Harvard School of Public Health admitting these shots did not stop transmission, on page 2 of his decision the judge *arrogantly* and *foolishly* says: "Kaiser has presented strong empirical evidence about the efficacy of the vaccine."[45]

> Against the backdrop of these health concerns, the plaintiffs have made a weak showing in support of their contention that Kaiser's

> vaccination policy unreasonably infringes their privacy rights. The plaintiffs have submitted declarations contesting the safety and efficacy of COVID-19 vaccines (as well as asserting that the vaccines are not "vaccines" at all), but it appears unlikely that much of this testimony would stand up under Rule 702 of the Federal Rule of Evidence. Indeed, Kaiser has presented strong empirical evidence about the efficacy of the vaccine, and "compulsory immunization has long been recognized as the gold standard for preventing the spread of contagious diseases." *Love v. State Department of Education*, 29 Cal.

Of course we were right. In May 2024, Kaiser gave up their mandate. One of Kaiser's motivations was to have a financial advantage by eliminating employees' options for alternative employment.[46] So, while their policy finally backfired, for two and a half years, Kaiser succeeded in threatening its staff because the judge failed to do his duty.

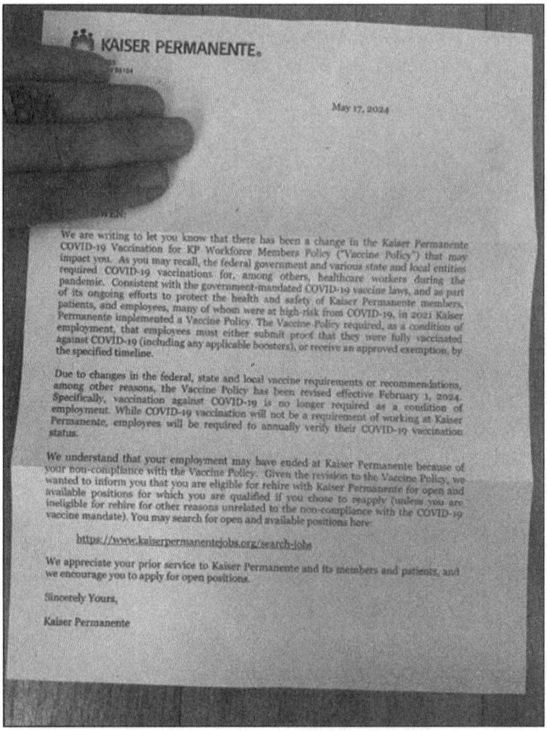

KAISER PERMANENTE.

May 17, 2024

WEN:

We are writing to let you know that there has been a change in the Kaiser Permanente COVID-19 Vaccination for KP Workforce Members Policy ("Vaccine Policy") that may impact you. As you may recall, the federal government and various state and local entities required COVID-19 vaccinations for, among others, healthcare workers during the pandemic. Consistent with the government-mandated COVID-19 vaccine laws, and as part of its ongoing efforts to protect the health and safety of Kaiser Permanente members, patients, and employees, many of whom were at high-risk from COVID-19, in 2021 Kaiser Permanente implemented a Vaccine Policy. The Vaccine Policy required, as a condition of employment, that employees must either submit proof that they were fully vaccinated against COVID-19 (including any applicable boosters), or receive an approved exemption, by the specified timeline.

Due to changes in the federal, state and local vaccine requirements or recommendations, among other reasons, the Vaccine Policy has been revised effective February 1, 2024. Specifically, vaccination against COVID-19 is no longer required as a condition of employment. While COVID-19 vaccination will not be a requirement of working at Kaiser Permanente, employees will be required to annually verify their COVID-19 vaccination status.

We understand that your employment may have ended at Kaiser Permanente because of your non-compliance with the Vaccine Policy. Given the revision to the Vaccine Policy, we wanted to inform you that you are eligible for rehire with Kaiser Permanente for open and available positions for which you are qualified if you chose to reapply (unless you are ineligible for rehire for other reasons unrelated to the non-compliance with the COVID-19 vaccine mandate). You may search for open and available positions here:

https://www.kaiserpermanentejobs.org/search-jobs

We appreciate your prior service to Kaiser Permanente and its members and patients, and we encourage you to apply for open positions.

Sincerely Yours,

Kaiser Permanente

Nonetheless, we didn't give up. On the contrary, the judge's claim that evidence supporting the injections was "strong" made it all the more urgent for Americans to see the original Pfizer documents. We pressed forward and helped pack the courtroom in a suit brought by dozens of medical school professors, as members of the Public Health and Medical Professionals for Transparency (PHMPT), to force the FDA to release the documents submitted by Pfizer to request licensure of its COVID-19 vaccine.

The FDA refused to release the documents, and after being sued by PHMPT, offered, without a hint of insight, to release them over the next fifty-five-plus years. One of the members of PHMPT, Dr. Aaron Kheriaty, did not miss the irony of the government claiming to need decades to scrutinize the documents before releasing them for public viewing, while it needed only a few months to sufficiently review them to authorize their use by the American public![47]

Aaron Kheriaty, MD
@akheriaty · Follow
I submitted this FOIA request to the FDA: they now claim it will take them 55 years to release the data on which Pfizer's vaccine approval was based, though it only took them 108 days to review this data for the approval process. New heights of absurdity.
israelnationalnews.com
FDA asks for 55 years to release data on Pfiz...
The FDA promised "full transparency" due to "tremendous public interest" in a drug that it...
8:55 PM · Nov 18, 2021
Read the full conversation on Twitter
12.6K
See the latest COVID-19 information on Twitter
Read 390 replies

AFLDS brought doctors from all over the country, each of whom dropped everything with only twenty-four-hours' notice in order to appear at the January 2022 hearing of the case to show solidarity for the lawsuit. We too had been fighting from the onset of the injection campaign to give the public the information it needed to make informed decisions. As AFLDS affiliate physician Dr. John Thomas (second from left), who was in the courtroom, explained after the hearing:

> People are not being informed of the grave dangers of the vaccine. Informed consent means having information about deaths and adverse events, the kind of data Pfizer has, and provided to the FDA. The documents the FDA has should tell us a lot.[48]

Dr. Brian Procter (sixth from left), another AFLDS affiliate physician who made the trip to the federal courthouse in Texas, added:

> The significance of the information and the urgency in obtaining it cannot be understated.[49]

Just days later, the Texas court ordered the FDA to provide documents in an expedited fashion on a monthly basis.[50]

Aaron Siri, the attorney who represented PHMPT and who led the fight to force the FDA to release the Pfizer and Moderna COVID-19 vaccine documents, in lawsuits supported by Informed Consent Action Network (ICAN), also brought a lawsuit to strike down an OSHA rule requiring employers with more than one hundred employees to require their employees to receive a COVID-19 vaccine.[51] In a reply brief to the Supreme Court, Siri summed up the government's overreach:

> The Government envisions a world in which an omnipotent federal overlord has the power and authority to regulate the smallest details of everyday American life, wielding a virtually unlimited general police power, all premised on the economic activity of employment—something that, for the vast majority of Americans, is a prerequisite of providing the necessities of life for themselves and their families.
>
> To accept the Government's arguments in this case, as explained below, is to permit the federal government to regulate American's diets, their medications, and their medical procedures—at least if they want to be gainfully employed.[52]

A Doctor and Lawyer Speaking Law to Power

Because of my dual training as a physician and an attorney, I was able to see a flaw in how the courts were deciding COVID cases. In any litigation, each side supports their arguments by citing (referencing) prior cases (precedent). Because these shots were called "vaccines," both sides were looking at prior vaccine litigation. But that was factually inaccurate, because the COVID shots *did not work like a vaccine* as the word "vaccine" had been historically defined. All prior vaccine cases were about drugs that *stopped interpersonal transmission of a contagious disease.*

Jacobson, a Supreme Court smallpox vaccine case from more than a century ago,[53] held that a person could be required to take a vaccine (hence anti-freedom persons cited it), but if the person did not want to take the shot he could pay a modest fine (~$150 in today's value) or obtain an exemption (hence, pro-freedom persons also cited it). But the Supreme Court's reasoning in *Jacobson* was that the government only gets to interfere if there is a general public interest. *Jacobson* stated:

> In every well-ordered society charged with the duty of conserving the safety of its members, the rights of the individual in respect of his liberty may at times, under the pressure of great dangers, be subjected to such restraint, to be enforced by reasonable regulations, as the safety of the general public may demand.[54]

Thus, *Jacobson,* to the extent that it is still good law, established that "only in the protection of the public from harm does any possible legitimate state interest in compelling vaccines arise."[55]

AFLDS was the *only* party to ever argue to the court that the COVID shots should *not* be analyzed through the lens of prior vaccine cases, because the COVID shots did not stop transmission or prevent disease. We argued that COVID legal cases should be analyzed through the lens of personal medical treatment cases. In other words, because the COVID shots were called a vaccine, the courts naturally wanted to apply vaccine law, but the principle of vaccine law is to balance the public and private interest, which was not the case with the COVID shots.

We were able to make this argument because that is exactly what the scientific facts showed. Consider the following facts: During the initial Pfizer and Moderna applications to the FDA in 2020, the pharmaceutical companies admitted the shots were not known to stop transmission. In August 2021, CDC Director Rochelle Walensky admitted the shots did not stop transmission. In 2022, the majority of hospitalized patients had received the vaccines. In 2024, Fauci and prior CDC Director Robert R. Redfield acknowledged under oath that the shots did not stop transmission. COVID lawsuits should never be compared to any other prior vaccine cases, but only to what the shot was: possibly helpful medical treatment. There had never been a vaccine legal case where the injection *was not stated to stop the transmission of the disease.*

Vaccine cases have to balance the public interest of the entire population vs. an individual's right to determine what is best for his or her own best medical interest. Personal medical treatment cases have no such balancing requirement. The landmark precedent for vaccine law is the *Jacobson* case and the landmark precedent for medical treatment is the *Cruzan* case. If the relevant law is "vaccine," it is judged under the "rational basis" standard. If the relevant law is "medical treatment," it is judged under the "strict scrutiny" standard. This is critical: It is the difference between winning and losing.

Almost any law can meet the "rational basis" standard, and conversely, almost no law can meet the "strict scrutiny" standard. Our long national legal history acknowledges that if a rule is rational and not infringing on an inalienable right or targeting a protected class (usually race), then it's likely going to be legal. But if a rule infringes on an inalienable right (such as deciding what drugs to take), it has to pass a *much* higher standard of judicial review, known as *strict scrutiny.* It's almost impossible to meet the strict scrutiny standard. Speaking as a physician-lawyer who taught this subject, I was very aware that moving the *medical* standard from "vaccine" to "treatment" was the difference between winning and losing, specifically because the *legal* standard between the two was entirely different.

The *Kaiser* case was the first time anyone presented my unique theory, that COVID cases should not be decided under the "gold-standard" vaccine case *Jacobson*. At the time, other lawyers rebuffed my idea, but as a physician, I knew they were wrong. I hired a litigator to bring my unique theory in a lawsuit. He recognized my legal theory as "brilliant," and I did the bulk of the work of the *Kaiser* lawsuit while the attorney perfected the procedural aspects and added his own theory of "state-action." (If you are interested in understanding this better, please watch the video referenced in the hyperlink for e-readers and in the notes for all readers.)[56]

When the judge so quickly dismissed our strong case, I was very disheartened. The litigator advised me not to appeal. While I knew my legal theory was correct, by then I had encountered so many subpar judges that I accepted his judgment, and we did not appeal. I would not let that legal theory go, however! So I presented the same argument in an *amicus curiae* to the Supreme Court, submitted November 4, 2021. I used Tony Fauci's own words as proof that the injections are not vaccines but, rather, medical treatments, since they do not create immunity:

> We know now as a fact that [vaccinated people with COVID-19] are capable of transmitting the infection to someone else.[57]

Once we established that this is not a *vaccine* case, I then quoted the landmark Supreme Court decision that ensures an individual's right to decide their own *medical treatment*:

> . . . a competent person has a constitutionally protected liberty interest in refusing unwanted medical treatment.[58]

We further stated:

> . . . this Court observed that "no right is held more sacred, or is more carefully guarded, by the common law, than the right of every individual to the possession and control of his own person, free from all restraint or interference of others, unless by clear and unquestionable authority of law. . . . Every human being of adult years and sound mind has a right to determine what shall be done with his own body; and a surgeon who performs an operation without his patient's consent commits an assault, for which he is liable in damages." The informed consent doctrine has become firmly entrenched in American tort law. The logical corollary of the doctrine of informed consent is that the patient generally possesses the right not to consent, that is, to refuse treatment. 497 US at 269–270.[59]

We argued that COVID cases should not be analyzed under *Jacobson* but rather analyzed under *Cruzan,* a landmark medical treatment case in which it was decided that it is a person's right to choose what to do or not to do with their own medical treatment.[60] We argued that the judiciary incorrectly assumed COVID-19 injections were conferring immunity, but as they did not, and as they were merely treatments that may reduce the severity of symptoms, the proper analysis stems from *Cruzan.*

Unlike the *Kaiser* case, we succeeded, as the court stayed the OSHA rule on the grounds that the plaintiffs were "likely to succeed on the merits of their claim that the Secretary [of Labor] lacked the authority to impose the [injection] mandate."[61] So mandates did not become law of the land.

There is a postscript, however, to the *Kaiser* case, foreshadowing betrayal to come. After the *Kaiser* case, the attorney I hired drafted a lawsuit with another plaintiff using my unique legal theory regarding the COVID mandates, that the shots are not vaccines but medical treatment. The following timeline proves how this attorney took my work and passed it off as his:

> Spring-Summer 2021—I hired the attorney to file a lawsuit using my *Cruzan* theory. I wrote the content for the *Cruzan* theory, and the attorney added the "state-action" theory.
>
> Fall 2021—The attorney and I filed the *Kaiser* lawsuit on October 7, 2021, with both our theories, and the judge dismissed almost immediately. We then filed an *amicus brief* in a different lawsuit using only my *Cruzan* theory, and we won (see DrGoldReferences Appendix D, p. 2 and p. 23).[62]

Case 4:21-cv-07894 Document 1 Filed 10/07/21 Page 23 of 40

82. Those who recover from infection from COVID, over 99% of those who are infected, enjoy robust and durable natural immunity. Natural immunity is superior to vaccine-induced immunity resulting from the COVID vaccines, which do not prevent re-infection or transmission of COVID, and do not prevent infection, re-infection or transmission of the current Delta strain.

B. Mandatory COVID Vaccines Are Contrary to Public Policy.

83. COVID vaccines are not vaccines in the traditional sense. In fact, the FDA classifies them as "CBER-Regulated Biologics" otherwise known as "therapeutics" which falls under the "Coronavirus Treatment Acceleration Program."[50]

84. The vaccine is misnamed since it does not prevent either re-infection or transmission of the disease, the key elements of a vaccine. The CDC has publicly stated that the vaccine is effective in reducing the severity of the disease but not infection, re-infection, or transmission. The injection is a treatment and not a vaccine.

85. The current strain of COVID is the Delta strain.[51] The CDC Director has stated

e. The CDC Director acknowledged that the COVID vaccines do not prevent infection or transmission of COVID: "[W]hat the vaccines can't do anymore is prevent transmission."[1]

f. The CDC acknowledged that the vaccinated and unvaccinated are equally likely to spread the virus.[2]

g. The vaccines only reduce symptoms of those who are infected by COVID, but not transmission of the virus. They are, therefore, treatments, and not vaccines as that term has always been defined in the law.

h. The CDC changed its definition of "vaccine" in August 2021. The CDC formerly described vaccination as "the act of introducing a vaccine into the body to produce immunity to a specific disease." The definition has since been changed and now reads: "the act of introducing a vaccine into the body to produce protection to a specific disease."

i. This is a critical factual and legal distinction. Legal authority to mandate medical treatment only derives under public health regulations. As the CDC holds that Delta is the only strain; that the shots do not stop the transmission of Delta; and that vaccination is mere "protection" against a disease and not "immunity" against the disease; claiming this is a public health mandate is fallacious.

2022—The attorney filed a different lawsuit for another plaintiff using my theory.

2024—On June 7, 2024, the Ninth Circuit *agreed with my legal theory and declared these shots are not a vaccine!* (see DrGoldReferences Appendix E, p .2 and p. 9)[63]

> Addressing the merits, the panel held that the district court misapplied the Supreme Court's decision in *Jacobson v. Massachusetts*, 197 U.S. 11 (1905), in concluding that the Policy survived rational basis review. *Jacobson* held that mandatory vaccinations were rationally related to preventing the spread of smallpox. Here, however, plaintiffs allege that the vaccine does not effectively prevent spread but only mitigates symptoms for the recipient and therefore is akin to a medical treatment, not a "traditional" vaccine. Taking plaintiffs' allegations as true at this stage of litigation, plaintiffs plausibly alleged that the COVID-19 vaccine does not effectively "prevent the spread" of COVID-19. Thus, *Jacobson* does not apply.

[1] Plaintiffs consist of the State of Missouri, the State of Louisiana, Dr. Aaron Kheriaty ("Kheriaty"), Dr. Martin Kulldorff ("Kulldorff"), Jim Hoft ("Hoft"), Dr. Jayanta Bhattacharya ("Bhattacharya"), and Jill Hines ("Hines").

[2] Defendants consist of President Joseph R Biden ("President Biden"), Jr, Karine Jean-Pierre ("Jean-Pierre"), Vivek H Murthy ("Murthy"), Xavier Becerra ("Becerra"), Dept of Health & Human Services ("HHS"), Dr. Hugh Auchincloss ("Auchincloss"), National Institute of Allergy & Infectious Diseases ("NIAID"), Centers for Disease Control & Prevention ("CDC"), Alejandro Mayorkas ("Mayorkas"), Dept of Homeland Security ("DHS"), Jen Easterly ("Easterly"), Cybersecurity & Infrastructure Security Agency ("CISA"), Carol Crawford ("Crawford"), United States Census Bureau ("Census Bureau"), U. S. Dept of Commerce ("Commerce"), Robert Silvers ("Silvers"), Samantha Vinograd ("Vinograd"), Ali Zaidi ("Zaidi"), Rob Flaherty ("Flaherty"), Dori Salcido ("Salcido"), Stuart F. Delery ("Delery"), Aisha Shah ("Shah"), Sarah Beran ("Beran"), Mina Hsiang ("Hsiang"), U. S. Dept of Justice ("DOJ"), Federal Bureau of Investigation ("FBI"), Laura Dehmlow ("Dehmlow"), Elvis M. Chan ("Chan"), Jay Dempsey ("Dempsey"), Kate Galatas ("Galatas"), Katharine Dealy ("Dealy"), Yolanda Byrd ("Byrd"), Christy Choi ("Choi"), Ashley Morse ("Morse"), Joshua Peck ("Peck"), Kym Wyman ("Wyman"), Lauren Protentis ("Protentis"), Geoffrey Hale ("Hale"), Allison Snell ("Snell"), Brian Scully ("Scully"), Jennifer Shopkorn ("Shopkorn"), U. S. Food & Drug Administration ("FDA"), Erica Jefferson ("Jefferson"), Michael Murray ("Murray"), Brad Kimberly ("Kimberly"), U. S. Dept of State ("State"), Leah Bray ("Bray"), Alexis Frisbie ("Frisbie"), Daniel Kimmage ("Kimmage"), U. S. Dept of Treasury ("Treasury"), Wally Adeyemo ("Adeyemo"), U. S. Election Assistance Commission ("EAC"), Steven Frid ("Frid"), and Kristen Muthig ("Muthig").

I am so glad that this is now the precedent as it is extremely important that the courts understand these shots are not, and never were, vaccines. However, the intellectual theft by my own attorney is infuriating. The attorney whom I hired to argue to the court that these shots should not be viewed as vaccines from a legal perspective did not complete the job for which he was handsomely paid. Then he took my work and filed it for another plaintiff, presumably they also paid him, and he and they took credit!

I confronted this attorney about this in a phone call in June 2024 and, in front of many witnesses, he claimed that he "already knew about this theory." That is categorically false. Everyone litigating COVID-19 issues from 2020–2022 only relied on *Jacobson* because they believed relying on *Cruzan* was either irrelevant or harmful. And "everyone" demonstrably includes him. In addition to the timeline listed above, in addition to directly comparing my earlier language to their later language, here is the smoking gun from his email to me on August 26, 2021. Six weeks prior to the *Kaiser* filing, he was still wanting to proceed under the silly *Jacobson,* not comprehending my superior legal theory of *Cruzan.* Note his erroneous belief that the *rational basis* analysis would be victorious. No. It would not. He was blinded by his own bias that there is no rational basis for mandatory vaccines. In fact, that is the exact law under *Jacobson.* The legal flaw during the COVID years was that these mRNA shots were not vaccines. The attorney I hired did not know this until I taught this to him, and then he took intellectual credit.

Liars always need to be exposed. This is his email from August 2021.

My approach is to use Jacobson to our benefit since the judiciary seems dead set on reviving that 1905 rational basis analysis. But we can win under that analysis as there is simply no rational basis for mandatory vaccines. That is what we must allege and support to survive dispositive motions. This approach can be used for several challenges, whether private or public.

Properly structured allegations remove the case from the hands of the judge, and place it in the hands of the finder of fact. That is what we must do, and that is why I need your experts. We can prevail if we do what I am suggesting. Your team of experts is critical to this however.

Many thanks.
[redacted]
Partner
[redacted]

The Ministry of Truth

As it soon became obvious to everyone that the COVID shots did not prevent interpersonal transmission of SARS-2, the CDC changed the definition of "vaccine" and "vaccination" in 2021 with no public announcement. An article in the *Miami Herald* documented these changes as follows: The CDC's definition of vaccine changed from "a product that stimulates a person's immune system to produce *immunity* to a specific disease" to "a preparation that is used to *stimulate* the body's immune response against diseases." The CDC's definition of vaccination changed from "the act of introducing a vaccine into the body to produce *immunity* to a specific disease" to "the act of introducing a vaccine into the body to produce *protection* to a specific disease."[64] In other words, the CDC simply *disappeared* the word *immunity* from the definition of vaccine, and then they denied this was a significant change!

Representative Thomas Massie documented these vaccine definition changes in his September 8, 2021 tweet: [65]

A CDC spokesperson said that the "coronavirus vaccines are doing exactly what they were designed to do, which is to prevent severe disease. . . ."[66] That is true; they never stopped transmission, only *(possibly)* reduced severity from severe to moderate and moderate to mild with the initial strain. But I cannot stress strongly enough how dishonest our government is. Our government (the CDC) *changed* the definition of the

> **Thomas Massie**
> @RepThomasMassie
>
> Check out @CDCgov's evolving definition of "vaccination." They've been busy at the Ministry of Truth:
>
> **Vaccination (pre-2015):** Injection of a killed or weakened infectious organism in order to prevent the disease.
>
> **Vaccination (2015-2021):** The act of introducing a vaccine into the body to produce immunity to a specific disease.
>
> **Vaccination (Sept 2021):** The act of introducing a vaccine into the body to produce protection from a specific disease.

key word, they did not announce this change, and then they *denied* this change was significant.

Here's just one way the change is incredibly significant: The rest of the world, including the courts, was laboring under the impression that the word "vaccine" means something entirely different than what the CDC says. By a sleight of hand (i.e., name change), the pro-government side instantly oriented the courts to think about these cases as "vaccine cases" instead of "medical treatment cases." How important is that distinction? It is everything. Under vaccine law, there is a balancing of public vs. private interest. Under medical treatment law, there is only the private interest of one's own bodily integrity.

Once the SCOTUS held it unconstitutional for the federal government to mandate everyone take the shots,[67] only the Centers for Medicare and Medicaid Services (CMS) mandate had yet to be canceled, with challenges still being litigated. The Biden administration, however, fought to continue its plans to mandate shots for all federal employees.[68]

AFLDS opposed this and submitted an *amicus brief* in June 2022.[69] The brief detailed personal admissions by public health officials that the injections did not prevent transmission of COVID, removing the only argument the government had for imposing the mandate. As we waited for a decision on this appeal, state mandates were falling across the country.

The Public Grows Weary and Suspicious of the Government

By August 2022, the nation was nearing one hundred million positive PCR (polymerase chain reaction) tests,[70] which the government dishonestly labeled as "cases." At this point, virtually everyone knew someone who had tested positive but never developed any symptoms. Many had tested positive multiple times, so the report of a positive test no longer led to the kind of panic that had first been achieved by fearmongering over the airwaves. Even *The New York Times* ran a front page story that the PCR tests were overwhelmingly inaccurate due to far too many false positive results.[71]

Less fear meant less compliance. Even where required, people commonly wore face masks on their chins. The CDC had long since been relegated to putting out videos "reminding" the public that chin masks don't help . . . the sort of pestering that you do when you know no one is listening anymore.[72] The public didn't need a medical or law degree to utilize their own common sense: These theatrics had nothing to do with science and everything to do with *cult compliance*. In other words . . . The Religion of Public Health.[73]

The government, however, remained undeterred by the evaporating support for mask and vaccine mandates.[74] After a federal court knocked down the CDC's transportation mask mandate,[75] which covered practically every form of public transportation, government lawyers appealed to a higher court to reinstate the requirement.[76] The stakes were high, with

Tweet

CDC
@CDCgov

Wearing a cloth face covering correctly can help prevent the spread of #COVID19 to others. When you go out on essential trips, follow these "do's". If you have a child, remember those under age 2 should not wear a face covering. See bit.ly/2R9av5m.

Cloth Face Covering Do's & Don'ts
Wearing a cloth face covering correctly can help prevent the spread of COVID-19 to others.

hundreds of passengers not only fined up to $3,000 for noncompliance,[77] but also frequently placed on no-fly lists, something usually reserved for suspected terrorists[78] (and dissident doctors, as it turns out).

By then, many people knew about or had seen videos of people injured or killed by the injections.[79] Unfortunately, far fewer were yet aware of the harms of masking, which was both an infringement on civil liberties and continued casual cruelty, not to mention potential child abuse. Mounting evidence of significant harms to childhood development brought about by senseless masking[80] should have given responsible adults more pause.

This was overcome by incessant public relations messaging; rejecting the talisman of a face mask was defined by the media as "selfish," even though many decades of research had already conclusively established the lunacy of believing a basic covering could influence a virus that is 0.1 micron in size—that is 1/1000 the size of a hair. You might as well use a chain link fence to keep out a mosquito.[81]

And how can it *not* be an infringement of a person's civil liberties to demand they wear an article of clothing against their will? Donning these useless (and in fact, harmful) masks was only a demonstration of a person's obedience to The Religion of Public Health.

Finally, there was neither outrage nor lawsuits against the discriminatory mandates produced against the disabled. I traveled frequently with a hearing-impaired physician who could not wear the mask due to the ear straps making scratching noises amplified in her hearing aids. On top of that, she needed to see her companion's face to communicate. She faced discrimination everywhere she went. She even brought a clear plastic shield with her to the airport to wear instead of the cotton mask, but was still forced to suffer the impairment of masking because American workers had internalized the practice of casual cruelty. It was inconceivable to me that everywhere across the nation large and small employers suddenly all felt empowered to disregard the federal Americans with Disabilities Act, which protects the disabled against rules that impair their ability to participate in public life.

Finally, a federal judge in Florida tossed the mask mandate—and the government appealed. AFLDS opposed the federal government's attempt to overturn the injunction on the mask rule by submitting a brief to the appellate court.[82] We argued that it is not just ineffective, inconvenient, and annoying to wear a mask, but it is an outright health hazard! We publicized this very danger in our *amicus brief*:

> Masks have been found to have measurably harmful effects such as increased incidents of life-threatening bacterial pneumonia, decreased oxygen levels in the brains of mask-wearers, and speech deficits in children. Masks are also unsanitary, and function as bacteria-collectors.

> "Mandatory" mask wearing has also become the source of numerous disruptive and sometimes violent conflicts between passengers and transportation workers, and among transportation workers themselves, creating veritable chaos in the skies.[83]

More than one year after the judge ruled that masks could not be forced on federal transportation, the Biden administration terminated the national emergency. The anti-freedom side then filed to get this precedent thrown out. The only reason to do that (now that the "emergency" was over) was so this freedom ruling could not be relied upon in some future mask-mandate situation. Fortunately, their attempt failed, and Judge Kathryn Mizelle's trial court opinion invalidating the transportation mask mandate remains the law of the land.

YouTube even dropped[84] its ban on videos containing "claims that masks do not play a role in preventing the contraction or transmission of COVID."[85] Despite our best efforts, especially related to masking, we will continue to feel the impact of allowing this abusive travesty to harm our children. Physiological development and social interaction have all taken a severe turn for the worse relating to mandatory mask wearing.[86]

In all, we have initiated or supported more than a dozen federal and state lawsuits to prevent and roll back the advancing medical police state.[87] We sued state and local governments, federal agencies, universities, and health sector giants, pressuring public and private employers alike.[88] We sued on behalf of children who did not want to take the shot. We sued on behalf of COVID-recovered college students and soldiers. We sued the federal departments of Health and Human Services and the Food and Drug Administration (HHS and FDA). We sued on behalf of workers whose employers were firing them, such as Kaiser Permanente. We sued on behalf of workers whose local and county government were firing them such as San Francisco firefighters. We sued on behalf of small business owners whose local government was blocking their business such as New York City. We opposed mandates of all types and showed the nation that doctors on the front lines aren't willing to rely on FDA summaries of data when the FDA hides the data itself.

While we scored some outright wins, our primary goal was not winning litigation but preventing vaccine *mandates* from becoming law and *slowing* the rushed rollout of injections. We knew mandates would far outlive COVID, and the shots would reveal themselves over time to be worthless and sometimes dangerous.[89] We only needed to buy the American people a delay. Our strategy was to throw enough sand in the gears until the negative shot data started to appear, and in that time, prevent any version of a vaccine mandate from becoming accepted and normalized. This approach proved successful, and I believe AFLDS was a critical factor in preventing the total loss of what we've always known to be our inalienable rights to life, liberty, and the pursuit of happiness. And our theory that these were *never* vaccines, but treatment only, finally was recognized by the courts.

Nevertheless, the government's ongoing disregard and distortion of the law continues to severely erode our Constitution. Regarding COVID litigation, the judiciary's reluctance to examine the evidence, choosing instead to kowtow to unsubstantiated (false) statements made by Executive Branch agencies, is disheartening and violative of our separation of powers. And as a two-tiered justice system is implemented, accepted, and normalized, as evidenced by the treatment of January 6 defendants, our sacred separation of powers is further subverted. This subversion is producing a disruptive double standard, which, like most historical conflicts of power, is perfectly by design.

CHAPTER SIX

COVID Crimes and Misdemeanors

A lie told once remains a lie, but a lie told a thousand times becomes the Truth.

—Chief Nazi Propagandist Joseph Goebbels

"If you can make someone believe absurdities, you can make them commit atrocities."[1] This is why it is worth fighting the absurdities. My life would have been much easier over the last few years had I simply accepted the government's nonsensical narrative. But, ultimately, freedom is lifesaving for all of us. And for me, honesty is like oxygen—I cannot breathe without it.

The answer to how to fight the absurdities of the last few years was simply to refuse. Lockdowns, face masks, and experimental injection mandates are irrational and harmful to both individuals and society at large, and not just physically harmful, but psychologically as well. A good reference to look up is the National Citizens Inquiry of Canada.[2] The onslaught of propaganda resulting from the "pandemic" led to an unfortunate chain reaction of what became known as "mass formation psychosis."[3] Worldwide indiscriminate social compliance led to baseless, contagious fear and hatred of fellow human beings.[4] It enabled the practice of casual cruelty. It made us *inhumane*.

Ideally, we would have all stood against absurdity together. I would have been thrilled had the doctors in the two emergency rooms where I worked united in refusing to follow dangerous protocols such as isolating anyone with a false positive PCR test and rushing to put them on ventilators and refusing to give our patients lifesaving medicines.

Follow the Money

But we were fighting uphill. The people who generated those absurdities didn't only control the media, they also controlled the purse strings of what Americans have been trained to call healthcare. During COVID, hospital administrators were handed a financial challenge and a quick fix. The challenge of treating COVID patients forced hospital controllers to minimize patient volume and cancel highly profitable "elective" surgeries like knee replacements, bringing them to the brink of, or into, bankruptcy. *Becker's Hospital Review* reported on this in November 2020:

> At least 32 hospitals across the U.S. have filed this year, and the financial challenges caused by the COVID-19 pandemic may force more hospitals to enter bankruptcy in coming months.
>
> Lower patient volumes, canceled elective procedures and higher expenses have created a cash crunch for hospitals, many of which were already operating on thin margins. U.S. hospitals are estimated to lose more than $323 billion this year, according to a report from the American Hospital Association.[5]

A hospital facing the loss of a third of its revenue would need to reduce payroll by that same percentage, whether by layoffs, salary reductions, or both. Or the bureaucrats could provide it with a quick fix. In this case, the lost revenue could be made up through hospitals providing protocol-based treatment to every patient with a positive PCR test result. This was an engineered problem and solution, centered around the lifeblood of a hospital: revenue.

The federal government (HHS, the Department of Health and Human Services) gave hundreds of millions of dollars to doctors and hospitals to not see patients.[6] For example, Cedars-Sinai Medical Center in Los Angeles, Northwestern Medical Center in Chicago, and Texas Children's Hospital in

Houston each received more than $200 million. New York University received more than $400 million. So, of course, hospital administrators complied with codifying the propaganda into bedside numbers by the employee-doctors who staffed their hospitals. I should know; I was one of them. Regardless of the actual reason for each patient's hospitalization, wildly inflated numbers were classified as COVID patients. Dissension by anyone within this chain would, of course, endanger everyone else's salaries. Subsequently, dissent was seldom expressed, and the cruelty and devastation grew.

You Get What You Pay For

This same compromise infected researchers, who are even more directly controlled than doctors. Scientists are acutely aware that they would be personally blacklisted from government funding if they failed to tow the party line.[7] As a result, researchers began publishing studies with preferential results to fit the narrative (i.e., propaganda) vs. studies with conclusions based on data (i.e., research).

To have any chance of winning a fight, you must understand precisely what you are fighting. Rather than a distinct enemy in the form of a rival nation or tribe, stakeholders control scientific funding, politicizing it to the point that it is almost impossible to rely on even peer-reviewed studies in (previously) prestigious medical journals. Likewise, it is now impossible to rely on government statistics (CDC, NIH, FDA, the US Surgeon General, etc.).

Researchers are informed of what their government or pharmaceutical industry-backed studies are funded to find, and, not surprisingly, they make sure to find it. They ensure that their conclusions support the government goal, often by "adjusting" the data with some ambiguous statement about why they made the adjustment, sometimes without even releasing the original data points, and sometimes in direct contradiction to the data itself. If they can't fudge the results enough to outright support the politically correct theory, they might dutifully conclude that their results "could be consistent with" that theory, or offer a conclusion that "additional research should be conducted" in their chosen field. Thus, the researcher stays on good terms with the funding government agencies and provides justification for additional research grants for themselves and their colleagues.

And the money flows in all directions. The NIH funds researchers, and Big Pharma donates and/or profit-shares with NIH. It's really a "you scratch my back, I'll scratch yours" relationship.

> New data from the National Institutes of Health reveal the agency and its scientists collected $710 million in royalties during the pandemic, from late 2021 through 2023 . . . Almost all that cash—$690 million—went to the National Institute of Allergy and Infectious Diseases, the subagency led by Dr. Anthony Fauci, and 260 of its scientists . . . the royalties paid from September 2009 to October 2021 were $325 million . . . Payments skyrocketed during the pandemic era: more than double the amount of cash flow to NIH compared to the prior 12 years combined. [Or 13 times the previous annual amounts.] All told, it's $1.036 billion. . . . It's unknown if any of the COVID vaccine royalties from Pfizer and Moderna is even included in these numbers—earlier this year Moderna paid $400 million.[8]

This corruption happened with almost every scientific article written about early treatment for COVID.[9] The corruption was so universal that I stopped reading any journals. If the scientific deception was so blatant that I, a mere bedside clinician and not a researcher, could spot it each time, it really was trash. The biggest scandal was "Lancet-Gate" involving the medical journal *The Lancet* and the non-data it published from the nonexistent company Surgisphere, now wiped clean off the Internet.[10]

Two of the most prestigious medical journals in the world, *The Lancet* and *The New England Journal of Medicine* (*NEJM*), had to retract their studies. This fact was well documented in a series published in *The Guardian,* starting with the headline: "The Lancet has made one of the biggest retractions in modern history. How could this happen?"[11] Other articles were eventually published with comments on the retraction:

> It sounds absurd that an obscure US company with a hastily constructed website could have driven international health policy

> and brought major clinical trials to a halt within the span of a few weeks. Yet that's what happened earlier this year, when Illinois-based Surgisphere Corporation began a publishing spree that would trigger one of the largest scientific scandals of the COVID-19 pandemic to date.[12]

This could not have happened by accident. The sheer number and magnitude of the things that went wrong or missing are too enormous to attribute to mere incompetence. There are many layers of double-checking before an article is published in some of the most prestigious medical journals in the world. The data upon which these studies were based were so ridiculously erroneous that it only took two weeks for an eagle-eyed independent physician to publicly demand an explanation. The company that "gathered" the alleged data (Surgisphere) is now wiped clean from the Internet. The most likely explanation is that the data were all fabricated. But the result of having published these fraudulent studies was that, all across the world, studies of hydroxychloroquine for early treatment were halted.

Big Pharma Controls the Medical Journals

There have been many whistleblowers over the years who have pointed out that the pharmaceutical industry is rigged. Pharmaceutical companies control the research that is published and the regulators who are tasked with overseeing them. Sell products to consumers. Rinse and repeat.

Consider what Dr. Philippe Douste-Blazy, the former French health minister, under secretary general of the UN, and candidate for director of WHO, has said. Dr. Douste-Blazy has publicly stated that *The Lancet* and the *NEJM* editors admitted to being pressured by pharmaceutical companies to publish certain results:

> *The Lancet's* boss . . . said . . . the pharmaceutical companies are so financially powerful today and are able to use such methodologies as to have us accept papers which . . . in reality manage to conclude what they want . . . I have been doing research for 20 years of my

> life. I never thought the boss of *The Lancet* could say that. And the boss of the *NEJM* too. He even said it was "criminal."[13]

Consider the warning by Dr. Marcia Angell, a former editor-in-chief of the *NEJM* who spent twenty years there. Dr. Angell has written several books and articles about how Big Pharma took control of medical research, education, and doctors, including *The Truth About the Drug Companies: How They Deceive Us and What to Do About It.*[14]

Consider the detailed research presented by Robert Kennedy Jr. in his book *The Real Anthony Fauci,*[15] which reveals how Anthony Fauci nearly single-handedly controlled the $6.1 billion annual taxpayer funding for scientific research. Kennedy investigated the murky relationship between Anthony Fauci, Bill Gates, and the $60 billion global vaccine market, revealing the corrupted relationship between Big Pharma and Big Government.

Consider the observation made by the surgeon general of Florida, Dr. Joseph Ladapo, MD, PhD, who points out that our medical students and doctors don't understand and are not well trained on how to methodically examine pharmaceutical studies.[16]

Before turning to the pharmaceutical industry corruption regarding the COVID shots specifically, I want to briefly address the issue of vaccine propaganda. I am not an expert on this. I personally had taken every shot until COVID and so had my children. But, over the years, I observed two vaccine lies that I was told in all of my training and journal reading. The first lie was that vaccines prevented the illness they targeted. But every day in my work as an ER physician I observed that virtually every single patient I admitted into the hospital with influenza had taken the influenza shot. In almost twenty years as an emergency doctor, I'm not sure I hospitalized a single person with influenza who *hadn't* taken the influenza shot. That's *weird.*

The second lie was the exaggeration of the dangers of the illnesses. I watched doctors proselytize parents about the chicken pox shot, which was introduced when my kids were young. Pediatricians exaggerated the threat of chicken pox to get parents to comply. I was fascinated watching the disinformation unfold in real time. The parents, who'd all had chicken pox themselves as children, were easily propagandized to believe something different from their own life experience! People just meekly followed what the doctor said, even when it contradicted their own life experience. Doctors were coercing patients by failing to give informed consent. And our society had become crushingly incurious and obedient to "experts."

If you are interested in the subject of pharmaceutical manufacturer corruption, consider reading *Plague of Corruption*.[17] If you are interested in understanding the science of vaccines and making an informed decision, consider reading *Turtles All the Way Down*.[18] If you are interested in learning the story of an early whistleblower, CDC scientist Dr. William Thompson,[19] who protested the CDC omitting data that showed that black babies were susceptible to autism from the MMR vaccine, consider reading *Vaccine Whistleblower*.[20]

I now turn attention to COVID shots propaganda, misinformation, and whistleblowers. I want to acknowledge Senator Ron Johnson, who held countless congressional hearings on the subject,[21] wherein the most esteemed scientists and bedside clinicians gave testimony in sharp contrast to Big Pharma. The nation and world owes him a debt of gratitude, because while Big Pharma lies a lot in general, they lied *continuously* during the COVID years.

Big Pharma Controls the Federal Agencies . . . and the Neighborhood Doctor

Let's start with the foundational lie that the COVID shots stopped transmission of the SARS-2 virus. This is the lie that bothered me the most because this disinformation was so severe it nearly toppled our Constitution. Additionally, it confused judges to adjudicate COVID cases as vaccine cases (see Chapter 4). Moreover, "everyone" said everyone *else* had to take the shot because "no one is safe unless everyone is safe." This was the most dangerous lie—*and our government knew it was lying.*

So judges, lawyers, news anchors, and celebrities felt morally righteous in portraying people who didn't want to take an experimental shot as immoral grandma-murderers, and everyone piled on. How infuriating to know that none of the elite who showered people like me with hate ever bothered to research or *read* the original paperwork.

These shots *never stopped transmission.* Which is worse, if Big Pharma lies to the FDA or if the FDA lies to the public? Big Pharma has a long and odious history of lying to the FDA and to the public. In 2009 Pfizer had to pay "the largest health care fraud settlement in the history of the Department of Justice, to resolve criminal and civil liability."[22] But it seems that now, Big Pharma doesn't even have to lie, as Big Pharma now controls our government agencies so completely that the government itself will do the lying. When Pfizer and Moderna submitted their applications to the FDA, they plainly told the FDA that these shots did not stop transmission but reduced symptoms only. Which was true (with the first variant). But then our *government* lied to us by telling us that the shots stopped transmission.

"Regulatory capture" is when the agencies that are supposed to regulate an industry are instead *captured* (controlled) by the industry itself. At this point in time, Big Pharma controls the FDA. Taxpayers funded the FDA from its creation in 1906 until 1992 when Congress passed the "Prescription Drug User Fee Act." Now, the pharmaceutical companies provide the majority of the FDA budget, which is charged with regulating those same pharmaceutical companies.

As *The New York Times* reported, Big Pharma finances about 75 percent of the FDA's drug division budget and about half of the overall FDA budget.[23] This is a deliberate choice made by our Congress, which must reauthorize this act every five years. So when executives from Pfizer, Moderna, Johnson & Johnson, and a slew of other pharmaceutical companies sat down to negotiations in 2022 with the FDA, the result was that Big Pharma provided money to hire specific staff for the FDA and then submitted applications for its own new products to be approved by this same staff.

Were Pfizer and Moderna innocent during COVID? Absolutely not. Their behavior has been despicable and lucrative.[24] But they are working for their shareholders, whereas the FDA is supposed to be working for *us.* The FDA read their applications, so why did they approve these shots in the middle of a pandemic? In the notes, I have provided one article from

November 2020, one month *prior* to the CDC unleashing the shots on the world, regarding questions about the effectiveness of the shots,[25] and here is an excerpt from the 2020 AFLDS white paper on the subject (see DrGoldReferences Appendix B).[26]

1. No Proof the Vaccine Stops Transmission of the Virus.
The trial data on the vaccinations released so far has not addressed the issue of *transmission* of the virus. That is, the efficacy data is primarily based on ***symptoms***, not on transmission. Could the vaccine create asymptomatic carriers that can unknowingly transmit the virus? The scientists are very upfront about the fact that they don't know if the vaccine even stops the spread of the virus![32] Dr. Corey who oversees the vaccine trials for the NIH COVID-10 Prevention Network says: "the studies aren't designed to assess transmission. They don't ask that question and there's really no information on this at this point in time."

Scientists involved in oversight of the Operation Warp Speed COVID-19 vaccine trials are tempering excitement about efficacy, noting that the studies haven't shown yet whether the products can prevent transmission of the SARS-CoV-2 virus.

"We don't know if people can become infected and thus also transmit even with vaccination," said former US Food and Drug Administration

Commissioner Margaret Hamburg, MD, in a November 18 briefing on COVID-19 vaccines sponsored by the American Public Health Association (APHA) and the National Academy of Medicine (NAM).

For that reason and others — including if there isn't significant uptake of vaccine — "people can expect to still be wearing masks, still be asked to follow non-pharmaceutical public health measures that we've all come to know so well," she said.

Another clever lie enabled the government to keep manipulating data to frighten people into submission. In September 2022, a peer-reviewed paper on COVID transmission was released by *Nature Communications*, which could be said to have brought scientific research to a new low. The study included the following definitions, which went completely unchallenged by those tasked with conducting its peer review:

> The definition of **fully vaccinated included individuals that had been infected** more than 14 days previously but was otherwise defined according to the vaccine used as follows: 7 days after second dose of Comirnaty (Pfizer/BioNTech); 15 days after second dose of Vaxzevria (AstraZeneca); **14 days after second dose of Spikevax (Moderna)** . . .

> **All other individuals, including 59 partially vaccinated individuals, were regarded as unvaccinated.**" [Emphases added].[27]

In other words, if someone had a positive PCR test before the study, did not test positive during the study, and *never* received any vaccination shots, they were listed as *vaccinated*, and thus as a vaccine success for not testing positive during the study. At the same time, someone who received *two doses* of the Moderna shot and tested positive thirteen days after the second shot was listed as *unvaccinated*, and thus as a COVID case due to *not* being vaccinated.

Dr. Simon Goddek,[28] holding a PhD in biotechnology, had this reaction to *Nature Communications*'s inversion of vaccinated and unvaccinated statuses:

> Academia is dead and the peer-review process is a joke . . . a study published in the "renowned" journal *Nature Communications* declared vaccinated people unvaccinated and vice versa. Unvaccinated people with a previous infection counted as fully vaccinated! That's how they manipulate data to justify injecting us with that gene therapy. The publication includes 20 authors and no objections were raised? Even the peer reviewers had nothing to claim about. I feel ashamed of being a scientist. From now on, I define myself as an independent science journalist.[29]

Scientists will go to extreme lengths to avoid #MedicalCancelCulture.[30] Consider Dr. Michel Goldman, a leading Belgian immunologist, who played the absurdity card when he reported on his *very own* vaccine injury—an extraordinary spread, "like fireworks," of lymphoma on the right side of his body just eight days post-injection near the injection site. Despite the clear implication of the title of his case report, "Rapid Progression of Lymphoma Following Moderna Vaccine Booster Shot," Goldman added:

> At this time, extrapolation of the findings of this case to other patients with AITL or other peripheral T cell lymphoma involving TFH cells is premature . . .

> Patient Perspective: The patient is the corresponding author of this case report . . . He remains convinced that mRNA vaccines represent very efficient products with a favorable benefit-risk ratio.[31]

A case report is a type of scientific publication where a physician or scientist notices something unusual in a specific patient or situation and reports it to the medical community. It is not an overall conclusion. A case report is an early question in the scientific process. Enough case reports on a specific issue typically lead to more in-depth study. This researcher, suffering from cancer that appeared to be linked to the shot, felt ethically obliged to report this to the medical community. However, he also felt obliged to put in a disclaimer to protect himself from #MedicalCancelCulture. The medical community is aware that a case report is just a single observation, and the fact that the author felt obliged to protect himself in this way is a sad commentary on where we are as a nation.

Mainstream Media Suppression of Cancer-Causing Data Linked to the Shots

In fact, there ended up being so many similar case reports worldwide that it did lead to further study, and even the coining of a new phrase for people whose cancer returned aggressively following the shots: turbo cancer.[32] There are increased cancer signals (early warning signs) across virtually all cancers and across the globe that are not being reported in the mainstream media. In fact the phrase "turbo cancer" itself is called a conspiracy theory. (Joke: What is the difference between a conspiracy theory and the truth? About six months.) Wikipedia currently says the following about turbo cancer:

> **Turbo cancer** is an anti-vaccination conspiracy theory alleging that people vaccinated against COVID-19, especially with mRNA vaccines, are suffering from a high incidence of fast-developing cancers. Although the idea has been spread by a number of vaccine opponents, including several health professionals, turbo cancer is not supported by cancer research, and there is no evidence that COVID-19 vaccination causes or worsens cancer.[33]

I checked the references on this page and, amusingly, the references are from "fact-checkers" or opinion writers and one government issue brief. But no scientific reference supports their headline that turbo cancer isn't real. One opinion writer criticized a scientist who recommended that the manufacturers show their product is not the cause of the increased rate. In other words, the scientist observed the higher rates, and the opinion writer, who cannot dispute the increased cancer rates, instead attacked the scientist's suggestion that Big Pharma or the government should have to show the shots are safe.

This demonstrates how irrelevant the elite believes the single individual is. Never lose sight of the fact that an individual's decision to take a medication depends heavily upon their personal risk assessment. If a person has a disease, they are more accepting of taking a risk. Because vaccines are given to healthy people, they must be extraordinarily safe. But in the world envisioned by our government and media, the collective is what matters. The individual is roadkill. This idea will be discussed later in the chapter.

Instead of parroting falsehoods and opinion like what Wikipedia presents, let's examine one recent scientific study titled "Increased Age-Adjusted Cancer Mortality After the Third mRNA-Lipid Nanoparticle Vaccine Dose During the COVID-19 Pandemic in Japan."[34] The study used a database of millions of people and distinguished between the injury to the body from the disease and the injury to the body from the shots. It also reviewed several mechanisms by which these shots increase the risk of cancer. The scientists used the official death statistics from Japan, comparing 2010–2019 to 2020–2022, and concluded:

> Statistically significant increases in age-adjusted mortality rates of all cancer and some specific types of cancer, namely, ovarian cancer, leukemia, prostate, lip/oral/pharyngeal, pancreatic, and breast cancers, were observed in 2022 after two-thirds of the Japanese population had received the third or later dose of SARS-CoV-2 mRNA-LNP vaccine. These particularly marked increases in mortality rates of these ERα-sensitive cancers may be attributable to several mechanisms of the mRNA-LNP vaccination rather than

> COVID-19 infection itself or reduced cancer care due to the lockdown. The significance of this possibility warrants further studies.[35]

Let's start with a quick science lesson. First, clots, called "thrombus" by doctors, are deadly. They are often the final step that causes death of a person or an organ. Second, these shots (they are not vaccines)[36] have two components: the spike protein (S protein) and the lipid nanoparticle (LNP) that surrounds it and facilitates (greases) its entry into organs. Third, LNPs can cross the blood-brain barrier (BBB), which is shocking. Almost nothing can cross the BBB, including no vaccines, but these shots do. The long-term effects of this are as yet unknown. Fourth, the biggest reason we don't all have cancer all the time is that our body's immune system is constantly surveilling and destroying cancer cells. The mechanisms by which these mRNA shots increase the risk of cancer include the following:

1. The shots increase clots. "The thrombus-forming tendency noted with the mRNA-LNP (lipid nanoparticle)" is a major cause of death in cancer patients' "cancer-associated thrombosis."
2. The shots suppress cancer immunosurveillance. "[S]tudies have shown that type I interferon (INF) responses, which play an essential role in cancer immunosurveillance, are suppressed after SARS-CoV-2 mRNA-LNP vaccination . . . suppresses the function of type I IFN and BRCA2, which are critical factors against cancer cells . . . These findings might explain excess mortality for all cancers, especially excess deaths for pancreatic cancer and breast cancer in our study."
3. The shots allow latent cancer-causing viruses to reactivate. "The shots cause immunosuppression and lead to the reactivation of latent viruses . . . considered oncogenic."
4. The S protein encourages estrogen-sensitive cancer cell growth. "In our study . . . ovarian cancer, leukemia, prostate, lip/oral/pharyngeal, pancreatic, and breast cancers increased significantly beyond the predicted rates, especially in 2022.

All of these cancers are known as estrogen and estrogen receptor alpha (ERα)-sensitive cancers. . . . that S-protein specifically binds to ERα. . . . Breast cancer cells grow when S is added instead of E2 . . ."

5. The S protein causes dysfunction of crucial cancer suppressor genes BRCA2, P53, and BRCA1. "Impaired BRCA1 activity is associated with higher risk of breast, uterine, and ovarian cancer in women and prostate cancer in men, as well as moderately higher risk of pancreatic cancer in both men and women. BRCA2-associated cancers include breast and ovarian cancer in women, prostate and breast cancer in men, and acute myeloid leukemia in children."
6. The LNPs cluster in highly sensitive areas. "LNPs accumulate particularly in the ovaries and bone marrow and could better explain our findings of excess mortalities from ovarian cancer and leukemia in 2022."
7. Other theoretical etiologies: "Accumulation of vaccine mRNA and reverse-transcribed DNA molecules in the cytoplasm [cell] could be expected to induce chronic autoinflammation, autoimmunity, DNA damage, and cancer risk in susceptible individuals." "This is a concern because studies have shown that the SARS-CoV-2 RNA could be reverse-transcribed to DNA and integrated into the human cell genome in vitro [petri dish.]" And the FDA already had previously warned that residual DNA could be oncogenic (cancer-causing). "There are several potential mechanisms by which residual DNA could be oncogenic, including the integration and expression of encoded oncogenes or insertional mutagenesis following DNA integration."[37]

Then there are the observed death rates due to cancer. The United Kingdom has a robust database that has provided raw data used by scientists all over the globe for years to measure various effects of the SARS-CoV-2 virus and the COVID-19 injections on populations. Their medical report titled, "Excess adjusted deaths from malignant neoplasms for ages

15 to 44, in England and Wales," provides a snapshot of what they have found regarding cancer in young people. You won't need a microscope, or a PhD, to understand the result:[38]

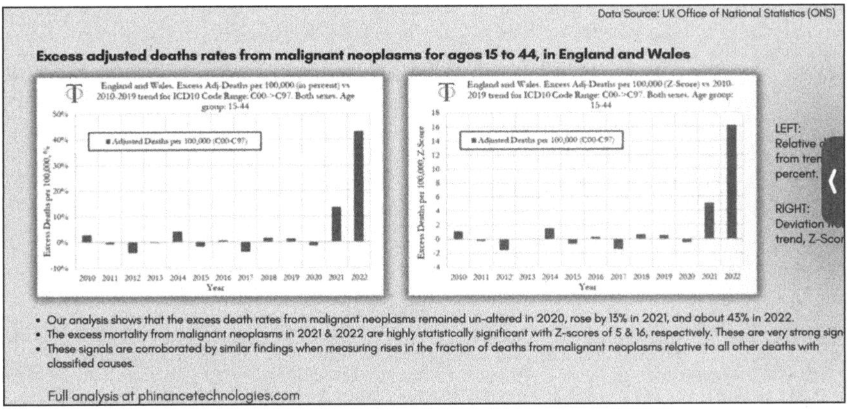
Data Source: UK Office of National Statistics (ONS)
Excess adjusted deaths rates from malignant neoplasms for ages 15 to 44, in England and Wales
England and Wales. Excess Adj-Deaths per 100,000 (in percent) vs 2010-2019 trend for ICD10 Code Range: C00->C97. Both sexes. Age group: 15-44
Adjusted Deaths per 100,000 (C00-C97)
Excess Deaths per 100,000, %
Year
England and Wales. Excess Adj-Deaths per 100,000 (Z-Score) vs 2010-2019 trend for ICD10 Code Range: C00->C97. Both sexes. Age group: 15-44
Adjusted Deaths per 100,000 (C00-C97)
Excess Deaths per 100,000, Z-Score
Year
LEFT:
Relative
percent.
RIGHT:
Deviation
• Our analysis shows that the excess death rates from malignant neoplasms remained un-altered in 2020, rose by 13% in 2021, and about 43% in 2022.
• The excess mortality from malignant neoplasms in 2021 & 2022 are highly statistically significant with Z-scores of 5 & 16, respectively. These are very strong
• These signals are corroborated by similar findings when measuring rises in the fraction of deaths from malignant neoplasms relative to all other deaths with classified causes.
Full analysis at phinancetechnologies.com

Another recent scientific study from June 2024 shows a strong link between the shot and death. A systematic REVIEW of autopsy findings in deaths after COVID-19 vaccination found "73.9 percent of deaths were directly due to or significantly contributed to by COVID-19 vaccination," and "data suggest a high likelihood of a causal link between COVID-19 vaccination and death."[39]

Following the Political Science

The introduction of bias in the science community is not a recent development.[40] In 1593, British admiral Sir Richard Hawkins found that oranges and lemons cured the deadly disease scurvy among his sailors during a stop in Brazil.[41] Independently, French navigator François Pyrard discovered the same in 1602 during a stop in Madagascar, concluding, "it is especially necessary before setting out to make provision of orange and lemon juice in order to [provide] their protection against this scurvy."[42]

The scientific establishment, however, was unwilling to give up its belief that scurvy was contagious. Sailors continued leaving for long voyages without the fruit juices they would need and continued falling ill. One sailor who fell extremely ill, more than a century after Hawkins's discovery, was abandoned on an island by his crew to protect them from him. His recovery and return to England on a passing ship led British naval surgeon James Lind to rediscover the healing power of citrus fruits in 1753.

However, Lind's research was rejected by the British medical establishment for some four decades, until lemon juice began to be provided to sailors in 1795. Even then, the story was far from over, particularly outside England. In 1874, Jean-Antoine Villemin, a member of the Académie Impériale de Médecine, argued that:

> Scurvy is a contagious miasm, comparable to typhus, which occurs in epidemic form when people are closely congregated in large groups as in prisons, naval vessels and sieges . . . We have many examples of well-fed sailors and soldiers going down with scurvy, while others less well fed do not.[43]

More than a century ago, in 1898, the American Pediatric Association blamed hundreds of new scurvy cases in young children on bacteria. The scurvy was actually caused by the new pasteurization process that destroyed the vitamin C in milk. Even in World War I, doctors blamed scurvy in soldiers on bacteria when outbreaks took place in divisions that had poor food rations. Only the isolation of vitamin C in the 1930s put an end to the idea that scurvy was contagious. Unfortunately, the same story played out with other vitamin deficiencies, including beriberi, caused by vitamin B1 deficiency, and pellagra, caused by niacin deficiency. Scientists refused to drop the idea that these diseases were contagious, and untold numbers of people got ill and died long after their cures were known.

The Great AIDS Debate You Didn't Know Existed

In retrospect, it's even more interesting to discuss why research into the etiology of AIDS was aggressively blocked by Anthony Fauci. For forty years it has been dogma that HIV causes AIDS. And from that point onward, many drugs have been sold. But many incredibly high-profile researchers have said, since the beginning of the AIDS epidemic, that HIV is not the etiology.

Immunologist Michael Gottlieb, at the UCLA School of Medicine, diagnosed the first five cases of AIDS in 1980 and described them in the *Morbidity and Mortality Weekly Report* of June 5, 1981:

> The patients did not know each other and had no known common contacts or knowledge of sexual partners who had had similar illnesses. The 5 did not have comparable histories of sexually transmitted disease . . . All 5 reported using inhalant drugs . . .[44]

Those inhalants, known as poppers, had been discussed by the *Canadian Journal of Psychiatry* shortly before the appearance of AIDS in a 1978 paper "Poppers, A New Recreational Drug Craze":

> Amyl nitrite is a volatile yellow liquid [that] comes in fragile glass ampoules which are crushed or "popped" in the fingers and then inhaled: hence the colloquialism "poppers. . ." the current poppers "craze" began only within the last two to three years.[45]

Poppers work like Viagra (years prior to that 1998 release) by relaxing sphincter muscles and were ubiquitous in the gay community in the 1980s.

> Now the use of poppers has reached almost "epidemic" proportions in major North American cities. However, it has been centered so far among those persons who frequent homosexual bars, discotheques, and steam baths.[46]

Professor Duesberg had this to say about poppers in *Inventing the AIDS Virus*:

> Few chemicals are more toxic than nitrites. Sodium nitrite, a much weaker, related compound used in tiny amounts as a preservative in meats, has been regulated for years as a potential cancer-causing agent. The alkylated nitrites (poppers), on the other hand, react more violently with almost anything.

> Upon mixing with water, as in the human body, these nitrites form the unstable nitrous acid, which in turn destroys any biological molecules within reach. The nitrites and their breakdown products have long been known to scientists for their ability to mutate DNA, a point recently verified by direct experiment. In addition, nitrites are some of the most powerful cancer-causing chemicals in existence.[47]

Several laboratories followed up on Professor Gottlieb's findings about poppers and found "clear destructive effects on the immune system, especially after a few months."[48]

And there are many others. Dr. Robert Willner, MD, PhD, a medical doctor so convinced of the harmlessness of HIV, injected himself with HIV-positive blood on live television.[49] Repeatedly. And Professor Luc Montagnier, who was awarded the Nobel Prize in Physiology or Medicine for being the one to discover HIV,[50] came to the shocking conclusion that "the HIV virus is harmless and passive, a benign virus."[51]

But Anthony Fauci, head of the NIH's National Institute of Allergy and Infectious Diseases and in charge of determining federal health policy for AIDS, blocked Duesberg (and others) from continuing research into non-HIV causes of AIDS, declaring the science to be "settled." Then, an NIH staffer flew Duesberg to NIH headquarters, where a senior government scientist took him to the opera and bribed him with continuing his research funding if he would sign a prewritten paper saying that HIV does in fact cause AIDS. Duesberg scornfully declined.[52]

Once HIV was the "accepted" etiology of AIDS, Big Pharma could sell even very toxic drugs to treat it. Jerome Horwitz, who invented azidothymidine (AZT), found it to be too toxic even for chemotherapy, killing healthy cells together with cancer cells.[53] He never even published the results of his experiment and did not seek a patent for his discovery.

I am not expert enough to know the scientific truth about AIDS, but I do know the NIH funds pretty much anything. In medical residency I once had to review a paper that reported on who suffers foot burns when walking on hot sand. The answer was as follows: people who couldn't get off the beach on their own (little children) and people with impaired sensation in their feet (diabetics). This stunning conclusion was funded by the NIH.

Where there's censorship, I'm suspicious, and when there's hundreds of billions of dollars at stake, I'm even more suspicious. HIV being the etiology of AIDS correlates to trillions of dollars in anti-HIV drug sales ($30 billion in 2023).[54] Poppers, being the etiology of AIDS, does not. Our federal government is massively funded specifically to present profitable man-made solutions that they can control. That this manipulation has spread from celebrities, politicians, and the media to take root among scientists and physicians is a very bad prognosticator.

Dr. Kary B. Mullis was a Nobel Prize winner who challenged the narrative on HIV, meaning he challenged Fauci. He stated:

> If people think I'm a crazy person, that's okay. But here's a Nobel Prize winner trying to ask a simple question from those who spent $22 billion and killed 100,000 people [with a lethal drug (AZT) for a harmless virus (HIV)].[55]

COVID Lies: The Corruption of Federal Public Health[56]

Five years later, my 2020 speeches sound downright prophetic.[57] Now everyone agrees with everything I have said since 2020: Lockdowns and masks don't work, but early treatment does work.[58] There were many lies told by our public health officials. Let's start, first, with confessions from the tyrants themselves.

In May 2024 Dr. Redfield, the former director of the Centers for Disease Control and Prevention (CDC), publicly acknowledged the shots are not safe and they should never have been forced on all persons.[59] The CDC is the agency that pushed the lies on the entire world; and, in 2024, the CDC director admitted the whole thing was a scam.

And then, of course, there's Anthony Fauci. He is the person most responsible for nearly destroying the nation, permanently shuttering small businesses, decimating the middle class, keeping kids out of school, causing increases in depression and drug use and abuse, and destroying millions of human lives. To people who think I'm being too harsh, I have five words: *I'm not being harsh enough.* Only a person who believes in fascism and believes himself the anointed king could have done this. I'll share just one short clip of a leaked video that came out under congressional questioning, years after Fauci forced horrific policies that seemed specifically designed to destroy America. In the leaked video, you hear Anthony Fauci saying the following:

> Once people feel empowered, and protected legally, you are going to have schools, universities, and colleges are going to say you want to come to this college, buddy, you're going to get vaccinated. Lady, you're going to get vaccinated. Yeah, big corporations like Amazon and Facebook and all of those others are going to say, you want to work for us, you get vaccinated. And it's been proven that when you make it difficult for people in their lives, they lose their **ideological bullshit.** And they get vaccinated. [Emphasis added][60]

Remember six-foot social distancing? For most of us, it was annoying and a reminder we were no longer free. But the most harmful effect of six-foot social distancing was forcing schools to close. It was not possible for most schools to comply with the six-foot distancing rule, due to the amount of space in a given classroom. The harm that has resulted to our youth and young adults is incalculable.

And, of course, the mask was also a lie. For his entire career spanning more than forty years, Fauci said masks do not work to stop tiny respiratory viruses. On March 8, 2020, he did a *60 Minutes* interview advising people *not* to wear a mask.[61] Then, he did all he could to force every American to wear a mask. Never forget what he did to children and babies.[62] And, of course, the shots didn't work, and they are not vaccines (see: Chapter 16).

Fauci made things up that suited his political and financial agenda and called them science. When put under oath, however, he told a completely different story, and it's worth reading. He admitted there was no scientific basis for the harmful policies he forced on the world. Below is a screenshot of his words from his congressional testimony, under oath, in January 2024:[63]

Q Do you recall when discussions regarding, kind of, the at-least-a-6-foot threshold began?
A The 6-foot in the school?
Q Six-foot overall. I mean, 6-foot was applied at businesses --
A Yeah.
Q -- it was applied in schools, it was applied here. At least how the messaging was applied was that 6-foot distancing was the distance that needed to be --
A You know, I don't recall. It sort of just appeared. I don't recall, like, a discussion of whether it should be 5 or 6 or whatever. It was just that 6-foot is --
Q Did you see any studies that supported 6 feet?
A I was not aware of studies that -- in fact, that would be a very difficult study to do.

SOCIAL DISTANCING

Q Do you recall reviewing any studies or data supporting masking for children?
A You know, I might have, Mitch, but I don't recall specifically that I did. I might have.
Q Since the -- there's been a lot of studies that have come out since the pandemic started, but specifically on this there have been significant on kind of like the learning loss and speech and development issues that have been associated with particularly young children wearing masks while they're growing up. They can't see their teacher talk and can't learn how to form words.
Have you followed any of those studies?
A No. But I believe that there are a lot of conflicting studies too, that there are those that say, yes, there is an impact, and there are those that say there's not. I still think that's up in the air.

MASKING

How could Fauci have been so effective? It's almost as if he had experience knowing how to pull off an insider coup. Indeed, he did. COVID-19 was not his first time up at bat. COVID-19 was Fauci 2.0. AIDS was Fauci 1.0. Let us compare the three most consequential lies Anthony Fauci told during the COVID pandemic to the three most consequential lies Anthony Fauci told during the AIDS epidemic decades earlier: social distancing, no current available treatment, pursue a vaccine above all other priorities.

	Proclamation		**Effect**	
	Fauci 2.0 (COVID-19)	Fauci 1.0 (AIDS)	Fauci 2.0 (COVID-19)	Fauci 1.0 (AIDS)
Lie	Avoid all people; six-feet social distancing.	*Avoid gay people; casual contact with gay people is risky.*	Schools & businesses closed. Fear. Isolation.	*Decade of fear of gay men and AIDS patients.*
Lie	Can't use cheap, safe meds. (e.g. HCQ, IVM); inexpensive and safe treatments blocked.	*Can't use cheap, safe meds. (e.g. Bactrim); inexpensive and safe treatments blocked.*	Many deaths. Also enabled rapid shots.	*Many deaths.*
Lie	We need a vaccine; we'll be safe after a vaccine.	*We need a vaccine; we'll be safe after a vaccine.*	Faulty non-vaccine rushed to market.	*No functional vaccine. Huge money for the NIH.*[64]

I'm old enough to remember what it was like in the 1980s and 1990s with AIDS. Everyone was taught to panic if coming in contact with a gay man.[65] Everyone put gloves on just to touch an AIDS patient, including AIDS babies. Fauci knew, or should have known from the very beginning, *that AIDS could not be transmitted casually*. Bless Princess Diana. She was the first public personality to hold an AIDS baby without gloves. This started the renormalization of the treatment of gay men.

I was in medical school and residency at this time. Very often, the final fatal illness for an AIDS patient was a specific "pneumocystis carinii pneumonia," or PCP, which had been seen in other immune-compromised conditions. Therefore, Fauci knew, or should have known, a cheap, safe, old antibiotic was very effective for PCP (e.g., Bactrim). Fauci blocked safe antibiotics for more than ten years in pursuit of a vaccine. The picture below is a screen shot of the article in this note, discussing PCP and its treatment before AIDS.[66] I can attest to having personally experienced difficulty in correctly treating PCP in my professional practice due to this issue.

> Because there are a number of immunological disorders that result in a susceptibility to similar opportunistic infections that are characteristic of AIDS, PCP had been well studied before AIDS appeared. When the epidemic began we knew how to diagnose this particular opportunistic infection, we knew how to treat it and we also knew how to prevent it.
>
> As early as 1977 it had been well established that PCP could be prevented by an inexpensive medication, yet official recommendations for the use of this and other interventions as prophylactic agents against PCP in people with AIDS did not appear until 1989.
>
> This long delay is a strange episode in the history of medicine, although it is barely remembered today. But anyone who experienced the first decade of the epidemic in the US will remember the scourge that was PCP.

When AIDS came along, the NIH was practically broke, but Fauci created extreme and unwarranted hysteria (AIDS was not casually transmitted), which led to an enormous influx of money. Due to bringing in so much money to NIH, Fauci became very powerful. Instead of helping the existing patients, almost exclusively gay men, Fauci spent his time and money trying to develop a vaccine, which proved elusive. Fauci knew, or should have known, AIDS was never a threat to the general population. After about a decade of failure on the vaccine, he permitted the use of the cheap, old antibiotic.

Because of his total neglect of a disenfranchised group (gay people) for years, Fauci was quite despised. He was perceived to be incompetent, uncaring, and arrogant. For example, in 1988, the prominent gay activist Larry Kramer called Fauci a murderer, an idiot, and pompous. The image below is a clip from Larry Kramer's 1988 article published in *The San Francisco Examiner*:[67]

SAY By Larry Kramer

I CALL YOU MURDERERS

An open letter to an incompetent idiot, Dr. Anthony Fauci, of the National Institute of Allergy and Infectious Diseases:

I have been screaming at the National Institutes of Health since I first visited your Animal House of Horrors in 1984. I called you monsters then and I called you idiots in my play, *The Normal Heart*, and now I call you murderers.

You are responsible for supervising all government-funded AIDS treatment research programs. In the name of right, you make decisions that cost the lives of others. I call that murder.

At hearings on April 29 before the House Subcommittee on Human Resources, after almost eight years of the worst epidemic in modern history, perhaps to be the worst in all history, you were pummeled into admitting publicly what some of us have been claiming since you took over some three years ago.

You admitted that you are an incompetent idiot.

Over the past four years, $374 million has been allocated for AIDS treatment research. You were in charge of spending much of that money.

It doesn't take a genius to set up a nationwide network of testing sites, commence a small number of moderately sized treatment efficacy tests on a population desperate to participate in them, import any and all interesting drugs (now numbering about 110) from around the world for inclusion in these tests at these sites and swiftly get into circulation anything that remotely passes muster. Yet, after three years, you have established only a system of waste, chaos and uselessness.

To quote Rep. Henry Waxman, D.-Los Angeles: "Dr. Fauci, your own drug selection committee has named 24 drugs as high priority for development and trials. As best I can tell, 11 of these 24 are not in trials yet. Six of these drugs have been waiting for six months to more than a year. Why the delays? I understand the need to do what you call 'setting priorities,' but it appears even with your own scientists' choices, the trials are not going on."

Now you come bawling to Congress that you don't have enough staff, office space, lab space, secretaries, computer operators, lab technicians, file clerks, janitors, toilet paper; and that's why the drugs aren't being tested and the network of treatment centers isn't working and the drug protocols aren't in place. You have $374 million and you expect us to buy this garbage bag of excuses.

The gay community has been on your case for three years. For 36 agonizing months, you refused to go public with what was happening (correction: not happening), and because you wouldn't speak up until you were asked pointedly by a congressional committee, we lie down and die and our bodies pile up higher and higher in hospitals and homes and hospices and streets and doorways.

Meanwhile, drugs we have been begging that you test remain untested. The list of promising untested drugs is now so endless and the pipeline so clogged with NIH and FDA bureaucratic lies that there is no Roto-Rooter service in all God's Christendom that will ever muck it out.

The gay community has, for five years, told the NIH which drugs to test because we know and hear first what is working on some of us somewhere. You couldn't care less about what we say. You won't answer our phone calls or letters or listen to anyone in our stricken community. What tragic pomposity.

The gay community has consistently warned that unless you move quickly your studies will be worthless because we are already taking drugs into our bodies that we desperately locate all over the world (who can wait for you?), and all your "scientific" protocols are stupidly based on utilizing guinea-pig bodies that are "clean." You wouldn't listen. Why should those who can obtain the drugs take the chance of receiving a placebo?

How many years ago did we tell you about aerosol pentamidine, Tony? This stuff saves lives. And we dis-

In 2014, the play, *The Normal Heart*, based upon Larry Kramer's observation of Fauci's NIH, was turned into an HBO movie.[68] Furthermore, gay activist Randy Shilts outed Fauci in the book, *And The Band Played On*,[69] a real-time page-turner historical account of the AIDS epidemic. Notably, Randy Shilts developed AIDS while writing the book. I read Shilts's book when it first was published in 1987, and it forever changed me. Until I read this book, it had never occurred to me to question any widely accepted medical narrative. I had no idea that powerful government and corporate interests were influencing doctors to hurt patients. I am very grateful I read this book in my early twenties—it made me a much better doctor to all my patients.

I personally remember a protest in San Francisco where they burned Fauci in effigy in 1988. The picture below is a clip from these protests from a BBC article on Anthony Fauci.[70]

Clearly, during the AIDS epidemic, there was tremendous hatred of Anthony Fauci. Fauci was evil personified to millions of gay people all across the world. With very rare exception, the media failed to provide *any* of this context in their adoring coverage of him during COVID, which is pure disinformation propaganda through the form of *omission bias*.

It would not be possible to list the innumerable government lies, but a few examples will demonstrate that the corruption is so deep and so broad that an enormous swath of the American people, myself included, no longer believe any of the three-letter federal agencies. Not the CDC, NIH, FDA, HHS, CMS. (And in other chapters it's clear we don't trust the FBI, DOJ, BOP, CIA, DHS, and TSA either.) I'll share four of my "favorite" lies to demonstrate.

a. *LIE: Ivermectin is horse medicine.* The FDA tweeted to the entire world that ivermectin is "horse" medicine and mocked anyone who took it. It was a remarkably low moment for the United States government. Ivermectin won the Nobel Prize in (*human!*) medicine in 2015; it is listed on the WHO's List of Essential Medications that all nations should have available; and it has been in constant use in our country since receiving FDA approval more than thirty-five years ago. Frontline doctors, led by Dr. Mary Talley Bowden, sued the FDA over this egregious disinformation campaign and won.[71] But it took two years, enormous effort, funding, and countless loss of lives.
b. *LIE: Hydroxychloroquine is dangerous.*[72] HCQ has been FDA approved for seventy years. It, too, is listed on the WHO's List of Essential Medications that all nations should have available. In the federal government's database FAERS (FDA Adverse Events Reporting System), HCQ has far fewer adverse events than Tylenol.[73] There are more than 500 million prescriptions written for this drug annually in the United States, typically for lupus or rheumatoid arthritis. It is over-the-counter in the majority of the world, excluding First World nations.
c. *LIE: The COVID shot stops transmission.* No, they never did. Pfizer and Moderna never even claimed it did in the paperwork they submitted to the FDA. Knowing this, the CDC still unleashed the shots on Americans in December 2020. Note the Medscape article from November 2020.[74] Not surprisingly, because so many people took the shot and promptly got COVID themselves and gave it to others, by

July 2021 the CDC had to admit they lied.[75] Of course their press release confession was in doublespeak. But the CDC published a study in August 2021 showing that vaccinated persons had a higher rate of infection and higher viral loads than the unvaccinated.[76]

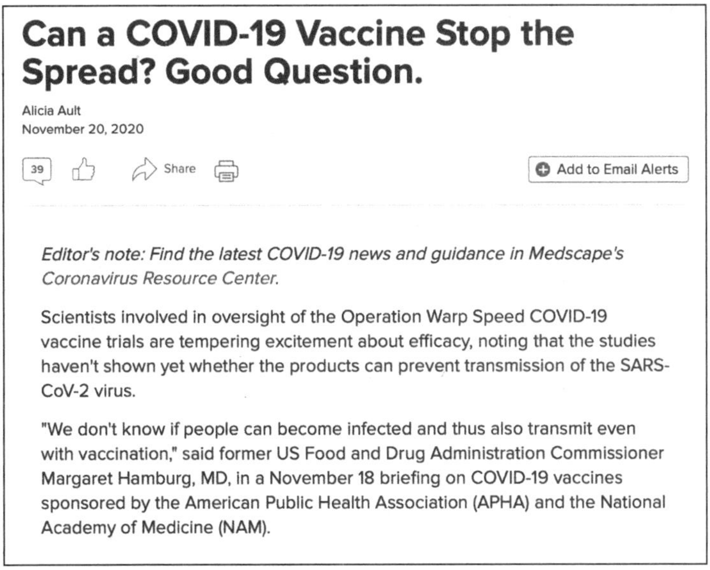

Can a COVID-19 Vaccine Stop the Spread? Good Question.

Alicia Ault
November 20, 2020

39 Share Add to Email Alerts

Editor's note: Find the latest COVID-19 news and guidance in Medscape's Coronavirus Resource Center.

Scientists involved in oversight of the Operation Warp Speed COVID-19 vaccine trials are tempering excitement about efficacy, noting that the studies haven't shown yet whether the products can prevent transmission of the SARS-CoV-2 virus.

"We don't know if people can become infected and thus also transmit even with vaccination," said former US Food and Drug Administration Commissioner Margaret Hamburg, MD, in a November 18 briefing on COVID-19 vaccines sponsored by the American Public Health Association (APHA) and the National Academy of Medicine (NAM).

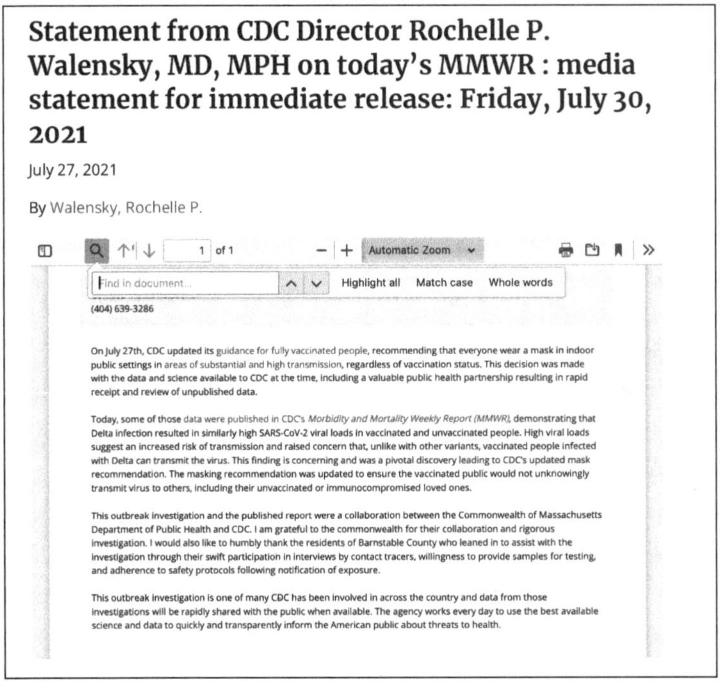

Statement from CDC Director Rochelle P. Walensky, MD, MPH on today's MMWR : media statement for immediate release: Friday, July 30, 2021

July 27, 2021

By Walensky, Rochelle P.

1 of 1 Automatic Zoom

Find in document... Highlight all Match case Whole words

(404) 639-3286

On July 27th, CDC updated its guidance for fully vaccinated people, recommending that everyone wear a mask in indoor public settings in areas of substantial and high transmission, regardless of vaccination status. This decision was made with the data and science available to CDC at the time, including a valuable public health partnership resulting in rapid receipt and review of unpublished data.

Today, some of those data were published in CDC's *Morbidity and Mortality Weekly Report (MMWR)*, demonstrating that Delta infection resulted in similarly high SARS-CoV-2 viral loads in vaccinated and unvaccinated people. High viral loads suggest an increased risk of transmission and raised concern that, unlike with other variants, vaccinated people infected with Delta can transmit the virus. This finding is concerning and was a pivotal discovery leading to CDC's updated mask recommendation. The masking recommendation was updated to ensure the vaccinated public would not unknowingly transmit virus to others, including their unvaccinated or immunocompromised loved ones.

This outbreak investigation and the published report were a collaboration between the Commonwealth of Massachusetts Department of Public Health and CDC. I am grateful to the commonwealth for their collaboration and rigorous investigation. I would also like to humbly thank the residents of Barnstable County who leaned in to assist with the investigation through their swift participation in interviews by contact tracers, willingness to provide samples for testing, and adherence to safety protocols following notification of exposure.

This outbreak investigation is one of many CDC has been involved in across the country and data from those investigations will be rapidly shared with the public when available. The agency works every day to use the best available science and data to quickly and transparently inform the American public about threats to health.

d. *LIE: The COVID shot is safe and effective.* Physicians are by nature, training, and experience very risk-averse. We are the professionals who recommend pregnant women not take a single alcoholic drink or a bite of sushi. We require years of research prior to approving medications or treatments. We teach patients to avoid new and unproven remedies. But when the government and media told doctors to comply with a new and experimental treatment modality, the doctors silently obeyed. There are infinite sources who have attested to the shots being unsafe and ineffective, but here are two die-hards who have done an about-face: the former director of the CDC[77] and former CNN anchor Chris Cuomo.[78]

e. *Bonus LIE: Vaccines stop the transmission of viruses.* On September 5, 2023, FDA propagandist Dr. Peter Marks stated: "It is important to note that FDA's licensure standards for vaccines do not require demonstration of the prevention of infection or transmission . . . There is no requirement that the vaccine also prevents infection with the pathogen that can cause the disease or transmission of that pathogen to others."[79] Wow.

I Followed the Science

With most doctors and scientists willingly (if perhaps awkwardly) pretending not to see clear signs of danger, and with the media shutting out any divergent views, average laypeople found themselves chastised by public health officials. Anyone who dared to oppose pandemic policies as illegitimate was accused of refusing to "follow the science." Many people in the general public who exercised even a little independent thought and common sense realized things were not adding up. Yet, it was nearly impossible to find straight answers.

In that void of honest scientific review, it was more important than ever to advise the public that science is not unilaterally defined by the CDC or by any government agency. So, for example, I told the world in April 2020 that the world-famous medical journal *JAMA* had published fraudulent data to block hydroxychloroquine usage.[80] This was a necessary step by them so the vaccines could be rushed to market a few months later.

On top of that, these alphabet agencies had fallen far short of providing accurate information and the necessary transparency required to maintain public trust. Indeed, it became increasingly clear that this was not an accidental failure but a coordinated, intentional effort to consolidate all authority and public trust into a centralized point of state control. It was the modern advent of medical Marxism, and where Marxism flourishes, genocide follows. Essentially, the NIH appears to have knowingly contributed to funding the Wuhan Institute of Virology to make the virus. Then, the NIH used the most toxic part of that virus to sell shots that they co-patented.

The CDC pushed these shots on every man, woman, and child in America. They are the entity most responsible for allowing teenagers, children, and even infants to receive an experimental and unnecessary shot that led to many young people dying and being harmed. As stated above, in 2024, the former director of the CDC acknowledged his errors, but he did not take personal accountability.[81] Among other things, he admitted the shots don't work and people younger than age fifty shouldn't take them.

I mention this here not to state the obvious errors in his current words, but because his 2024 words are exactly what I said *3.5 years earlier* in October 2020 when I published a white paper decrying the experimental shots (see DrGoldReferences Appendix B).[82] At that time, I only very cautiously allowed for the shots to even be considered in one subset: frail elderly. Why in the world does anyone put their trust in these alphabet agencies, whose regulators are captured by Big Pharma? I was an ordinary bedside clinician who gleaned this information solely by reading publicly available documents. I reject that CDC Director Dr. Redfield knew less than me: that degree of incompetence is just not possible.

Finally, we have to at least mention the amount of money the pharmaceutical industry pours into propagandizing pediatricians. Pediatricians earn a huge percentage of their salary from complying with the vaccine schedule.[83] The way the companies coerce this is particularly clever. The doctor gets money for every child who takes a shot. But the doctor only gets this money if a certain percentage of his entire practice takes various shots. This financial "trick" makes the doctor very aggressive toward making sure each and every patient takes a shot. If Johnny's mommy doesn't want a particular shot, the doctor doesn't internalize that he may lose $70. Rather, he thinks he may have lost a few hundred thousand dollars if Johnny's failure to comply puts him under a certain percentage line! Your doctor almost certainly is not thinking only of your best interest; she has been wittingly or unwittingly corrupted.

The best predictor of future behavior is past behavior.
—Dr. Phil McGraw

Lies, Lies, and More Lies

I am a big fan of exposing corrupt people. I don't care if their actions are intentional and deliberate or willfully ignorant. Millions died, worldwide economies faltered, middle-class businesses were wiped out, children lost IQ points, families were fractured, fear gripped Americans and moved us closer to communism, #TeamLunacy took over, and the political results were catastrophic.

From major public and private officials and institutions, there was an endless stream of false information, COVID propaganda, and outright lies during the pandemic. For example, this graphic from July 2020 shows that there was never justification for the widespread fearmongering over SARS-2.

Per the CDC, without any treatment at all, the overwhelming majority of people survive. It was only a significant cause of death in people with multiple other medical conditions. Some of these lies were caused by mere negligence, careless incompetence, and a lack of data. But many lies were told purposely and knowingly by officials intending to mislead. Many of those official lies killed countless numbers of people. Perhaps history and future courts, such as a Nuremberg 2.0, will give us the answers to those questions.

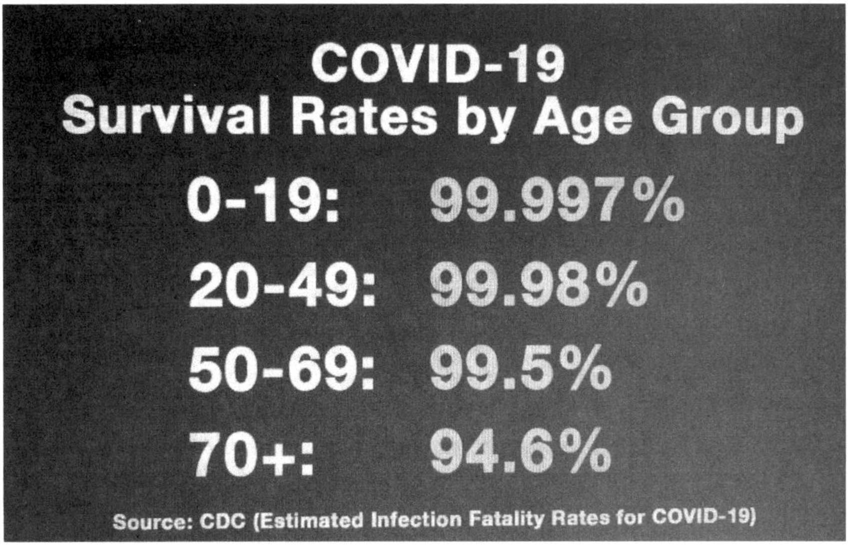
COVID-19
Survival Rates by Age Group
0-19: 99.997%
20-49: 99.98%
50-69: 99.5%
70+: 94.6%
Source: CDC (Estimated Infection Fatality Rates for COVID-19)

Who's Who of Propagandists

It helps to realize that different people have very different motives for repeating the same lie. There are several reasons why truthful and accurate medical information was aggressively labeled as disinformation while official COVID lies were promoted. I believe there were four different types of propagandists, who, in concert, made it appear like a uniform narrative. I attach an incomplete table of some offenders.

1. Useful Idiots = the media, many doctors
2. Smug Intellectuals = doctors and influencers
3. Financial Self-Interest = big pharma, big tech, politicians
4. Truly Nefarious = small elite who benefit from central control

Useful Idiots ←→Smug Intellectuals		Self-Interest ←→Truly Nefarious	
Media	Doctors	Politics/Business	Money/Power
Chris Cuomo	Francis Collins	Justin Trudeau	Klaus Schwab, WEF
Sanjay Gupta	Peter Hotez	Andrew Cuomo	Bill Gates
Don Lemon	Neil Ferguson	Rachel Levine	Tedros, WHO
Rachel Maddow	David Fisman	Rishi Sunak	CCP
Joy Reid	Christin Grady	Boris Johnson	**Anthony Fauci**
Marc Siegel	Mandy Cohen	James Clyburn	Albert Bourla
Neil Cavuto	Paul Offit	Gretchen Whitmer	Stephane Bancel
Nicola Sturgeon	Andrea Horwath	Alex Azar	Ugur Sahin
Nicole Saphier	Xavier Becerra	Jack Dorsey	
BBC	Drew Weissman	Mark Zuckerburg	
NY Times Editorial	Anthony Fauci		
Leana Wen	Howard Njoo		
	Scott Gottlieb		
	Janet Woodcock		
	Peter Daszak		
	Ashish Jha		
	Rochelle Walensky		
	Ralph Baric		
	Stephen Hahn		
	Deborah Birx		
	Vivek Murthy		
	Peter Marks		

The Deadly Disinformation Dozen

In 2020, I found myself in the company of fellow truth-tellers and medical experts who were all focused on exposing the numerous COVID lies. For freely speaking true and accurate medical information, we were all persecuted to various degrees. We were targeted by the media, employers, and professional accreditation societies. We were accused of spreading "misinformation, disinformation, and malinformation." Many of us were labeled as the "Disinformation Dozen" by the Biden White House, as discussed in Judge Terry A. Doughty's landmark 155-page opinion in *Murthy v Missouri, fka Missouri v. Biden*, the major First Amendment case discussed in Chapter 4.

But who were the *actual* "Deadly Disinformation Dozen," those who chose to spread their official COVID lies with often fatal consequences? America's Frontline Doctors answers this key question by giving you the propagandists' own words in this video entitled *The Deadly Disinformation Dozen*.[84] How are these people not in prison?

The Deadly Disinformation Dozen may go down in infamy for their crimes against humanity. Here is but a sample of their official COVID lies covered in the video:

NIAID Director Anthony Fauci:[85]

Fauci lied about masks, natural immunity, lockdowns, experimental mRNA injections being safe (hint: they are experimental) and effective (hint: they did not prevent transmission and infection). He also lied about the origins of the virus and about his agency financing dangerous gain-of-function research, and he admitted to pressuring people to give up their inalienable rights, which he calls "ideological bullshit."

CDC Director Rochelle Walensky:

Rochelle Walensky lied about the experimental mRNA injections preventing transmission and infection. She also lied about them being safe for pregnant women, despite huge increases in miscarriages and stillbirths, a 1,200-fold increase in menstrual abnormalities, and a 57-fold increase in miscarriages.[86]

Biden through Jen Psaki (spokesperson):

The Biden administration lied about the mRNA injections preventing transmission and infection, and about not mandating vaccines, masks, and social distancing, all of which they ended up mandating.

Religion of Public Health Adherent Dr. Ashish Jha:

Dr. Ashish Jha, head of the Biden White House COVID response, lied about masks working, even though it was clear he knew that masks did not work.

Industry Shill Dr. Peter Hotez:

Dr. Peter Hotez, mainstream-media-virologist-whore, lied about the accelerated development timeline of the mRNA injections not being an accelerated timeline at all and falsely claimed that these injections would "stop asymptomatic transmission."

NIH Director Dr. Francis Collins:

Dr. Francis Collins fabricated "six-foot social distancing," which was the main reason schools were forced to close; he mocked the Chinese Wuhan Institute of Virology lab leak theory as a "conspiracy theory"; he lied about the billions of dollars of profit from the mRNA shots. But under oath on January 12, 2024, he testified to the opposite of all this:[87]

> Question: "Putting aside de nova, the possibility of a laboratory or research-related accident, a researcher doing something in a lab, getting infected with a virus, and then sparking the pandemic. Is that scenario a conspiracy theory?"
> Dr. Collins: "Not at this point."
> Question: "Is the origin of COVID-19 still unsettled science?"
> Dr. Collins: "Yes."
> Question: "Moving on to social distancing and the various regulations surrounding that. On March 22, 2020, the CDC issued guidance describing social distancing to include remaining out congregant settings, avoiding mass gatherings, and maintaining approximately six feet from others when possible. We asked Dr. Fauci where the six feet came from, and he said, 'It kind of just appeared,' is the quote. Do you recall science or evidence that supported the six-feet distance?"
> Dr. Collins: "I do not."
> Question: "Is that 'I do not recall,' or 'I do not see any evidence supporting six feet?"
> Dr. Collins: "I did not see evidence, but I'm not sure I would have been shown evidence at that point."
> Question: "Since then, it has been an awfully large topic. Have you seen any evidence since then supporting six feet?"
> Dr. Collins: "No."

Moderna CEO Stéphane Bancel

Stéphane Bancel lied about the vaccines causing myocarditis (heart inflammation). He was spectacularly exposed by Senator Rand Paul.

Pfizer CEO Dr. Albert Bourla

Albert Bourla lied about the Pfizer "vaccine" being extensively tested for preventing transmission before it was launched into the marketplace.

WHO Director General Tedros Ghebreyesus

Tedros lied about China's role in the COVID pandemic, stating that China's actions helped to reduce the spread of coronavirus to other countries.

Deborah Birx

Member of the White House Coronavirus Task Force, she lied about these injections protecting against infection.

Bill Gates

Entrepreneur Bill Gates, self-appointed vaccine expert, lied about not making money on vaccines.

WEF (World Economic Forum) Executive Chairman Klaus Schwab

Klaus Schwab lied by stating that "nobody will be safe if not everybody is vaccinated."

New York Governor Andrew Cuomo

Cuomo specifically enacted the most lethal policies in the nation leading to the highest death rate in the nation. His policies were so patently risky, including forcing nursing homes to comingle COVID and non-COVID patients, that even the *NY Times* and *WaPo* had to write about his callous disregard. While many deaths were unavoidable, the majority *were* avoidable if only Cuomo hadn't been empowered. Dr. Peter Breggin wrote:

> I cannot think of any COVID policy that Cuomo enacted that didn't kill massive numbers of New Yorkers. He ordered multiple deadly nursing homes policies and he prevented physicians and pharmacies from using early treatment medications. He also clearly thought he was King. For example, he wanted to contact trace *everyone,* and he attempted to force people to stay in their homes *or worse.* His

aggressive "social distancing" policies revealed his total contempt for Americans and the Constitution. He did keep the NYC subway system open—despite scientific evidence showing that *was* contributing to higher rates. For these reasons, New York ended up with just about the worst record on every single COVID measure.[88]

Truth Always Wins in the End

In 1794 George Washington said: "Truth will ultimately prevail where pains [are] taken to bring it to light." What I have said has stood the test of time. From 2020 until today, I was censored and defamed for making the following nine statements:

1. Lockdowns cannot stop the spread of tiny (0.1 micron) respiratory virus.[89]
2. Lockdowns are extremely detrimental to individuals and the nation.[90]
3. There is no scientific basis for six-feet social distancing.[91]
4. Surgical masks don't keep out tiny respiratory viruses.[92]
5. Early treatment works very well for SARS-2.[93]
6. SARS-2 is not dangerous except for the frail.[94]
7. Experimental medications are inherently risky.[95]
8. As a physician: the shots do not stop transmission.[96]
9. As a lawyer: medical treatment decisions are always a personal choice.[97]

In 2024 everyone agrees:

1. Lockdowns don't stop viral spread.[98]
2. Lockdowns caused harm.[99]
3. There is no basis for six-feet social distancing.[100]
4. Masks don't work.[101]
5. Early treatment works.[102]
6. Persons who died from SARS-2 had four other severe conditions.[103]

7. The government database shows tens of thousands of serious adverse events.[104]
8. As a matter of science, the shots do not stop transmission.[105]
9. As a matter of law, these shots are not a vaccine.[106]

Medical Whistleblowers = Truth-Tellers

Despite the great personal and professional risk, a large number of doctors besides myself issued grave warnings about the dangers lurking within the draconian public health approaches to pandemic response. Many highly credentialed experts knew these approaches were lies built on top of lies, but the experts who spoke against them were censored and mocked. Consider the following.

Dr. Luc Montagnier won a Nobel Prize in Medicine in 2008 (co-discovering the HIV virus as causing AIDS).[107] In 2021, he said, ". . . the vaccine program for the coronavirus is an 'unacceptable mistake'. The history books will show that, because it is the vaccination that is creating the variants."[108] In 2020, Dr. Montagnier said the virus "was produced by a laboratory. It is what is known as a recombinant, perhaps produced by a Chinese laboratory. It was a job for molecular biologists. It's a very meticulous job. You could say a clockwork of sequences. There is enormous pressure for everything that is at the origin of the virus to be hidden."[109]

Dr. Didier Raoult is one of the most cited scholars in the world, with an astounding 235,087 citations to his name on Google Scholar at the time of this writing.[110] In February 2020, he published that hydroxychloroquine appeared to be helpful in early treatment of SARS-2, similar to its effectiveness in SARS-1 fifteen years earlier. Raoult's hospitalized patients had a fraction of the death rate compared to the rest of France,[111] which blocked hydroxychloroquine. In short, he is a hero. For this, he has been mocked, ridiculed,[112] and persecuted.[113]

Dr. Robert Malone,[114] who was credited as the original inventor of mRNA vaccination technology[115,116] until he publicly opposed vaccine mandates, was joined by seventy-five fellow physicians to sign onto a July 2022 letter warning:

> Data for clinically useful efficacy in small children are scant or absent. In older children, for whom the vaccines are already licensed, they have been promoted via ethically dubious schemes . . . [117]

Dr. Malone, who has approximately 100 scientific publications with over 12,000 citations of his work, not only accused mRNA injection pushers of "ethically dubious schemes" in reaction to the progression of the pandemic, but he maintains that the scheming was premeditated, with a disregard for potential dangers,

> using . . . flawed pre-clinical trials to support a platform technology was PLANNED from the beginning . . .
>
> The protein levels being produced by [mRNA] vaccines is not known, the duration of protein production isn't known, and the biodistribution of protein production is not known. And the FDA and other global regulatory authorities are all comfortable with this??
>
> As an example of one of the dangers with not knowing the protein levels, distribution and duration of transgene expression, we know from many prior immune tolerance studies that too much antigen (protein in this case), can cause "tolerance." That is essentially where the immune system stops seeing the threat." [Emphasis in original post][118]

Dr. Michael Yeadon,[119] who served as the chief scientist and vice president of the allergy and respiratory research division for Pfizer, which gives credibility to his opinion on treatments for potential respiratory illnesses like COVID, publicly denounced the administration of the mRNA injections. He declared:

> Now here's the real problem I've got, and I'm a father and a grandfather, young people are not susceptible to COVID-19. If they acquire the virus, they usually have no symptoms and they shrug it off very easily. So they're not at risk. It's a crazy thing then, to vaccinate them with something that is actually 50 times more likely to kill them, than the virus itself.[120]

Like Dr. Malone, Dr. Yeadon was not reluctant to express his concern that those behind the injections were not making innocent mistakes.

> If this was to do with public health, you wouldn't have done any of the things they're doing, and you can't come up with a benign explanation.

Likewise, Dr. Peter McCullough, a cardiologist and epidemiologist with over 1,000 publications and over 500 citations in the National Library of Medicine and "the most published scientist in the history of his field," labeled the public health policy on COVID "a complete and total failure AT EVERY LEVEL!"[121]

McCullough also didn't stop at merely accusing health officials of negligence. He went ahead and reinforced a warning by Dr. Malone:

> And it's clear, there is a manifold increase across many disease categories among our servicemen year over year. The only thing that's changed is the administration of the vaccines in large numbers. So data transparency at this point in time will be an area that I believe Dr. Malone is correct, will be intensively investigated. And for those who are close to the data, I think they do have a choice coming up and it's going to be a matter of them making the right choice and where they want to end up on what side of history.

The surgeon general of the State of Florida took steps to protect Floridians from the harmful pro-injection propaganda. In 2022, Dr. Ladapo recommended against males under age thirty-nine receiving the shots (due to the risk of myocarditis). In 2023, he expanded to not recommending the shots to persons under age sixty-five. He said:

> Once again the federal government is failing Americans by refusing to be honest about the risks and not providing sufficient clinical evidence when it comes to these COVID-19 mRNA shots. In Florida, we will always use common sense and protect the rights and liberties of Floridians, including the right to accurate information.[122]

The surgeon general also publicly advised the risk of something I had warned about since October 2020: the negative effectiveness of the shots. Essentially, taking the shots made a person more likely to get COVID-19. This is not true for any other vaccine.

Then, as new data emerged regarding contaminant DNA integration into human DNA, Surgeon General Ladapo went a step further, calling for a complete halt to the mRNA injections. On January 3, 2024, the Florida Department of Health issued Dr. Lapado's statement in a press release titled, "Florida State Surgeon General Calls for Halt in the Use of COVID-19 mRNA Vaccines."

> The FDA's response does not provide data or evidence that the DNA integration assessments they recommended themselves have been performed. . . . DNA integration poses a unique and elevated risk to human health and to the integrity of the human genome, including the risk that DNA integrated into sperm or egg gametes could be passed onto offspring of mRNA COVID-19 vaccine recipients. If the risks of DNA integration have not been assessed for mRNA COVID-19 vaccines, **these vaccines are not appropriate for use in human beings**. [Emphasis added][123]

There are actually too many whistleblower doctors to list here. A particular mention goes to Dr. Mary Talley Bowden,[124] who forced the FDA to retract Lie #1 (Ivermectin is horse medicine), and attorney Aaron Siri,[125] whose skill in vaccine law brought the FDA to its knees.[126] At the time this book goes to press, there is a long list of people and groups who are now vociferously protesting the shots. The Arizona GOP declared COVID-19 injections biological and technological weapons and stated that there are "186 elected officials, 103 candidates and 7 physician organizations publicly demanding the shots be pulled off the market."[127]

Although you wouldn't have known it by watching the medical mouthpieces invited onto cable news, there were many notable physician experts on the dissident side from the beginning. I was joined on the world stage in July 2020 by thousands of doctors from across the globe. At that time, there were already fifty-seven scientific studies from all across the world showing that early treatment worked (and lockdowns didn't). Later, the Great Barrington Declaration included nearly one million healthcare professionals.

There was Dr. Lynn Fynn, Dr. Richard Urso, Dr. Stella Immanuel, Dr. Pierre Kory, Dr. Bryan Tyson, Dr. Jane Orient, Dr. George Fareed, Dr. Aaron Kheriaty, Dr. Joseph Ladapo, Dr. Scott Jensen, Dr. David Martin,[128] Dr. Lee Merritt, Dr. Ryan Cole, Dr. Jeff Barke, Dr. Mark McDonald, Dr. Jay Bhattacharya, Dr. Stephen Ionnides, Dr. Renata Moon, Dr. Mary Talley Bowden, Dr. Kulvinder Kaur, Dr. Scott Atlas, Dr. Harvey Risch, Dr. Sunetra Gupta, Dr. Martin Kuldorff, Dr. Zev Zelenko, Dr. Jay Bhattacharya, Professor Paolo Marindo de Andrade Zanotto, the World Doctors Alliance, Doctors 4 COVID Ethics, AAPS,[129] FLCCC,[130] Great Barrington Declaration,[131] America's Frontline Doctors, Israeli People's Committee, and many others. There were doctors in New Zealand, Australia, UK, Israel, Canada, Portugal, and a leader of the Japanese Medical Association.

What's particularly notable is that no one on the medical freedom side ever switched to the government propaganda side, but despite the very high price of #MedicalCancelCulture, so many have fled the other side. For example, Dr. Aseem Malhotra and Dr. Drew Pinsky and Dr. Molly Rutherford and Dr. Peter McCullough come to mind as physicians who used to support the shot but changed their mind. A partial list of truth-tellers and a rueful (and truthful) observation is shown on the next page.

From the inventor of the mRNA technology itself to a top Pfizer scientist to a world-renowned epidemiologist to a state surgeon general—each of them was, in a way, acting, where others failed to act in their respective fields. As an ER physician, I did the same by taking action.

The Haters Keep On Hating

Of course we were vindicated, but the most vitriolic people have refused to apologize. They instead ask for "amnesty," but it is impossible to move forward with people who refuse to even acknowledge their mistakes, let alone apologize for their misdeeds and course-correct. That we have been proven correct is not in dispute. The non-apologies started in 2022 in *The*

I'm "SAFE & EFFECTIVE" Today BECAUSE
I Listened to "Conspiracy Theorists"
Dr. Geert Vanden Bossche
Dr. Robert Malone
Dr. Peter McCullough
Dr. Jay Bhattacharya
Dr. Ryan Cole
Dr. Francis A. Boyle
Dr. Pierre Kory
Dr. Sucharit Bhakdi
Dr. Carrie Madej
Dr. Vladimir Zelenko (RIP)
Dr. Lawrence Palevsky
Dr. Sherri Tenpenny
Dr. Walter Chesnut
Dr. Mary Bowden
Dr. Aaron Kheriaty
Dr. Teck Khong
Dr. Jane Ruby
Dr. Ben Tapper
Dr. Ahmad Malik
Dr. Jane Orient
Dr. Stella Immanuel
Dr. Mattias Desmet
Dr. Retsef Levi
Dr. Joseph Fraiman
Dr. Richard Urso
Dr. David E. Martin
Dr. Eli David
Dr. Kelly Victory
Dr. Jessica Rose
Dr. Mollie James
Dr. Claire Craig
Dr. Rashid Buttar (RIP)
Dr. James Thorp
Dr. Tom Cowan
Dr. Kevin Jenkins
Dr. Lawrence Palevsky
Dr. Tom Cowan
Dr. Joseph Mercola
Dr. Bryan Tyson
Dr. Dan Stock
Dr. Drew Pinsky*
Dr. Aseem Malhotra *
Dr. Judy Mikovits
Dr. Simone Gold
Dr. Joseph Ladapo
Dr. Mike Yeadon
Dr. Vernon Coleman
Dr. Scott Jensen
Dr. Dolores Cahill
Dr. Mohammad Adil
Dr. Andrew Kaufman
Dr. Sabine Hazan
Dr. Theresa Long
Dr. Paul Alexander
Dr. Sunetra Gupta
Dr. Tess Lawrie
Dr. Meryl Nass
Dr. Theresa Long
Sen/Dr. Rand Paul
Sen. Ron Johnson
Dr. Paul Marik
Dr. Kevin Bass*
Dr. Naomi Wolf
Dr. Christina Parks
Dr. David Cartland
Dr. George Fareed
Dr. Vinay Prasad
Dr. Syed Haider
Dr. Lynn Flynn
Dr. Andrew Huff
Dr. Martin Kulldorf
Dr. Peter Breggin
Dr. Steven LaTulippe
Dr. Marty Makary
Dr. Kary Mullis (RIP)
Dr. Bret Weinstein
Dr. Heather Heying
Rep. Thomas Massie
Rep. Jim Jordan
Robert F. Kennedy, Jr.
Christine Anderson
Del Bigtree
Mike Adams
Alex Jones
Russell Brand
Joe Rogan
OPENVAERS
Sharyl Attkisson
Steve Kirsch
Michael Senger
Joshua Hartley
Kyle Becker
Tom Renz
Reiner Fuellmich
Jeffrey Tucker
Mikki Willis
Jefferey Jaxen
Erin Elizabeth
Alex Jones
Russell Brand
Elon Musk *
Whitney Webb
Alex Berenson
Janet Ossebaard
Mikki Willis
Ezra Levant
Avi Yemeni
Rizza Islam
Artur Pawlowski
Ed Dowd
JP Sears
Tucker Carlson
@Catturd2
@TheVigilantFox
@thevivafrei
@TexasLindsay_
@KanekoaTheGreat
James O'Keefe
Novak Djokovic
Sayer Ji
Maajid Nawaz
Aaron Rodgers
(* = recently awake)
ABOVE LIST IS FAR FROM COMPREHENSIVE
A year ago
Now
Vaccinated can spread COVID
Hoax
Truth
The NIH funded GOF research at Wuhan through EcoHealth Alliance
Hoax
Truth
Vaccinated are susceptible to new variants and reinfection
Hoax
Truth
More vaxxed are dying than unvaxxed
Hoax
Truth
COVID vaccines can cause blood clots and other serious side effects
Hoax
Truth
Shots can cause myocarditis
Hoax
Truth
3rd and 4th shot
Hoax
Truth
Shots may disrupt mentrual cycles and can get into breast milk
Hoax
Truth
New shots every year/half a year
Hoax
Truth
mRNA from shots can go to organs & tissues all over the bocy
Hoax
Truth
Shots for young children
Hoax
Truth
Ivermectin & Hydroxychloroquine can be effective for early treatment
Hoax
Truth
Total segregation of the society
Hoax
Truth
Jabs are NOT safe and are NOT effective.
Hoax
Truth
Camps for the unvaccinated
Hoax
Truth
Natural Immunity is robust and durable
Hoax
Truth
Unvaccinated unable to work
Hoax
Truth
Shots may impair your immune system
Hoax
Truth
Harder access of medical care for unvaccinated
Hoax
Truth
Virus leaked from a lab
Hoax
Truth
Secret contracts between Pfizer and governments
Hoax
Truth
Shortened link (caps-sensitive) to my ever-expanding google-document (over 1000 pages) on which I've documented 3 years of links to "conspiracy theory interviews, data, studies, videos, expert opinions, whistleblowers, opinions, speculations, heresay, misinformation, disinformation"
https://bit.ly.TheyCantAllBeWrong
"Trust the Science"
@1StacyPhillips

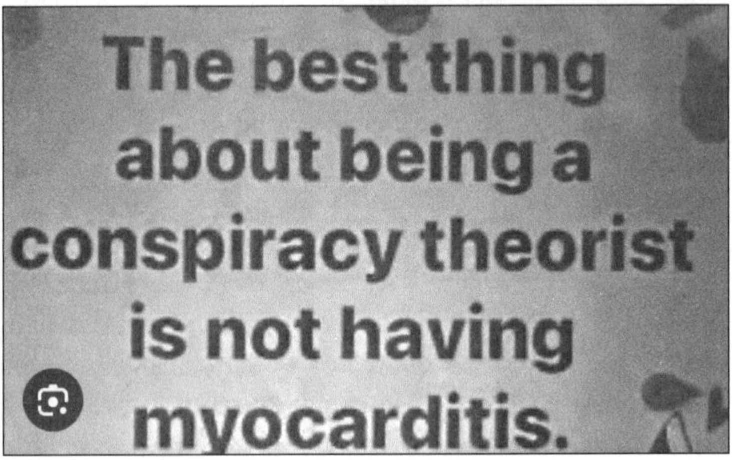
The best thing about being a conspiracy theorist is not having myocarditis.

Atlantic.[132] In May 2024, *The New York Times*[133] very belatedly acknowledged the shots hurt a lot of people but without apologizing. For example, former New York Governor Cuomo[134] and his brother, CNN news anchor Chris Cuomo, argued vociferously and nastily against people they pejoratively called "anti-vaxxers." Then, in May 2024, Chris Cuomo went public with his own COVID-19 vaccine injury! But neither apologized for their words and policies that killed so many, which shows a lack of self-reflection.

This was no innocent misunderstanding. There was pure venom from the elites to the public. This was a religious cult for them. They truly wanted people like me dead or ridiculed into submission. Here are typical examples[135] from news anchors, celebrities, and public health officials, talking about their fellow citizens with pure contempt. Although the hate was worse from the left, it is important to note the hate was definitely bipartisan. These words should be understood to fall into three types of groupings (explanation to follow).

> MSNBC's Mika Brzezinski: "It is the unvaccinated who are the problem, period, end of story."
>
> CNN's Don Lemon: "The only people you can blame–this isn't shaming, this is the truth–are the unvaccinated. Maybe they should be shamed. *Oh, you can't shame them, you can't call them stupid.* Yes, they are!"
>
> Alabama Republican Governor Kay Ivey: "Start blaming the unvaccinated folks, not the regular folks."
>
> MSNBC's Jonathan Capeheart: "Anyone you came into contact with will blame you, as will the rest of us who've done the right thing by getting vaccinated . . . Don't get me started on the lunatics who won't take any of the COVID vaccines."
>
> CNN and commissioner of the Baltimore City Health Department Dr. Leana Wen: "Because frankly we know that we can't trust the unvaccinated . . . We need to start looking at the unvaccinated the same way we look at driving while intoxicated."
>
> Jimmy Kimmel: ". . . we're going to have to make some very tough choices about who gets an ICU bed. That choice doesn't seem that tough to me. Vaccinated person having a heart attack? Come

right on in, we'll take care of you. Unvaccinated guy who gobbled horse goo? Rest in peace, wheezy."

Joy Ann Reid: "The anti-vaxxers, they seem to have a thing for death and home remedies."

Fauci: "We're going to see two types of America: the vaxxed and the unvaxxed."

Fox's Neil Cavuto: "Life is too short to be an ass. Life is way too short to be ignorant of the promise of something that is helping people worldwide."

CNN: Maybe you're doing it because you're antisocial.

MSNBC: The unvaccinated should be taxed. They should pay more for healthcare.

Stephen Colbert: "The unvaccinated include children and a group that are acting like children. And the rest of us are starting to get pissed off."

Arnold Schwarzenegger: "Oh . . . 'my freedom is being kind of disturbed here.' No! Screw your freedom!"

Howard Stern and Whoopi Goldberg: "When are we going to stop putting up with the idiots in this country and just say it's mandatory to get vaccinated? F*ck them, F*ck their freedom. I want my freedom to live. I want to get out of the house already. I want to go next door and play chess."

CNN: You're treading on our freedom and you're . . . killing other people.

CNN's Don Lemon: "We have to start doing things for the greater good of society and not for idiots who think they can do their own research."

Joe Biden: "We've been patient, but our patience is wearing thin. This is not about freedom or personal choice."

MSNBC: All the vaccinated folks are going to start wearing masks to protect the unvaccinated folks. It's called a Christian value.

CNN's Anderson Cooper: "I think it's time that we get our moral house in order, it's the unvaccinated who are the threat."

CNN: Basically, we're punishing the vaccinated for the sins of the unvaccinated.

> Commissioner of the Baltimore City Health Department Dr. Leana Wen: "People are not behaving honorably. The unvaccinated are basically, it's open season for me, I can do what I want."
>
> MSNBC's Chuck Todd: "Literally, the only people dying are the unvaccinated. And for those of you spreading misinformation, shame on you. I don't know how you sleep at night."
>
> MSNBC's Mika Brzezinski: "Going back to the unvaccinated, who are really creating a problem in this country . . . every death that we are seeing from COVID could have been prevented."[136]

Of course there can be no "amnesty" without an apology for speech like this—not because we're unwilling to forgive, but because there's no forgiveness without self-reflection and correction. Forgiveness is a two-step process: asking by the one, granting by the other. How can it be granted if it's never requested?

It is important to listen carefully to exactly what these elitists on the right and the left said, because you can hear three steps of fascist propaganda:

1. Positioning the unvaccinated as "the other."[137]
2. Claiming the group is more important than the individual.[138]
3. Claiming moral superiority if you follow the group.

The United States of America is built on the inalienable rights of the individual. Our Founding Fathers agreed on the Bill of (Individual) Rights because the founders knew the biggest threat to all of us is from an extremely powerful government vs. an individual. We have always been a society that prioritized the individual. Our individual freedom created the environment for the most human creativity in history. The citizens of most other countries cannot really comprehend the scope of individual rights the way Americans do. If you have a conversation with a native Chinese person, you will quickly learn that they always know and feel their first loyalty is to the State, not themselves and not their family. These basic communist principles exactly match the words said by the talking heads.

This type of propaganda would never have even been considered a generation ago. Americans would have been immune to the divisiveness of the first tactic, disinterested in the second tactic, and unswayed by the third tactic.

The Cure for Corruption

This repeating pattern of government and media propaganda (instead of releasing data to be independently analyzed) is a serious threat to public health. States must reclaim their sovereignty and refuse to acquiesce to the bullying of federal overreach. Individual counties and states should independently analyze all relevant data. This means that health data must be unequivocally released, not just secretly shared with the federal government. States should take steps to empower researchers without the threat of defunding "dissident" scientists (i.e., persons who disagreed with Fauci, in charge of NIH research budgets for forty years). The government should have no interest in a particular outcome, other than it be accurate.

It is only when multiple independent researchers analyze that data that we can determine if there might legitimately be new dangers not previously seen, and if new measures are indeed warranted, as opposed to the time-tested truths of optimizing holistic, healthy lifestyles. If the complete data on death and illness *from*, and not just *with*, COVID did indicate a need for such measures, we would still need a proper series of unbiased studies to determine an effective public health response.

Obviously, we must thoroughly debunk the propaganda surrounding lockdowns, face masks, inappropriate PCR testing protocols, frequently fatal treatments like remdesivir, and mRNA shots. We must excoriate the cruelty and insanity of needlessly isolating patients, withholding water and nutrition, failing to test for common illnesses, and moving patients from wards that specialize in their underlying illness (such as heart disease) to senseless COVID wards with patients suffering from a full range of illnesses.

We certainly didn't have sufficient findings on the mRNA shots' mutagenicity, teratogenicity, fertility, carcinogenicity, immunogenicity, and more. In addition, it is obvious that the apoplectic fear was unwarranted. There was no reason to deviate from previous standard approaches without critically necessary long-term safety data. Virtually every public health recommendation during the COVID years was the opposite of public health textbooks. For example, doctors had known for many decades that it is harmful to vaccinate an entire population during a viral respiratory pandemic.

We are in a fight for our freedoms and for the health and safety of our future. Our opponents are miscreants willing to engage in casual cruelty, misbehavior, and criminality in order to achieve their agenda. In response, we must practice common sense, alongside compassion and humility. We should choose freedom over fear. We should live each day granted to us with gratitude and with purpose, always pursuing what we know to be good and true and honorable. That is the path forward to transformative healing and a future of lasting health and success.

My Father's Warning

My father was a survivor of the Holocaust, from a part of the world that was taken over by the USSR. He taught me that communists specifically promote people who are willing to serve as a cog in the system. These are typically mediocre people who don't see much beyond their salary and living quarters. If they can be recruited to operate the nuts and bolts of an evil system, it will be difficult to slow down the machine. My father taught me that, after World War II, the Russian method to gain control was to avoid picking people who were bright (they could be convinced with facts) or stupid (they could be manipulated), but to pick the most average people, as they would just follow what they were told.

In America, this method is seen in the rise of the bureaucratic state. It is happening even faster in Canada, which now has eliminated free speech in so many areas. For example, doctors in Canada cannot express medical opinions,[139] Canadian citizens must speak certain pronouns,[140] the government can censor misinformation and online harm,[141] and comedians may not tell certain jokes.[142] What all these rules have in common is the theoretical elevation of the collective over the individual. I say "theoretical," because unless you were born yesterday, you're old enough to know that the myth of "do this for the greater good" always ends in oppression or slavery.[143]

I was presented with a choice in 2020: to practice medicine in service to individual humans or to practice cruelty in service to the State. I simply did the right thing in the moment, which was to take care of the person in front of me. The result, years later, is an organization that has provided real help, healing, and inspiration to millions as they join the fight for what's right.

I choose to fight because freedom must be fought for, and my children and your children deserve the freedom and opportunity that God designed them to experience. We fight so they might flourish. The ancient text *Ethics of the Fathers* teaches us: "It is not incumbent upon you to finish the task, but neither are you free to absolve yourself from it."[144]

CHAPTER SEVEN

Selective Prosecution

Government is not reason, it is not eloquence—it is force! Like fire it is a dangerous servant and a fearful master; never for a moment should it be left to irresponsible action.

—George Washington

While managing litigation to defend Americans from medical tyranny, there was one case that I was neglecting—my own. Despite the overzealousness of the FBI and the increasing demonization of January 6 (J6) protestors, I knew one thing for sure: I was totally unaware of the legally restricted status of certain grounds or the building on that day and equally unaware of any supposed "conspiracy" or coordination of any kind to commit illegal activity.

Like most others in DC on January 6, I never dreamed that anyone, including myself, might venture inside the Capitol. By the time I might have considered the question, I had already been swept inside by a crowd of extraordinary size, after watching doors being opened from within. That afternoon wasn't preplanned; it was me reacting to events.

Most significantly, January 6 was overtly planned and advertised in advance as a political protest event, government-approved permits on Capitol grounds included. In other words, it was the exact type of activity that is explicitly protected by the First Amendment. Therefore, the burden of proof placed on the government to demonstrate specific criminal activity in spite of those protections should have been very high. Unlike a guilty person, I put no energy into the defense of a case for which I didn't even need an alibi. I expected the case to be dropped or hastily concluded as a misunderstanding. This would have been true at any point in our nation's history for such a First Amendment event, but even more so in the context of so many recent precedents.

Three months after my arrest, in April 2021, the DC government agreed to pay $1.6 million to more than two hundred protestors who claimed to have been wrongfully arrested on Inauguration Day in 2017.[1] While many protestors were innocent, laws were broken on Inauguration Day 2017. Six police officers were injured,[2] and 210 protesters were charged with felony rioting after causing more than $100,000 of property damage and torching a limousine.[3] These protestors argued that,

> . . . in response to vandalism and property damage caused by a small number of protesters, MPD officers rounded up, or "kettled," more than 200 protesters—including many who had broken no laws . . .[4]

The prosecutors acknowledged in court that they had no evidence that the handful of people they had actually put on trial had personally caused any property damage or physical injuries. Those protesters' successful lawsuits maintained that the **mass arrests** "violated the First, Fourth and Fifth Amendments and DC law."[5] So the standard in that situation was as follows: charging protestors with felony rioting, admitting the people charged were not the persons who committed violence or caused damage, jurors acquitting for lack of evidence, prosecutors dropping all charges, and then taxpayers giving a cash payout to the people who were arrested.

The 2017 protesters didn't just come out ahead financially. Aside from a single person who was sentenced to four months of prison for assaulting a police officer, *none of the remaining 209 inauguration rioters were sentenced to even a single day of jail.* In fact, after twenty additional protesters pled guilty to misdemeanor rioting, paid a small fine, and were placed on probation with no jail time, all charges against the remaining defendants were dropped.

That same month, the US Attorney's Office in Oregon dismissed charges against Antifa and BLM protestors who were arrested after those groups "barricaded federal officers inside a courthouse—and tried to set the building on fire," while throwing fireworks and rocks at the officers.[6] The Oregon violence was severe and continued for many days and nights. At the time of the protests, federal prosecutors reported:

> . . . acts of violence towards law enforcement and first responders include a Portland firefighter being shot in the chest with a steel ball bearing launched from an arm-mounted slingshot, a man dousing several police officers with high-powered bear deterrent spray, a man punching a female police officer in the face, and a woman striking a police officer in the head from behind with a wooden shield . . .[7]

The prosecutors pointed out that the nightly violence would take place "after peaceful demonstrations end,"[8] claiming to take issue only with violent protesters:

> The US Attorney's Office is committed to prosecuting people who impede or assault law enforcement officers, damage federal property, and set fire to buildings. Make no mistake: *those who commit violence in the name of protest, will be investigated, arrested, prosecuted, and face prison time.*[9]

But even that turned out to be an overstatement:

> Of 96 cases the U.S. attorney's office in Portland filed last year charging protesters with federal crimes, including assaulting federal officers, civil disorder, and failing to obey, prosecutors have dropped 47 of them, government documents show.[10]

In all, about half of the protestors had their charges dropped, including four charged with felony assault of a federal officer![11] For the half who did receive a penalty, many were sentenced to a "punishment" of . . . continuing their partisan operations:

> The penalties levied so far against any federal defendants, most of whom were arrested in clashes around federal buildings in Portland including the courthouse, have largely consisted of *community service,* such as working in a food bank or *encouraging people to vote.* [Emphasis added][12]

No points for guessing in which political party they were registered.

To summarize, violent assault and widespread destruction of government property was instantly excused for anyone serving as a left-wing soldier. Even leftist defendant David Bouchard was surprised.

> [Bouchard] showed up at a nighttime protest with a leaf blower to disperse police tear gas and ended up on the ground with two police officers, according to an affidavit . . .
>
> Bouchard . . . completed 30 hours of community service . . . "I did that and they immediately dropped the charges," he said. "I was kind of amazed by that."[13]

Another instance in 2018 saw almost six hundred people arrested by Capitol Police for swarming into Congress for a "sit-in" during the Women's March protest. They were intentionally breaking the law in a demonstration of civil disobedience against President Trump's management of immigration policy. These protestors were openly supported by several Democrat senators, including Elizabeth Warren, Tammy Duckworth, and Ed Markey. Their punishment for this "insurrection"?

ABC News reported:

> US Capitol Police arrested 575 people at the protest in the Senate building and charged them a $50 citation for unlawfully demonstrating. Rep. Pramila Jayapal, D-Wash, and actress Susan Sarandon both tweeted they were arrested.[14]

Protesting on the side of the Hollywood elites always seems to end happily ever after.

Same Capitol, Different Results

I had no reason to assume the latest protests at the Capitol would be handled any more aggressively than previous protest activities on federal property. During the 2018 protests against the nomination of Judge Brett Kavanaugh to the Supreme Court, government-funded National Public Radio explained that "shows of protest are nothing new on Capitol Hill" and described those interfering with Senate hearings as "The Resistance."[15]

Kavanaugh protestors "busted through police barricades"[16] and "even *invaded the offices* of some Senators."[17] Celebrities like Amy Schumer demanded to be arrested rather than follow orders to leave. In just one day of this effort,[18] 128 people were arrested for "unlawfully demonstrating" outside of senators' offices and in the main rotunda of the Russell Senate Building.[19]

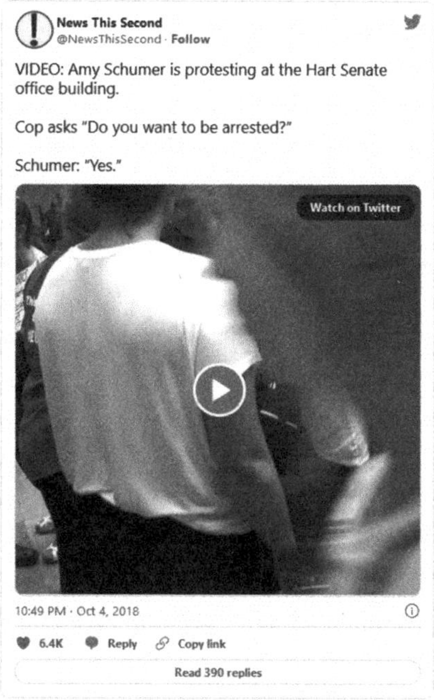

The Russell Building[20] is where many Senators have their offices and is the part of the United States Capitol Complex. Yet, the DOJ did not seek any convictions for "entering and remaining in a restricted building or grounds."

> Apparently all [Kavanaugh protestors] were treated in accordance with the established *post and forfeit procedure.* They posted and forfeited $50 and were promptly released without a conviction, without having to hire a lawyer, and without ever having to set one foot in a courtroom.[21]

It turns out that for many years up until January 6, *the release of trespassing and even disruptive* (nonviolent) *protestors without charges is, in fact, standard federal procedure* on Capitol Hill.

> The U.S. Attorney's Office does not make this charging decision on an ad hoc basis. Instead, it and the D.C. law enforcement agencies have a developed policy about how protest cases involving minor disorderly conduct are handled. Under this procedure, *protestors are arrested and charged with a local (D.C. Code) misdemeanor disorderly conduct offense, not with a federal misdemeanor offense.*
>
> The cases are disposed of, often en masse, using a procedure known as "post and forfeit." *The protestor is permitted to "post" $50 at the police station to resolve the matter, at which point they are released, and the case is effectively concluded.* The money is shortly thereafter "forfeited," which is the legal conclusion of the case.
>
> The protestor ends up with only an arrest on his or her record in D.C. Superior Court, but *no conviction.* There is no court appearance, no need to hire an attorney, no conviction on the person's record, no possibility of jail or being put on probation, only a modest fee to pay, *and the possibility of sealing the record of the case.*
>
> This procedure is so well-established that the ACLU has a page on its website explaining it to protestors who are heading to D.C. for the first time to engage in civil disobedience (although the ACLU wrongly advises that the records of such cases cannot be sealed after the fact).[22]

January 6 was not such a radical shift in our national conscience that it caused a *permanent* change in this policy. The federal government's "without conviction" policy for nonviolent trespassers at the Capitol is just as alive today, post-J6, as before. In June 2022, nine members of the production team of *The Late Show with Steven Colbert* were arrested while trespassing in the Longworth House Office Building, an office building for House Representatives that is part of the Capitol complex.

The Colbert staffers were illegally let into the Capitol, according to Tucker Carlson.[23] They trespassed again "after hours" in a restricted space, without a required congressional escort, despite having "been told at various points by the US Capitol Police that they were supposed to have an escort,"[24] and actively harassed sitting members of Congress by banging on their doors,[25] being "loud" and "disruptive."[26] There is no dispute that the television crew continued to trespass after being told by police that they could not be in the Capitol without an escort, nor that they were arrested by Capitol Police near the offices of Rep. Lauren Boebert and House Minority Leader Kevin McCarthy. They were charged with trespassing, but stopped short of committing outright assault. Thus, as nonviolent trespassers, *their charges were all dropped.*[27]

In other words, pre-January 6 and post-January 6 protestors are treated similarly; it is *only* January 6 defendants who are treated so uniquely.

The Loss of Equal Protection

The meticulous hunting and vicious wrangling of nonviolent J6 protesters was unprecedented before and after that fateful day. Only protestors on that singular afternoon would be prosecuted by the US Attorney's Office with absurd felonies carrying twenty-year prison penalties. Hundreds of protesters seeking to exercise their sacred First Amendment right of political protest, most of whom never committed any violence or intended any criminality, would now become the victims of **selective prosecution**. Specifically, the government **selected to prosecute** them for a nonviolent infraction that virtually all others are excused for on a regular basis.

The US Attorney's Office in DC is no doubt aware that this practice is unconstitutional. The US Supreme Court has held citizens to be constitutionally protected from selective prosecution, stating:

> Under the equal protection component of the Fifth Amendment's Due Process Clause, the decision whether to prosecute may not be based on an arbitrary classification such as race or religion. [Emphasis added][28]

There have been rare glimmers of hope that the judiciary is starting to recognize selective prosecution as an existential threat to our nation's constitutional republic. In March 2024, *USA v. Rundo* found that the anti–free speech violent protestors who set off munitions, broke windows, and beat people were not prosecuted, but the free speech protestors were prosecuted. Judge Cormac J. Carney wrote:

> . . . prosecuting only members of the far right and ignoring members of the far left leads to the troubling conclusion that the government believes it is permissible to physically assault and injure Trump supporters to silence speech. It is only when those tactics are deployed against those on the left that the government brings charges under the Anti-Riot Act. That is not permissible under our Constitution.[29]

On May 2, 2024, the comprehensive 178-page "President Trump's Motion to Dismiss the Indictment Based On Selective and Vindictive Prosecution" was filed in the federal district court for the Southern District of Florida in *United States of America v. Donald J. Trump, et al.*, 23-80101, SDFL.[30] In his detailed motion, President Trump contrasts his disparate treatment concerning his handling of classified documents with numerous other examples of very different treatment given to other high level government officials. President Trump then examines the many-legal precedents that prohibit such selective prosecution, beginning with:

> The government may not pursue cases "with an evil eye and an unequal hand so as practically to make unjust and illegal discrimination between persons in similar circumstances."[31]

President Trump's motion to dismiss the indictment based on selective and vindictive prosecution was granted.

What distinguished the nonviolent J6 protesters from protesters at other events that ensured the most severe possible prosecution of their criminal charges, if not their political and/or religious beliefs? Those beliefs, of course, would in fact constitute the "arbitrary classification" prohibited by the law. US District Judge Trevor McFadden, for one, ruled that the beliefs of the J6 protestors caused their unequally harsh treatment.

In one case where prosecutors sought prison time for a J6 protester charged with trespassing, McFadden found that the defendant, a Texas florist named Jenny Cudd, was indeed being treated worse than recent protesters in Portland and at the Supreme Court. McFadden specifically rejected the argument by the US attorney that the defendant should be punished for the behavior of a minority of violent protestors and found the DOJ's sentencing recommendation disproportionate.

"It does feel like the government has had two standards here, and I can't abide by that," McFadden said. The judge added that before January 6, 2021, he could not remember seeing a nonviolent, first-time misdemeanant "sentenced to serious jail time . . . regardless of their race, gender or political affiliation."[32]

And what about those, like me, who didn't encounter a police barrier or any other indication that the Capitol was currently restricted as closed to the public and who peacefully complied with police orders? This presented a serious obstacle to prosecutors. They would then need to prove an element of a crime that did not exist—that we *knowingly* trespassed.

You've likely heard the translation of the legal principle of *ignorantia juris non excusat*: "ignorance of the law excuses not." That phrase, however, has a complementary Latin pair, *ignorantia facti excusat*: "ignorance of the fact excuses." So while a person cannot claim to have believed it was okay to possess a stolen stereo, they could claim that, having received it from a friend, they had no idea it was stolen.

This principle helped Harold Staples out of a conviction on a charge carrying a potential ten-year sentence for possessing a gun that was more advanced than he knew. His gun had been modified to allow it to shoot more than one bullet with one squeeze of the trigger. This modification made it an automatic weapon, which must be registered with the federal government. In their prosecution, however, the government didn't try to prove that Staples knew about the modification or ever used it. Instead, they insisted that possessing it was enough. The court instructed the jury likewise, and Staples was convicted.

Justice Clarence Thomas stepped in with a majority opinion that the government simply cannot jail a man for a prohibited act without proving that he was aware that he was committing the act.[33] The man was acquitted.

Mens rea, literally meaning "guilty mind," is another requirement limiting the government's ability to jail the innocent. Under this twelfth-century principle of English law, to obtain a conviction the government must prove that a person acted with "criminal intent." If a person runs onto a highway, for example, and a driver is unable to stop before hitting him, the driver would be innocent despite having knowledge of both the facts of the accident and illegality of killing another man since he lacked even a minimal level of criminal intent.

The Supreme Court considers the mental component so critical that it reads a minimal level of *mens rea* into even those criminal statutes that do not specifically list it as an element of the crime:

> [w]hen interpreting federal criminal statutes that are silent on the required mental state, we read into the statute "only that *mens rea*" which is necessary to separate wrongful conduct from "otherwise innocent conduct."[34]

The courts do not normally need to "add" a *mens rea* element to a statute, however, because most criminal laws already include it:

> Under most statutes, to win a conviction, the government must prove beyond a reasonable doubt that the defendant acted "knowingly."[35]

The True Meaning of Trespass

When it comes to trespassing, many jurisdictions have strict requirements for landowners to put potential trespassers on proper notice. Consider Montana and then Vermont, for example:

> The Montana unlawful trespass statute . . . requires no-trespassing signs be "conspicuous" and placed on a "post, structure, or natural object . . . with not less than 50 square inches of fluorescent orange paint . . ." [requires] signs to be at least 11.5 inches wide and 8 inches high, with lettering and background of contrasting colors [and] requires that signs be set "upon or near the boundaries of lands to be affected with notices at each corner and not over 400 feet apart . . .[36]

While the government reported that signs saying "Area closed by order of the United States Capitol Police Board" would be "passed" by one who "crossed from the west to the east side of the Capitol grounds,"[37] I didn't see *any* such signage as I made my way along Constitution Avenue from the Ellipse to the northeast corner of the Capitol through an enormous crowd. Interestingly, the government said the signs would be "passed" by, not "visible" to, a person coming from the west side, conceding that the signs were not deployed in a way that could be seen by everyone, or even most, in a crowd as large as that of January 6.

At my codefendant's trial, at which time the government presented the same evidence it would have presented against me, the government was forced to admit that there was no evidence (via signs or barricades) that the area in which we were located was closed or restricted when we were there. The government disingenuously submitted evidence of the existence of a handful of such signs over a large geographic area. But, on cross examination, the government was forced to admit the pictures they submitted came from much earlier in the day, but that by the time we arrived at the Capitol around 2 p.m., there was no signage or barricades. Thankfully, the criminal defense attorney was familiar with such treachery and forced the government to admit its duplicity.

Walking to the east side of the Capitol, I never passed or saw a single police barrier to indicate that the area was restricted. The absence of warning signs is even more curious in light of Congress's clearly expressed intent that unknowing trespassers should not be included in the scope of the federal trespassing statute. That very law, used to prosecute hundreds of nonviolent J6 protesters, myself included, defines a trespasser as one who,

> knowingly enters or remains in any restricted building or grounds without lawful authority to do so . . .
>
> . . . the term "restricted buildings or grounds" means any posted, cordoned off, or otherwise restricted area . . . of a building or grounds so restricted in conjunction with an event designated as a special event of national significance . . .[38]

I assumed that entry was allowed because there was no signage or any obvious indication of any area being restricted, I saw the doors opened from the inside, and I experienced the law enforcement officers and uniformed building staff present not giving any indication that people should leave. Whether that was intentional at the *beginning* of the day or whether that was a decision *made in the moment* of crowd control, neither thought ever occurred to me.

My specific trespass charge was 18 USC §1752(a)(1), which is "entering and remaining in a restricted building or grounds."[39] I ask the reader to decide for him or herself if I voluntarily or intentionally entered. Specifically, I invite you to watch as if you are a juror and decide if you think I had the *mens rea* (the requisite criminal intent) to *criminally* enter. I can tell you how I *felt* in the moment, and that was that when the doors swung open from the inside, the crowd surged, and I was pushed and tumbled over the threshold. That was how it *felt* to me, and I don't recall having any intentional thought process about it. A videotape (minute 5:20) of the event does exist, and you can decide for yourself.[40] This was the sole charge that at least had some relationship to my actions. The other charges were vertical and horizontal overcharges, and will be discussed in the next chapter (see Chapter 8).

Minute 5:20 on the videotape is the "entering" part of the statute. The other half is "remaining." As I attested to in court, there was simply no way to leave. Hundreds of people were continuously pouring into the building through the single visible entrance/exit, and it was impossible to leave. So I "remained," and while "remaining," I gave my peaceful speech twice. But when eventually asked to leave by law enforcement (minute 10:25), I peacefully complied. This voids the final element of "remaining." This was, therefore, a classic case of unknowingly or unintentionally trespassing, which is not a crime.

Upon Reflection

Later, in prison, I was visited by the prison rabbi at Miami Federal Detention Center. He began his discussion by asking me which lessons I might want to take from, essentially, "getting caught." It took quite a while for him to understand that I didn't get caught "doing" anything. We talked for a while, with me trying to explain what I was experiencing, which was the collapse of the rule of law, that the government was persecuting political dissidents.

Even if you ignore all the times the government tolerated much worse behavior referenced in this chapter and honestly think I was guilty of criminal trespass, how can the government justify selectively arresting me among thousands of others? My actions were indistinguishable from thousands of peaceful others in the building *except* that I gave a speech and am known to publicly protest our government being weaponized.

From my perspective, my taking the Hippocratic Oath as a doctor meant I had to speak up when people were being harmed. My training as a lawyer meant I recognized in real time that the Equal Protection Clause of the Constitution was being violated. Ultimately, the necessity I feel to help people as a doctor and my absolute reliance on the Constitution as a lawyer led to my experiencing the most massive betrayal by my own government.

My father's being a Holocaust survivor has always had a big impact on who I am and how I see the world. I am aware that in pre–World War II Germany Jews were highly assimilated and valued German citizens, including thousands of German Jews who fought honorably for their nation in World War I. When Hitler took power, Jews were about one third of the nation's professors and doctors. Within just a few years of Hitler taking power, Jews were stripped of all their property, all their rights, all their professions, and finally, their lives. I am acutely aware that it only takes a shift in the political winds for an entire nation with a too-powerful government to deprive targeted citizens of all rights.

When I was young, a group of neo-Nazis decided to stir things up and petitioned to hold a march in Skokie, Illinois. They claimed First Amendment protection to chant hateful Nazi slogans as they marched through the streets in SS uniforms. They chose Skokie, Illinois, specifically to cause the maximum amount of pain to its large population of elderly Jewish Holocaust survivors who had settled there. The ACLU defended the neo-Nazis' right to march through Skokie at the time.

Back then, the "elites" were in favor of free speech, and the neo-Nazis were permitted to march. I concurred. Even as a young girl and the daughter of a Holocaust survivor, I sided with the neo-Nazis' legal right to march and speak. I knew instinctively, even as a child, that silencing people would always lead to much worse permanent results than temporarily hearing hateful words. I have never changed my position. But the elites have now completely reversed themselves, and they are the ones aggressively leading the fight to destroy the First Amendment.

Above all else, our Constitution guarantees our legal right to speak freely. We have no need for a First Amendment to say roses smell sweet. We need a First Amendment to say things *other people don't like.* If I cannot say something you don't like without fear of the government targeting me, there is no free speech—exactly what the DOJ and FBI appear to want.

The rabbi clearly knew absolutely nothing about me. He asked his standard question about what changes I could make to change my criminal lifestyle. The failure of a prison chaplain to recognize that the infrastructure for fascism has already been implemented in the United States was so alarming that it became the impetus for this book.

After all, I was talking to him in a prison jumpsuit.

CHAPTER EIGHT

Dirty Lawyers

Show me the man and I'll show you the crime.
—Lavrentiy Beria, chief of secret police under Joseph Stalin

The federal government aggressively disputed the explanation given by many J6 protesters that they were unaware that the Capitol building was closed to the public. Then, in August 2021, the Department of Justice was forced into an eye-opening disclosure under a Supreme Court precedent dictating that prosecutors have a constitutional duty to turn over material evidence favorable to a defendant.[1] Known as "Brady material" after the name of the defendant in that SCOTUS ruling, the DOJ's revelation was indeed exculpatory:

> . . . the Justice Department . . . admitted it possesses at least some images of police officers taking pictures with and fist-bumping Capitol rioters on January 6 but has not given it to the defense . . .[2]

Federal prosecutors had evidence that J6 protesters had reason to believe they were permitted to be in the Capitol. Yet those prosecutors failed to uphold their legal duty to share the evidence. Not only did they possess these photos, but they also had at least forty-four thousand hours of video evidence, much of which still remains hidden from the public, including J6 defendants who are legally entitled to use it for their defense.

This egregious Brady violation was further exposed in March 2023 by the Tucker Carlson bombshell revelations of previously hidden footage, including footage of Jacob Chansley, the now infamous horned helmet-wearing protester dubbed the J6 "Shaman" who was shown on CCTV footage being chaperoned inside the Capitol by a handful of United States Capitol police officers. The officers calmly led him through multiple areas, even ushering him into the Senate chamber and listening as he offered a prayer of thanks for the police officers' assistance in guiding the protesters safely through the building. His legal defense was never provided with this footage, and Chansley was sentenced to a nearly four-year prison term in spite of the overtly exculpatory evidence withheld by the DOJ.[3] Some of this evidence was summarized, as I mentioned in Chapter 3, by Judge McFadden in an April 2022 decision acquitting New Mexico resident Matthew Martin of trespassing and all other charges he faced:

> . . . it was reasonable for Martin to believe that outnumbered police officers allowed him and others to enter the Capitol through the Rotunda doors on Jan. 6 . . . video shows two police officers standing near the Rotunda doors and allowing people to enter as Martin approached. One of the officers appeared to lean back before Martin placed a hand on the officer's shoulder as a possible sign of gratitude . . . Martin's testimony [was] "largely credible."[4]

The Brady violations, however, went disturbingly unchallenged. No amount of exculpatory evidence prompted any of the prosecutors to drop so much as a single trespassing charge, even as that evidence showed police behavior giving credence to the protesters' belief that they had been granted entry into the building. On the contrary, the US Attorney's Office in DC continues to demand that defendants enter into a plea bargain by signing a standard "Statement of Offense." Such a deal includes a paragraph of this nature:

> When the defendant entered the U.S. Capitol Building on January 6, it was a restricted building. The defendant **knew** at the time she entered the U.S. Capitol Building that she did not have lawful authority to enter the building.[5]

This Statement of Offense was pushed even when defendants repeatedly claimed the very opposite to be the reality. How did prosecutors get hundreds of American citizens who did not knowingly conspire to break the law to acquiesce to such an admission? How can hundreds of nonviolent protesters, who did not know they were trespassing at all, be "convinced" to confess to having done so with sincere foreknowledge? Why would defendants who consistently claimed to have believed they were allowed to be somewhere, suddenly confess to the opposite? Did the government find new evidence, like a text message to their spouse saying, "I knew we weren't allowed on the Capitol grounds, but I went there anyway?"

No. Such evidence did not exist, so the feds created something else.

Legal Leverage

Lavrentiy Beria, the ruthless head of the Soviet secret police during Stalin's "Reign of Terror" against his own population, openly bragged about gaining convictions of innocent civilians. His infamous declaration, "Show me the man and I'll show you the crime," set the stage for his attack on dissidents, both real and imagined.

What would Beria have done to get around the nuisance of a legal requirement to prove J6 defendants "knowingly" trespassed? It's likely he would have approved of the Biden DOJ's fascist-style strategy. Prosecutors just piled additional criminal charges (deficient in supporting evidence) onto each defendant, each with serious penalty implications. Given the government's nearly 100 percent conviction rate, there was now a powerful incentive for the defendant to give a false statement—confessing to something they didn't actually do in order to get the most serious charges dropped. Many protesters were charged with five separate crimes, bringing their total maximum prison sentence, based on one act (i.e., being present in the Capitol), to:

1. **Entering** and Remaining in a Restricted Building - 1 year[6]
2. **Disorderly** and Disruptive Conduct in a Restricted Building - 1 year[7]
3. **Disorderly** Conduct in a Capitol Building - 6 months[8]

4. **Parading**, Demonstrating or Picketing in a Capitol Building - 6 months[9]
5. **Obstruction** of an Official Proceeding - 20 years[10]

Just like that, a protester who was otherwise willing to defend their innocence at trial on the single trespassing charge, and who had little to gain by insincerely pleading guilty to that charge, suddenly has a huge incentive to confess—even falsely—that, on second thought, they were totally aware of the restricted status of the Capitol. Accepting this plea bargain "carrot" would immediately reduce the "stick" of their potential prison term from a shocking 23+ years down to 0–12 months.

This is similar to a dishonest business negotiation where one side adds superfluous demands in order to make the other side feel as if they have gained concessions when those demands are eventually dropped. This, however, is not an arms-length commercial transaction angling for the best deal. First of all, the prosecution is supposed to be on the side of truth, not on the side of conviction. In fact, they are required by law to be dispassionate and follow (and share) the actual evidence. The prosecution works for all of us collectively, including the defendants. Second, the defendants are not free to walk away from the prosecution. The stakes involve prison and devastating felony records, and the Department of Justice boasts an unlimited budget to exploit surveillance footage, witness statements, and social media materials to secure these consequences.

It's one thing to turn a denial into a confession after presenting a defendant with witness testimonies or other admissible evidence to prove the crime was actually committed. It's entirely different to produce no evidence at all and simply hang additional charges over the defendant's head, squeezing them into "confessing" to the lesser charge. Such an approach inherently creates a strong likelihood that defendants will confess to something that is not true. For that reason, overcharging is prohibited and illegal in America, at least on paper (see discussion below). Nevertheless, it remains a common prosecutorial tactic and one that is frequently abused by the government, but never more so than with the DOJ's J6 witch hunt.

The DC Appellate Court, which oversees the DC District Court in which all of these plea bargains are submitted, has, for half a century, banned the practice of overcharging defendants to coerce a guilty plea to a lesser charge:

> . . . the prosecutor clearly cannot have carte blanche to apply whatever tactics he wishes to induce a guilty plea. A policy of deliberately overcharging defendants with no intention of prosecuting on all counts simply in order to have chips at the bargaining table would, for example, constitute improper harassment of the defendant.[11]

University of Chicago law school professor and Justice Department official Albert Alschuler describes the two different ways prosecutors can overcharge defendants: horizontal and vertical. Horizontal overcharging is:

> . . . multiplying "unreasonably" the number of accusations against a single defendant . . . prosecutors may fragment a single criminal transaction into numerous component offenses. In Cleveland, "bad check artists" are usually charged, not only with one, but with three separate offenses for each check: forgery, uttering [passing or using a forged document], and obtaining property by false pretenses. In Boston, the pattern is the same, except that a fourth offense is occasionally added; the defendant may also be charged as a "common and notorious thief."[12]

It's almost as if the US Attorney's Office is determined to prove that horizontal overcharging has become standard operating procedure, demonstrating, on a webpage dedicated to J6 cases, how to "fragment a single potential criminal transaction" of entering the Capitol into "numerous component offenses," including the first four charges listed above: entering and remaining, disorderly conduct in a restricted building, disorderly conduct in the Capitol, and picketing or parading.[13]

After the initial shock of being charged with five variations of one act, the reality of the government's unchecked power quickly sinks in, and an offer to plead to only one of the redundant charges sounds almost generous. Next, the professor defined *vertical* overcharging as:

> . . . charging a single offense at a higher level than the circumstances of the case seems to warrant . . . prosecutors charge robbery when they should charge larceny from the person, that they charge grand theft when they should charge petty theft, that they charge assault with intent to commit murder when they should charge some form of battery, and that they charge the larceny of an automobile when they should charge "joy-riding," a less serious offense that does not involve an intention to deprive the car owner permanently of his property.[14,15]

The idea of punishing someone more severely than their actual behavior is repugnant to any reasonable person. But it happens routinely in America, and it happened to J6 defendants especially severely, including being vertically overcharged with a twenty-year felony.

The US attorney charged hundreds of J6 trespassers with the twenty-year felony of 18 U.S. Code §1512(c)(2), a statute with the name: "Tampering with a witness, victim, or an informant." *Tampering*? With a *witness*? How in the world did a statute relating to "tampering with a witness" become part of a political protest? I have thought about that a lot since my own indictment with this statute.

Licensed to Lie

This §1512(c)(2) statute was passed by Congress to close what became known as the "Arthur Andersen loophole" following the 2002 Enron debacle, which was the biggest corporate financial scandal of its time. Enron's accounting firm, Arthur Andersen, was accused of corruptly persuading its employees to destroy documents with the intent to hide evidence in a government investigation. That this technical evidence shredding statute has morphed unrecognizably into prosecuting political prisoners, in my opinion, cannot be a coincidence. The lawyer for the case that led to the creation of this technical §1512(c)(2) statute is Andrew Weissman, a professional fascist, a rabid elitist who suffers from a severe case of Trump Derangement Syndrome.

This prosecutor repeatedly argued for and persuaded the federal judge to instruct the jury it could convict Arthur Andersen even if the firm honestly and sincerely believed its conduct was lawful. Eventually, the Supreme Court rejected this abuse of prosecutorial power in a unanimous 9–0 reversal. Essentially the most esteemed jurists in our nation scorned this lawyer, noting that the very words of the statute specifically contradicted what he instructed the jury. His arguments to the jury removed all criminal intent from the requirements for a conviction. Sidney Powell's book *Licensed To Lie: Exposing Corruption in the Department of Justice* describes exactly how this lawyer spent his career obtaining convictions at any cost and the effect of his abuses on the lives of innocent people he destroyed.[16]

Attorney Andrew Weissmann was known as "the driving force" for causing a multi-billion-dollar worldwide company to collapse and eigthy-five thousand people to lose their jobs. Weissmann distorted the evidence and the written words of a statute to obtain a conviction without criminal conduct. That is who Andrew Weissmann is. Weissmann's prosecutorial misconduct (misleading the jury) caused the DOJ to suffer a humiliating unanimous loss in front of the United States Supreme Court. That is a professional disgrace. But, just as would be expected in fascist regimens, his unethical and low-quality work kept earning him promotions. After being deputy director and general counsel of the FBI and head of the fraud division of the DOJ, he became "Mueller's boy" in special investigations targeting Paul Manafort and President Trump.

Where is Weissmann now? He is in the position deemed most important to fascist regimes: communications. Fascist entities use disinformation and propaganda campaigns to control people. That Weissmann is so ethically challenged that a divided Supreme Court unanimously ruled against *him* is the type of black mark that would prevent his promotion in a free society. So naturally he is an on-air correspondent for MSNBC, co-hosting *Prosecuting Donald Trump*—a prosecution for which he has long salivated.

Following the Enron scandal, Congress passed a statute to make sure corporations did not shred documents or intimidate witnesses to corruptly influence a trial outcome. Here is the actual text of the §1512(c) statute:

> Whoever corruptly (1) alters, destroys, mutilates, or conceals a record, document, or other object, or attempts to do so, with the

> intent to impair the object's integrity or availability for use in an official proceeding; or (2) otherwise obstructs, influences, or impedes any official proceeding, or attempts to do so, shall be fined under this title or imprisoned not more than 20 years, or both.[17]

President George W. Bush, who signed this bill into law, warned of the potential misapplication and abuse of the statute:

> . . . the purpose of the Act was to "adopt tough new provisions to deter and punish corporate and accounting fraud and corruption" . . . To ensure that no infringement on the constitutional right to petition the Government for redress of grievances occurs in the enforcement of section 1512(c) of title 18 of the U.S. Code.[18]

President Bush's warning about how this statute must not be used has turned out to be exactly how the statute is being misused against J6 defendants. It is hard to understand how a nonviolent bystander at a protest could ever be charged with evidence tampering or witness obstruction related to a legal proceeding.

Charging §1512(c)(2) was so startlingly irrelevant to the events of January 6 that in the three years since then, many observers have wondered how the government even came up with this charge—and so rapidly? The common reading of this statute, including its title, "Witness tampering and evidence shredding," has literally nothing to do with the thousands of "mostly peaceful" protestors in DC on January 6.

In retrospect, it is clear that this vertical overcharging was planned months *prior* to January 6. There is simply no way a completely irrelevant statute could have been so rapidly weaponized against so many average Americans within two days of the event. It takes malicious legal wizardry to convert our First Amendment-protected right to political protest into an "evidence tampering crime" of legal obstruction punishable by an outrageous twenty years in prison. The FBI and DOJ is led by many of the same group of people who methodically targeted Trump and General Michael Flynn[19] and anyone who supports Trump, such as Steve Bannon, Peter Navarro, and J6 defendants.

This brings me back to the rabid anti-Trump activist, MSNBC media correspondent and attorney Andrew Weissmann, who was reprimanded by the Supreme Court 9–0 for prosecuting a case using illegitimate jury instructions that simply disappeared the concept of criminal intent—the very element that makes an act criminal. Weissman is one of only a handful of people who would have been able to conceive how to distort a highly technical witness tampering statute into an indictment against hundreds of Trump protestors and Trump himself. This abuse of power had Weissmann written all over it.

In case the reader wonders if the government innocently charged this twenty-year felony statute because they could not find a better fit . . . no. Just a few pages away in the same United States Code, 18 U.S.C. §1505 enumerates a statute and penalty that more closely resembles J6 conduct. For J6, the government is alleging under 18 U.S.Code §1512(c)(2) that several thousand uncoordinated and unarmed American citizens who assembled to protest were in fact conspiring to "obstruct justice" by preventing an official proceeding in Congress from being conducted. Although the DOJ lacked any evidence to prove such a conspiracy, there is a law that would at least apply accurately to such an allegation. The text of statute 18 U.S. Code §1505 states:

> Whoever corruptly, or by threats or force . . . obstructs, or . . . endeavors to . . . impede the due and proper administration of the law under which any pending proceeding is being had before any department or agency of the United States . . . shall be fined under this title, imprisoned not more than 5 years.[20]

When comparing the text and legislative history of this §1505 statute to the one that was actually charged against me (and hundreds of others), it is obvious that the government purposely chose the irrelevant one. Why? I think it is because §1512(c)(2) carries a twenty-year penalty and §1505 carries a five-year penalty. Five years just wasn't enough to force defendants into accepting a plea deal immediately, so they reached past this statute to find a stronger form of legal leverage. The quicker the plea deals accumulated, the more the government could brazenly tell the public that there had been a widespread conspiracy and feed their insurrection story. Getting defendants to roll over, and fast, was important for the Biden DOJ.

Disproportionate and Insincere

A test for whether the government is engaged in overcharging was developed by Santa Clara University law school professor Kyle Graham, using three criteria:

1. Charging without adequate proof
2. Filing charges disproportionate to the crime
3. Prosecutorial insincerity[21]

All of these applied to the J6 prosecutors. Nonviolent protestors who spent a short time taking selfies in the Capitol have been charged with a twenty-year obstruction felony without any evidence of obstruction, any proportion to what they actually did, or any indication of a sincere effort by prosecutors to later prove the claimed obstruction. How else would they even begin to prove the *mens rea*, or criminal intent, for obstruction in such cases, except to "incentivize" an abrupt reversal of the defendants' mindset?

It is illegal for a prosecutor to charge any crime for which they do not *already* possess proof that the defendant met the elements of the crime. The nation's highest court not only describes the parameters of acceptable plea bargain strategy by prosecutors, it also articulates what is not permitted:

> . . . the [unacceptable] situation where the prosecutor or judge, or both, deliberately employ their charging and sentencing powers to induce a particular defendant to tender a plea of guilty. In [this] case there is no claim that the prosecutor threatened prosecution on a charge not justified by the evidence . . . to induce him to plead guilty.[22]

The court asserts that such a prosecutorial threat would, in fact, be both illegal and unacceptable. In another Supreme Court decision, a dissenting justice noted bluntly that:

> . . . plea bargaining . . . presents grave risks of prosecutorial overcharging that effectively compels an innocent defendant to avoid massive risk by pleading guilty to a lesser offense . . . [23]

The American Bar Association also rejects overcharging:

> The prosecutor should not file or maintain charges greater in number or degree than can reasonably be supported with evidence at trial and are necessary to fairly reflect the gravity of the offense or deter similar conduct.[24]

Federal prosecutors themselves have even been warned about overcharging, alerting defense attorneys to the problem as part of their Office of Justice Program.[25]

Despite such opposition, the practice continues. It was viciously used by federal prosecutors to not only coerce J6 defendants into false confessions of "knowingly" trespassing, but also to waive their right to appeal their sentences as part of their written plea bargain:

> Your client also agrees to waive the right to appeal the sentence in this case, including but not limited to any term of imprisonment, fine, forfeiture, award of restitution, term or condition of supervised release, authority of the Court to set conditions of release, and the manner in which the sentence was determined, except to the extent the Court sentences your client above the statutory maximum or guidelines range determined by the Court.[26]

Mark Twain is credited with the quote, "If you tell the truth, you don't have to remember anything." Prosecutors rely on the difficulty of remembering a lie in their cross-examinations of witnesses. It should have come as no surprise that a J6 defendant pressured to falsely confess that they knowingly entered the Capitol might later state the opposite.

Jenny Cudd, the Texas florist I mentioned in Chapter 7, did just that. As part of her plea agreement, she legally confessed, via a statement written for her by the DOJ, to knowing that she wasn't allowed in the Capitol.[27] Later, when she had to meet with a probation officer for a presentencing interview, she told the officer,

> I did not realize, at the time, that I was breaking the law when I walked inside through open doors to the Capitol. When I said on TV that I didn't do anything unlawful, I genuinely meant that I did not believe that I did anything illegal.[28]

One might think that prosecutors would weigh the sincerity of Cudd's claims of innocence and consider recommending a lighter sentence. Such a conclusion would be wrong. Prosecutors filed a *new* motion arguing Cudd may have "repudiated" her plea agreement and opened herself up to a *new* prosecution on the dropped charges! The judge didn't buy it, luckily, and sentenced Cudd according to the plea agreement, including no jail time at all. Cudd's lawyer called the US attorney's attempt to reintroduce charges "malicious."[29] With dirty lawyers like this, who needs enemies?

Literal Heartbreak

Matthew Perna, a thirty-seven-year-old from Pennsylvania who was an English teacher overseas, a runner, a photographer, a writer, and a devoted son, spent just twenty minutes inside the Capitol building on January 6. He entered the building long after Congress adjourned. When he heard a mere rumor that the FBI wanted to talk with him, *he* contacted *them* to turn himself in. He was charged with two misdemeanors and released that same day without bail. Later, the government added the twenty-year felony to his charge. He was bullied into signing a plea agreement admitting that he knowingly entered a restricted space, despite the fact that he entered through an open door and was welcomed by police. His family reported these facts in his obituary after he took his life under extreme prosecutorial pressure:

> Matt's heart broke and his spirit died, and many people are responsible for the pain he endured. . . . He entered the Capitol through a previously opened door (he did not break in as was reported), where he was ushered in by police. He didn't break, touch or steal anything. He did not harm anyone, as he stayed within the velvet ropes taking pictures. For this act he has been persecuted . . . [30]

Not only was the Capitol door open, but Perna, after immediately turning himself in to the FBI upon learning they were looking for him, clarified that he did not enter the Capitol voluntarily, as recorded by an unnamed FBI special agent in an extraordinarily contradictory affidavit:

> PERNA indicated that he and a friend went to the top of the steps of the Capitol building's west side and was surprised that the door was open. Two U.S. Capitol police officers were inside the door. PERNA claimed that he was pushed into the building by a crowd that had gathered behind him. PERNA claimed that it was not his intention to enter the Capitol . . .
>
> Based on the foregoing, your affiant submits that there is probable cause to believe that PERNA violated 18 U.S.C. § 1752(a)(1) and (2), which makes it a crime to (1) knowingly enter or remain in any restricted building or grounds without lawful authority to do . . . [31]

That agent did not provide any evidence or rationale to justify his jump from Perna claiming to be pushed into the Capitol, through open doors in front of policemen who did not object, to his conclusion that there is probable cause to believe he knowingly entered a restricted space.

The government was not finished with Perna, though. They called him in for a follow-up interrogation in which he admitted that "at one point he [had] become frustrated, and, using a metal pole, tapped on a window of the Capitol building." That knock on the window did *not* break any glass, but was deemed sufficient evidence of violence to bring the weight of the Justice Department down heavily on Perna. He was then swept into the growing torrent of protesters who vigorously denied knowing they were disallowed entry into the Capitol before signing a confession to the contrary:

> The defendant knew at the time he entered the U.S. Capitol Building that he did not have permission to enter the building.[32]

That, sadly, wasn't the end of his confession. Under pressure to concede that his flagpole was a weapon (despite no violent actions), Perna also agreed to the much higher-level offense:

> The defendant, in concert with others, obstructed, influenced, and impeded an official proceeding . . .[33]

Federal prosecutors actually boasted on their website about the extraordinary punishment faced by Perna for his twenty peaceful minutes in the Capitol, one moment in which he tapped on a window notwithstanding, knowing the chilling effect this would have on others:

> [Perna] remained inside the building for approximately 20 minutes, in the Senate Wing Lobby. While there, he held a cellular device in his right hand and filmed and chanted with the crowd . . .
>
> Perna pleaded guilty in the District of Columbia to an indictment that charged him with obstruction of Congress, a felony, and three related misdemeanor charges . . .
>
> He faces up to 20 years in prison and a $250,000 fine on the felony charge and additional penalties on the misdemeanor offenses.[34]

Apparently twenty years for twenty minutes was still not satisfactory, so the Department of Justice informed Perna that they also planned to seek a "terrorism sentencing enhancement."[35] This was too much for Perna, who was informed this terrorism enhancement meant the DOJ would likely put him behind bars for at least five to ten years. Literally crushed by the corruption, Matthew Perna hanged himself in anguish. His family said, ". . . the justice system killed his spirit and his zest for life."[36] His aunt, Geri Perna, tells his story.[37]

After Matthew hanged himself, the family spoke with the DOJ prosecutors who did this. The lawyers seemed shaken up that they were the tools of so much evil and told the family that they did not believe the enhancement would have been accepted by the judge. It was the *threat* of the prison sentence—the vertical overcharge—that was impossible for this young man to endure.[38]

On March 1, 2024, Representative Marjorie Taylor Greene introduced the Matthew Lawrence Perna Act of 2024 named in honor of just one victim of the cruel and unusual treatment inflicted by Joe Biden's Department of Injustice, tragically leading to his untimely death. The press release explains that this vital legislation is a critical step to ensure that political persecution is curtailed by law.

Congresswoman Greene said, "Having personally witnessed the abuses in the DC jail, where patriotic Americans are left to suffer by the very government meant to protect them, it is evident that reform is urgently needed."[39] Matthew Perna's tragic death serves as a stark reminder of the consequences of unchecked government brutality.

Congresswoman Greene urges all of her colleagues to ensure no nonviolent political protestor is ever treated with such inhumanity in the United States again. The Matthew Lawrence Perna Act enacts several essential reforms, including:

- **Prohibition of Detention for Nonviolent Political Protesters:** This bill bars the unjust detention of nonviolent political protesters and allows for civil action against any violations.
- **Fair and Speedy Trials:** Ensures fair and speedy trials for defendants while providing remedies against malicious over-prosecution.
- **Limiting Government Surveillance and Investigation:** Restricts the government's ability to use national defense or foreign policy justifications to deny citizens knowledge of government surveillance or investigation.

- **Consistent Sentencing Guidelines:** Mandates that judges impose sentences consistent with applicable guidelines for defendants involved in covered political protest offenses.
- **Transfer of Venue:** Permits the transfer of venue in criminal trials for nonviolent political protestors in Washington, DC.[40]

All of the examples in this chapter are of lawyers and agencies funded by our citizens, but running roughshod over these same citizens. Some less experienced or bright lawyers may think they are just "doing their job," but it's clear most of them are aware that their actions are illegal and simply do not care. Stalin's secret police chief ruthlessly controlled his own population in exactly this way, by stacking the deck.

When American DOJ lawyers routinely engage in Brady violations, vertical overcharging, horizontal overcharging, charging without adequate proof, filing charges disproportionate to the crime, and coercing defendants into signing false statements of offense, they are using the Stalinist technique of stacking the deck. We think it cannot happen in the United States of America. It already has.

CHAPTER NINE

The Associated Propaganda

If you don't read the newspaper, you're uninformed. If you read the newspaper, you're misinformed.

—Attributed to Mark Twain

Nothing can now be believed which is seen in a newspaper. Truth itself becomes suspicious by being put into that polluted vehicle.

—Thomas Jefferson

The formal name of the AP is the Associated Press. The AP is a cooperative of hundreds of radio stations, television stations, and newspapers who provide content to 15,000 media outlets around the world.[1] They dominate all news, on the one hand, providing economic efficiency and, on the other hand, providing a single centralized source of news resulting in a tremendous lack of diversity in reporting in national newspapers. Over the past few decades, many people have come to learn that AP really stands for "Associated Propaganda."[2] The other big conglomerate in this space is Reuters, which is similar.

Before I wrote my first book, *I Do Not Consent,*[3] which details a cancellation operation carried out by a collusion of corporate media and government forces, I did not think the government was as entwined with media as I now know it is. I know from personal experience that the government widely deploys the media for various strategic attacks, including propaganda and censorship.

Printing Lies for Two Reasons

While unfamiliar to people like myself who were never pointedly "political," eliminating political opponents by propaganda has been a tried-and-true technique for many decades. The government leaks information on an opponent to certain media allies, who then run hit pieces on that dissident figure. The thrust of the article is often to give the public the impression that the government, the very source of the article in the first place, isn't doing enough to address the alleged "crisis" supposedly created by said dissident. They create the illusion of their own failure and thus the justification for swiftly rectifying it. This strategy is based on an age-old Marxist technique referred to by the acronym PRS: Problem, Reaction, Solution.

Sound familiar? The most famous recent example was when FBI Director James Comey orchestrated a media leak in 2017 to pressure the FBI to investigate supposed Russian collusion in Trump's election after he was fired as director. A common theme that has emerged from the FBI's Crossfire Hurricane investigation is bureau officials' use of media reports and leaks to initiate and advance the bureau's probe of the Trump campaign's possible ties to Russia. In at least five instances, FBI officials capitalized on the so-called news hooks as justification to open up new areas of the investigation. Essentially, a federal agency uses media reports to then open up a government investigation into the targeted person.

I don't believe this is what happens solely because I've learned about it through reading or hearsay. I personally experienced this type of propaganda attack. As I wrote in Chapter 4, the Congressional Select Subcommittee on the Coronavirus Crisis relied exclusively on a hit piece in *The Intercept* to open a congressional inquiry into me.[4] As *The Intercept* story was completely false, it is my belief it was a planted story from the subcommittee itself. In other words, it wasn't printed *just* to defame me and reduce my credibility, but also so the defamatory story could become the basis for a congressional investigation.

Familiar Plot

Soon after gaining fame for his reporting on the Watergate scandal, *Washington Post* journalist Carl Bernstein spent six months in the late 1970s researching the influence of the CIA on the press. He published his findings in a 25,000-word cover story for *Rolling Stone* titled "The CIA and the Media." His findings were astounding.

> More than 400 American journalists . . . in the past twenty-five years have secretly carried out assignments for the Central Intelligence Agency . . . full-time CIA employees [were] masquerading as journalists abroad. In many instances, CIA documents show, journalists were engaged to perform tasks for the CIA with the consent of the management of America's leading news organizations . . . Further investigation into the matter, CIA officials say, would inevitably reveal a series of embarrassing relationships in the 1950s and 1960s with some of the most powerful organizations and individuals in American journalism . . . By far the most valuable of these associations, according to CIA officials, have been with the *New York Times*, CBS and Time Inc.[5]

The journalists' cooperation, however, was not always voluntary. For example, two American journalists were even wiretapped, according to CIA files referencing "Operation Mockingbird," a name sometimes used to describe the entire CIA project to steer media messaging.[6]

Here is a disturbing example of this type of planted "propaganda leak" harming our national security. In February 2020, President Trump reached an agreement with the Taliban to end the nearly twenty-year conflict in Afghanistan, withdrawing all US and NATO troops.[7] Four months later, *The New York Times* ran the so-called "Bountygate" story about the Russian government offering money to Taliban-linked fighters to attack US soldiers in Afghanistan.[8] Within days, the story was cited by congressional representatives to justify an amendment to the defense spending bill that would limit the president's ability to reduce the number of US troops deployed in Afghanistan below eight thousand.[9] The bill passed.

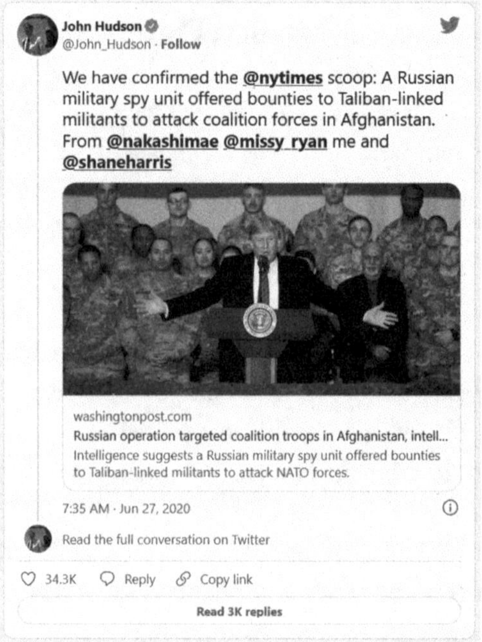
John Hudson
@John_Hudson · Follow

We have confirmed the @nytimes scoop: A Russian military spy unit offered bounties to Taliban-linked militants to attack coalition forces in Afghanistan. From @nakashimae @missy_ryan me and @shaneharris

washingtonpost.com
Russian operation targeted coalition troops in Afghanistan, intell...
Intelligence suggests a Russian military spy unit offered bounties to Taliban-linked militants to attack NATO forces.

7:35 AM · Jun 27, 2020

Read the full conversation on Twitter

34.3K Reply Copy link

Read 3K replies

After the vote in September 2020, the top US generals in Afghanistan announced that "a detailed review of all available intelligence has not been able to corroborate the existence of such a program."[10] In April 2021, *The Daily Beast* reported,

> Intel Walks Back Claim Russians Put Bounties; It was a huge election-time story that prompted cries of treason. But according to a newly disclosed assessment, Donald Trump might have been right to call it a "hoax."[11]

It is truly difficult to overstate the enormity of a leftist outlet like *The Daily Beast* printing the words "Trump might have been right." Needless to say, the leak was indisputably confirmed to be a lie.

That same day, *The New York Times* reported that the source of their bountygate "scoop" was the CIA. Independent journalist Caitlin Johnstone summed it up this way:

> They quite literally ran a CIA press release and disguised it as a news story. This allowed the CIA to throw shade and inertia on Trump's proposed troop withdrawals . . .
>
> In totalitarian dictatorships, the government spy agency tells the news media what stories to run, and the news media unquestioningly publish it. In free democracies, the government spy agency says, "Hoo buddy, have I got a scoop for you!" and the news media unquestioningly publish it.[12]

Joining the Cast of This Familiar Plot

Hit pieces on me didn't just start on January 6, 2021. They appeared much earlier, as soon as I began to have an impact on the debate over coronavirus responses. In May 2020, I received confirmation that President Trump himself had read my anti-lockdown letter to him outlining the "exponentially growing negative health consequences of the national shutdown." I had garnered the written endorsement of over seven hundred physicians for my plea to relax the lockdown, and that's just what happened. Tony Fauci appeared on national media the day after my letter was publicized to announce a rollback in the intensity of the shutdown.

This victory was followed, within hours, by an AP reporter[13] calling to ask whether I was working for the president's campaign. Prior to this question, the reporter had set a trap by "informing" me, without any basis, that he had absolute confirmation that I was on a short list for a position in the Trump administration. When I vehemently and repeatedly answered "no," verbally and in writing, that I was not working for the campaign and that we were grassroots doctors, the AP wrote: "Gold denied she was coordinating her efforts with Trump's reelection campaign."[14] They did so without explaining why such an allegation would even be imaginable. They might as well have written that I denied being a professional tennis player.

The AP even wrote that I said, "I'm honored to be considered," without explaining that they themselves were the source of the fabricated rumor that I was on some "short list" to work with the president.[15] And so, just like that, AP planted a seed in the minds of its readers that I was a Trump operative and stealthily turned what should have been a purely medical issue into a political one. The implicit message to their readers was that *unless you're a Trump supporter, you have no business considering alternative approaches to COVID treatments, lockdowns, masks, or vaccine mandates.*

I think, sadly, that it was (and is) inconceivable to most of today's journalists that ordinary Americans can think for themselves, would dare to think for themselves, or would want to think for themselves. I think this truly baffles them. I don't know how they explain away presidential candidate and lifelong Democrat Robert Kennedy Jr.,[16] who vehemently disagreed with Trump on the vaccines.

Additional disingenuous articles planted further baseless claims in the minds of readers, including a description of AFLDS as "a fringe group of self-proclaimed medical experts," implying that we failed to possess such credentials.[17] This was later parroted by Rachel Maddow in an openly defamatory segment perpetuating several such manipulations to undermine our credibility.[18] We were the most credentialed grassroots organization imaginable. Every one of us has multiple advanced degrees, decades of experience, not to mention hundreds of journal articles and government data supporting our statements.

A piece published by *The Intercept* attempted to frighten people with a headline about "hacked data" for "COVID-19 consultations promoted" by AFLDS.[19] This article was a complete hoax on multiple levels. For one, AFLDS did not have any patient data whatsoever since we do not treat any patients. Any persons interested in early treatment (and millions were) could choose to pursue this with third-party telemedicine providers, independent of AFLDS, through referrals on our website. More importantly, though, there was no evidence of a data hack as written by *The Intercept*. It appears the authors *literally made it up*. An expensive cybersecurity audit was performed, which failed to find a breach. Nevertheless, those who read the headline without verifying the details were undoubtedly filled with concern about a breach of their privacy, not realizing that there was no *fire* behind the media's *smoke*.

Crony Censorship

But is the **government** really involved or controlling such **media** malfeasance?

A source of many such attacks against me and other doctors is a group called "No License for Disinformation" (NLFD). Little would be known about them if not for the work of Rich Swier, PhD, the former chair of the Sarasota Better Business Council. In an investigative piece titled, "CALIFORNIA: New Witch Hunt to Strip Honest Doctors of Their Licenses," Swier connected the dots all the way back to 1600 Pennsylvania Avenue:

> Regulating the medical views a doctor can and cannot have is dangerous in the extreme, and . . . we must . . . push back against phony front groups that promote this kind of medical tyranny. This includes NLFD . . . which promotes the false information disseminated by the dark-money hate group known as the Center for Countering Digital Hate (CCDH).
>
> Just who is the NLFD? In November 2021, I wrote about the NLFD, pointing out that the bottom [disclaimer] of their website declared, "Created & Developed by EverydayAmericanJoe." At the time, I took a screenshot of it, in case they'd wise up and change it. Good thing, because that notice has since been deleted.
>
> And, no wonder, because it leads right back to the Biden White House. EverydayAmericanJoe, created by a marketing strategist named Chris Gilroy, was a website dedicated to supporting Joe Biden's presidential campaign. (That website has since been disabled).[20]

Where's the proof that Gilroy actually worked for Biden? In his archived LinkedIn profile.[21]

According to his LinkedIn profile, Gilroy created EverydayAmericanJoe.com—"the largest Biden-Harris grassroots website online"—*as a freelance senior marketing consultant and designer for the Biden campaign . . .*

Gilroy used a list of twelve people, dubbed the "Disinformation Dozen," that the CCDH deemed most responsible for "vaccine hesitancy" including personalities like Robert F. Kennedy Jr.[22]

Crony capitalism is a pejorative phrase which describes a business profiting from a close relationship with a state power. I would label what

Gilroy did as "crony censorship." A powerful and connected state power (i.e., the Biden campaign) tasked others (i.e., Gilroy) to execute propaganda and censorship. Dr. Swier summarizes Gilroy's propaganda:

> [T]he NLFD has promoted and relied on the CCDH's fabricated "Disinformation Dozen" report, which has even been denounced as biased and flawed in the extreme by Facebook.
>
> It's quite clear that the CCDH exists to fabricate "evidence" that is then used to destroy the opposition in order to control the information, and the NLFD uses the CCDH's fabrications as justification to suppress First Amendment rights. Indeed, Biden himself has publicly promoted and relied on this dark money CCDH report.
>
> The point of all this is that the censorship is being authorized and directed from the very highest level of our government.[23]

And who else also funds NLFD? Bill Gates.[24]

A little postscript about the defamatory "Disinformation Dozen": AFLDS produced a counter-video entitled the Deadly Disinformation Dozen.[25] In this video the viewer can listen to the speakers' words . . . and decide for themselves regarding who is spreading disinformation.

And if you are still skeptical about the coordinated propaganda and censorship that dominates this country, watch this short video.[26]

Patient First Medicine

Associating me with presidential politics was an obvious ploy to entice half the country into reactively opposing me, never mind my actual positions. "Patient First" *medicine* was to be disparaged by Democrats exactly the same as "America First" *politics.* By continuing to treat patients based on what they needed vs. what public health officials (wrongly) required, I would be labeled or canceled (just like America First advocates). Of course, debating the government "science" was not allowed.

For example, *The Intercept* falsely accused me of pushing HCQ treatment as a means of "currying favor with the president."[27] However, exactly what favor I could expect in return from President Trump was never clarified. *The Intercept* also falsely claimed that AFLDS is "a right-wing group founded last year to promote pro-Trump doctors."[28] Doctors are not questioned on their political affiliation before they join AFLDS. If they are qualified and credentialed doctors advocating for medical freedom, they are welcomed and supported, regardless of their political party, religion, race, or any other divisionary category.

AFLDS's nonpartisan reality doesn't provide the media with a useful angle for manipulation, so the "news" media has switched gears. *Time* quoted a Columbia University academic accusing me, ironically, of advocating for HCQ as a "21st century, digital version of snake-oil salesmen."[29] The article omitted a critical fact, which was that I attempted to make HCQ available to every single American *without* a prescription, removing the physicians' profit potential in prescribing it![30]

Had the *Time* writer been interested in honest reporting, she could have easily learned that the AFLDS website (AFLDS.org) sells neither drugs nor medical services. Rather, AFLDS.org has a huge amount of content for the public to self-educate. Users can also click through to a different site for an individualized consultation with an independent telemedicine company. When doing so, users are clearly informed that the telemedicine company may choose to donate money to AFLDS, but there is no obligation.[31] Apparently, those details were too tedious to share with the public; we wouldn't want facts getting in the way of a good story, would we?

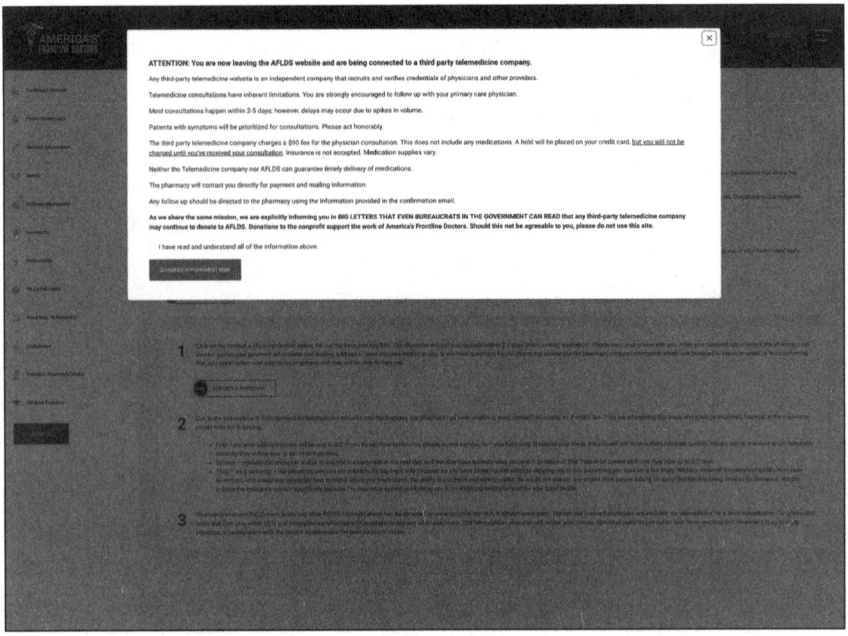

In the case of *The Intercept*, they simply invented a good story out of thin air. Their false statements became the basis for an ominous congressional inquiry into me and the work of America's Frontline Doctors, which dragged on for fourteen months before finally being abandoned.

As I wrote in Chapter 4, in October 2021 I received a letter from the Select Subcommittee on the Coronavirus Crisis accusing me of selling snake oil and profiting from it. Congress's factual basis for this accusation was *The Intercept* article. Congress accused me as follows: "America's Frontline Doctors (AFLDS) offers paid online consultations and prescriptions for drugs like hydroxychloroquine and ivermectin" (see DrGoldReferences Appendix 6).[32]

When Congressman James Clyburn and his cronies could find nothing against me from their baseless accusations started by the media and weaponized by Congress, they issued a 250-page report containing no evidence against me. They never sent an apology, or a thank-you-for-cooperating, or a public statement acknowledging their smear or their lack of evidence against me. In fact, they didn't say anything at all to me. It simply became a public document with no comment. Your tax dollars are hard at work.

Perhaps the most disappointing outcome to me was how many liberal-minded people seemed to suddenly drop the underlying principle of liberalism—support for the liberty of free thought and free speech—along with other previously held convictions of equality and empowerment.

In a piece amazingly bereft of self-reflection, *Mother Jones*, an online magazine named after a nineteenth-century female activist motivated by injustices like child labor and poor working conditions, published "Doctor, Lawyer, Insurrectionist: The Radicalization of Simone Gold."[33] I sometimes wonder if this is the left's idea of having a sense of humor!

In another hatchet piece, I found myself attacked by *Slate* for including a female West African doctor in my White Coat Summit.[34] Dr. Stella Immanuel held personal religious views, completely separate from the COVID debate and unknown to me at the time, which included the belief that negative spiritual forces can lead to physical ailments.[35] She was ridiculed for not being impressionable enough to change her views in favor of Western cultural preferences, while I was called "too independent-minded" to join the attackers who labeled her the "demon sperm" doctor. What happened to that short-lived rallying cry, "believe all women"?

Crony Capitalism

While the government holds serious blame for suffocating a proper scientific debate about COVID policy, it is not solely responsible. The role of mega-corporations related to COVID public policy is explained in the article, "Big Pharma Hunts Down Dissenting Doctors."[36] In the book, *The Truth About COVID-19*, Robert F. Kennedy Jr. wrote a foreword explaining how large pharmaceutical companies often block negative coverage in the media:

> Big Pharma's $9.6 billion annual advertising budget gives these unscrupulous companies control over our news and television outlets. Strong economic drivers (pharmaceutical companies are the biggest network advertisers) have long discouraged mainstream media outlets from criticizing vaccines manufacturers. In 2014, [Fox] network president, Roger Ailes, told me he would fire any

> of his news show hosts who allowed me to talk about [the lack of] vaccine safety on air. "Our news division," he explained, "gets up to 70 percent of its ad revenue from pharma in non-election years."[37]

When a single source is funding almost three quarters of your entire enterprise, it seems pretty fair to say they own you. It is certainly obvious that a newsroom in such circumstances has received a very specific directive about shaping their message. That would be suspect enough, but it gets much worse.

An article posted on the Fierce Pharma website in 2018 reported that, "In the past decade, members of Congress from both parties have received about $81 million from 68 pharma PACs."[38] OpenSecrets, a nonpartisan research group tracking the flow of money in American politics, revealed that the money is flowing to both sides of the aisle, with Senate Republicans actually receiving more than twice as much from Pfizer as Democrats.[39] This information makes it pretty difficult to believe the click-bait headlines that AFLDS is a "right-wing" political group.

Big Pharma is able to leverage its enormous resources in pressuring the media directly through advertising funds and indirectly through the politicians it bankrolls. This is the furthest thing from free-market capitalism.

Merriam-Webster defines *crony capitalism* as "an economic system in which individuals and businesses with political connections and influence are favored (as through tax breaks, grants, and other forms of government assistance) in ways seen as suppressing open competition in a free market."[40]

Exemplifying this crony "corporate cooperation," large pharmaceutical companies (i.e., Big Pharma) donate to politicians who then approve spending bills to provide those pharma groups with taxpayer-funded grants for their research, taxpayer-funded advertising to peddle their vaccines and other drugs, regulations allocating their vaccine products to government vaccination schedules, and mandating their vaccines for entry to schools and healthcare facilities. Big Pharma even secured a law protecting themselves from liability for vaccine injuries,[41] conveniently passed just as they were having difficulty obtaining liability insurance due to high payouts. Since President Reagan signed this law, taxpayers, instead of manufacturers, are responsible for the compensation of vaccine injury victims, which has added up to billions of dollars[42] On the other hand, the vaccine manufacturers only need to pay a 75 cent excise tax for each vaccine dose to the government's Vaccine Injury Compensation Program.[43] The closed system enabling Big Pharma's comprehensive protection is profoundly dangerous.

Operation Warp Speed, a federal effort that supported the speeding up of COVID-19 vaccines,[44] for example, provided billions in COVID vaccine research grants to six companies: Johnson & Johnson, AstraZeneca, Moderna, Novavax, Sanofi, and GlaxoSmithKline.[45] Meanwhile, Pfizer projected over $82 billion in revenue in a single year for its injections,[46] which are completely immune from any legal liability. How could any independent business or publication compete against that? Have you noticed that the majority of television ads are pharmaceutical ads?

The fallacious hit piece by *The Intercept* included a now-laughable quote from vaccine advocate Dr. Kolina Koltai. She alleged AFLDS to be "really good at manipulating science to seem like the vaccine is not safe, or is not tested, or is not necessary."[47] Dr. Koltai's position at the University of Washington's Center for an Informed Public now requires her to identify any digital information that would discourage or delay a person from accepting an mRNA injection.

At the time of this writing in 2024, it is widely known that mRNA injections actually *increased* the risk of death in every age group.[48] As I'm old enough to remember when doctors argued against injecting oneself with a medication that increases your chance of death, I stand *more* firmly by my early statements that these shots are very unsafe. A simple review of COVID-19's mortality according to the CDC is as follows: 0.3 percent without any treatment, and even lower when treated with mild medications like HCQ and ivermectin (see DrGoldReferences Appendix A).[49] Such information also renders the injections grossly unnecessary.

It's also known that Big Pharma manipulated the "science" in their favor. Pfizer, for example, falsely reported data from its clinical trials, and subsequently indicated that there was indeed a need for alarm or further study. An FDA court-ordered release of documents in November 2021 revealed that while Pfizer made a public announcement in July 2021 that more subjects receiving a placebo died than subjects receiving their injection, they actually told the FDA the opposite.[50] In other words, in Pfizer's internal study, more vaccinated subjects died than unvaccinated subjects! Pfizer either lied to the public or the FDA. Either way, "disinformation" would have to apply, and it was, quite literally, deadly disinformation.

A staggering 37,382 American deaths through March 29, 2024, have been attributed by medical professionals to the experimental mRNA injections, as reported to the CDC's Vaccine Adverse Event Reporting System (VAERS). And note that all experts agree that reports to VAERS likely are not even 10 percent of the real number, as it is a passive reporting system.[51] And the cancer detection signals have escalated exponentially, leading many to believe the worst is yet to come. This is not reported by the AP. As I said in Chapter 6 section "Mainstream Media Suppression of Cancer-Causing Data Linked to the Shots," you won't need a microscope, or a PhD, to understand this graphic from the United Kingdom's database (note: malignant neoplasms refers to cancer):[52]

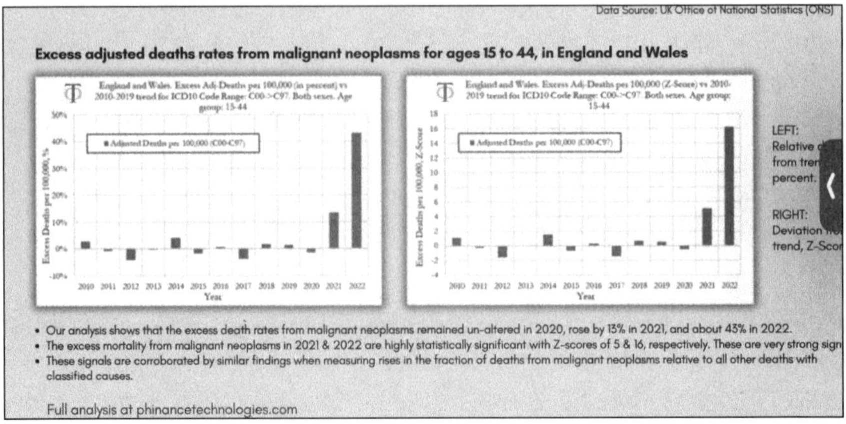
Data Source: UK Office of National Statistics (ONS)
Excess adjusted deaths rates from malignant neoplasms for ages 15 to 44, in England and Wales
England and Wales. Excess Adj-Deaths per 100,000 (in percent) vs 2010-2019 trend for ICD10 Code Range: C00->C97. Both sexes. Age group: 15-44
Adjusted Deaths per 100,000 (C00-C97)
Excess Deaths per 100,000, %
Year
England and Wales. Excess Adj-Deaths per 100,000 (Z-Score) vs 2010-2019 trend for ICD10 Code Range: C00->C97. Both sexes. Age group: 15-44
Adjusted Deaths per 100,000 (C00-C97)
Excess Deaths per 100,000, Z-Score
Year
LEFT:
Relative
percent.
RIGHT:
Deviation
• Our analysis shows that the excess death rates from malignant neoplasms remained un-altered in 2020, rose by 13% in 2021, and about 43% in 2022.
• The excess mortality from malignant neoplasms in 2021 & 2022 are highly statistically significant with Z-scores of 5 & 16, respectively. These are very strong
• These signals are corroborated by similar findings when measuring rises in the fraction of deaths from malignant neoplasms relative to all other deaths with classified causes.
Full analysis at phinancetechnologies.com

Adverse event reports were also manipulated. Twelve-year-old Pfizer clinical volunteer Maddie De Garay,[53] from Ohio, was left paralyzed from the vaccine.[54] Now she can only eat through a feeding tube. Getting around with a wheelchair, Maddie suffers crippling body pain, fingers and toes that turn ice cold and white, and sometimes feels like someone is "ripping her heart out though her neck."[55]

Maddie's parents were understandably shocked to discover that Pfizer listed her reaction as "functional abdominal pain" in its report to the FDA. Excuse me, but is being paralyzed ever mistaken for a stomachache? Maddie's horrific injury ensured that Pfizer's secret would now be anything but. She played a significant role in bringing the truth about Pfizer manipulation of statistics to light, bravely appearing at Senator Ron Johnson's 2021 press conference on adverse reactions to the mRNA injections.

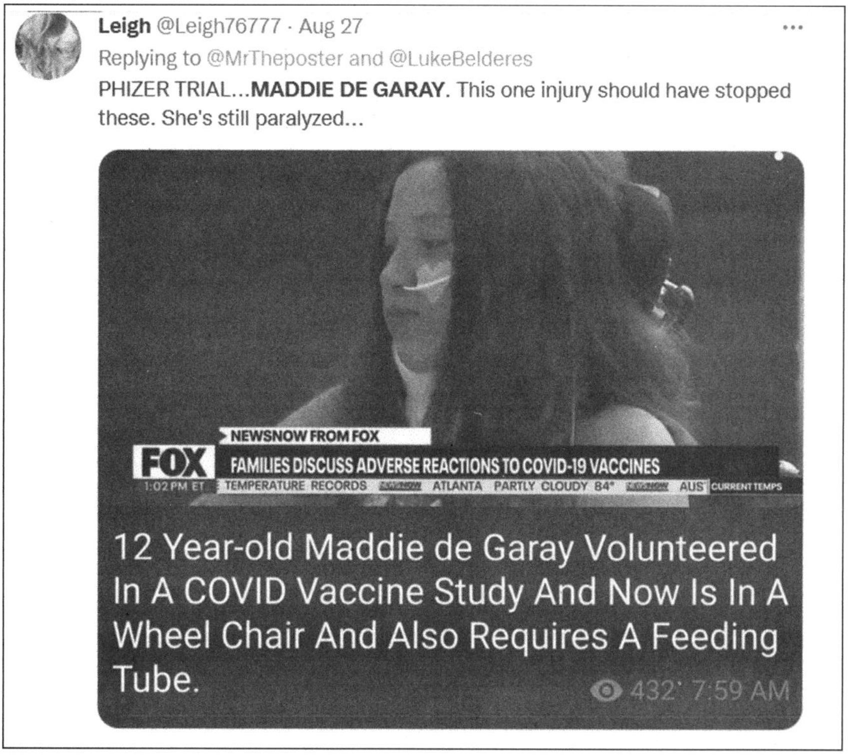

Leigh @Leigh76777 · Aug 27
Replying to @MrTheposter and @LukeBelderes
PHIZER TRIAL...MADDIE DE GARAY. This one injury should have stopped these. She's still paralyzed...
NEWSNOW FROM FOX
FOX
FAMILIES DISCUSS ADVERSE REACTIONS TO COVID-19 VACCINES
1:02 PM ET
TEMPERATURE RECORDS
ATLANTA PARTLY CLOUDY 84°
CURRENT TEMPS
12 Year-old Maddie de Garay Volunteered In A COVID Vaccine Study And Now Is In A Wheel Chair And Also Requires A Feeding Tube.
432 7:59 AM

It eventually holds true that there is no escape—a *lying tongue* is always revealed. The tragedy of Maddie's suffering is an inspiring example of courage, as she became an emissary for truth and accountability. Her suffering is also a somber warning of the consequences of crony corporatism. Let us all pray for her recovery and commit ourselves to preventing further tragedy by demanding integrity and transparency of ourselves and those we allow to hold positions of power.

The actual "pandemic" that threatens our survival as a free people is the rampant crony corruption found in governments and powerful corporations. The United States Constitution, as truly written, is the cure.

CHAPTER TEN

Antidote for Dishonesty

> *Sunlight is said to be the best of disinfectants.*
>
> —Supreme Court Justice Louis Brandeis

Americans have a long history of disdain for manipulated messages, whether by hit pieces based on falsehoods or today's cancellation on social media. This is particularly true when the impetus for the censorship or slander is government criticism. This was a paramount concern of our founding father Thomas Jefferson, who fought to reverse the restrictions on speech critical of the government found in President John Adams's "Alien and Sedition" acts.

In fact, in the 1964 libel case *New York Times v. Sullivan*, the Supreme Court expanded the First Amendment protection for those criticizing government officials.[1] It also established protection to publish even false defamatory statements against government officials and candidates for public office. This prevented the publisher from facing any liability except in the rare cases where the public officials could prove that slander was carried out with "actual malice."

This concern was recently echoed, poignantly, by my codefendant John Strand in his testimony before Congress at a June 13, 2023, field hearing hosted by Congressman Matt Gaetz of Florida,[2] exposing J6 fraud and government weaponization against citizens who publicly criticized the DOJ and the Washington court system.

No Legal Consequences to Defaming Others

After the 1964 *Sullivan* case, something interesting happened. In *Curtis Publishing v. Butts*, the Supreme Court extended the protection afforded to those who falsely slander public *officials* to those who slander public *figures*.[3] The protection against slander claims was so extensive that Justice Clarence Thomas called Sullivan and related decisions "policy-driven decisions masquerading as constitutional law."[4]

Sullivan allowed the publication of false claims against a police commissioner (in the absence of meeting the high standard of proving actual malice in the publication). *Curtis* allowed the publication of false claims against football coaches in the absence of meeting that high standard.

The disastrous end result of these rulings were as follows: The First Amendment right to criticize government officials with accurate information was now turned on its head to allow the unchecked defamation of non-government citizens who dared to criticize the government. Hit pieces attacking those critics could use even completely false allegations, and there would still be no consequences for the publisher.

The difficulty in meeting the "actual malice" standard precludes most lawsuits even when the allegations are demonstrably false. Therefore, doctors and other individuals who publicly criticized government COVID policies were open targets in "The Slander Games," and the defamatory hunting grew more vicious and more frequent.

"Dr. Gold, don't read it, but *The Guardian* ran a piece on you."

"You heard about the NPR article, right?"

"*Time* . . . CNN . . . Huffington Post . . . MSNBC . . . Politico . . . *The Intercept* . . . *WaPo* . . ."

Having terrible and dishonest smear pieces publicized one after the other while facing multiple criminal charges is enough to distract anyone from carrying on a productive life. That was their goal—I didn't let it happen.

That is not to say the defamation did not bother me or did not do damage. It did. I had enjoyed a pristine reputation my entire life, the logical and just result of working hard and ethically for decades. But my awareness of two things helped. The first is that God considers even true gossip, let alone false defamation, to be a very grave sin. In fact, Judaism considers gossiping about a person to be akin to murder. In the introduction, I shared a story attributed to Rabbi Levi Yitzhak of Berdichev that is used to explain the power and permanence of defamation.[5] The second is my legal knowledge that our courts would not protect people who were being massively defamed.

Like feathers carried by the wind, words you have said about others or words others have said about you can never be retrieved. The damage is done. Growing up with this spiritual education definitely protected me from great unhappiness in 2020. When it happened to me, I understood that I was being harmed and that, even if our courts had been wiser than *Sullivan*, defamation is essentially unfixable. So I never really became unhappy over the massive defamation.

Understanding Lashon Hara ("Evil Tongue")

I speak of the Halacha (Jewish Law) against *lashon hara* because it is so ubiquitous these days, understanding *lashon hara* will help people navigate their daily lives better. *Lashon hara* is Hebrew for "evil tongue" and does not only mean gossip. It is more broad. It means you shouldn't talk (or listen to talk) about people at all. There are two exceptions to *lashon hara*. The first is you are permitted to say something if the other person must be informed about something you know. This is kind of a "need to know" exception to *lashon hara*. If an acquaintance is considering marrying someone who you know is a wife-beater, clearly you are permitted to disclose this. If a friend is considering going into business with a person who cheated you in business, you are permitted to disclose this.

The second exception to *lashon hara* is that you are permitted to say something in confidence to another trusted person if your mental well-being depends upon it. Sometimes you need to express yourself and talk something over with another person. That could be a friend or a therapist. In this limited context, words that would otherwise be *lashon hara* are permitted. And, of course, you should continue to say nice things that you directly think, feel, or observe about a person or their spouse. In fact, it is considered a commandment (and a blessing) to tell a person something nice about their spouse.

Excluding these two categories, people are simply not permitted to talk about other people. But to see just how far away from following the rules of *lashon hara* we are, consider this trivial example. Let's say your friend invites you to a party, and you innocently ask another friend, "What time is the party?" That is *lashon hara* because you don't know if your friend has also been invited to the party. You can cause unnecessary hurt feelings even when you are talking innocently and accurately about people. So avoiding *lashon hara* means training yourself to simply not talk about other people, ever.

I think the best way to understand the concept of *lashon hara* in your own life is to think of it as avoiding "idle words." That means you yourself should not speak them or listen to them. People who engage in idle words risk hurting others as well as they are wasting their own time, which really means they are wasting their life. And sometimes you have to go the extra step and refute idle words said by others.

I don't think it is even possible anymore to live in the modern world and not be exposed or contribute to *lashon hara.* Entire industries are built around it, including higher quality media content providers who aim to be accurate and lower quality media content providers who don't even bother with accuracy. Ninety-nine percent of social media is *lashon hara.* At its very best, it is only wasting your time, but it is far more likely that you are being hurt by it and you are hurting others by it.

More than just mere gossip, there are real-world consequences of living in a world of *lashon hara.* During the height of COVID insanity, in my speeches I frequently included a joke:

Q: "Why don't the Amish get COVID?"
A: "Because they don't have television."

The joke isn't in the words as the words are just true. The joke is we ruefully recognize the influence of *lashon hara* in our own life. The ubiquitousness of *lashon hara* is like the old expression: "I don't know who invented water, but it wasn't a fish." Just like a goldfish doesn't "see" water, we cannot see our *lashon hara* environment as it is just normal twenty-first–century American life. So when people or websites or social media just throw around idle words about a person, we don't wonder if it is true or false; we don't even notice it for what it is. Whether an AP reporter truthfully says I am not a Trump operative or the president of the California Medical Board falsely says that I stalked her, almost all *lashon hara* eventually ends up hurting real people.

The only solution on a personal level to protect ourselves and our families in modern times is to deny *lashon hara* any entry points into your eyes and ears. Over time, I have trained myself to permit only a few "inputs" into my inner world. I simply don't let my eyes or ears ingest the vast amounts of garbage that other people do. A modern take on Proverbs 18:8 captures my approach:

> "Listening to gossip is like eating cheap candy; do you really want junk like that in your belly?"[6]

Assuming you don't listen or speak *lashon hara,* there is still one other aspect to consider. It is necessary to sometimes do the uncomfortable thing, which is to affirmatively refute *lashon hara.* From the school playground to the high school prom, from your daily job to a weekend with relatives, avoiding being gossiped about has always been an important social tool. But it is now, arguably, the most potent weapon deployed in society today.

It did not used to be this severe. In the past, almost everyone had some religious education attenuating gossip, so while always present, it was not as severe. There certainly weren't entire industries built on it. It wasn't *normalized.* Then came instant worldwide communication, which gave *lashon hara* a universal reach, both in geography and backward/forward in time.

The modern infinite breadth and depth of *lashon hara* has made *avoiding* becoming a victim of *lashon hara* a nearly all-encompassing life goal for most people. I saw that avoidance over and over again among doctors, lawyers, judges, and journalists. Cancel culture is so punishing it has caused almost everyone to refuse to speak up *when they should.* This avoidance to speak up when we should is costing us our freedom.

As a victim of severe *lashon hara,* I want to attest that living in fear of cancel culture is dead wrong. When you are silent in the face of idle words that you know are harmful, you deaden yourself and you kill others. Being talked about is not the worst thing that can happen to you. When I was given the choice between being gossiped about or saving lives, I understood that was not a serious contest. There is just too much at stake to keep being silent. Jordan Peterson says it well: "When you speak the truth, whatever happens is the best possible thing that could have happened."[7]

Spiritual Perspective

Despite witnessing miracles, secularism has become a near religion among doctors educated by statist institutions. Law school presented an environment even more detached from spiritual considerations. For me, I was always guided by an internal North Star found in my unshakeable belief in God. My father's deeply sincere Jewish faith always held him to maintain the highest ethical standard, which left an indelible mark on my life and family. Although I did not grow up in a religious family, as Jewish teachings have been advising humans for more than three thousand years, only a foolish or prejudiced person would think such a voluminous intellectual résumé is worthless. The hatred our elite espouses for religion is so irrational that it reveals its motive. And medical study after medical study consistently shows that having a spiritual connection is strongly connected to a happier life.

The value of this spiritual understanding became quite practical during the course of the attacks discussed in this book. As strong and healthy as we might intend ourselves to be, the forces of evil are very real and severe, with terrible destructive capacity. These forces are often brought to bear most intensely on those who maintain integrity and a pursuit of righteousness, thus requiring a greater strength of protection only found in God and friendship with other people of faith.

The difference in worldview between those who do and don't believe in God is additionally striking. It's becoming clearer by the day that if a person doesn't believe in God, they instead believe that they themselves (or perhaps another more talented human) *are* God. Awareness of a higher purpose in life sets a precedent for humility while its lack leads to a dangerously narcissistic worldview. Narcissism is rampant among the secular elites.

In contrast, I have continually been amazed at the warm reception and enthusiastic support I've found at Evangelical Christian churches across the country. This was unexpected as a Jewish person, but my strategy was simply to determine who was actively following God's law above illegitimate government mandates and cult-science propaganda. My litmus test: Did the church think God is prominent or preeminent? There is a world of difference between the two ideas, and the difference became crystal clear in 2020.

Churches who knew God is preeminent were reliably marked by a very early return to in-person gatherings in 2020, despite overwhelming government persecution in mandating or otherwise pressuring citizens of faith to abandon their religious practices. They were also eager to hear and share my message about medical hope and legitimate science, and poured their resources into furthering the reach and impact of the AFLDS mission. Numerous pastors and parishioners have frequently given me strength and encouragement at moments when I was suffering the greatest attack and slander. Pastor Rob McCoy of Godspeak Calvary Chapel in Southern California was especially bold. He freely shared his time and wisdom with me during personal hardships, and Godspeak became a spiritual home in that region. Pastor Mike McClure and Values Advocacy Council, persecuted by Governor Newsom, is another, as well as Pastor Jack Hibbs. Spiritually oriented leaders upon whom I have relied include Dennis Prager, Eric Metaxas, and Leon Benjamin.

The Era of Fake News

My concerns about the general public believing lies about me were attenuated by the realization that the vast majority of Americans no longer trusted the media anyway. After a couple of years of COVID, Gallup found that just 11 percent of those surveyed said they have a "great deal" or "quite a lot" of confidence in "television news."[8] Eleven percent! And it's not that the public thinks the media accidentally gets the facts wrong. An earlier Gallup/Knight study found that, "Eight in 10 Americans say that when they suspect an inaccuracy in a story, they worry it was intentional."[9] That's because it is. The upside to this is that traditional news organizations are collapsing or declining,[10] and tens of thousands of citizen-journalists have arisen on the Internet.

The dystopian "Trusted News Initiative" was announced December 10, 2020, and was a coalition of all major media, Big Tech, and government stakeholders in vaccination.[11] They coordinated with each other to not allow any negative information about vaccines (labeled as "vaccine hesitancy") to be published into the majority of popular media. They feared that "if Americans got balanced coverage on safety events they simply would not get the vaccine."[12] The Trusted News Initiative includes the following: Associated Press, AFP, BBC, CBC/Radio-Canada, European Broadcasting Union (EBU), Facebook, Financial Times, First Draft, Google/YouTube, *The Hindu*, Microsoft, Reuters, Reuters Institute for the Study of Journalism, Twitter, *The Washington Post*, and *The Wall Street Journal*.[13] These companies are supposed to be competitors!

Even though most of the public never heard of the Trusted News Initiative, its massive censorship effect was palpable to the public, as noted by the abysmal media trust survey results. There is a profound level of distrust of the media. The more I saw this divide between the media and the people, the less the defamation campaign against me weighed on my mind, and the more I felt an urgency to provide the public with accurate information.

Ironically, it was the Trusted News Initiative, Big Tech, and Big Gov who made me famous. I was just a good emergency room doctor. Then I started saying the quiet parts out loud, and they started censoring me. I now get one million views on many of my tweets. For example, note this tweet from February 2024.[14] People know the media is lying. I'm just a messenger.

Those media trust surveys cover the entire general population. Not incidentally, within a group of "believers," the percentage of people rejecting corporate propaganda seems to approach 100 percent. It's more than just a feeling: Those who regularly attend church, it has been found, are

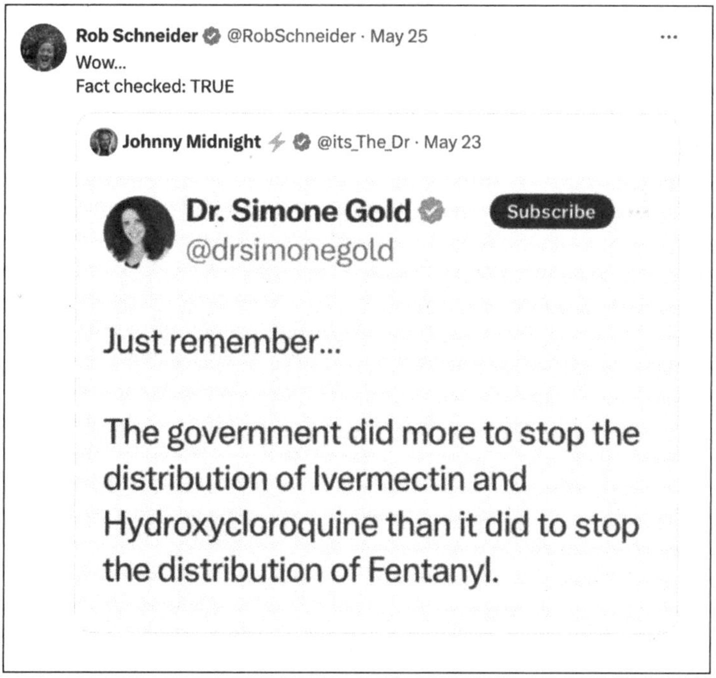
Rob Schneider @RobSchneider · May 25
Wow...
Fact checked: TRUE
Johnny Midnight @its_The_Dr · May 23
Dr. Simone Gold
Subscribe
@drsimonegold
Just remember...
The government did more to stop the distribution of Ivermectin and Hydroxycloroquine than it did to stop the distribution of Fentanyl.

significantly more likely to believe that mainstream media actively "promulgates fake news."[15]

At a time when academics, doctors, and others in the less religious crowds were doing little or nothing to challenge obviously skewed science (like the listing of people who died *with* COVID as having died *from* COVID), the few standing up for #TeamReality were overwhelmingly people of faith. I recognized this trend and made a very intentional decision to work primarily with churches, pastors, a few observant Jewish groups, and religious freedom attorneys.

As Dr. Vladimir Zelenko said during his efforts against pandemic measures, the more connected one is to his Creator, the more easily he will see through the lies at a time like this (see quotes that follow). God is the ultimate truth—connecting to Him gives a person that internal compass to remain free from the chains of self-interest, whether that interest stems from the fear of losing a job, the fear of being ridiculed, or any other worldly anxiety.

Born in the Soviet Union when communists banned religious education and ritual, Dr. Zelenko emigrated to the United States and radically changed his life, taking on the observance of kosher laws, the Shabbat, and studying the Bible intensely. The doctor summarized the challenge of the moment:

> [Human history is marked by a struggle between people] trying to live a God-conscious or God-centered life [and those] who have always attempted to be god-like and to have global control of the rest of humanity.
>
> We're made in God's image, our lives have sanctity just because they are—not because of any other reason [but those seeking to control humanity and play god can only do so by] enslaving [humanity] psychologically . . .
>
> Don't live in fear, don't live in isolation, don't take the poison death shot . . . live with God-consciousness. Improve yourself as an individual, and when enough individuals improve themselves—society as a whole improves and we move away from paganism, idolatry, and child sacrifice toward a world of truth, love, and the revelation of God . . . [16]

Taking Truth on the Road

Realizing that the antidote to the pandemic of lies was spreading as much truth as possible, and undeterred by government persecution and flight restrictions, I wrapped an RV with the AFLDS emblem and embarked on a nationwide "Uncensored Truth Tour."[17] Willing to speak wherever people were willing to listen, I was invited into and enthusiastically received by numerous community centers.

By the spring of 2021 I was speaking regularly at churches and venues from coast to coast[18] including Clay Clark's "ReAwaken America Tour."[19] Previously known for his Thrive Time Show on business development,[20] Clark redirected his efforts to promoting "Health and Freedom" events as lockdowns and restrictions darkened the skies over America.

Taking time out from his business and homeschooling his five children—including one who was born blind, whom doctors said would never see, yet who miraculously regained normal sight after his mother's nonstop prayers[21]—Clark attracted Eric Trump, former Ambassador Alan Keyes, retired General Michael Flynn,[22] Pastor Greg Locke of Tennessee, Lara Logan, Roger Stone, and many others to the tour. In my speeches, I emphasized that lockdowns are totally unsupported by science and that our freedoms are inalienable rights given to us by God, above any politician or power system.

In August 2020, I appeared on the faith-based Daystar Television Network together with Robert Kennedy Jr.[23] I returned to Daystar several more times, including appearing with Robert Kennedy Jr.[24] and Dr. Peter McCullough,[25] the most cited medical doctor on COVID-19 treatments at the National Library of Medicine, with more than 75,626 citations for his total body of work (according current Google Scholar data).

In total, I was on the road for most of 2021, speaking with notable leaders such as Dr. Jim Meehan,[26] chief resident of a Veterans Affairs medical center and associate editor for the *Journal of Ocular Immunology and Inflammation*, Pastor Leon Benjamin, founder of Harvest Bible College,[27] and Pastor Bill Cook, founder of the Black Robe Regiment, a national alliance of pastors and ministry leaders.[28] I met with Pastor Henry Hildebrant from Canada. I spoke alongside Pastor Tony Spell at his church in Baton Rouge following his landmark Louisiana Supreme Court victory (he refused to shut down services during the pandemic and was arrested for preaching), and I shared stages with other esteemed religious leaders throughout the country. Del Bigtree featured one of my speeches on his show, The HighWire.[29] During this time, I learned that General Michael Flynn works ceaselessly in his support of the Constitution and human rights.[30]

With any spare minutes, I poured into our religious freedom litigation efforts with several prominent attorneys: Robert Tyler, founder of Advocates for Faith & Freedom, a nonprofit law firm dedicated to the protection of constitutional and faith-based liberties,[31] former Liberty University law school dean and Liberty Counsel founder Mat Staver,[32] and First Liberty Institute President Kelly Shackleford.[33] We focused on developing the legal strategies we would pursue to place obstacles on the government's road to tyranny.

We also made sure to deliver our message with joy! In San Antonio, we produced a heartwarming re-creation of the historic song, "We Are the World," during the 2021 anniversary of the White Coat Summit.[34] The creative performance culminated with an unmasking of the children participants and a symbolic burning of the most identifiable mark of the growing tyranny: the masks themselves. We most definitely made fun of the lunacy! Watch this hilarious video we produced (e-readers can click on the link, all readers can see the link in the notes): The Normal Symbol.[35]

The resounding success of this and other enjoyable approaches to connecting people together with positive ideas reminded me of another divine truth: the healing power of joy.

A joyful heart is good medicine, but a broken spirit dries up the bones.
—Proverbs 17:22

I had been giving a speech that year titled "The Religion of Public Health."[36] It revealed that the scientifically baseless policies of the public health institutions meant complying with the government was essentially a religious sacrament. Through enduring my own struggles with slander, persecution, and fatigue, I recognized that a key tenet of the false religion of the government was to eliminate joy, because unhappy people are easier to control. Joy was replaced with isolation, anxiety, and depression (the inevitable result of lockdowns and malicious "distancing" propaganda). Lack of joy is a consistent hallmark of tyranny.

Similar to the control gained by subverting physical health, the bureaucracy produced further compliance of the masses by diluting their spiritual strength and crippling them with fear and dependence. I made sure to urge audiences to be mindful of this spiritual antidote by making a practice of choosing joy and gratitude. I also encouraged our local Citizen Corps chapters to pursue various activities that would facilitate joyous family and community fellowship.

The crowds at every gathering were warm and energetic in their reception during speeches and in their comments as I mingled with audience members afterward. I gained at least as much from each appearance as anyone in attendance did. It didn't take long to discover that our support went far beyond those who were able to show up in person at the events.

Beyond the walls of the churches and other venues was a veritable army of people who were committed to the struggle against tyranny. These supporters made themselves known by the thousands through emails, written letters, and donations to the organization. To this day, the average donation amount is about $29 a month—truly a grassroots populist movement. The more the media smeared and attempted to cancel us, the more the public support continued to grow. While I would have loved to continue The Uncensored Truth Tour without interruption, the future held other plans.

I was soon to embark on an unforeseen journey of injustice and impossibly difficult choices.

CHAPTER ELEVEN

The Path to a Plea

The great object of my fear is the federal judiciary. That body, like gravity, ever acting, with noiseless foot, and unalarming advance, gaining ground step by step, and holding what it gains, is engulfing insidiously the special governments into the jaws of that which feeds them.

—Thomas Jefferson

Escape from corruption and persecution and the search for fair treatment under the law have driven migration to our American shores since the time of the Pilgrims. However, the risk of authority figures using the law to their personal advantage long predates the seventeenth-century founding of Plymouth Colony. Consider this case from thousands of years ago, recorded in the Old Testament scriptures:

> Now it came to pass in those days that Moses grew up and went out to his brothers and looked at their burdens, and he saw an Egyptian man striking a Hebrew man of his brothers (Exodus 2:11).[1]
>
> That Egyptian man was a taskmaster. The Jewish slave he was beating, under the pretext of not working hard enough, was the husband of a woman who caught the taskmaster's attention.
>
> . . . the taskmasters would go to the houses of the [Israelite] officers at daybreak to make them go summon the workers. Once, an Egyptian taskmaster went to [do so to] an Israelite officer and

> he set his eye on his wife who was beautiful, without blemish. He called the man and brought him out of his house, then the Egyptian returned and had relations with his wife, who, thinking he was her husband, became pregnant from him.
>
> Her husband returned and found the Egyptian leaving his house. He asked her, "Did he touch you?" She said "Yes, but I thought he was you." When the taskmaster saw that the husband suspected him, he demoted him to hard labor [from his officer capacity], struck him, and sought to kill him.[2]

Equal Protection Under Law

Of course, the citizens of our constitutional republic rightfully expect a much higher standard of ethics from our authority figures than those in Pharaoh's Egypt. Thankfully, the Supreme Court affirmed as much in *US vs Armstrong*, holding Americans to be constitutionally protected from selective targeting:

> Under the equal protection component of the Fifth Amendment's Due Process Clause, the decision whether to prosecute may not be based on an arbitrary classification such as race or religion.[3]

In other words, Selective Prosecution is explicitly prohibited.

Despite such clear language, the Constitution's protections against a two-tiered justice system are only as good as the gatekeepers charged with upholding that Constitution. Unfortunately, most of that responsibility and power has consolidated over the years into the brutal bureaucracy of the DOJ. This has now metastasized into a full fourth branch of the federal government, an unconstitutional and highly dangerous national tumor. For years now, Americans have felt the sunlight of fairness fading behind the storm clouds of prejudice and political calculation.

These feelings solidified into fact with a 2017 NPR story where the "IRS Apologizes for Aggressive Scrutiny of Conservative Groups."[4] Judicial Watch summed up the scandal this way:

> Beginning in 2010 members of the IRS Tax Exempt and Government Entities Division began targeting "Tea Party" and other conservative groups for extra scrutiny and harassment. Some groups were forced to answer outrageous and arbitrary questionnaires, or were simply denied the critical tax exempt status they deserved . . .[5]

And that's where this scandal ended: with an apology and settlements but no criminal responsibility. Two years earlier, in 2015, FBI director James Comey had already closed the investigation into the IRS officials responsible, including Lois Lerner, the director of the Exempt Organizations Unit, without filing any federal criminal charges in connection with the controversy.[6] The federal government was establishing a clear precedent that favored one political class over another. Of course, they vigorously deny it every time the disparity is pointed out. "Nobody is above the law" has become the classic double-speak denial of a cheating spouse caught in the act . . . but without any mechanism for a "national divorce."

Partisan Privilege

It didn't take long for this political favoritism to be extended to violent rioters bearing the politically correct credentials. The *Tennessee Star* broke the story titled, "Feds Quietly Dismiss Dozens of Cases Against Antifa Extremists Who Terrorized Downtown Portland Last Summer."[7]

"Terrorized" was no overstatement. Notice the specifics of what the *Tennessee Star* reported:

> Cases being dismissed include felony charges such as assaults on federal officers . . . Antifa agitators clashed with federal agents in front of the Mark O. Hatfield United States Courthouse in Portland for weeks on end, costing the city at least $2.3 million . . .
>
> In addition to tagging the properties with graffiti, Antifa and BLM agitators set fires and broke windows, as well as deployed commercial grade firecrackers, powerful lasers, and Molotov cocktails at the police . . .

> More than 113 federal officers reportedly suffered eye injuries due to the lasers. In an interview last summer, a DHS agent who had been deployed to protect the courthouse, said the agitators were "catatonic with hate," and that officers were getting injured on a nightly basis . . .
>
> "I personally saw an agent get hit in the leg with a bottle and limp back from the skirmish line. I saw video of another agent hit similarly and limp back. One DHS law enforcement officer had irritant thrown on his arms, which turned them red and caused a burn. Another guy had a firework explode directly on his chest. The use of fireworks has increased every night," [a DHS agent who had been deployed to protect the courthouse] said.[8]

Not only did federal prosecutors drop these assault and battery charges, but most were "dismissed with prejudice," meaning the charges can never be refiled.

And what is the ideology driving these rioters, who were the beneficiaries of the DOJ's "discretionary" treatment? *The New American* found out:

> According to Professor Mike Isaacson . . . an Antifa leader who teaches at the City University of New York's John Jay College of Law, "Anti-communism is code for fascism." There you have it: If you're an anti-communist, if you're averse to living in a communist police state—24/7 surveillance, repression, torture, gulags, genocide, etc.—well, then, you're obviously a FASCIST.
>
> If you stand anywhere to the right of Mao Zedong or Fidel Castro, you are a FASCIST, and, according to the Antifa jihadists, you should be treated as such. Which means that not only have you forfeited your right to speak, but also your right to exist. It's "Off with your head!" Literally. The Antifa website "It's Going Down" wants to bring back the French Revolution's Reign of Terror, with a campaign to "Make the Guillotine Red Again." Communist megalomaniacs from Marx to Lenin, Mao Zedong, Ho Chi Minh, Fidel Castro, and Pol Pot have invoked the French Revolution's massive bloodletting as their inspiration for remolding society.

> Prof. Isaacson, a founder of Smash Racism DC, an Antifa group in our nation's capital that participated in the violent and disruptive "protests" during President Trump's inauguration, has gained infamy for his numerous public endorsements of Antifa violence and his many tweets supporting murder of police officers, some of whom are his law school students. Here are a few of his offensive tweets that have caused outrage . . .
>
> > August 17, 2017—"I hear their police stations catch on fire with an accelerant."
> >
> > August 23, 2017—"Some of y'all might think it sucks being an anti-fascist teaching at John Jay College but I think it's a privilege to teach future dead cops."[9]

This was a left-wing law school professor, openly encouraging terrorism and the killing of police officers.

The *Tennessee Star* also provided an illuminating comparison of the DOJ's treatment of Antifa protesters with the protesters at J6:

> As charges against dozens of violent left-wing insurrectionists are dropped, the Biden Justice Dept. is taking a tough stance against the Trump supporters who stormed the Capitol on January 6.
>
> So far, none of the cases against the Capitol Hill rioters and trespassers have been dismissed. In fact, federal prosecutors are adding "enhancement charges" and building sedition cases . . . [10]

Even *The New York Times* noted disturbing federal aggression toward J6 protestors:

> The House committee investigating the assault on the Capitol and what led to it is employing the aggressive tactics prosecutors use on mobsters and terrorists.[11]

The New York Times
@nytimes

The House committee investigating the assault on the Capitol and what led to it is employing the aggressive tactics prosecutors use on mobsters and terrorists.

nytimes.com
In Scrutinizing Trump and His Allies, Jan. 6 Panel Adopts Prosecution Tactics
The House committee investigating the assault on the Capitol and what led to it is employing techniques more common in criminal cases than in congressional ...

10:50 PM · Feb 5, 2022 · SocialFlow

Mostly Peaceful Insurrection

With the public becoming increasingly aware of the double standard applied to free speech advocates labeled as "right-wing," the DOJ needed to justify its heavy handed approach to those in and near the Capitol on January 6, 2021. They claimed that justification with a single word: "Insurrection." This, for an event devoid of weapons.[12] In a crowd reaching over a million people throughout the city, there were no real weapons at all, rendering the allegation of "insurrection" a total absurdity and an obvious political word weapon wielded by the DOJ against unarmed citizens.

In my case, I was at the Capitol to give a speech on health and freedom, not to focus on the election or political parties. Even so, how was insurrection even a relevant term for those who did come with the intention to protest for election integrity? Despite the incessant repetition of "insurrection" propaganda by the mainstream media, the Biden DOJ has not charged any J6 defendant with the actual crime of "Rebellion or insurrection" under 18 U.S. Code §2383.

According to the *Washington Examiner,* in this August 2021 headline, January 6 was not an insurrection: "FBI confirms there was no insurrection on Jan. 6."[13] They explained:

> The Cambridge Dictionary defines "insurrection" as: "an organized attempt by a group of people to defeat their government and take control of their country, usually by violence."
>
> By that definition, there was no "insurrection" at the United States Capitol on Jan. 6, according to the FBI. *Reuters* reports:
>
> "The FBI has found scant evidence that the Jan. 6 attack on the U.S. Capitol was the result of an organized plot to overturn the presidential election result, according to four current and former law enforcement officials . . ."
>
> "Ninety to ninety-five percent of these are one-off cases," said a former senior law enforcement official with knowledge of the investigation. "Then you have five percent, maybe, of these militia groups that were more closely organized. But there was no grand scheme with Roger Stone and Alex Jones and all of these people to storm the Capitol and take hostages."
>
> This report is a devastating blow to President Joe Biden and Democrats, who have attempted to make the existence of an "insurrection" on Jan. 6 a key issue in the 2022 midterm elections . . .
>
> Trying to politicize it and turn it into something it wasn't won't make the Capitol any safer. [14]

Conflict of Interest

The appalling irony is, making the Capitol safer was never actually the plan. Clear evidence of this was revealed by Kash Patel, chief of staff at the Department of Defense during that time. President Trump offered ten thousand National Guard troops, but the responsibility for safety of the Capitol of course does not fall to the president of the United States. Establishing proper precautions fell ultimately on House Speaker Nancy Pelosi and DC Mayor Muriel Bowser. They both declined the increased security, despite the Capitol Police's intelligence unit having "knowledge of the potential for violence,"[15] and FBI intel making it clear that additional security measures and resources were warranted.

After declining the extra police, following January 6, 2021, Nancy Pelosi publicly blamed Chief of the US Capitol Police Steven Sund and demanded his resignation. He became the public "fall guy" even though, on January 6, 2021, Pelosi admitted it was her responsibility in a video taken by her daughter and released to the public in June 2024.[16]

Pelosi also publicly stated, "He [Sund] hasn't even called us since this happened." But video exists of Sund's congressional testimony proving Pelosi's lies.[17] There is also a timeline of Sund's (and others) attempt to secure January 6, 2021, many days prior to that day, and his frantic requests for backup and encountering active stonewalling throughout the day itself.[18]

Furthermore, as I described earlier, the government had a number of federal agents apparently provoking, not preventing, violence on January 6. *The New American*, in "January 6 Melee: Insurrection or Fedsurrection?" relates the efforts of several congresspeople to examine the extent of the federal role in the violence:

> Was the January 6, 2021, "invasion" of the U.S. Capitol a "coup attempt" by President Trump and his supporters? Or was it a choreographed setup by federal officials and their MAGA hat-wearing *agents provocateur* to create an incident used to smear Trump followers as terrorists and justify more oppressive legislation and police-state powers targeting conservatives? Mounting evidence points to the latter. This [entrapment] is the central issue that must be settled; *all other expressions of concern about the January 6 affair are distractions* . . . [emphasis added]
>
> In a press conference at the Capitol on January 6, Representatives Matt Gaetz (R-Fla.) and Marjorie Taylor Greene (R-Ga.) hit these

> issues head-on, particularly calling out House Speaker Nancy Pelosi, the House January 6 Committee, and the media for blatantly ignoring the evidence of federal agents provocateurs inciting and leading the "insurrection" [concluding] "it very well may have been a Fedsurrection."[19]

Later, in a stunning admission, a federal prosecutor confirmed in court documents that several "D.C. Metropolitan Police Department undercover officers acted as provocateurs."[20] In other words, a Fedsurrection . . . *literally*.

In addition, Julie Kelly,[21] intrepid senior writer at *American Greatness*, has doggedly covered most of the concerning behavior by various government officials throughout the J6 propaganda and persecution campaign waged by Mob Boss Merrick's DOJ. She commented on Twitter that continued evidence raises questions of government entrapment:

> As evidence continues to emerge about massive numbers of uniformed, undercover, and CHSs (Confidential Human Source) from multiple agencies were on the ground on Jan 6—why did they not stop the "insurrection?" . . . and the role of police to instigate what happened that day is being covered up . . .[22]

And finally, it has now been revealed that an unknown number of undercover FBI agents were present, and neither the FBI or DOJ will reveal the number.

Not only did the government illegally and selectively prosecute thousands of J6 protestors while excusing violent left-wing rioters, but they planted operatives—mysteriously ignored and never charged or even publicly reviewed—in the J6 crowd. These operatives instigated violence, which led to harm and destruction and created an opportunity for inflicting long prison sentences, not to mention the demonization of a disfavored political party.

The drama doesn't end there.

It's hard to imagine how J6 investigators can keep a straight face knowing the galling double standard that's being applied to the protesters, but no one is doing a better job of unblinkingly carrying the hypocritical charade forward than the chairman of a congressional commission "reviewing" the protest:

> Rep. Bennie Thompson, the Mississippi Democrat who chairs the congressional commission investigating the Jan. 6 Capitol riot . . . in 1971 . . . placed himself on the opposite side, openly sympathizing with a secessionist group known as the Republic of New Africa [RNA] . . .
>
> Thompson's affection for the RNA and its members—which FBI counterintelligence memos from the 1970s warned were threatening "guerrilla warfare" against the United States—was still intact as recently as 2013, when he openly campaigned on behalf of the group's former vice president to be mayor of Mississippi's largest city . . .[23]

Thompson isn't the only former insurrectionist sitting in Congress:

> Thompson's Democratic colleague in Congress and the Congressional Black Caucus, Rep. Bobby Rush of Illinois, famously cofounded the extremist Black Panthers chapter in Illinois in 1968 before he entered politics. Both the RNA and the Black Panthers were avowed supporters of insurrection, and at one point in 1967, armed Black Panthers stormed the state capitol in California.[24]

The prosecution of my speaking publicly about health freedom in a jurisdiction that censors my political views is like an investigator prosecuting a person who possessed legal medical marijuana while himself being intoxicated. It made no sense, it was offensive, and the investigators were more guilty than the defendant. I certainly believed I had a clear case for getting my charges dismissed on a violation of the previously described *Armstrong* decision barring prosecution based on an "arbitrary classification."[25]

I and many others present at J6 were clearly prosecuted with extreme harshness based on the arbitrary classification of our political beliefs. Nevertheless, like almost every other victim, I eventually found myself in the unconscionable position of being coerced into waiving my right to argue that this selective prosecution was a violation of my Fourth and Fifth Amendment rights to due process. The terrifying force of a runaway federal prosecution hurtling down the hill pinned us to the only available, and strategically positioned, off-ramp: a plea deal.

Federal Roulette

The main consideration driving most J6 protestors to accept a plea deal was to escape the lengthy prison sentences threatened by the prosecutorial overcharges I described earlier. Despite a lack of factual basis for those extra charges, the political perspective of the DC jury pool and of the DC judges all but guaranteed that J6ers would face an automatic conviction if they went to trial. Thus far, there have been no jury acquittals out of over a thousand indictments and counting. None. That is astounding!

The Epoch Times reported on March 6, 2024, that the DOJ historically has a 65 percent conviction rate in the District of Columbia.[26] And recall that the protestors who went to trial for rioting during Trump's inauguration were all *acquitted* by DC juries. Fifty percent of J6 defendants come from six states: Florida, Texas, Pennsylvania, California, Ohio, and New York. Virtually all of these defendants requested a change in venue, a motion that becomes more compelling over time, not less, as the obviousness of the jury pool bias cannot be denied. If the government has a 100 percent conviction rate for any one group (such as all blacks, all whites, all women, all men, all Christians, all Muslims), by definition, that is a rigged trial system. That means merely being accused is the same as a conviction. Why bother with a trial? Most J6 defendants have not bothered with a trial.

As one criminal defense attorney put it in the *Epoch Times* article, "The way the question needs to be framed today and put before the judges again is, 'How many trials and how high a conviction rate is necessary before the judges start to consider that maybe it's not the evidence but it's the jurors?'"

The risk was so dangerously high that the government even succeeded in getting defendants to sign an admission that we had clear and complete knowledge of our criminality when we did not, AND to waive our right to appeal the sentence that would be handed down pursuant to that plea. That meant we were subject to the maximum under the guidelines. In most criminal cases, the maximum is rarely given.

Another factor in accepting a plea was that, while the Supreme Court clearly prohibited selective prosecution, it sets a nearly impossible standard for proving it:

> In order to prove a selective-prosecution claim, the claimant must demonstrate that the prosecutorial policy had a discriminatory effect and was motivated by a discriminatory purpose.[27]

The court specifically left the burden of proof on the defendant as noted in the language below.

> A selective-prosecution claim is not a defense on the merits to the criminal charge itself, but an independent assertion that the prosecutor has brought the charge for reasons forbidden by the Constitution. Our cases delineating the necessary elements to prove a claim of selective prosecution have taken great pains to explain that the standard is a demanding one . . . [28]
>
> "So long as the prosecutor has probable cause to believe that the accused committed an offense defined by statute, the decision whether or not to prosecute, and what charge to file or bring before a grand jury, generally rests entirely in his discretion."[29]

The selective-prosecution claim is so difficult to prove that it's nearly impossible to find a successful case (a 1997 scholarly article noted that no defendant since 1886 has proved a race-based claim of selective prosecution).[30]

The Plea Itself: To Plea or Not to Plea

So how does a plea deal work? One day your lawyer tells you that the government (US Attorney's Office) has offered you a plea deal. For me, this was in December 2021. Until then, I had appeared in approximately monthly Zoom hearings at which time nothing was ever accomplished, and I had to call in weekly to let the court know I was present. The purpose of these calls was never clear to me because they had my passport and, even if I had fled somewhere, I could still call in. The defendant has to reach a person on the phone and not leave a message. If no one picks up, it is the defendant's responsibility to keep calling or be sent to prison for not complying. This weekly call was surprisingly stressful as I don't have a regular schedule. I set multiple alarms on my phone.

I had about a month to decide to accept or reject the plea deal. Until then, I had not paid much attention to the legal proceedings, did not understand the implications of the charges, and thought I would go to trial. When we received the plea offer, my attorney had a long conversation with me, and I learned that the 18 USC §1512(c)(2) indictment carries a potential twenty-year sentence. I was absolutely stunned.

That was a game changer for me.

I did not fully understand the 18 USC §1512(c)(2) charge then (see Chapter 15), but I knew it was nonsensical. What I did understand was that the government was going to put all its efforts to put me into prison for decades. For a few weeks I vacillated between going to trial and accepting the plea. It sounds naive now that I even considered going to trial, but it's extremely difficult for a person like me to participate in a corrupt proceeding. In addition, I *was* naive. I did not understand that no J6 defendants would be acquitted. I did not understand that DC judges were treating J6 defendants completely differently than other defendants. For that hard dose of reality, I thank my criminal defense attorneys.

There are about three dozen criminal defense attorneys actively defending J6 defendants, so they develop a lot of experience with the judges, the charges, the evidence, and the prosecutors. The defense attorneys run the gamut politically. Many are (classic) liberal, some are raging leftists who truly hate their clients, and a handful are libertarian-conservative. Regardless of their political views, it seems almost all of them are stunned by the total departure from precedent and reality evidenced in these court proceedings.

When initially conferring with my lead attorney, I was weighing the decision "to plea or not to plea" as if I were an attorney in a just system.

There was video evidence of me walking, staying within tourist ropes, no damage or violence, giving a speech, and waiting patiently to exit. To me, this evidence was exculpatory of all the charges except, perhaps, the trespass charge. Everything else was complete fiction. At the time, I thought I would roll the dice on the trespass charge and let a jury decide if I had the *mens rea* (criminal intent) to trespass. But my academic analysis hadn't included two things: a twenty-year felony threat and a DC jury. This I learned from my attorney.

By vertically overcharging me with a twenty-year felony with a hostile jury pool, I was deprived of my chance to go to trial on the real issue, which was to answer the following question: Were my actions criminal trespass? While I should not have to go to trial on this trespass issue—as virtually all political protestors who even get arrested are never prosecuted and have their charges dropped (see Chapter 7)—I was not given that chance. And lest any naysayer say I was given the chance to go to trial, I will state the obvious: When there is a loaded gun held to your head, you cannot exercise free will. A twenty-year felony[31] is a loaded gun.[32]

For about eighteen months, I was angry at being forced to take a plea. At the time, I would have gone to trial on the trespass. I thought that was "fair." Now, two years later, having seen that 100 percent of J6 defendants are vertically and horizontally overcharged and then convicted, I am grateful to my attorneys for strongly advising me to accept a plea, because what I had naively welcomed was a *fair* trial. But I have no need to waste my time or energy on a show trial (see Chapter 16), and the plea spared me from that. I am more at peace with having taken a plea now than I was at the time, but I am far more pained for our country, having learned it is so corrupted.

I had no professional experience in taking a plea deal. Because it is called a plea *deal*, I always assumed there was a negotiation process. Turns out: No. There isn't. The government says, "Take it or leave it." It doesn't matter if it is inaccurate. It doesn't matter if it is prejudicial. It doesn't matter if the information it contains is accurate and prejudicial—but not about *you*. This really surprised me and is another reason why having such a lopsided (more than 95 percent) conviction rate is dangerous for the system. There is no motive to be honest.

Before I get to the actual plea as written on paper, I must share something very shocking that also contributed to my taking this false plea. The prosecutor threatened to additionally charge me with assaulting a police officer. As far as I know, this is not written anywhere. I learned this from my criminal defense attorney who conferred several times with the prosecutor about the language of the plea. During these conversations, the AUSA told my attorney that I was "lucky" she did not charge me with assaulting a police officer. She did this to apply more pressure on me to sign the plea as she falsely wrote it.

This type of duplicity was the same as my experience in Pueblo, Colorado, when federal agents attempted to plant narcotics on me, described in Chapter 4. A lying government official with all the power to destroy my reputation. Of course I did not assault an officer, but the mere allegation of that would cause irreparable harm. That the AUSA would lie and threaten like this is so shocking that I knew there was nothing they would not do, no line they would not cross, no moral boundary they would respect. That was the environment in which I was "negotiating" my plea.

The plea deal the government offered me was both inaccurate and prejudicial. I did not mind the minor inaccuracies so much (it does bother me to know that government lawyers are sloppy), and my lawyer educated me that the government is allowed to add irrelevant prejudicial statements that were not about me. But I vehemently protested one line in the plea deal because the way the government chose to write it was to besmirch my reputation. In my plea, the government implied that I didn't help an officer who was assaulted.

That I now possess absolute proof that the government lied in presenting me this plea deal has caused my lawyers to caution me not to write of this or speak of this, lest the government accuse me of having signed my name to a statement that I knew at the time was false. Get that? Let me say that again. The *government* lied, the *government* withheld exculpatory evidence that they are required by law to show me, the *government* knowingly presented me with a false plea deal, and if *I* speak about it, *I* could be charged with the crime of perjury.[33]

I must start with the disclaimer that I am bound by the plea deal not to say anything that contradicts my plea deal, and I am not contradicting what I signed. Rather, now I have absolute proof that the government lied to me when they coerced me to sign the plea deal. At the time the government offered me the plea, they had proof they were lying, and they failed to provide me with that proof. That does not mean *I* lied in signing the deal. Not at all. I made the best decision I could with the limited evidence I was provided.

The plea deal that was presented to me is in the DrGoldReferences Appendix 10,[34] and in the "Statement of Offense" on the bottom of page 4 is a sentence that says: "Directly in front of GOLD and Strand a law enforcement officer was assaulted and dragged to the ground." This is not even close to what happened. I will now relay what happened, including proof of the events of the day. I will then explain how I never committed perjury when I signed my name to a paper that said something false, and I include that specifically because our government is so dishonest that they tried very hard to lead me into saying I perjured myself.[35]

First, note that everything the government is referring to is visible on government closed circuit TV video (CCTV), and you should watch this video yourself.[36] It is one thing to believe that your government lies because I am telling you. It is another to see the proof yourself. The government's CCTV videotape captured virtually every moment I was in the Capitol. You be the judge of what I am saying.

Starting at minute 3:00, you can see what the prosecutor is referencing. Just prior to this, my codefendant and I were hugging the wall because the crowd was so large, albeit peaceful. When the police set off a flash-bang, the crowd became agitated, which is evident in this frenetic moment of the video.

As you see in the video, the area is packed, we are like sardines in a can. About ten feet away from me, I saw a police officer look light-headed, like he would faint. He was trying to get through the crowd but it was slow going. Then he did faint into the crowd. For a fraction of a second, his pathway was about two people-deep away from me, and when he fainted, there were about ten people between him and us. The crowd immediately chanted, "Get him up!" and within five seconds or so, he was standing up. You can see in the video that he is still woozy with his eyes closed, but the crowd did *not* want him to get trampled and got him up immediately.

This entire episode is perhaps five or ten seconds. When I first started working with my criminal defense attorney, she asked me to exactly relay to her the events of the day. I told her what is evident in the video: I saw a cop who had fainted, had been helped up by the crowd, and walked off uninjured. This was a very minor detail of the day, and I did not think of it again until the government presented me with the dishonest plea deal. They not only mischaracterized what I had directly seen but implied that I did not help an officer who was assaulted! It was *outrageous.*

At the time I was presented the plea, I did not have any evidence to substantiate my recollection. Specifically, I did not have this video, and I did not have the evidence the government possessed proving my recollection was exactly correct. All I had was my recollection, which never wavered. I did not see an officer being assaulted and dragged to the ground. I saw him faint. So how could I sign a legal document that I knew was a lie? That is the quandary that people who sign false plea deals find themselves in. For the rest of their lives, they must hold out in public that what they signed was the *truth.* This is another reason you want the government to deal honestly. Why would you want our citizens to be dishonest? What does that serve? As I too signed this false plea deal, how can I write of the government's lies here and now without admitting I perjured myself then?

I was able to sign this document without perjuring myself because the government used the word "assault." As an attorney, I knew the legal definition of the word. We all think of the word *assault* as meaning a physical assault. Someone hitting someone. But assault is broader and less specific than that. The phrase "assault and battery" captures the totality of such a violent incident. The word "battery" refers to the actual physical interaction, while the word "assault" is causing someone to reasonably fear harm. The government used the word *assault* specifically to besmirch my reputation because they knew everyone would assume battery. The meaning of these two words has become conflated in our culture.

At the time the government presented this plea, I had not seen this video, but the government had. They knew I would eventually see this video, so they knew they had to proceed very carefully with how they described my actions in this plea. They knew I never came near this officer, and they knew they couldn't say ***I*** assaulted him, because I would easily get such a plea thrown out in the future when this evidence inevitably became public. So they chose a word that could possibly, technically, somehow, be true, because they were eager to get me to sign a piece of paper that would cause maximum damage to my reputation. "Dr. Gold admitted she didn't help an officer who was assaulted!" I can hardly think of a more harmful sentence coming from the government. Of course, if you've read Chapter 3, you'll recall the government also attempted to plant narcotics on me.

When I signed the plea deal, however, I was under the impression that the government had some mysterious evidence I did not have, such as the officer being assaulted (e.g., threatened or Maced) prior to my seeing him. This is because, as a trained lawyer, I knew that the government was required to turn over all evidence that could help the defense. As discussed in Chapter 8, that is called turning over "Brady evidence." As a practicing ER physician, I assessed that the officer simply fainted because he was so pressed by the crowd. Though I believed I was likely right, I did not rule out that I could have been wrong and that the government could have had other evidence I did not have. I was, therefore, able to sign the plea without lying.

Imagine my shock at learning almost a full year later that the DOJ had been flat-out lying about this sentence in the plea deal they offered me. And the government prosecutor lied again in court at my sentencing. This is explained in Chapter 12.

Double Jeopardy (Adjacent): *California Medical Board vs. Dr. Gold*

If you think I am splitting hairs with this description, know that I share this because of what the government attempted to do next, which was to entrap me in a perjury charge. I speak of this in this section of the book because it provides additional confirmation that taking a plea was the correct decision. Since taking a plea, I have repeatedly been presented with evidence that our government actively works to entrap its citizens.

The government took the words that they crafted in the plea and threatened me with these same words in yet another trial (and a third trial still pending). About a year after my release from prison, I was in trial against the California Medical Board (see Chapter 4), which was attempting to revoke my physician's license over free speech issues. Because their case was so weak (obviously you cannot restrict a person's speech by threatening to revoke a professional license), they shifted into making this a second J6 trial. If you thought the average law-abiding American citizen should not face a second trial for the exact same events, you have not walked in my shoes.

Please note that I am taking creative license by saying that I was tried twice for the same events. Of course I was not criminally tried twice. I am saying that the California Medical Board took the same events for which I already endured a criminal process and used that to attempt to revoke my physician's license and to attempt to entrap me into perjury. I am facing a similar trial with the New York Bar over my attorney's license.

Just a short aside before I proceed. I believe it is indisputable that the California Medical Board (CMB) exceeded its authority in targeting me. As I explain in Chapter 4, the CMB initially targeted my license for exercising free speech. During the trial, they pivoted to saying I had acted unprofessionally by being present at the Capitol on January 6. Problematically for the prosecution, the California Code of Regulations (CCR) Title 16 section 1360 (CCR Title 16 §1360)[37] provides that to constitute professional misconduct, an alleged act must be *substantially related* to the qualifications, functions, or duties of a person holding a license.

Cal. Code Regs. Tit. 16, § 1360 - Substantial Relationship Criteria

State Regulations Compare

(a) For the purposes of denial, suspension or revocation of a license pursuant to Section 141 or Division 1.5 (commencing with Section 475) of the code, a crime, professional misconduct, or act shall be considered to be substantially related to the qualifications, functions or duties of a person holding a license if to a substantial degree it evidences present or potential unfitness of a person holding a license to perform the functions authorized by the license in a manner consistent with the public health, safety or welfare. Such crimes, professional misconduct, or acts shall include but not be limited to the following: Violating or attempting to violate, directly or indirectly, or assisting in or abetting the violation of, or conspiring to violate any provision of state or federal law governing the applicant's or licensee's professional practice.

(b) In making the substantial relationship determination required under subdivision (a) for a crime, the board shall consider the following criteria:

(1) The nature and gravity of the crime;

(2) The number of years elapsed since the date of the crime; and

(3) The nature and duties of the profession.

According to CCR Title 16 §1360, the CMB is empowered to regulate acts by license-holders that show evidence of licensees' potential unfitness to perform the functions authorized by the license in a manner consistent with public health, safety, or welfare. A later court case held that the purpose of California's Medical Practice Act, which authorizes the California Medical Board, "is not penal but to 'protect the life, health and welfare of the people at large and to set up a plan whereby those who practice medicine will have the qualifications which will prevent, as far as possible, the evils which could result from ignorance or incompetency or a lack of honesty and integrity.'"[38]

In other words, the CMB has a specific and narrow lane. Their powers are not all-encompassing. By law, the CMB is only permitted to delve into matters concerning a physician's abilities, practice, or judgment. Exactly how was my Capitol presence substantially related to the practice of medicine? Even the J6 judge who despised me agreed that my presence at the Capitol that day had nothing to do with my ability to practice medicine. He seemed surprised to learn that a state medical board would even attempt such a thing. From page 35 of my Sentencing memo June 16, 2022:

> MR. YOUNG: But as a result of that allegation, actions were commenced against her in California and in Florida concerning her continued ability to practice medicine. So, I mean, that was obviously a mistake, to include the word "treason."
>
> THE COURT: Has she lost any medical license or any other professional license as a result of her involvement in this case?
>
> MR. YOUNG: No, but those actions are pending, to suspend her or sanction her. So that's not over with, and I would think that they're waiting to see what the outcome of this proceeding is to make a determination.
>
> You know, I might suggest, too—
>
> THE COURT: I'm sorry, out of curiosity, is a misdemeanor conviction a grounds to rescind anyone's medical license anywhere in the country?
>
> MR. YOUNG: I don't believe it is.
>
> THE COURT: If it doesn't involve patient care?

> MR. YOUNG: Well, we were party to conversations with Dr. Gold's counsel that represents her in these proceedings, and he was extremely concerned that the record in this case not include anything about treason because that is—my understanding—
>
> THE COURT: Well, the statute number speaks for itself. The statement of facts speaks for itself regardless of what label you put on the statute. I don't think anyone could reasonably suggest—certainly the government doesn't suggest that Ms. Gold has pled guilty to anything approaching treason, okay?
>
> MR. YOUNG: But the actions as a result of those allegations are pending against her.
>
> THE COURT: Those bodies will now have the benefit of the transcript of this proceeding.

The California Medical Board prosecutor knew it angered me that the plea deal contained a sentence that was such a slander to my reputation as a doctor. As an ER physician for twenty-five years, I have taken care of many wonderful people. I have also taken care of plenty of mediocre people, such as deadbeat dads, cheating spouses, aggressive teens, and lousy parents. I've also taken care of many truly horrible people, including repeat drunk drivers, pedophiles, domestic abusers, robbers, rapists, and murderers. There has never, and never will be, a scenario where I don't help a person. I upended my entire life to help millions of people I'll never even meet. So to have been publicly smeared as a person who didn't help a *police officer* offended me to my core. And the CMB prosecutor knew I had publicly disputed this sentence in the plea. So she tried very hard to get me to say that I signed a plea that I did not believe when I signed it. But this would mean I had committed perjury, and I am quite certain the government would have indicted me for that. This is definitely worth reading yourself, and again, it is in the DrGoldReferences Appendix 9.[39]

The Plea Itself

Here, I address a few more comments about the plea I accepted for misdemeanor trespass. There are twelve clauses in the Statement of Offense (see

DrGoldReferences Appendix 9), and the first seven are the government's version of J6 generally. These extraneous (and prejudicial) clauses were about events that had nothing to do with where I was geographically or with me personally. Paragraph 9 contains what I have just described: The lie that I was near an officer who was assaulted. Please note that, in this paragraph, the government was forced to acknowledge that I was there to give a speech against vaccine mandates and government-imposed lockdowns.

Paragraph 9 then continues with the government stating that, "Multiple law enforcement officers had to intervene before Gold stopped giving her speech." This is another example of the government purposefully attempting to mislead the public, the court, and the media. I cannot imagine how much more severe the government's lies are when there is no video evidence. Fortunately, in my case, you can and should watch the video yourself, at approximately 9:22.[40] Before you do, form a picture in your mind to match the words the government used. Then watch the video and ask yourself, "Did that look like 'multiple law enforcement officers having to intervene'?" Not quite.

If you watch the video, here is what you will see. While I was giving my speech, an officer tapped me on the shoulder and told me to move along. I was startled for a moment, and *then I moved along*. This entire interaction is about three peaceful seconds in duration. These three peaceful seconds are what is described in the plea as "Multiple law enforcement officers had to intervene before Gold stopped giving her speech." It's really shameful that our government feels the need to mislead like this, by overstating the facts. It's so dishonest and so unnecessary.

The last line of the plea I would like to point out is in paragraph 11, which states, "Gold was arrested by FBI agents executing a lawful search warrant." Again, form a picture in your mind that matches the words the government used. Do their words sound *remotely* like what I endured—twenty heavily armed FBI and other officers executing the most violent SWAT team arrest imaginable, one worthy of arresting El Chapo? They broke down my door with two battering rams, they aimed several massive rifles at my chest from three feet away, then they handcuffed and shackled me and perp-walked me through the street (I describe this arrest in detail in Chapter 3). Again, it's really shameful that our government feels the need to mislead like this, this time by understating the facts. It's so dishonest and unnecessary.

Conclusion

It became clear early on, as the malice of the J6 witch hunt grew more and more extreme, that battling the DOJ virtually guarantees the devastation of a defendant's career, family, and future. I struggled with the injustice of this coercion and the hopeless feeling of being unable to overcome such egregious government weaponization. An eighteenth-century maxim helped to remind me of a positive approach to overwhelming circumstances: "A little bit of light dispels a great deal of darkness."[41]

I had a critical mission with America's Frontline Doctors and GoldCare® from the onset of the government's rollout of the "pandemic" and the ensuing "new normal." I could not afford to be sidelined. Even if I were ultimately successful in a long and arduous legal battle, I didn't believe I could justify being incapacitated for so long by a Supreme Court contest over selective prosecution. I certainly couldn't afford to spend two decades in prison. In fact, I'm not sure we have even five years to derail this current dash toward despotism and to establish an alternative. GoldCare.com,[42] the medical freedom platform that prioritizes the doctor-patient relationship, was now my clear and present mandate from the American people, who were pleading for a path of escape from the trap of the Medical Industrial Complex.

As I was forced to do business with a dishonest broker, I chose to take the rational path of a plea bargain.[43] It is heartbreaking[44] that our own government is the dishonest broker, putting me (and thousands of others) in a position of choosing between fulfilling my obligations or abandoning those obligations for the noble purpose of telling the truth. I concur with this comment posted on the AFLDS website:

> I'm sad Dr. Gold took a plea deal. The Capitol police waived [sic] people to come into the building. They removed barricades. They stood there as people walked past them. They were set up. It makes me furious.

CHAPTER TWELVE

Rotten Inside

You shall set up judges . . . in all your cities. . . and they shall judge the people with righteous judgment. You shall not pervert justice; you shall not show favoritism... You shall not plant for yourself an idolatrous tree.

—Deuteronomy 16:18–21

The juxtaposition of the commandment to appoint righteous judges and the prohibition of an idolatrous "tree" (as opposed to a chiseled idol which looks like an idol from the outside), teaches that, like an idolatrous "tree," a corrupt judge looks like other judges on the outside, but is rotten on the inside.

—Chaim Brisker

A few weeks after my January arrest, they scheduled the district court judge to preside over my case. Judge Christopher Cooper's name meant nothing to me, but I was shocked when I saw his face on the screen during our first remote hearing. Casey (Christopher) Cooper had been my classmate at Stanford Law School. We were two of just 147 graduates in the class of '93.

Cooper hadn't been just a classmate. I joined him on a few casual dates at the campus cafeteria, and he asked me out on a formal date. I declined. I recalled him as ambitious and bright, but soulless, and thus not for me. I remained as friendly to him, though, as I was to the rest of our classmates.

I had assumed the friendly feeling ran both ways, so it didn't even occur to me he might have held a grudge. I also wasn't sitting next to my attorney, to glance at them quickly and perhaps whisper something about it. We were thousands of miles away and only connected by Zoom. Before I could formulate my thoughts or attempt a private text message to my attorney, the moment passed. My defense attorney had mentioned this judge was likely to be as "fair" as any other DC judge.

The Standard for (Judicial) Recusal

Should this judge have recused himself? The Code of Federal Regulations makes recusal *mandatory* in situations:

> A judge **shall** recuse themself under circumstances that would require disqualification of a Federal judge under Canon 3(C) of the Code of Conduct for United States Judges.[1]

The referenced canon of the Code of Conduct for United States Judges provides:

> A judge shall disqualify himself or herself in a proceeding in which the judge's impartiality might reasonably be questioned, including but not limited to instances in which: (a) the judge has a personal bias or prejudice concerning a party . . .[2]

And the same canon of the Code of Conduct provides a second instance in which a judge must disqualify himself, namely when:

> the judge's spouse . . . has a financial interest in the subject matter in controversy . . . or any other interest that could be affected substantially by the outcome of the proceeding . . . [3]

It would undoubtedly be justifiable to question Cooper's impartiality when he is deciding whether or not to incarcerate someone he knows personally and used to be friendly with. The above precepts recommend recusal for: appearance of lack of impartiality, bias or prejudice, or spouse financial/other interest. Let us consider how Cooper has handled potential recusal situations in the past.

CNN contributor and former Syracuse University professor Dr. Boyce D. Watkins published a report according to which Cooper declined to recuse himself from a Judicial Council that was looking into a judicial misconduct claim against . . . Cooper himself.

Former military Legal Specialist Holly Clark, an administrator at the Harvard University Graduate School of Education, brought the complaint. Clark says she witnessed Cooper violate the canons of the Judicial Code of Conduct during a 2018 hearing. She appealed the initial dismissal of her complaint to the nine judges on the Circuit Judicial Council for Cooper's circuit, as required by judiciary rules. One of those nine judges was Cooper himself. Despite the mandatory requirement for a judge to recuse himself where his "impartiality might reasonably be questioned:

> "In this case, the complained-of district court judge (Cooper) was voluntarily assigned to the 28 U.S.C. § 352(d) Panel of the Judicial Council empaneled to rule on the Petition for Review of a complaint against himself," the petition stated, producing in an appendix Circuit-furnished proof that Cooper was present and voting on himself.
>
> "It then invoked '*Nemo iudex in causa sua*,' a Latin expression, to indicate that 'a lawyer or judge is not supposed to sit in judgment of oneself in a disciplinary proceeding, for it is one of the cardinal rules of natural justice that no one should act as judge in a case in which they have a personal vested interest.'"

The DC jury pool and most federal judges in Washington were openly hostile to J6 protestors (Trump received just 5 percent of the vote in DC in 2020).[4] But even among this group, you could hardly find a DC couple more contemptuous of J6 defendants than Cooper and his attorney-wife.

Judge Cooper is married to Amy Jeffress, an attorney heavily involved in Democratic DC politics. Merrick Garland presided over their wedding in 1999. Yes, Attorney General Merrick Garland—the single person most culpable for the "DC Gulag" and brutal treatment of January 6 defendants, the single person who violently abrogated the rule of law to wreak havoc and destruction on thousands of very ordinary Americans—is a close personal friend. From Jeffress's blog, which strongly supports Garland's brutality and compares J6 to the KKK:

> The storming of the Capitol, Judge Garland continued, was "the most heinous attack on the democratic processes that I've ever seen and one that I never expected to see in my lifetime." He explicitly identified the role of white supremacy: "If anything was necessary to refocus our attention on white supremacists, that was the attack on the Capitol. There is a line from Oklahoma City [to January 6], and there's another line from Oklahoma City all the way back to the experiences that I mentioned in my opening with respect to the battles of the original Justice Department against the Ku Klux Klan.[5]

In fact, Jeffress[6] appears to find Garland's approach too mild. She bemoaned his reluctance to support "a growing chorus of support for a domestic terrorism statute,"[7] as he opted to make do with current laws. She clearly fantasizes about destroying many, if not all J6 protestors with felonies and staggering prison sentences.

In addition to his wife's public hatred and contempt for J6 defendants, Cooper also knew that his wife was getting paid by clients who actively oppose the J6 protestors' political efforts. Her client list includes fired FBI lawyer Lisa Page.[8] Page famously texted with "her lover" Deputy Assistant Director Peter Strzok about how they would use their FBI positions to prevent Trump from being elected. Page's Twitter profile[9] even includes a photograph of herself with Cooper's wife.[10]

Cooper also presided over the trial of Michael Sussmann, a lawyer who handled documents falsely accusing the Trump Organization of wrongdoing while Sussmann hid his connection to the Hillary Clinton campaign.[11] Legal scholar Jonathan Turley noted that Cooper allowed three Clinton donors, an AOC donor, and a woman whose daughter is on a sports team with Sussmann's daughter onto the jury for Sussmann's case, calling it the worst jurors the prosecutor could face short of DNC staff members.[12] The trial seemed rigged to many people.[13]

Fox News headline:[14]

> "Will judge in Sussmann case consider recusal after wife represented Lisa Page?"

Interestingly, while not recusing himself, Cooper did have this to say about himself and Sussmann at a hearing in September 2021:

> . . . we were professional acquaintances. I don't believe that this creates a conflict, but my regular practice is to disclose these sorts of relationships with lawyers or with parties on the record. [15]

These examples show a clear pattern that was replicated in my case: an apathetic acknowledgment of a "casual acquaintance" that nullifies any possible conflict of interest in his own mind, which appears to be the standard he uses.

A Career Favoring Leftists . . . and Terrorists

Cooper himself, while required to "refrain from political activity" during his tenure as a federal judge,[16] has nonetheless created severe doubts about his impartiality by applauding left-wing efforts to disrupt Supreme Court hearings:

> Cooper said . . . he did not doubt the sincerity of the defendants' beliefs, and that he applauded their commitment to participating in the political process . . .[17]

The demonstrators Cooper applauded were anti–free speech operatives. They were protesting a Supreme Court decision striking down a federal law that infringed on the First Amendment right to post political ads.[18] In an attempt to pressure the high court to reverse that decision and allow the government to censor ads, the anti–free speech operatives joined with the group 99Rise[19] that carried out a year-long "coordinated" effort to disrupt Supreme Court proceedings.[20] Cooper acknowledged that these protestors "interfered with the right of lawyers to argue on behalf of their clients" but gave them a weekend in jail (i.e., a *very* light sentence).[21]

And Cooper's cozy approach extended past leftists to include actual terrorists. He issued a sentence to one of the Benghazi terrorists that was *so* unreasonably light, it was overturned by the Appellate Court.[22] Read the previous sentence twice.

> The D.C. Circuit Court of Appeals on Tuesday ruled that Ahmed Abu Khatallah's sentence is "substantively unreasonably low in light of the gravity of his crimes of terrorism. . . . In sentencing Khatallah to just twelve years for the two support-of-terrorism counts and the property destruction count, the district court [i.e., Judge Cooper] did not—and could not on this record—sufficiently justify its additional variance so far below the sentencing range that would have been appropriate . . .
>
> U.S. District Court Judge Christopher Cooper in 2018 could have imposed a greater sentence on Khatallah—because two of his convictions pertained to terrorism—offering up the possibility of life in prison. But Cooper went with the lesser sentence of 22 years . . . The decision instructs Cooper to re-sentence Khatallah. [23]

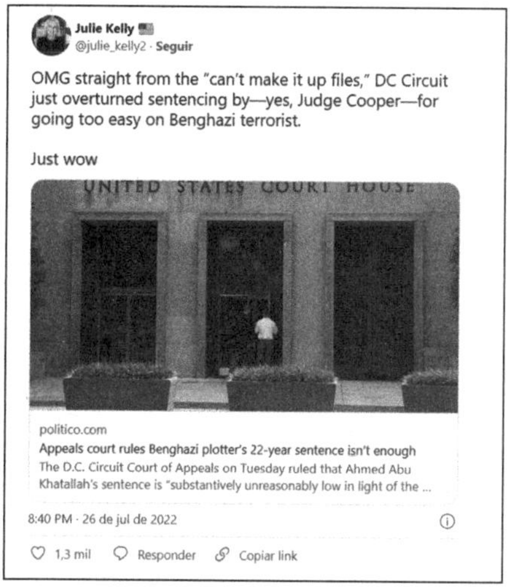

Julie Kelly
@julie_kelly2 · Seguir
OMG straight from the "can't make it up files," DC Circuit just overturned sentencing by—yes, Judge Cooper—for going too easy on Benghazi terrorist.
Just wow
UNITED STATES COURT HOUSE
politico.com
Appeals court rules Benghazi plotter's 22-year sentence isn't enough
The D.C. Circuit Court of Appeals on Tuesday ruled that Ahmed Abu Khatallah's sentence is "substantively unreasonably low in light of the ...
8:40 PM · 26 de jul de 2022
1,3 mil
Responder
Copiar link

And at least one case Cooper had litigated as a lawyer was uniquely disturbing.[24] Prior to being appointed a judge, Cooper was the attorney defending the rights of three of the elite rulers of Saudi Arabia against the families of 9/11 victims. The litigation that spanned eight years (2002–2010) was work that Cooper was clearly very proud of. In contrast, such work would either make nearly any other American's blood boil or run cold.

While all litigants deserve representation, it was particularly concerning to learn that a classmate apparently had no hesitation in taking a paycheck to represent a wealthy foreign nation against the interests of American citizens who died under circumstances that appeared to implicate that foreign nation. Cooper succeeded in getting the cases against the Saudi defense minister and two other Saudi government officials' defendants thrown out.

While I spent the majority of my career working in the inner cities helping the poorest and most disenfranchised (mainly black) Americans, the irony of a man who, while in law school, portrayed himself as a champion of "black" rights but who actually grew up to defend the wealthy over the poor—punishing a white woman who actually grew up to *serve* poor black people—was not lost on me.

Man in the Mirror

After I decided to accept the plea deal, revelations of suspicious government activity on J6 grew worse by the day. That, plus Cooper's decision to not recuse himself, gave me hope that sentencing would be proportionate and fair. I was mistaken.[25] Instead, I became the latest person to object to the way Cooper conducts his courtroom.

Judge Cooper has a mantra he repeats as he sentences Jan 6 protesters: "You're not being singled out for your political views." Really. My classmate Casey Cooper may believe that this lofty pronouncement shields him from any query into the political influence of his judicial decisions. Rather than granting him the immunity he desires, it actually brands him as a black robe gaslighter. Note the Cleveland Clinic definition for gaslighting: "Gaslighting is a form of emotional manipulation by someone to make you feel like your feelings aren't your feelings or what you think is happening isn't really happening."[26]

When Texas businesswoman Jenna Ryan appeared in Cooper's courtroom for her sentencing, she may have been relieved when the judge indicated that her politics were not an issue. That is, until he revealed that they were. HuffPost reports his language:

> "You're not being singled out for your political views or anything like that," Cooper said. "It's how and where you decided to express them . . ."
>
> At the end of the hearing, Judge Cooper also advised [Texas businesswoman Jenna] Ryan to think about what sources she relied upon for her news in the future.[27]

Buffalo News reported that in the case of New Yorker Traci Sunstrum, Cooper specifically noted the role of her political views in determining her sentence after saying that she's not being punished for those views:

> The judge noted Sunstrum was wearing a QAnon hat during the riot.
>
> Cooper said he was not punishing her for her political views or personal associations, but he expressed concern whether some conspiracy theory would cause her "to answer this kind of call again . . ."
>
> "In light of her statements for being there because 'my POTUS called me to be there,' it seems to me those facts warrant a period of probation or supervision to ensure that she is free from these sorts of *influence* going forward," Cooper said.[28]

The gaslighting may already be disorienting or you may not even notice it. But a judge just informed the world that a defendant's choice of clothing was a factor in their judgment. And a judge gaslit a defendant while saying he is not punishing her political views while also saying he is punishing her so she isn't influenced by what he considers a conspiracy theorist.

Take a step back and really consider this. Aren't judges supposed to punish based upon *criminal behavior*? I must have missed that day in law school when judges like Cooper were taught that our country empowered judges to reprimand citizens for their beliefs. One of the most beautiful things about America is that anyone can think or believe anything, per their own judgment. They just can't *act* criminally, and that admonition used to include prosecutors and judges. Dizzy yet?

Frontline News reported that former West Virginia city councilor Eric Barber received a:

> special kind of self-contradictory sentencing speech from Cooper—in sandwich form, getting berated for his political views both before and after being told that his political views were irrelevant. These wildly conflicting pronouncements effectively gaslights the defendant with an impossible paradox he's expected to either accept, or to think he's lost his mind because he can't understand the judge's implausible reprimand. [29]

Mediaite reported the gaslighting this way:

> The judge also offered the former elected official a reality check. "You're too old and you're too accomplished and you're too smart to get involved in nonsense like this," Cooper said after he handed down the sentence.
>
> "This is not about the First Amendment. You are free to express your views. You're free to support any political candidate or positions or issues that you want. I encourage that. But enough of this nonsense, OK?"[30]

Gaslighting in Black (Robes)

Cooper not only chastised defendants in contradiction to his claim that he doesn't consider politics when sentencing, but his actual sentencing record shows the falsity of his words. BuzzFeed reported on the weekend jail time Cooper gave out to the left-wing protesters, following their year-long "coordinated" effort to disrupt Supreme Court proceedings:

> Five protesters arrested for staging a demonstration at the US Supreme Court in 2015 were sentenced to jail time . . . Four of the defendants will spend one weekend behind bars, with the fifth person sentenced to two weekends . . . the sentences were minimal . . .[31]

The report noted that the stage had already been set for Cooper's lenient trespassing sentences:

> The protesters faced a maximum of a year in jail, but in reality the stakes were lower. The US attorney's office in Washington, DC, had asked for a sentence of 10 days in jail for each defendant. Lawyers for the defendants asked for no jail time beyond the two days they spent in custody after their arrest.
>
> Still, given earlier cases in which protesters arrested for similar conduct received no jail time—beyond what they'd already served after their arrest—the case represented a test of whether and when demonstrators could go to jail for this type of civil disobedience.[32]

BuzzFeed even pointed out how "longer" sentences were reserved for particularly extreme protest actions:

> A Texas man, Rives Grogan, was sentenced to 21 days in jail in 2015 for interrupting Supreme Court proceedings, but defense lawyer Jeffrey Light said on Monday that Grogan's case was different because he had been arrested numerous times for protest activity, and because his conduct at the Supreme Court had been more "inflammatory."[33]

Three weeks in jail for the most "inflammatory" of the protesters because, after all, political protest is a sacred and specifically protected type of activity, right?

Selective Sentencing

What better indication of future sentences could there be other than prior sentences for similar conduct? I expected the prosecutors in my case to recommend no jail time, similar to other (past) protesters who received no jail time even when purposely disrupting government proceedings. But my lawyer told me the shocking news: "Dr. Gold . . . they're asking for ninety days in prison."

Ninety. From the same US attorneys in DC who suggested only ten days for truly disruptive, organized, and repeat protesters. They'd requested ten days for the left-wing protesters, expecting that a weekend or two would be the final sentence Cooper issued. By suggesting ninety days for me, they were clearly predicting an extreme departure from past sentencing by Cooper, anticipating he would land on several weeks or months. How could the prosecutors have been so confident in securing the judge's cooperation in such aggressive penal escalation?

Somehow, my case became even more extreme. In what the *Washington Post* called "a rare move," the court's probation officer (PO) recommended even more prison time than the prosecutors: *six months* for trespassing![34] This, for a first-time nonviolent misdemeanor, committed by a doctor and lawyer exercising free speech with a government-approved permit,[35] and no allegations of violence, vandalism, or anything beyond simply *being there*. The raw appearance of ***in***justice in the Department of Justice's behavior was truly nauseating.

As an aside, I learned that this particular PO, Robert Walters, was universally scorned. It was apparent that prosecutors, defense attorneys, and even judges routinely ignored him. That is because, even among his peers, he had an exceptional level of laziness. For example, he cut and pasted among different defendants' paperwork. He didn't make or keep mandatory appointments. He lied to lawyers and judges. And as I have said throughout this book, I *welcome* a defamation lawsuit by any individual I have specifically named. An absolute defense to defamation is if the statement is true. So to Robert Walters, I say: Bring it.

Truth Derangement Syndrome

Although I generally managed to put the upcoming sentencing hearing out of my mind, on the morning of the hearing I began to wonder, "Is prison a real possibility?" Refusing to accept any "new normal," I reiterated to my staff, "Anything more than probation would be a travesty, obviously."

A travesty it was. The moment Casey Cooper began speaking, I could feel the hatred emanating from his face and body like a radiant heat source.[36] In person, it became obvious that he had a huge vendetta. Whether it was the politics of J6 protesters or because of my rejecting his romantic advances many years ago, I'll never know, but he exuded the rage of a judge cracking down on a violent vagrant. You could feel his fury from across the COVID-Social-Distancing room, where everyone except the judge was forced by the judge to wear a mask. *Rules for me but not for thee* was the literal law regarding masks in DC courts. The policy is stated as: "masks will be required unless the presiding judge permits otherwise."

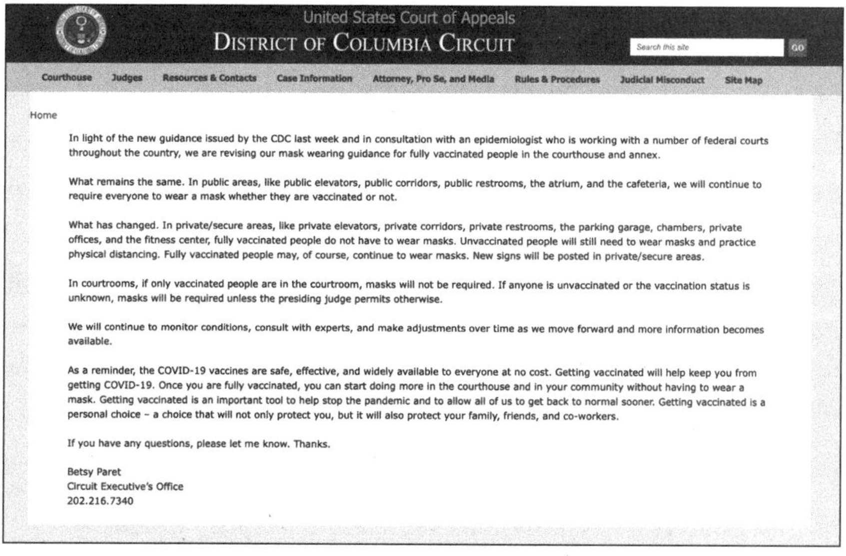

United States Court of Appeals
DISTRICT OF COLUMBIA CIRCUIT

Search this site GO

Courthouse | Judges | Resources & Contacts | Case Information | Attorney, Pro Se, and Media | Rules & Procedures | Judicial Misconduct | Site Map

Home

In light of the new guidance issued by the CDC last week and in consultation with an epidemiologist who is working with a number of federal courts throughout the country, we are revising our mask wearing guidance for fully vaccinated people in the courthouse and annex.

What remains the same. In public areas, like public elevators, public corridors, public restrooms, the atrium, and the cafeteria, we will continue to require everyone to wear a mask whether they are vaccinated or not.

What has changed. In private/secure areas, like private elevators, private corridors, private restrooms, the parking garage, chambers, private offices, and the fitness center, fully vaccinated people do not have to wear masks. Unvaccinated people will still need to wear masks and practice physical distancing. Fully vaccinated people may, of course, continue to wear masks. New signs will be posted in private/secure areas.

In courtrooms, if only vaccinated people are in the courtroom, masks will not be required. If anyone is unvaccinated or the vaccination status is unknown, masks will be required unless the presiding judge permits otherwise.

We will continue to monitor conditions, consult with experts, and make adjustments over time as we move forward and more information becomes available.

As a reminder, the COVID-19 vaccines are safe, effective, and widely available to everyone at no cost. Getting vaccinated will help keep you from getting COVID-19. Once you are fully vaccinated, you can start doing more in the courthouse and in your community without having to wear a mask. Getting vaccinated is an important tool to help stop the pandemic and to allow all of us to get back to normal sooner. Getting vaccinated is a personal choice – a choice that will not only protect you, but it will also protect your family, friends, and co-workers.

If you have any questions, please let me know. Thanks.

Betsy Paret
Circuit Executive's Office
202.216.7340

I must have missed the day in medical school when doctors were taught that viruses "obey" judges. This very arrogant man required every single person to wear a mask. How I wish photographs were permitted.

It would have been eye-opening for Americans who consider themselves sovereign to see a judge acting exactly like a king. Cooper ordered every person except himself to wear a mask. For hours and hours, the bailiffs, court clerk, stenographer, defendant, two prosecutors, two defense attorneys, and observers were all masked, while the judge was unmasked. It was the pictorial representation of the fascism that I despised.

Cooper began his explanation of the impending sentence by accusing me of failing to express remorse for (unknowingly) entering a restricted public space, entering the building (swept in by the crowd through open doors, all visible on CCTV), and disrespecting the supposed memory of policemen killed during the protest. Casey Cooper literally said, from the bench, "But what I haven't heard is about the five people who died that day. The four people who committed suicide because of the trauma they suffered that day at the hands of the mob." Page 55 of my sentencing memo from June 16, 2022:

```
persecution, about how you've lost your job, about how you
haven't been able to get on a flight.  But what I haven't
heard is anything about the five people who died that day,
the four people who committed suicide because of the trauma
that they suffered that day at the hands of the mob, or the
```

Cooper was admitting to sentencing *me* for what he claims *other* protesters did. That's really inappropriate for a judge. But far worse, it was all based on a myth, so I was being "judged" by a person who was incredibly ignorant and/or biased. Either way, such a person lacks judicial temperament. These myths had been debunked many months earlier, including by *The Western Journal*:

> This claim that the pro-Trump protesters on January 6 went on to "kill five cops" is 100 percent fiction. In truth, *not a single police officer died* that day. Even left-wing PolitiFact had to admit that no police officers died during the events of January 6.

> Only one officer died in the immediate aftermath of the protest, and that was Capitol Police officer Brian Sicknick, who *died of natural causes one day after* the protests ended. The best that left-wingers can do to claim that Sicknick was a "victim" of the protests is to claim that the stress of the protests "contributed" to the strokes that took his life. But even that is conjecture, not medical fact. The other four officers who died—long after the protest ended—all died from suicide. *Not a single officer died during the protests and none died as a direct action of any protester.*" [Emphases added][37]

There *were* deaths on the day of the protest—four protesters in the crowd never came back.[38] All four were unarmed.

1. Ashli Babbitt, a petite woman and Air Force veteran, was shot to death by USCP officer Michael Byrd, who shot Ashli to death even though she was flanked by three other armed USCP officers—who were *not* threatened by her nonviolent presence;[39]
2. Rosanne Boyland, a woman viciously bludgeoned to death with a stick by DC Metro police officer Lila Morris;
3. Kevin Greeson, killed by cardiac arrest caused by flash-bang grenades fired into the crowd by police; and
4. Benjamin Phillips, suffering the same fate as Greeson.

Cooper did not suggest that the Capitol Police should express any remorse for the protesters who were killed, nor did he voice concern that the officers who killed the two women or who launched deadly flash-bang grenades were never charged with any crimes or otherwise disciplined. Not only that, but just moments prior, I had in fact publicly expressed my remorse for being in proximity of the turmoil as I addressed the judge directly.

While he made sure to gaslight *me* about failing to express remorse right after I did, Cooper did not have a problem with the actual lack of remorse from one of his favored left-wing protesters who disrupted SCOTUS hearings. Cooper sentenced Matthew Kresling to just one weekend in jail and skipped the lack of remorse speech despite Kresling's astonishing arrogance:

> Matthew Kresling, of Los Angeles, told Cooper that if protests were an annoyance, "it's an annoyance in the same sense that a fire alarm is."[40]

Cooper continued gaslighting me with the "it's not about your political beliefs" trope, right after letting me know that he's read my organization's material and doesn't approve of it. As quoted by CNN, he told me, in open court:

> Your organization is leaving people with the misimpression that this is a political prosecution or that it's about free speech. It ain't about free speech. January 6 was about a lot of things, but it wasn't about free speech or COVID vaccinations . . . the only reason you are here is where and when and how you chose to express your views . . .[41]

So Cooper says it's only about the trespass—the wrong place at the wrong time—and not about anything else, but just a moment earlier he mentioned getting upset after reading through the AFLDS website, and he explained how much it bothers him. Then, after clearing himself of considering politics, he goes right back to attacking free speech that has no relation to trespass, as reported by the *Washington Post*:

> I find it unseemly that your organization is raising hundreds of thousands of dollars for its operations, including your salary, by mischaracterizing what this proceeding is all about. People need to know this is not acceptable.[42]

Having sandwiched his claim of ignoring politics in between his scoldings on politics, Cooper was deeply offended that millions of American citizens freely chose to support my policy positions in defending medical choice and freedom of speech, both long before and after J6. He complained about my organization exercising its First Amendment right to free speech at the very moment that he insisted, "it ain't about free speech."

Did Cooper read through the websites of his political allies before sentencing them? Did he research the socialist group organizing the SCOTUS protestors whom he sentenced to a single weekend in jail? Does he find it "unseemly" that the founder of the organization 99Rise, Kai Newkirk,[43] boasts that he "led . . . 12 days of state capitol sit-ins," or that he supports a "democratic socialist political vision [which] demands a radical, structural redistribution of wealth and power?"[44] And Cooper didn't even do a very good job on understanding my work: all my public speaking is focused on medical freedom issues, not politics.

Gaslighting Guzzler

Cooper also impugned me over video footage that, until recently, was hidden from the public.[45] Like secret evidence in a proceeding against terrorists held in Guantánamo Bay,[46] prosecutors have withheld, for several years,[47] more than forty thousand hours of J6 surveillance video at the Capitol,[48] which "could be used to defend the innocence of both lawmakers and civilians accused of wrongdoing."[49] Now that this has been shared publicly in various reports by Tucker Carlson, Julie Kelly, and Jon Solomon, it's clear this footage paints an entirely different picture than the mainstream narrative of the events of J6. It proves the peaceful nature of most and implicates numerous government agents, both undercover and uniformed. Hiding Brady (exculpatory) material is illegal and a serious concern for defendants who have a legal right to receive all such exculpatory evidence in advance of being tried.

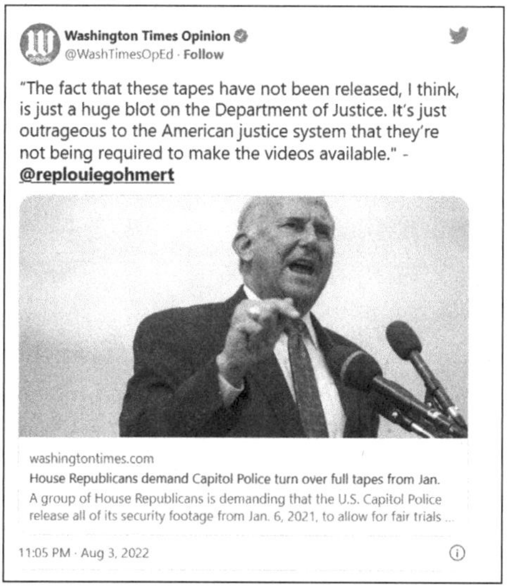
Washington Times Opinion
@WashTimesOpEd · Follow
"The fact that these tapes have not been released, I think, is just a huge blot on the Department of Justice. It's just outrageous to the American justice system that they're not being required to make the videos available." - @replouiegohmert
washingtontimes.com
House Republicans demand Capitol Police turn over full tapes from Jan.
A group of House Republicans is demanding that the U.S. Capitol Police release all of its security footage from Jan. 6, 2021, to allow for fair trials ...
11:05 PM · Aug 3, 2022

I saw select moments of this video footage for the very first time at my sentencing, because the prosecutors showed it. It was highly irregular to show evidence at a sentencing hearing. It was like a trial without cross-examination. The prosecution was trying to justify a harsh sentence by showing I was present at a frenetic moment. The prosecution did *not* show that the crowd was peaceful until just before this frenetic moment when the police had thrown a flash-bang into the crowd, causing the crowd to become agitated.

The video shows an officer who fainted outside the Capitol. I had informed my criminal defense attorney at the outset, eighteen months earlier, that I witnessed an officer who fainted. That officer later testified, in my codefendant's trial, that he had indeed fainted. This exactly matched his statement following the J6 event where he was interviewed by the FBI.

Shortly after falling, I heard the crowd yelling to those standing by him, "Get him up!" and I saw the bystanders help the officer get back on his feet within seconds, his baton still in hand. There was no dispute: He fainted, he got up as the crowd lifted him up within seconds, and he continued on without assistance. The officer did not seek medical attention. When debriefed by the FBI three days post-J6, he told FBI agent Sara Smither that he fainted and was uninjured.

I had no way to get to him through the dense crowd, nor did I need to. The nearby protesters succeeded in quickly getting him back to his feet within seconds. But despite that video clearly showing my inability to assist, the lack of need for assistance, and the absence of any malice toward the fallen officer, Cooper berated me for not magically flying over ten people to help him, while ignoring that he was quickly helped to his feet by those nearby. He also faulted me for not (magically) escaping the crowd after a "violent assault" of the officer—again, *an event which did not occur.* Cooper thus repeated three falsehoods told by the prosecutor, ignoring footage that clearly showed what happened.

It was incredible to witness a federal judge's inability to be rational while watching a video that directly disputed the prosecution's lies. It was infuriating to witness a federal judge show specific malice toward a defendant. Cooper is an incredibly arrogant human being. More than any other quality, this is why he is not a "judge." A judge possesses the ability to see clearly and rationally and dispassionately despite his own biases.

Licensed to Lie: United States Prosecutors[50]

Also very disturbing is the realization that federal prosecutors appear to lie routinely. The prosecutor in my case repeatedly defamed me and misinformed the court that I did not help an officer who was assaulted. All the while, she herself knew the officer wasn't assaulted. How do I know *she* knew he wasn't assaulted? *Because she had the evidence in her possession since the very beginning.* The officer was interviewed by the FBI three days after J6, as I mentioned, and stated to the FBI that he fell due to fainting, and eighteen months later he said the same thing in trial testimony. His story never changed, and there was also video evidence supporting what he consistently said. The prosecutor knew his story. The prosecutor had the officer's FBI interview in her possession. But listen to her words at my sentencing:

> "The U.S. Capitol Police officer has now been dragged to the ground . . ." and ". . . he is then . . . pulled down to the ground . . ." and "they do not help the officer. They do not administer any sort of medical care" and "The police officer went through a very traumatic experience. He was pulled down into a mob. Defendant Gold . . . do[es] not help the officer."

This is a lie, and Assistant US Attorney April Ayers-Perez knew it was a lie as she said it. I challenge her now, publicly, to dispute this. Her only defense would be that she never reviewed the evidence in her possession. April Ayers-Perez, a fetchingly beautiful woman who speaks in dulcet tones, a woman who appears to be the picture of joy and mental stability, is now in the Houston Texas DOJ office. How embarrassing for Texans to have government attorneys who lie to the court.

The facts, as testified to by the officer three days after the event and multiple times during various J6 trials years later, never changed. He testified that he fainted and was uninjured (meaning he was never assaulted, not dragged to the ground and not pulled to the ground); the crowd helped him get up; he walked away of his own volition; and he did not need medical assistance.

All these facts are in the DrGoldReferences Appendix 11.[51] The statement the police officer Joshua Pollitt, *who was never assaulted,* gave to FBI agent Sara Smither on January 9, 2021; the testimony the police officer Joshua Pollitt, *who was never assaulted,* gave at my codefendant's trial on September 21, 2022; and some of the lies Ms. April Ayers-Perez said at my sentencing on June 16, 2022, specifically about *my not helping a police officer who had been assaulted.*

My criminal defense attorney complained to the more senior Assistant US Prosecutor Jason Manning about this (and other) lies. After all, attorneys are prohibited from "perpetrating a falsehood upon a tribunal." Because if prosecutors lie, and lie so brazenly, we have worse than a poorly functioning legal system. We have a corrupt charade that the uninformed public *thinks* is a legal system. When I was released from prison and I learned of April Ayers-Perez's lies, I tried mightily to hold her responsible. I share the technical details here, because it would be a shame for anyone reading this to think I did not try to expose a government liar.

I knew of the prosecutors' lies because I was in a unique position. I was both a J6 defendant myself and a lawyer who assisted the legal team for my codefendant John Strand. During my case, April Ayer-Perez did not give this exculpatory information to my defense team. So I did not know of its existence at the time she lied about me. But while reviewing all the evidence for John Strand's trial, I found Officer Pollitt's FBI statement from three days post January 6—confirming what I had said all along, and directly refuting the liar, Ms. April Ayers-Perez. It was shocking to have absolute proof that our government lawyers ***lie.***

But it was very clear to me that the US Attorney's Office and DC Bar would be completely disinterested in a lawyer lying in a J6 trial. So I write of her lies here, and *I challenge The Liar April Ayers-Perez to sue me for defamation.* She will not because truth is an absolute defense against defamation, and the proof is now being shared with the public for all to see and in the DrGoldReferences Appendix 11.[52] She is a disgrace. Her lies were repeated by the media, and I cannot sue the media for defamation if they are merely quoting a legal proceeding.

As soon as John's trial was over, I informed my criminal defense attorneys that I wanted to file an ethics complaint against Liar April Ayers-Perez. My attorneys confirmed the facts and then contacted the more senior AUSA Scoundrel Jason Manning. At that time, the end of 2022, the evidence was still not permitted to be viewed by the public. I only had been granted access to it as part of John's legal team. My attorneys asked Jason Manning to waive the government privilege over Officer Pollitt's January 9 FBI statement, and of course, being an unethical scoundrel, he *refused* to allow the truth to see the light of day.

In other words, sitting at my sentencing in June 2022, listening to April Ayers-Perez lying, I knew she was lying, but I didn't have the proof. In September 2022, I saw proof that April Ayers-Perez lied (or was guilty of gross incompetence), but that proof was "owned" by the government, and the government prohibited me from using that proof to file an ethics complaint against one of their own lying attorneys.

All paid for by your tax dollars.

A word about scoundrel Jason Manning. Jason has been the lead prosecutor in many January 6 trials. He uses his abilities and position with no wisdom at all. He seems motivated by power. My observation is that the US Attorney thug Matthew Graves, who declined to prosecute 72 percent of those arrested for misdemeanors and 53 percent of those arrested or felonies in DC in 2022[53] and who agreed to a no-jail plea bargain in the 2023 case of a man who slammed a female officer against a wall and punched her in the face during a pro-Hamas riot,[54] delegated to Jason Manning (and others) the job of relentlessly hunting peaceful J6 protestors. Manning, then, likely jumped at the opportunity. Manning's signature move is to conflate a specific defendant's actions with *other* people's actions. He routinely said or implied to many juries that the specific defendant they were judging was guilty because *other* unrelated people did something.

My codefendant John Strand, introduced in Chapter 2, will tell his own story one day,[55] but many observers believed that John was going to be the first J6 defendant to be acquitted. His case was that egregious. Jason Manning was *frantic.* A random courtroom observer, whom I do not know and with whom I have never spoken, was so offended by Jason Manning that she took it upon herself to file an ethics complaint against Jason Manning because his behavior was so disturbing. That is in the DrGoldReferences Appendix 12.[56] She alerted the Office of the Inspector General, the DC Bar Association/Office of Disciplinary Counsel, the judge, the New York State Bar Association, two Congressmen, and a nonprofit.

This courtroom observer noted that Jason Manning falsely portrayed John to the jury. Jason Manning implied that John used a grenade launcher, implied that John disrupted the Senate, and implied that John interacted with traumatized officers, knowing that neither John nor I were anywhere near traumatized officers or anything else he implied.

Matthew Graves. Jason Manning. Paid for by your tax dollars. Remember these names and *never allow them to be promoted.* They are the problem personified.

Sixty Days in Prison

Cooper also chastised me for fund-raising to support my legal defense, even while that would have been legal, and he howled his indignation at my "profiting" from a "deadly" criminal event. Both are bald-faced lies. I voluntarily paid my legal expenses out of my personal funds, attested to by my attorneys in open court to Cooper.

But in Cooper's courtroom, the truth is whatever he claims it to be. Finally, with all the scathing anger and arrogance of his errant diatribe, he announced my sentence: sixty days in federal prison—same as many repeat sexual assailants—for a first-time, nonviolent, class A misdemeanor of a peaceful protester. The harsh reality of Judge Cooper's eyebrow-raising sentence was shocking. And yet, it was the vitriolic delivery that stunned me even more than the punishment itself.

This was clearly politicized: *Frontline News* reported that zero jail time was given to 209 of the 210 "politically correct" left-wing protesters charged with felony rioting for violence at the 2017 inauguration of President Trump.

> . . . of the 210 protestors charged with felony rioting during the 2017 inauguration, injuring six police officers and causing more than $100,000 in damage, only one inauguration rioter was sentenced to any jail time, despite their violence; 20 were placed on probation and the rest saw their charges dropped, with the government actually paying the remaining defendants $1.6 million for having detained them![57]

George Washington University Law School professor Jonathan Turley noted that even an ax attack on a sitting senator's office was insufficient to earn a prison sentence, when the perpetrator supported the political left:

> The self-avowed Antifa member took an axe to the office of Sen. John Hoeven in Fargo on Dec. 21, 2020. Federal sentencing guidelines suggested 10–16 months in prison but he was only sentenced to probation and fined $2,784 for restitution . . . he then reportedly mocked the FBI for returning his axe.[58]

Turley was referring to a Facebook post by the defendant featuring a picture of his ax with the caption: "Look what the FBI was kind enough to give back to me."

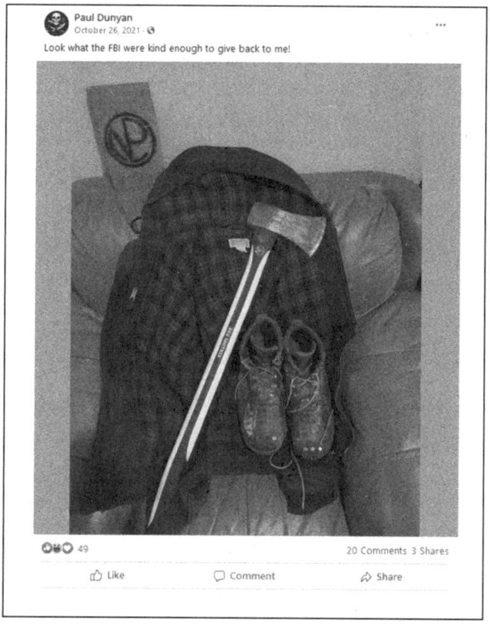

How does sixty days in federal prison compare to how Cooper sentences other defendants? I could not find a single case in his entire career where he sentenced a nonviolent first-time misdemeanor conviction to *any* prison time (other than a J6er). And believe me, I looked.

Who would "normally" get sixty days in federal prison? Consider Maxwell Berry, an Ohio man who had to be restrained in his airplane seat with tape during a flight in which he was "drinking alcohol . . . came out of the bathroom without his shirt on . . . groped the breasts of multiple flight attendants and then punched a male attendant in the face . . . [He] had pleaded guilty to three counts of assault and faced up to 18 months in prison."[59] A federal judge gave Berry sixty days in prison for this behavior.[60]

Or watch this random video I found when I typed "60 days in prison" into the YouTube browser.[61] This guy was stopped for a domestic situation, had just been released from jail a week earlier, and then repeatedly assaulted the officers, and then repeatedly resisted arrest.

After the sentence, I continued to speak publicly and often asked my audience, "Have you ever heard of a person going to prison for trespassing?" Or "Have you ever heard of a person going to prison for a misdemeanor?"

No one has ever raised their hand.

Gaslighting in Black Robes (Gaslighting in the Extreme)

The gaslighting effect of such double standards is quite disorienting. The government repeatedly claimed that they were harshly prosecuting all J6 protesters because even nonviolent participants were facilitating an "insurrection" just by being present. But. There. Was. No. Insurrection. That word was hijacked to gaslight everyone. No actions were taken that were consistent with insurrection. No person has been charged with insurrection. This fiction was the pretext which enabled the DOJ and judges to indulge their preexisting bias against Trump supporters and treat J6 defendants completely differently from all other defendants.

Make no mistake about it: The harsh treatment of political conservatives was possible only because the prosecutors and the judges categorized J6 defendants in their mind as "other." Judges do *not* categorically discriminate against groups of criminal defendants like "all rapists" or "all drunk drivers." Judges do *not* tolerate jurors who categorically discriminate against an entire group, whether it be gang members or cops.

But just like the doctors, nurses, and hospital executives mistreated patients during COVID (Chapter 1), just like the media mistreated the unvaccinated (Chapter 9), just like the prison guards mistreated the prisoners (Chapter 13), the DOJ and judges mistreated the J6 defendants by segregating people into "us" and "them."[62] The media perpetuated the gaslighting fantasy of "insurrection," which enabled the DOJ and judges to indulge their preexisting biases. The contrast is stark compared to minimizing or complete dismissal of criminality by left-wing activists.

When lawmakers and judges feel they need to have entirely new and different processes for a specific defendant or incident that is a clue that these lawmakers and judges are hopelessly biased and need to be replaced. In Chapter 4, I shared that the California State Legislature and California Medical Board created new laws and policies just for me. That is extreme bias. And J6 defendants in DC criminal court were facing new policies. Here are examples from two different J6 judges.

Judge Reggie Walton sentenced Daniel Goodwyn of Texas to the same misdemeanor trespass as me. But this judge was so incensed, that he also *illegally* ordered that the defendant's computer be monitored by the government for "disinformation!" (You would think a United States judge would be aware that there is no law known as "disinformation" in the United States of America.) Walton took great offense that Goodwyn had done a *Tucker Carlson Tonight* interview on March 14, 2023, and "gave the impression that individuals who have been charged in January 6th have been treated unfairly. And I [Judge Walton] see no evidence that, in fact, was the case." The appellate court ruled Judge Walton "plainly erred." How can this person still be a judge?! A person who is so hopelessly biased that he cannot see his bias should be permanently disqualified from judging—not to mention that he clearly is not familiar with the First Amendment of the Constitution.[63]

And the former chief judge of the DC federal court, an incredibly despicable, corrupt, and hateful person Beryl Howell, said this:

> And I start with this historical fact because what happened on January 6th was a chilling new type of criminal conduct to which our criminal laws have never before had to be applied.
>
> "For the reasons I will explain, even though the attack on the Capitol on January 6 was never planned for or imagined by the Congress when it enacted the criminal statute at issue in 18 U.S. C. §1512(c)(2), this law fits the charged criminal conduct, and Defendants motion to dismiss will be denied.[64]

It would be laughable if it weren't so tragic. She would fail out of law school. This "judge"—*a judge!*—without any shame whatsoever, without any insight whatsoever, and apparently without any intellect whatsoever, confesses in broad daylight that *she is going to make the crime fit the defendant even if it doesn't.* She is a disgrace to her nation.

You might be thinking the First Amendment made mention of a right to assemble—and specifically to petition the government for a redress of grievances—but that just might be your "extremist" imagination getting the best of you. Is our current DOJ genuinely concerned about an unruly protest with no weapons, no organization, and no intention of overthrowing the government? Or were they instituting a two-tiered justice system in which one party's activists are granted clemency for literally seditious plans to subvert government operations, while a disfavored party's nonviolent protesters with no connection to actual sedition are rounded up, disparaged, and destroyed like terrorists?

Where, exactly, is this Department of Justice trying to take us?

CHAPTER THIRTEEN

Prison

[Biblical] law does not employ prison sentences as punishments. Rather, people are immediately punished monetarily or corporeally. Nevertheless, one can be incarcerated until the facts surrounding his case are clarified.

—Adin Steinsaltz

Within minutes of entering the prison system, it becomes obvious why the Almighty did not include extended incarceration as a recommended punishment for crimes, providing instead that confinement be used only to prevent defendants from fleeing before their judgment is finalized. Prison literally destroys a person's soul. Even the reasonable guards—and there are some—bark out commands: "Everyone out of your cells! Inspection!"

Always at the top of their lungs. There is no slow building up the volume of their voices to correlate with a lack of compliance. Disconcertingly, straight to yelling. Not yelling, actually. Screaming. It's quite disorienting.

Then there's the monotony. It's mentally challenging to push yourself to overcome the urge to lie down in bed all day, given the lack of options for doing anything productive, particularly where I served my sentence. The Bureau of Prisons (BOP) determined that despite being a "minimum security risk," I would be sent to the only class of facility where minimum security detainees could be placed alongside high security risk criminals: a *transitional* facility.

On July 26, 2022, I entered the Federal Detention Center of Miami to serve my sentence alongside all ranges of serious offenders.[1] This was despite the BOP itself assigning me a minimum security designation, which was based on my lacking any previous record of aggressive behavior or criminal activity, my short sentence length, my voluntary surrender for confinement, and my lowest-level offense (nonviolent misdemeanor trespass).[2] In fact, this choice of facility apparently violated federal law and BOP policy, both of which prohibit placing those convicted only of misdemeanors with violent felons.[3]

People always ask: "What was it like?" Have you ever seen films depicting prisoners marking each new day with a scratch on the wall? It was pretty close to that. It was certainly not a minimum security "camp" like the one housing child-trafficker Ghislaine Maxwell, found guilty of harming multiple minors.

Frontline News contrasted my conditions with Maxwell's. Prisoners in Maxwell's location had access to in-person classes, a library, outdoor space, and regular access to video phone calls. FDC Miami, for women, had essentially nothing. Women who were assigned to FDC Miami for a longer term were placed on laundry or kitchen detail. Beyond that, for all of us, there was actually nothing to do.

Even with nothing to do and nowhere to go, we had very frequent lockdowns. The recent conviction of a prison guard at our facility, for the rape of a female inmate, illustrates how women must be on guard against fellow inmates and staff members alike. To top it off, all visitation at my facility had been suspended "until further notice," because, you know, "COVID." Throughout the nation, most COVID-related restrictions had ended about a year earlier.

With hardly any productive minutes scheduled in each twenty-four-hour period, the women shifted between idle chatter, idle board games, and the constantly running televisions (from 9 a.m. till 10 p.m.), which had no sound. In addition to the punishment of being away from one's life, friends, and family, the BOP clearly and mistakenly believes its role is to punish each prisoner as much as possible by making each day a wasted day as much as possible. This is the opposite of the mission statement for the BOP, which repeatedly emphasizes that it intends to prepare inmates for a productive reentry into society.

The purpose of the BOP is ostensibly to carry out the incarceration term safely and prepare the inmate for that moment of reentry, but inside prison, the BOP defines everything as a safety risk. It is a foreshadowing of what will happen throughout society if the mantra of "safety" continues to be prioritized above every other value. Merely using the word "safety" has become enough to deprive all the humans involved in the BOP system (the prisoners, the sadistic guards, and the normal guards) of any other goal or purpose. The BOP sacrifices all goals on the altar of "safety." Any agenda can be achieved by using the justification of "safety." Everyone knew the reason prisoners had no visitors in the summer of 2022 was because it was more convenient for the staff. There was not even the pretense of a public health issue. Prisoners were powerless, so there were no visitors, end of story. The BOP practices casual cruelty with no apology or accountability.

In a closed system with no accountability and virtually no oversight, there is no way to argue against the disingenuous call for "safety" that resulted in no visitors, no movement, no progress, and no life. If the warden had decided it was "safer" to eat only out of paper cups, I can assure you that is exactly what would have happened. It is not only the decisions that are problematic; it's the decision-making process itself that is fatally flawed. With "safety" claiming the only priority, there is no possibility of the BOP making appropriate decisions. As in life, safety is only one goal that should be balanced against other goals—and the humane treatment of all humans should be equally high on the priority list.

After what I witnessed, I am determined to tell the world that anyone who makes it through a long prison sentence with their humanity and work ethic intact is a person who any employer should strongly consider hiring.

COVID Confinement

I voluntarily surrendered at the scheduled time at FDC Miami, and I went through an intake process complete with a second mug shot and second smirk.

Then I was shackled and handcuffed, and much to my shock and horror, I was unceremoniously dumped into the "SHU" (pronounced like shoe): the dreaded punishment cell reserved for prisoners put into solitary confinement, something that is supposed to be used only as an extra maximum punishment when a prisoner is violent or found with contraband. All day and all night, I was not allowed out of my tiny six-by-ten-foot cell, and I did not know how many days I would be in this cell. A tray was pushed through a slot in the solid steel door three times a day (yes, like in the movies). The door remained locked twenty-four hours a day. My isolation cell had a fluorescent light on the ceiling, and within the solid steel door, a narrow vertical window (perhaps eight by sixteen inches), and a narrow horizontal slot for the food tray (perhaps four by twenty inches). The opposite wall was a metal shelving unit like you might find at Home Depot if you were looking for storage space for your garage. There was a narrow vertical window to view the outside and each metal rack had a thin (two-inch) foam pad. The cell had a steel sink–toilet, which was also the drinking water—but there was no cup in the cell. Whenever I saw a guard, I asked for a cup. I was mostly ignored, although one sadistic guard (Officer Santos) mimed using his hands. I said, "For weeks?" and he mimed using two hands. You have to check out mentally and live with no hope.

I've pondered how to convey the isolation experience to the typical American, and the closest psychological experience to the SHU in normal American life would be like being in an MRI machine/room for an extended period.

When a patient enters an MRI machine, the patient feels total isolation and total dependency on another person. It is so intolerable that about one third of patients require IV sedation to withstand just twenty minutes. That is the closest feeling to being dumped in the SHU. Of course, the physical space of an isolation cell is bigger than the coffin size of an MRI (as noted, it was a tiny closed six-by-ten cell with steel doors all around). But the feeling of total dependency and total isolation is the closest comparison in American life.

Later, the guards explained I wasn't being punished; I had been in *quarantine*. This was semantics and false. I was treated *exactly* the same as women on punishment. This "quarantine" policy was specific to FDC Miami and only to the women. I recognized the truth of the situation immediately: This was a warden staffing decision. The facility did not want to open up another ward for incoming women as that would have necessitated another staff person assigned to the quarantine ward. Instead of the more humane quarantine ward—standard policy for the men, standard policy for other prisons—the FDC Miami warden decided to put the women in isolation; it was cheaper. It was exactly the same decision-making I experienced throughout my career as an emergency physician. Hospital executives would claim they had "no beds" when that was a total lie: They were taking a cost-saving measure by having fewer nurses on duty.

What really bothered me about this from a policy perspective is that it is such an excellent example of why decisions must not be made in closed environments where only one side is heard. In this case, no one, absolutely no one, cares about the inmates, or for that matter, the law. Of course my treatment was illegal—if for no other reason than this policy was only applied against *women.* Even if you believe that inmates should have no rights at all, which is not the law, you can begin to see how completely disregarding the truth that there are two sides to a situation always leads to corrupt results.

Once released from isolation, I had an opportunity to speak with an assistant warden and advocate against this illegal and unethical use of isolation cells. The assistant warden had clearly already considered the points I made. But his stated reasoning was that the guards were *supposed* to be treating quarantine prisoners differently than punished prisoners. We were *supposed* to have books, paper and pencil, phone calls, and outside time. The conversation was very depressing because it was clear that everyone in the BOP was just playacting a role. The assistant warden knew the guards would treat quarantined prisoners exactly the same as punished prisoners if they were placed in the exact same isolation cells as punished prisoners.

To avoid facing the reality that they are complicit with throwing nonviolent misdemeanor women into isolation cells, which might make them feel bad about themselves, the wardens and guards must convince themselves that they themselves aren't complicit in evil by mouthing the false words—"of course prisoners in quarantine are not being punished"—all the while knowing that of course women prisoners in quarantine *are* being punished. This is dehumanizing for the guards—and certainly why so many guards were sadistic. Normal people would have a hard time staying at a job that required such a massive disconnect between stated words and actual reality.

I am very sensitive to observing such "small" examples of dehumanizing behavior, because I saw hospital personnel shift toward this same dehumanizing behavior in 2020. The more we allow dehumanizing policies to spread throughout society, as we already have done for the hundreds of thousands of people who work in the BOP, the worse off we all are. How we treat the weak and vulnerable is exactly who we are as a people.

If this wasn't a punishment, as they repeatedly claimed, they would have allowed for some level of movement within a twenty-four-hour period. They made no such accommodation. I also repeatedly asked for books; again ignored. Finally, a young psychology intern brought me some. I assumed obtaining books was a challenge for the guards—perhaps the books were on another floor or another ward. In other words, I attributed their lack of bringing me books to laziness. When I finally was released from isolation, I was shocked to discover there was a bookcase about twenty feet from my cell. It was a moment I'll never forget—most of the guards were either sadists or prisoners were so decidedly "other" to them that a human request didn't even register at all.

Like millions of prisoners before me, I read the Bible. To be perfectly honest, I started with the Bible because I had absolutely nothing in the cell and I thought a guard might think he "had" to bring me a Bible. The other reason was that I had so much difficulty getting any books at all, I thought if I had the opportunity to get even one book, I should request the Bible because it's long and at least it would be thought-provoking. Reading the Bible is the very best way to get oneself out of self-pity. My favorite story, naturally, was of Joseph, the son of Jacob, wrongfully imprisoned.[4] My favorite inspiration was Joshua 1:9: *Have I not commanded you? Be strong and courageous. Do not be afraid, do not be discouraged, for the Lord your God is with you wherever you go.*

In the middle of quarantine, I received a roommate. I was not excited about this because I was in a six-by-ten cell with metal slats for a "bed" and an upper-bunk metal slats "bed" with no ladder. This was another example of over-the-top unnecessary dehumanization. Exactly how are middle-aged women supposed to get to an upper bunk five feet off the ground with no steps? Guards informed us she could sleep on the ground, which exhausted the entirety of floor space in the cell.

Her arrival turned out to be a blessing for both of us. As noted, I did not know how long isolation would last. No guard seemed to know, so I feared it would be the entire incarceration. I found out later just how incredibly likely that had been. During intake, when asked if I had any reason to fear being in the general population, my final answer was "no." Had I said "yes," I would have been stuck in that torturous cage for the entire two months. There were traps and pitfalls everywhere, and I barely dodged this one, the worst of all.

Unbeknownst to me, this "trivial" routine question during intake held huge significance for the quality of my incarcerated life. When the guard asked if there was any reason I could not be in the general population, I initially had said yes. I knew I did not belong in a maximum security prison, I had no prison experience, and I was the target of much scrutiny.[5] Many people had told me ahead of time that they believed I would be specifically targeted.

Blessedly, the intake guard advised me to change my answer to "no" since I had no *specific* threat. I still thank God for this mercy. If that checkbox had remained a "yes," I would have been in isolation for my entire incarceration. This is inconceivable. I simply cannot imagine it. Unfortunately, this was the destiny of many women, including my new "cellie," Ana. And later on, I met women who had been in the SHU for *months.* I cannot convey how horrific an experience this would be. Do not be so arrogant as to think you can imagine what it feels like. You cannot.

The severity of isolation is unimaginable. It is so severe that it should be prohibited except in the most extreme of situations. Amnesty International and Human Rights Watch correctly label isolation over fourteen days as torture, and I would argue anything over two days. Fluorescent lights turn on at 6 a.m. sharp, even though all you want to do is sleep away as much time as possible. The empty day stretches ahead, not hour by hour, but minute by endless minute.

How bad is isolation? Consider the following social experiment by Mr. Beast.

Mr. Beast, who has 221 million subscribers on YouTube and 25 million followers on X (Twitter), offered a random person $10,000 for every day he could last—alone—in a well-stocked giant supermarket. Alex, the random person selected, grilled a steak on one of the store's barbecues his first night in isolation and said he'd easily be able to last for years. One year would earn Alex $3.65 million.

By day ten, Alex was already on shaky ground, and he downward revised his goal to 100 days, hoping to earn $1 million. On day twenty-one, Alex downward revised his goal again, this time aiming to last fifty days, to earn $500,000. On day thirty-four, Alex turned destructive. On day forty-five, Alex was just acting in a repetitive fashion, and when asked how much longer he could hold out, he said he didn't think he could make it even one more hour.

Mr. Beast suggested that he try to last five more days, to make a total of fifty days and a half a million dollars. To which Alex said: "It's not worth staying, and I'm leaving." And he walked out.

This is a remarkable social experiment. Alex was in a well-stocked and very large supermarket; he could cook whatever and whenever he liked; he had a normal bathroom; he chose to be there; he knew he could leave anytime; he could use anything the store sold, including an aboveground pool he assembled and used; he had visitors; he had a productive job to do; and he was earning $10,000 a day. He also had no sadistic guards tormenting him multiple times per day. Essentially had a really good physical setup, but no friends, family, or work that provided a greater sense of purpose and attachment. Prior to starting, he believed he could do "years," but when actually enduring the experiment, could only last forty-five days. If interested in this very public social experiment, watch the whole video (linked here for e-readers with the URL in the notes for all readers).[6] In the video, you can see the deterioration of a human being due to loneliness.

In comparison, the solitary cell I was in was a six-by-ten concrete closet that was totally barren. That is about the size of a parking space.

The United Nations calls solitary confinement torture and to be used only in very exceptional circumstances, as a last resort only, and for as short a time as possible. The (US) Bureau of Prisons technically agrees—official BOP policy states that the SHU is to be used rarely and only when necessary for "security." The reality on the ground, though, is vastly different.

It's really not known how many men and women are being held in isolation in United States prisons and jails right now.[7] Estimates range from 50,000 in the federal prison system to 130,000, including jails. Even a short amount of time in solitary is linked to severe psychological problems. Isolation is not linked to reduced violence or recidivism, which is also why the BOP pays lip service to not using it. In May 2022, Biden pledged to "end the practice of solitary confinement with very limited exceptions."[8] Call me cynical, but the numbers have gone up 7 to 11 percent during Biden's tenure. Johnny Perez, the director of the US prisons program at the nonprofit National Religious Campaign Against Torture[9] said: "It is beyond disappointing that despite President Biden's and Vice President Harris's pledge to end solitary confinement, this administration has doubled down on the use of this torturous practice."[10]

The whole time I was in the SHU, I never knew when I would be let out. No one tells the prisoners anything, but by yelling with other prisoners in other cells in the SHU, I learned that "quarantine" could be seven days, ten days, fourteen days, twenty-one days, or months. It sounds "short" to the reader, but each minute is intolerable during the ordeal.

On my eighth day in prison, the guard screamed my name and ordered me to face the wall (back to him) and crouch down and put my hands in the slot in the door so he could handcuff me. Then he unlocked the door and I stepped into the outer room where he shackled my ankles. He told me to bring my "things" (blanket, towel, and mail I had received). I couldn't tell if this request was serious or a joke because he had just handcuffed me. He was serious.

So there I was, with my hands cuffed behind my back, clutching my blanket and papers, shackled at the ankles, walking to who knew where. As I walked through the outer room, I was shocked to see two bookcases of books, not twenty feet from my cell. That moment is seared into my memory and conscience.

Whiling Away the Hours

I want to stress that where I was, FDC Miami, I did *not* feel at physical (security) risk. I think this was the positive side of being at a maximum security facility. The guards took assault very seriously, and the women knew that any hint of conflict would send them to the SHU. So if a person kept to herself and avoided any interpersonal negative experience, other prisoners generally did not bother her.

I had steeled myself for the fact that prison was going to be exceedingly boring, and I had goals for myself. I set out to interview every woman who would talk to me, which turned out to be nearly everyone. It was an opportunity I was not going to miss. Much like being an emergency physician, in prison I met people from every walk of life.

Among the white prisoners there was a doctor, two lawyers, a paralegal, a marketing consultant, a mortgage banker, a small business owner, a housewife, an artist, and women involved in prostitution and sex trafficking. Among the Spanish prisoners there was a member of the El Chapo family, a government consultant, and many on drug trafficking charges. Almost every black prisoner had a more severe backstory and was there for drug dealing, sex trafficking, or a prostitution-related crime.

We were locked in our cells 50 percent of the day: 9:30 p.m. to 6:30 a.m., 10 to 11 a.m., and 3:30 to 5:30 p.m. I used that to set a schedule for myself. I ignored the 6:30 a.m. bells and tried to stay "in bed" until almost 8 a.m. when an inspection might be called. Inspection was very strict. My cellie and I were both very neat, but inspection was an impossible task: We were not allowed to have anything on the counter, not even the hand towel or soap.

The guards throw out people's personal belongings and remove anything "extra," like a second "mattress" or blanket. Of course, many women went to very extreme and creative lengths to hide things they wanted to keep. It was a game of cat and mouse, but ultimately, it was pointless. I never broke any rules. It would never have been worth it to me to get into trouble. Unfortunately, that also meant I was very cold most of the time (no extra blanket) and had no pillow. Prisons are kept cold as a form of environmental control and thought to keep prisoners calmer.

Suffocation of the Soul

As I learned firsthand, most federal inmates are not individuals who committed violent or easily identifiable offenses, but those who breached government regulations. There were essentially two categories of women at FDC Miami: women caught with drugs or money or prostitution (often erroneously overcharged as sex trafficking) and white-collar women. The overwhelming majority of the latter were accused of a healthcare fraud kickback scheme. This was incredibly eye-opening to me and a huge warning to anyone who works in the healthcare space. What I am about to relate is extremely alarming, and I heard variations of this story a dozen times.

If a doctor's office accepts Medicare or Medicaid, the FBI and DOJ can look over their shoulder, and if there is any kind of fraud—intentional, accidental, or merely suspected—the doctor and his staff are going to prison. The reason I found this so alarming is because it was nothing like I would have expected. One woman was a front desk clerk in a doctor's office where everyone was charged and took pleas. In another case the DOJ/FBI pursued a doctor for five years, but then charged his seventy-year-old wife who took a plea. There was a marketing consultant who was charged with a kickback scheme, but still doesn't know what she supposedly did wrong. She had decided she would never work in healthcare again. In prison she was reading books on homebuilding as she decided she would become a contractor upon her release.

To clarify how aggressive the healthcare kickback example is: If Medicare or Medicaid funds laboratory tests and the laboratory sends a $20 referral fee to a doctor's office, anyone who handles the paperwork could be imprisoned for five years per charge.[11] The problem is that since the government has a nearly 100 percent conviction rate, an accusation is all that is needed—and the threat itself convinces people to plead and give up other people—guilty or not.

There's actually a lot more to the kickback law and to other regulations adding to the quickly growing list of federal crimes.[12] The Heritage Foundation says that no one even knows how many federal crimes have been created.

> [Once there were] fewer than a dozen common law felonies, and all those crimes stemmed from and mirrored a commonly-shared moral code [but] no one even knows how many federal criminal laws there are [today], much less what they require. The last time the Congressional Research Service was asked to quantify the number of federal crimes, it told Congress that it could not do so with any certainty . . .
>
> . . . federal crimes are scattered across almost all of the 51 titles of the [U.S.] Code, making it effectively impossible for an average

> citizen to find them all . . . One expert, Professor John Coffee of Columbia Law School, has estimated that there are more than 300,000 separate federal regulations that might be the basis for a criminal prosecution.[13]

Just how big of a problem is it to have three hundred thousand potential crimes to carefully navigate at home, at work, and in between? Depends on who is asking.

Three Felonies a Day

When it comes to an act prohibited by the Bible, like murder, determining who to prosecute is typically straightforward: follow the evidence to find the killer. When it comes to so-called victimless crimes, however, nearly everyone has violated some regulation at one time or another, giving law enforcement agents and prosecutors a lot of discretion in choosing who to prosecute. That decision often means following the path of least resistance—preferring defendants who are poor, have previous records, or are on probation. That describes the vast majority of the women I was in prison with. It seems quite easy to wind up there.

In *Three Felonies a Day: How the Feds Target the Innocent*, Harvard Law School lecturer Harvey Silverglate explains how the explosion in the number of acts outlawed by federal statute makes it possible for the government to prosecute just about anyone:

> The average professional in this country wakes up in the morning, goes to work, comes home, eats dinner, and then goes to sleep, unaware that he or she has likely committed several federal crimes that day . . .[14]

Most assuredly, the poor aren't the only ones at risk of being targeted by the government. With three hundred thousand options to choose from, prosecutors can easily target political or business opponents if desired. As Silverglate notes:

> . . . federal criminal laws have become dangerously disconnected from the English common law tradition . . . prosecutors can pin arguable federal crimes on any one of us, for even the most seemingly innocuous behavior.[15]

A Case of Mistaken Priority

When the FBI reassigns a large quantity of agents from child pornography, rape, or theft investigations to create elite teams for hunting and raiding protesters accused of misdemeanor trespassing, those FBI agents are not *replaced.* The child abuse and other violent crimes continue unrestrained, and the word gets out that it's easier and easier to get away with those "victim crimes."

We are typically a few years behind the supposedly more "progressive" (i.e. "woke") nations of Canada and numerous European countries, where officers are often removed from violent crime investigations in order to surf the Internet and interrogate citizens about Facebook posts supporting Freedom Convoys[16] and tweets criticizing "gender reassignment"[17] surgery for minors or "misgendering"[18] others. This shift in priorities has led to a prosecution rate for rapes of about 0.3 percent,[19] just one example of a crime that has lost its criminal deterrence for potential attackers.

Steve Friend, a SWAT team member with the FBI for twelve years, refused to remain silent as the FBI shifted even more dramatically into prosecuting alleged crimes against the government while neglecting very real crimes against children and other victims.[20]

Journalist Miranda Devine summed up her disturbing conversation with the whistleblower:

> He just could not live with his conscience after he was dragged off these very important child porn, child exploitation, and human trafficking investigations he was working on, and put on the very bogus January 6 cases he has been working on . . . He could see from the ground how the FBI Washington DC Field Office was manipulating these cases to try and expand and pretend the problem was bigger than it was. And he also didn't want to participate

House Judiciary GOP
@JudiciaryGOP · Follow
#BREAKING: New whistleblower information reveals that the FBI is moving agents off of child sexual abuse investigations to instead pursue political investigations.
The whistleblower recounted being told that "child sexual abuse investigations were no longer an FBI priority."
Congress of the United States
House of Representatives
3:31 AM · Sep 20, 2022

> in SWAT raids on people who were being accused of misdemeanors at worst . . . Steve Friend stood up and said, "I will not do this."[21]

I am wiser for having had firsthand experience with the fraud that is the federal BOP. It is as broken as every other federal bureaucracy: It exists to feed itself; and, along the way, it promotes staff who dehumanize the people they preside over.

CHAPTER FOURTEEN

Tales of Injustice

Justice, justice you shall pursue . . .

—Deuteronomy 16:20

While the modern legal system has prisons at the core of its establishment, the Torah never features prison as a form of punishment, even as a deterrent . . . The idea of locking someone up is antithetical to the nature of humanity. According to the Torah, a person was put on this earth for a purpose. Withholding one's ability to achieve that purpose is the most inhumane treatment he can possibly suffer. We're responsible to make sure that criminals are helped in their lives, rehabilitating them to a productive life in a moral and just society. We must ensure that prison acts not just as a punishment, but as an opportunity for positive growth.

—Rabbi Menachem Schneerson, The Lubavitcher Rebbe

At FDC Miami we were locked in our cells 50 percent of each day. The cells were on the perimeter of the general area and on two levels, one level slightly above and one level slightly below. The common area is most similar in appearance to a school gym, perhaps thirty feet wide and seventy feet long. There were perhaps thirty steel tables/benches bolted to the floor in the common area.

There was nothing to do all day, and I mean absolutely nothing. FDC Miami is an administrative facility, more transitory than most prisons, which was the reason I was given for its lack of programming. In the past they did have substantial programming, so I'm not sure why there isn't any now. Women who were assigned to FDC Miami for an extended period worked either in the laundry or kitchen for a few hours a day. But most of the women at FDC Miami did absolutely nothing productive. I had read some books about adapting to prison life, so I knew the importance of having a plan. My plan was focused on finding value or purpose to this experience.

If you don't accomplish anything in life, you won't have happiness or inner peace. My goal for my time in prison was to interview as many women as possible to better understand our federal prison system.

It seemed to me about 25 percent of the women were incarcerated for some kind of business violation "fraud," often when they were working for businesses owned by their husbands. About 50 percent were for drug-related crimes. And about 25 percent were in for some sex-related activities—surprisingly, sex trafficking and not mere prostitution.

I met most of the sixty or so women who ended up with me in FDC Miami. The women all seemed to have a sentence that simply didn't match their crime. Some were in for fifteen years, some for twenty-five, as if they were the ringleaders of criminal conspiracies. It should have been obvious to any judge that they were far from the masterminds of their crimes. Most had received little or no profit from their infractions, and many had this fact acknowledged by their trial judge.

So many seemed to be overcharged: The elevated "human trafficking" designation instead of the more accurate "aiding prostitution" was one very common example. Conspiracy to traffic drugs instead of drug possession. Conspiracy to commit fraud when the government couldn't prove fraud. The overcharging by the prosecutors is so aggressive that virtually everyone takes a plea, as I had recently learned myself.

I want to add that I did *not* do additional research to verify the truth of these stories. The stories I relate are to demonstrate prosecutorial processes and misconduct, not to plead innocence on behalf of these prisoners. We need a system that is fair.

Inchoate Crimes

As far back as law school, I was very concerned about what are called "inchoate" crimes. Inchoate, which is pronounced "in-KO-eight," means something being started but not completed. So an inchoate offense is an additional crime that you can be charged with if you take a step toward the commission of another actual/completed ("target") crime. It is very easy to see how this can be severely abused.

Let us imagine a man conspiring with two friends to rob a bank, and their plan includes several steps such as driving a car to the bank, buying a toy gun, wrapping duct tape over the teller's mouth, taking the money, and driving off.

- If this crime actually occurs, the man and his friends can be charged with the target offense, which is *bank robbery*.
- If this crime partially occurs (i.e., they start the process but it's foiled), the man and his friends can be charged with the target offense, which is *attempted bank robbery*.
- If this crime never occurs (i.e., the man and his friends only talk about it and buy a toy gun), the man and his friends can be charged with the inchoate crime of *conspiracy to bank robbery* (because they conspired *and* took the step of buying a toy gun).

But *in addition*—

- If this crime actually occurs and the man's wife bought duct tape, in addition to the man and his friends being charged with the target offense of bank robbery, the wife also can be charged with the *inchoate crime of conspiracy* to bank robbery.
- If this crime partially occurs and the man's wife bought duct tape, in addition to the man and his friends being charged with the target offense of attempted bank robbery, the wife also can be charged with the *inchoate crime of conspiracy* to attempted bank robbery.
- If this crime never occurs and the man's wife bought duct tape, in addition to the man and his friends being charged with the

inchoate crime of conspiracy to commit bank robbery, the wife also can be equally charged with the *inchoate crime of conspiracy* to bank robbery.

You commit an inchoate crime if you take a meaningful step toward the commission of another crime. Buying the duct tape is the meaningful step. If she is charged, it will become the wife's obligation to prove her innocence.[1] She will have to prove she did not know about the bank robbery, attempted bank robbery, or the conspiracy to rob the bank.

It is very hard to prove that you *didn't* know something. ("I don't have proof that I *didn't* know my husband was planning that bank robbery.")

It is even harder to prove that you *didn't* know something about something that didn't actually happen. ("I don't have proof that I *didn't* know my husband was planning a bank robbery that didn't actually happen.")

But all these charges would be valid the way the law is written right now. The above examples were from my law school class in criminal procedure at Stanford Law School. Even twenty-five years ago, this bothered me. I remember raising my hand and asking, "What if the mom bought duct tape for their child's school project? Would she still be guilty?"

The criminal law professor corrected my question, as follows. "I can't say if she would be *found* guilty or not guilty in court. But she would be charged, unless the prosecutor *chose* not to charge her. He has enough evidence to charge her."

Using "inchoate offenses," many additional people—both innocent and guilty—can be indicted and then used as pawns against other defendants. If there was a crime that included duct tape, in a system where the prosecution virtually always wins, the prosecution doesn't have to prove *anything* but that the additional person bought duct tape.

The three basic inchoate offenses are conspiracy, attempt, and solicitation. The actual intended crime is referred to as the target offense.

Conspiracy Charges

We can easily see that inchoate crimes are fraught with abuse potential. Certainly there can be a role for these types of charges in sophisticated, complicated criminal enterprises where evidence and proof is multifactorial and multilayered. But I was stunned at how often our federal prosecutors are relying on inchoate (incomplete) crimes instead of actual (complete) crimes. Obviously, our prisons should not be filled with people incarcerated for incomplete crimes! Inchoate convictions should be the exception. I realize my experience is skewed because indictments for inchoate crimes are surely more prevalent among women than men. But still, the large majority of female prisoners were there for an inchoate offense.

To me, in law school, being genuinely guilty of an inchoate offense implied a certain level of . . . sophistication. Planning, thought, skill. If there was an *action* that led to a crime, I assumed prosecutors were charging the actual crime (the target offense), not the inchoate crime. I don't know the statistics when I was in law school twenty-five years ago, but in the summer of 2022 at a federal prison in Miami, women being incarcerated for inchoate offenses were the majority, and they appeared to be charged thusly to enhance the severity of the actual action that the person had taken.

For example, obviously a lot of the women were mixed up in drugs and sex. Overwhelmingly this was personal drug use, smaller amounts of drug possession, and consensual sex traded for something else (money, drugs, housing, friendship). Even though it's excessive by my standards (I'm mostly libertarian when it comes to personal freedom), I can concur with society charging drug possession and even prostitution in these cases. I think it's heavy-handed and not ideal, but I don't think it's evil.

I interviewed almost all of the sixty women, and here are some of their stories. These low-level acts were so often overcharged as much harsher crimes that it cannot be a coincidence. Instead of prostitution, aiding prostitution, drug use, drug possession, etc., these acts were charged as conspiracy to traffic drugs, conspiracy to traffic sex, conspiracy to traffic minors for sex, attempt to traffic drugs, etc. The twin existence of hundreds of thousands of federal statutes and an enormous prosecutorial machine that routinely overcharges is antithetical to a free society. (If you are wondering why this happens, keep reading.)

Conspiracy to Traffic Drugs

"Christina" was a twenty-three-year-old girl with an extraordinarily short attention span and drug problems. I had been in the general population for about two weeks when she was brought in. She was jittery, constantly looking around, had a hard time focusing, and her natural way of interacting with everyone—me included—was to open every door to offering sexual favors in exchange for something she wanted. I found her friendly nature to be both endearing and sad. She clearly needed a good mom more than anything. She approached me because she wanted advice and/or assistance as to her legal situation. (No one knew I was a lawyer, but I was known to be educated.)

This young girl had just been sentenced to twenty-five *years*. She told me this almost offhandedly, practically as soon as she sat down. It was such a shock to hear. *Twenty-five years?* How could our government have thought this girl needed to be locked up for twenty-five years? Law-abiding people just assume that if a judge proclaims "twenty-five years' incarceration," surely that person must be one of the most threatening persons we could possibly encounter in our whole lives. But all I could think about while she prattled on about the details of her case was: Is our government completely crazy?

Well, young Jedi, if there is one thing I would like to impress upon the reader, it is that all of us average law-abiding American citizens have been hoodwinked by federal agencies who are doing what they must to guarantee the continuation of massive and lengthy incarceration to maintain their large budgets. I saw too many examples of this to believe otherwise.

As I listened, I learned about a weird set of circumstances in which the federal agent on Christina's case was himself recently arrested and convicted of fraud. (I did verify that upon my release.) That fact may (ironically) assist her at her appeal. But mostly I was stunned that this girl, who is not mentally capable of masterminding anything, was sentenced to a quarter century in prison. She was a high school dropout at age fifteen, pregnant at seventeen, assaulted by her boyfriend while five months pregnant, lost the pregnancy, and fell into drug abuse. No father, no high school education, early sex and drugs . . . no chance.

I was an ER doctor for a long time. This girl was indistinguishable from so many of my patients. She was young, addicted to drugs, and at this age/stage, making terrible life choices. How did she get twenty-five years? The government succeeded in getting her to accept a plea for *conspiracy to traffic* drugs. I found this astonishing. Whatever she did, and I'm certain she did a lot of illegal things including using drugs and buying and selling some quantities of drugs and prostituting herself to support this, it is surely disproportionate to the boasting of the US Attorney's Office that they apprehended another "drug trafficker." She should have never been charged so aggressively. Shame on our US prosecutors. She is a mixed-up girl-junkie with a sad backstory while all the rest of us watch the news at home, secure that our "United States Government Is Keeping Us Safe From Serious Criminals Who Are Conspiring To Traffic Drugs."

Of course, it's necessary to punish and deter negative behavior in order to uphold society. But the punishment must be fair and proportional. Prosecutors have an ethical responsibility to abstain from unjustified overcharging and dishonest tactics, and that has vanished. Whatever you practice, you will become; and what I had witnessed in hospitals and now in the justice system was the constant practice of cruelty and corruption.

Conspiracy to Sex Trafficking

Many of these women's stories are so similar, I'll relate them as one story. I met "Lavonne" when she was first incarcerated at age eighteen. I also met "Lavonne" when she was twenty-one. I also met "Lavonne" after she had been inside for eight years at age thirty-eight. "Lavonne" personifies everything that could go wrong for a girl.

Starting when Lavonne was eight, she was repeatedly sexually assaulted, first by her mother's boyfriend, then at age eleven by her older stepbrother. By the time she was thirteen, she figured out that she could get favors and clothes/money for sex. She dropped out of school at thirteen and a half when her stepbrother got her pregnant, and he paid for her first abortion. She had her first boyfriend (the reader would call this person a pimp) at age fifteen, and she thinks he was about twenty. She has no expectation of monogamy or contraception. She has had four abortions so far. She's had chlamydia twice, doesn't know if she has herpes, and tested negative for AIDS when she was incarcerated.

She was having sex with her boyfriend/pimp whenever he wanted, and about twice a week she would also have sex with his friends as a favor for her boyfriend who would buy her things. One day, when she was sixteen, her boyfriend wanted to also have sex with her friend, and she thought that was "cool." The friends decided among themselves that Lavonne was the "real" girlfriend but that her friend would have sex with Lavonne's boyfriend to also get some clothes. Lavonne giggled hysterically at telling me this "scam" they did on her "boyfriend." Her friend was fifteen at the time. Lavonne did this two other times; one friend was also fifteen, the other friend was sixteen.

When Lavonne was incarcerated at age eighteen, it was for "conspiracy to traffic minors for sex." (She had been arrested as a minor, too.) She had not been given a long sentence as the judge (properly) also considered her a victim. However, why was she charged with "conspiracy to sex traffic" at all? Why was she not simply charged with . . . nothing? Prostitution?

The Lavonne I met at age thirty-eight had grown up in the foster system as a child, had been sexually abused throughout her teens, was a high school dropout, had multiple abortions, had two children with two baby daddies, and had been incarcerated about eight years for solicitation for prostitution and conspiracy to sex traffic. Like the younger Lavonne, older Lavonne just was further along. She, too, brought in friends who traded sex for money and/or favors. The people Lavonne brought in were neighbors or friends, local adult women, and there was no allegation of force or youth. Because she had been arrested (and incarcerated) multiple times in the past, this time Lavonne was sentenced to ten years.

Another Lavonne was a pretty, slender twenty-one-year-old foster child graduate to prostitute who was no longer young enough to satisfy predatorial appetites, who, in conversation with me, did not seem to understand that she was being used to provide her pimp with younger girls. She herself had been sexually abused as a preteen and sexually active by age twelve. She related, "That guy took me and my fren' to live at his house." She said, "He don't even want sex or nuthin'." She then related her crime: She brought fourteen- and fifteen-year-old girls to the pimp and other clients. It's like she thought she was higher on the totem pole (at age twenty-one) and not even eligible herself anymore to be pimped out. This was a *promotion* that the younger girls can expect one day. Depravity now seems to be so pervasive that today's men generally don't even want pretty prostitutes in their twenties. Customers want fourteen- and fifteen-year-old girls. From what all these women said, that is becoming the norm. It's deeply disturbing.

Many of the women serving time for these "trafficking" offenses did not seem overly bothered by their move from the pimp's home to prison. (Most of them had long moved from their natal home to foster care or couch surfing.) Of course, that's my subjective observation, but they are more or less cheerful, treating prison a bit like a dorm. I was also surprised at how *local* the sex trafficking convicted prisoners were. These are not girls or women trafficking illegal aliens; they are American girls in their teens or very early twenties inviting in their American friends and neighbors who are one to four years younger than they are.

Before prison, I would never have thought our country felt the need to lock people away for a decade based upon these types of actions. I am not condoning their actions. But . . . whatever happened to the crime of prostitution? It seems to have been supplanted by "sex trafficking, a twenty-year felony.

Another woman was inside because she took a plea for "grooming a minor." Now this sounded serious to me. Lavonne was thirty-eight and said that she had a "boyfriend" (she knew he was a pimp). One day, he asked her to come to his apartment to braid someone's hair. She says the girl whose hair she was braiding looked to her to be sixteen or seventeen and was six months pregnant. Her exact words to me were, "She be f*cking already. She be sixteen or seventeen."

I'm not excusing what would have been obvious to Lavonne if she were innocent (i.e., why should a bachelor have an unrelated young pregnant teen in his home who needed her hair braided?). But here's the rest of the story: Her sentence was eighteen years, and the man's sentence was four years.

Even if she was conning me and eliminating critical details of her complicity, what was obvious to *anyone* who met this woman was that she was no mastermind. Wearing my physician hat, I would have called this woman mildly or moderately mentally retarded. I doubt her IQ reached eighty. She was . . . slow. She was obviously a minor player in someone else's trafficking scheme. It is simply *not possible* that a prosecutor could have thought she was clever enough to pull off any scheme at all. She could not have masterminded her way out of a paper bag. But the rest of us watch the news at home, secure that our United States Government Is Keeping Us Safe From Serious Criminals Who Are Conspiring To Human Trafficking.

These convicted women were also, without exception, prostituting themselves. They were so dysfunctional that they willingly attached themselves to a predator who took them under his wing and provided them with a home, a social group, and clients. As the women age, the predator stops offering clients and instead grooms them to invite younger girls into the "family." The predators themselves even stop touching these women when they become too "old." The shocking part was how old was "too old": about age twenty. The other shocking part was how typically the feds charge these dysfunctional women as sex traffickers.

It sounds to those of us watching the news that these prisoners kidnapped young immigrant girls and held them in a back room somewhere. Without excusing what they *were* doing, it wasn't *that*. They were, without exception, recruiting their friends or neighbors who were already sexually active and many already engaged in prostitution to work for a new boss. No coercion. The recruited women came and went whenever they pleased.

In my career in medicine, there is a common phrase: "buffing the chart." Buffing the (medical) chart means the physician adds a narrative, comments, details into the patient's chart that make the physician look "good" in case of a future lawsuit, a future complaint, an irate patient or administrator, etc. Resident physicians would say to each other: "Did you buff the chart?" Or "Don't worry about it, I buffed the chart."

I think the same thing is happening here. I don't necessarily think career prosecutors hate people like Lavonne. Rather, I think they are overcharging because it helps their own careers. They write on their résumé that they convicted a child sex trafficker . . . wow! Impressive! They are "buffing" their own career chart.

But here's the difference. In medicine, I never saw *lies* in the chart; it was just tedious padding. In today's legal environment, the prosecutors are lying. I suspect vertical overcharging has become so habitual, most don't even recognize their own lies.

Conspiracy to Commit Fraud: Another View of Our Broken "Healthcare" System

In the prison, there were many examples of "conspiracy to commit fraud," and every single example I encountered was in the healthcare space. This is an alarming warning for any doctor or mere office staff who chooses to work with government payors or insurance. When the government sets its sights on you as a person or business who has committed fraud, but is unable to *prove* actual fraud, it does not accept defeat. Ultimately, the government will still indict you or your loved one on the inchoate crime "conspiracy to commit fraud."

The prosecution's focus is to chase the next person and the next one and the next; but also to jail the low-level participants along the way. This is the part I didn't realize. It seems credible that various people indicted in these criminal conspiracies are indeed cutting corners in their jobs or businesses, but the government then spins a tale that portrays each individual as far more involved and nefarious than they actually are. US Attorney Offices issue provocative statements about uncovering large criminal enterprises, when many involved are just overhearing things or otherwise implicated in petty acts.

One prisoner was a consultant who helped business people who were seeking licenses to operate "medical equipment" companies. Like everything in healthcare, there's a lot of details and paperwork, so her business helped with the setup. One business she worked with also had a marketing company and, apparently, both the marketing company and the business were allegedly doing things that would violate anti-kickback laws. This consultant was charged with *conspiracy to commit healthcare fraud* together with the owner, the owner's marketing person, and many others.

She says she accepted a plea deal because they confiscated all her money and threatened to also indict her young adult son who worked at her business unless she testified using evidence they handed her. During this conversation they slid her a picture of her son on the desk and told her to "think about" what she had said that day. They then said they would meet with her again the next day to see if she "remembered anything" additional about her client. She was bankrupted, took a plea deal, and has a twenty-eight-month sentence. While I cannot verify the facts, her story was consistent with others I heard, and I also personally witnessed severe mistreatment of this particular prisoner by the DOJ while she was in prison.

There were many stories like this. There was the forty-eight-year-old mother of five who was a minimum-wage office worker at a doctor's office when the whole office was indicted. She doesn't even know what they all supposedly did wrong, but her job was answering the phone, making appointments, and checking patients out. She took a plea deal for *conspiracy to commit healthcare fraud* and has a fourteen-month sentence.

There was the seventy-year-old wife of an orthopedist whose husband was investigated for Medicare fraud for five years but whom the government ultimately could not find sufficient evidence to charge. The government finally charged the wife instead with *conspiracy to commit healthcare fraud,* which is a lesser inchoate offense. I would say this was a made-up offense when the government was frustrated it couldn't get its pound of flesh on the doctor. She took a plea deal and has a one-year sentence.

There was the back office worker at a doctor's office who didn't know it was illegal to refer patients to a radiology center partially owned by her boss. She claimed she also didn't know her boss was even a partial owner of the radiation center. Whether that is true or false, she certainly made no money on this as her job was to fill out the forms. She was charged with *conspiracy to commit healthcare fraud.* She took a plea deal and has a sixteen-month sentence.

Double Jeopardy

The legal concept of double jeopardy[2] is that a person cannot be punished twice for the same crime. This is black-letter law in the United States, and everyone instinctively understands this concept to be a matter of basic fairness. Well, it turns out, the double jeopardy prohibition does *not* apply if the time you served was for the same actions but resulted in another charge in another country.

FDC Miami had many incarcerated women from South America. "Sylvia" was in her thirties, a mother of two preteens, and had an accounting background. She more or less admitted to me to "doing the books" for many narcotic transactions for the El Chapo family. She served seven years in a Colombian prison for money laundering (which she says was *much* better than FDC Miami, wow). She was free for about two weeks when she was arrested, this time by US federal agents.

Let me be perfectly clear that I do not pretend to know the facts about these issues or this case. All I can attest to is what I heard from her and then verified with two women in prison who knew her: She was either an accountant or a comptroller (I could not understand the translation); she had formerly worked for a large international company in that capacity; she has two preteen children; she served seven years in a Colombian prison for money laundering; and she was out two to three weeks when she was arrested at her home by US federal agents and flown to FDC Miami.

Here's my problem with this. I accept that her crimes almost certainly affected people in America. I'm an ER doctor. I know we have a huge narcotics problem in this country and that the narcotics are typically from elsewhere. But she wasn't arrested for a new crime. (She wasn't out long enough.) She wasn't arrested in America. She was arrested for the same crime, for which she had served seven years, while in her home country of Columbia.

Our American government is barred by law from doing this to an American. I never considered that our government might be doing this to other people just because they *could.* I thought we Americans don't do "double jeopardy" because we all collectively know it is *wrong.*

Turns out: I was the one who was wrong.

Diamond in the Rough

I cannot finish describing my prison experience without mentioning "Tara." I noticed Tara immediately out of all the women there. She stood out because she was disciplined. She kept to a routine, mostly to herself, yet she was cordial toward others. With striking blue eyes and rather amazing dreadlocks, she dressed neatly in her work uniform, which she ironed each morning, and went to her designated work area. When she was in the common area after work, she brought all the workout gear she needed to an open area (the closest thing we had to an "outdoors'") and exercised for about forty-five minutes, then returned all the gear, showered, re-dressed, and went to her cell to read. Occasionally, she'd come out and sit at the common tables and read there. She clearly had been there a while; I assumed a year or two. She was the only one in a prison work uniform who did not idle away her time just gossiping with others, playing cards, and so forth.

Then I learned that she had already served ten years of a fifteen-year sentence. Incredible. I observed her for a few weeks until one day we chatted in the common area. I learned enough from her to write an entire book on prison reform. In short, the recurring problem of prosecutors' overcharging is exacerbated by judges seeking to boost their tough-on-crime reputations by giving out multi-decade sentences for nonviolent crimes without a crystal ball to know which inmates might turn their life around at some point during incarceration. Even if the judge is right eight or nine times out of ten about someone, that still leaves many human beings who are truly rehabilitated languishing in prison, and this is an unacceptably high rate of error.

If I could unilaterally change something about the DOJ/BOP system, it would be to eliminate, in almost all cases, the possibility of decade-plus sentences. The other thing would be to offer every inmate at some point in the first few years of their sentence (depending upon its length) the opportunity to switch to an "earning freedom track," like a ladder to climb. I believe a third to a quarter would still choose to stay on the "standard track." It's easier, and after being institutionalized, many have no motivation beyond watching TV all day. But for those who wish to become people capable of living freely without harming others and are willing to take an opportunity to prove themselves, of course there should be a track to do so. At the end of that track, we could measure what the person had accomplished. Tara engaged in just such a self-improvement effort without any external incentive.

Tara is the poster child for everything that could go wrong. She dropped out of school in the seventh grade and suffered many serious family issues, including her dad's early death and feelings of abandonment by her mother. She had three children by three different men, with the third born when she was twenty-two, about four months before her conviction. That baby daddy ran a small prostitution ring. Feeling insecure, she says she preferred to join him in his business rather than have him go off in that world without her (she readily admits that she was driven to this poor decision by her own jealousy and does not blame others for that mistake). In the end, her involvement in her third baby daddy's business meant that when two women working for him were revealed to be fifteen and sixteen, she was charged together with him for sex trafficking.

Tara admitted to not checking their IDs, but thought that, if anything, they were aggressive and controlling toward her, not the other way around. In the end, she says that these two girls were so rude and nasty in court while acting as government witnesses against her that the judge had to threaten both women (the alleged *victims* of trafficking) with contempt. If the term "trafficking" makes anyone think of a kidnapped American like Elizabeth Smart or Guatemalan girls snatched from their hometowns and sold into the sex trade, this wasn't that. In the absence of force or coercion, the conviction was based solely on age, a statutory crime. But in Tara's world, girls had consensual sex when they were thirteen, babies when they were fourteen, several baby daddies, and these two girls were living the same life she was living, sexually active long before she met them. I can't imagine that at that time Tara even understood that age fifteen and sixteen is not an age to have sex. Tara herself had a two-year-old son by the time she was fifteen.

With Tara's traumatic childhood and a long sentence in front of her, checking out would make sense. But she turned things around. She saw what a great job her mother was doing raising her three children and became very humble and grateful for all of her help and support, repairing a great deal of the damage from her childhood. She even began to thank God for watching over her family. Though raised in the "Bible Belt," she converted to Islam in prison, being drawn to the frequency and routine of prayer and the rituals like handwashing before prayer. She did not explain it using those exact terms, but that was the attraction for her.

So this seventh-grade dropout, with three kids by three different men, is now a peaceful, humble, grateful woman who covers her hair when she leaves the unit, irons her uniform, reads, studies, avoids trouble, thanks her mother often, and stays in close contact on a regular phone schedule with her three children (her oldest is now in college). Tara earned a GED inside prison and took every class available to her—electrician, plumbing, carpentry, and culinary arts—until COVID lockdowns suspended everything.

Tara says she was angry for about five years, and she thinks around year six or seven is the point by which she was able to turn herself around. She thinks everything after eight years has been a total waste, and when I met her, she still had three more years to go.

I share Tara's story to underscore the actions of judges and prosecutors. First, judges do not have crystal balls, and they simply cannot predict the future. For this reason alone, I am strongly opposed to long sentences. Second, her story shines a spotlight on the very ordinariness of DOJ corruption.

A quirk of Tara's specific case is that her codefendant was running this escort service in West Palm Beach in the early 2010s. Does this time and place ring any bells? Wasn't there a federal indictment of someone . . . famous . . . in a sex trafficking case . . . in West Palm Beach in the early 2000s? And didn't those federal sex trafficking charges just disappear, negotiated down to only a single state prostitution charge and a thirteen-month sentence?

In 2009, US federal prosecutors decided not to prosecute Jeffrey Epstein despite a fifty-plus page indictment and credible accusations from thirty to thirty-five women, including many minors.[3] Instead, federal prosecutors approved a one-year punishment on a single state solicitation charge that included Epstein being able to keep flying on his private plane. There was a lot of local outrage at the feds that kept increasing, as it was the beginning of the "me too" movement—and because Epstein kept engaging in the same heinous behavior. In April 2012, the local papers were filled with outrage that Epstein's one-year probation was ending.[4]

So, just a few months later, when the feds found a tiny (five to six people) local prostitution ring in West Palm Beach, which included two local and experienced fifteen- and sixteen-year-old girls who willingly consented, they pounced.

With just a little tweaking (otherwise known as vertical overcharging; see Chapter 8), this case was charged not as prostitution but sex trafficking. How fortuitous for the feds to conveniently be able to find this *different* "sex trafficking" case to bring before the same federal judge in the same jurisdiction where they had just entered into a secret "non-prosecution" agreement that angered everyone.[5] This case would provide an opportunity for the feds to appear "tough on child sex trafficking," and in that way, walk back the massive criticism over not prosecuting Epstein.

Never mind that in this completely unrelated case, the judge noted that Tara was a "vulnerable, undereducated, insecure, weak individual who had a troubled past, just like the victims, [was] used as a victim of prostitution [herself], and then used [by her codefendant] to perpetrate the crimes."

Never mind that in this completely unrelated case, the judge told Tara: "I don't think I'll ever see you again in my courtroom. I think the only mistake you made was one I see over and over again: You picked the wrong man."

The important point is that the judge sentenced Tara to fifteen years.

That is the important point, because what matters most in our current system is the prosecutor's *scorecard.* By sentencing Tara to fifteen years, the federal prosecutors improved their "tough-on-crime" scorecard that was badly tarnished by allowing the serial pedophile Epstein off.[6]

Perhaps it is too optimistic to hope that billionaires are treated like ordinary people. But we must demand that our federal prosecutors stop illegally overcharging ordinary defendants. Ordinary people have become pawns used by prosecutors to improve their own résumé. It's clear that the federal prosecutors overcharged Tara with sex trafficking instead of solicitation or aid to prostitution to snag a "tough-on-crime" notch on their conviction belt after choosing not to prosecute Epstein at all.

Epstein's attorneys had argued that the fact that the girls servicing Epstein were minors (age thirteen to fourteen) didn't matter. They argued that they were willing participants, they knew what they were doing, that they were prostitutes before they interacted with Epstein. Exactly Tara's case—except Tara wasn't the actual perp, Tara wasn't the mastermind, Tara herself was a victim, Tara's girls were only a few years younger than her at age sixteen, and Tara wasn't a billionaire who paid everyone off. The federal prosecutors let Epstein off and gave Tara fifteen years.

Many years later, the US prosecutor who cut or approved the corrupt deal, Alex Acosta, had to resign from his Cabinet position over his role in approving this miscarriage of justice. But what of Tara? She sits in prison still. Because what matters most in our current system is the prosecutor's *career.*

Concluding Remarks

There are countless stories inside prison just like this. I'm not sure what the solution is for an enormous and careless federal government—the Department of Justice (DOJ) and Bureau of Prisons (BOP)—steamrolling over its citizens with so little accountability. The system is far too big and far too powerful. Seemingly, no one can fight back in any meaningful way.

In *The Rational Bible: Exodus* (a great prison read, should you need one), Dennis Prager mentions that Norway adopted a maximum jail sentence of twenty-one years. I firmly support that, and actually, far less. I'm not saying some crimes don't deserve a more severe punishment. I'm saying *at the outset the judge cannot distinguish who might take an opportunity to truly turn their life around.* We are dealing with human souls; we cannot be so cavalier about it. When some years in prison are insufficient, capital punishment is entirely appropriate *and* likely more effective for society as a whole. Biblical law makes criminal punishment *immediate,* whether capital, corporeal, or financial:

> *And whoever does not fulfill the law of your God and the law of the king promptly—judgment shall be inflicted upon him; whether to be executed, uprooted, fined, or beaten.*
>
> —Ezra 7:26

The last leader of the Jewish Chabad movement, Grand Rabbi Menachem Schneerson, publicly opposed the prison system:

> . . . when one is incarcerated, we rescind his ability to act . . . The purpose of existence is to make an abode for Godliness in this world: "I was created solely to serve my Maker." If you lock a person behind bars, you restrict him from fulfilling his responsibility. You deny him the opportunity to fulfill his mission; you negate his reason for existence . . .[7]

The most important prison reform in many decades was the bipartisan First Step Act of 2018, enacted by President Trump.[8] The Aleph Institute, a division of the Jewish Chabad movement, tried to convince many Democrat and Republican presidents to enact the First Step Act, but it languished until Trump.[9] This act has meaningfully reduced the amount of time nonviolent prisoners spend in prison by offering them programming as a way to reduce time/recidivism. It has been very successful: Persons released early under the First Step Act have a recidivism rate of 12 percent compared to overall 43 percent within the BOP. In contrast, under Biden, there has not only been no prison reform, the number of prisoners being tortured in isolation, which does not reduce recidivism, has actually increased.

It must be noted, *especially* for atheists reading these words, that the people who work tirelessly to help the most vulnerable, such as prisoners, are almost always committed believers. This should not be attributed to coincidence. Of course there are righteous atheists, but believers know it is a violation of God's law to treat fellow humans so disgracefully.

When I met Tara, she was thirty-three and ten years into her fifteen-year sentence; clearly she should not have still been incarcerated. It's easy to see that now. But I submit that we are making the wrong decisions at the outset.

I put myself in the judge's shoes when I assessed girl-junkie Christina's twenty-five-year sentence at age twenty-three. As a fellow prisoner, Christina talked to me openly. She certainly needs institutionalization now. But it is not possible, yet, for *anyone* to know if she will turn out well like the minority (Tara) or if she will continue to be a mess. Because there is no crystal ball and the stakes are so high, twenty-five years is unjust.

CHAPTER FIFTEEN

Elephant in a Mousehole

To ensure that no infringement on the constitutional right to petition the Government for redress of grievances occurs in the enforcement of section 1512(c) . . . which among other things prohibits corruptly influencing any official proceeding, the executive branch shall construe the term "corruptly" in section 1512(c)(2) as requiring proof of a criminal state of mind on the part of the defendant.

—President George W. Bush, signing statement for the Sarbanes-Oxley Act in July 2002

Fischer v. United States

On June 28, 2024, the Supreme Court of the United States issued its first decision on a January 6 case. The case was about the twenty-year felony vertical overcharging of a J6 defendant and required the SCOTUS to give the correct interpretation of the text of a statute that the DOJ threw at hundreds of J6 defendants, including me.

The case, *Fischer v. United States,* is an individual appeal of a felony charge against Joseph Fischer for obstructing an official proceeding. The specific subsection in question, 18 USC §1512(c)(2), is titled "Tampering with a witness, victim, or an informant." This felony charge is listed within the "Corporate Fraud Accountability Act of 2002," which is a part of the larger Sarbanes-Oxley Act of 2002 (named after Congressmen Paul Sarbanes and Michael Oxley who sponsored the bill). The Sarbanes-Oxley

Act of 2002 is a United States federal law that mandates certain practices in financial recordkeeping and reporting for public corporations. It was enacted in response to major corporate and accounting scandals like Enron and WorldCom, with the aim of improving the accuracy and reliability of corporate disclosures. There is even an accounting phrase about this bill with the first letter of each name Sarbanes and Oxley: To be "SOX compliant," corporate executives must individually certify the accuracy of financial information. If you are scratching your head as to how this act applies to J6 defendants, you are not alone. When Congress passed this law, it went to great lengths to state that the statute was designed to increase the criminal penalty against industry giants committing high-level fraud. Congress said: "We must crack down on the corporate criminals and rebuild America's confidence in our markets . . . we must punish the corporate wrongdoers and punish them harshly."[1]

When passing the law, both the Legislative and Executive Branches expressly stated that the intent of the (c)(2) subsection was to indict corporate bad actors who obstructed justice by "shred[ding] tons of paper documents and electronic information." In fact, §1512(c)(2) is universally known as closing "the Arthur Andersen loophole." Indeed, for two decades and in thousands of cases, the government never used this statute against ordinary citizens in a political protest. Not once *until* January 6.

Since January 6, however, over 350 individual protesters and President Trump have been charged with §1512(c)(2) and other offenses in connection with their actions on that day. As a result of these charges, there have been over 150 convictions and guilty pleas. Including mine.

On January 6, Fischer attended the scheduled rally. Prosecutors say that his actions there included egging on rioters, making several inflammatory statements, and engaging in a physical encounter with a police officer. At 3:25 p.m., after the Capitol had already been breached and Congress had recessed, Fischer allegedly entered the building, remaining inside for just four minutes before exiting.

Following the incident, Fischer was charged with three counts: assaulting a police officer,[2] disorderly conduct in the Capitol, and obstruction of an official proceeding under §1512(c)(2). In response, Fischer argued that charging him under the 18 USC §1512(c)2 was incorrect as a matter of law for two reasons.

Specifically, his actions were not "witness tampering or evidence shredding" or "corruptly obstructing," which is the actual text of the statute. In addition to the actual written text, at the time the law was drafted and the president signed it, Congress and the president both unequivocally and repeatedly stated its intent was to rein in corporate bad actors such as Enron. (see DrGoldReferences Appendix 16.)[3] Fischer also argued that he didn't act with "corrupt" intent, a key detail in the written language of the statute.

The entire section, 18 USC §1512(c) is written as follows:

> *(c) Whoever corruptly—*
>
> *(1) alters, destroys, mutilates, or conceals a record, document, or other object, or attempts to do so, with the intent to impair the object's integrity or availability for use in an official proceeding; or*
>
> *(2) otherwise obstructs, influences, or impedes any official proceeding, or attempts to do so,*
>
> *shall be fined under this title or imprisoned not more than 20 years, or both.*

It is clear that when read as a whole, section (c)(2) is an extension of (c)(1) as it relates to the impairment of evidence for use in an official proceeding. If read separately, section (c)(2) would be a broad generalization of a wide range of actions that *all* could be attached to the twenty-year sentence for (c)(2).

In March 2022, Fischer's §1512(c)(2) charges were dismissed by District Judge Carl J. Nichols. The judge ruled that the subset of the law charged, §1512(c)(2), had been improperly separated from its parent, §1512(c)(1), which specifies evidence tampering in reference to a "document, record, or other object."

In April 2023, the DC Court of Appeals reversed trial Judge Nichols's ruling and held 2–1 in a "fractured" decision that the government's interpretation of the (c)(2) statute as separate from (c)(1) *was* broad enough to include the "obstructing" actions of Fischer on January 6. The decision is "fractured" because all three judges disagreed with each other in lengthy separate opinions regarding the definition and application of "corruptly," among other issues.

The lead opinion by Justice Florence Pan opines that the allegations "appear" to be sufficient to meet any proposed definition of "corrupt" intent (p. 17). Justice Pan then goes on to discuss three potential definitions regarding the definition of "corruptly" in the context of §1512(c)(2) without expressing a preference for any of them. Justice Justin Walker argued that the court must define the corrupt mental state to make sense of (c)(2)'s act element (See p. 1 of Walker's opinion). He would apply the long-standing meaning of "corruptly" as requiring a defendant to act with an intent to procure an unlawful benefit either for himself or for some other person. Justice Gregory Katsas's dissenting opinion runs thirty-nine pages and argues that Justice Walker's definition of "corruptly" requiring an intent to gain an unlawful benefit does not save the lead opinion's view giving §1512 (c)(2) an improbable breadth. Thus, there was no agreement on the definition or application of "corruptly" from the D.C. Court of Appeals on this issue.

In September 2023, Fischer appealed his case to the United States Supreme Court. The Supreme Court receives approximately eight thousand petitions each year and hears only sixty to eighty, so every single case accepted by SCOTUS is considered essential to the national interpretation of the law. The decision in this case will impact the fate of hundreds of other J6 defendants, including former President Trump. Most importantly, though, it will set a precedent for *either* the legal persecution *or* the legal protection of future political protesters.

In April 2024, SCOTUS heard oral arguments in Fischer. Several of the justices seemed very curious that this statute had indeed been misapplied far too broadly.

Precedent

In his signing statement of the Sarbanes-Oxley Act (SOX ACT) in July 2002, President George W. Bush explicitly rebuked any intention to use the law against ordinary Americans by requiring the DOJ to require that each defendant had a "criminal state of mind."[4]

Statement by the President

Today I have signed into law H.R. 3763, "An Act to protect investors by improving the accuracy and reliability of corporate disclosures made pursuant to the securities laws, and for other purposes." The Act adopts tough new provisions to deter and punish corporate and accounting fraud and corruption, ensure justice for wrongdoers, and protect the interests of workers and shareholders.

Several provisions of the Act require careful construction by the executive branch as it faithfully executes the Act.

The legislative purpose of sections 302, 401, and 906 of the Act, relating to certification and accuracy of reports, is to strengthen the existing corporate reporting system under section 13(a) and 15(d) of the Securities Exchange Act of 1934. Accordingly, the executive branch shall construe this Act as not affecting the authority relating to national security set forth in section 13(b) of the Securities Exchange Act of 1934.

To ensure that no infringement on the constitutional right to petition the Government for redress of grievances occurs in the enforcement of section 1512(c) of title 18 of the U.S. Code, enacted by section 1102 of the Act, which among other things prohibits corruptly influencing any official proceeding, the executive branch shall construe the term "corruptly" in section 1512(c)(2) as requiring proof of a criminal state of mind on the part of the defendant.

Given that the legislative purpose of section 1514A of title 18 of the U.S. Code, enacted by section 806 of the Act, is to protect against company retaliation for lawful cooperation with investigations and not to define the scope of investigative authority or to grant new investigative authority, the executive branch shall construe section 1514A(a)(1)(B) as referring to investigations authorized by the rules of the Senate or the House of Representatives and conducted for a proper legislative purpose.

GEORGE W. BUSH
THE WHITE HOUSE,
July 30, 2002.

This law has been in effect for more than twenty years and used in thousands of cases. Not once prior to January 6 did the government ever use this statute in this way—against ordinary citizens in a political protest. Corporate bad actors falsifying or destroying documents—not regular citizens protesting the actions of their elected officials in a public government building—were specifically identified as the intended targets of that law.

Consider that none of the thousands of protestors who occupied the Hart Senate Office Building in October 2018 to protest Judge Kavanaugh faced an "obstruction of an official proceeding" charge.[5]

Consider that Senator Elizabeth Warren did not face "obstruction of an official proceeding charge" when she ignited a crowd that later stormed the Senate building and directly harassed US senators.[6] Neither did any of those protestors face this charge for their actions.

Consider that none of the thousands of protestors who rioted in the nation's capital during Trump's 2017 inauguration faced "obstruction of an official proceeding charge." While several hundred (mostly) misdemeanor charges followed the event, all except one were eventually dropped.[7]

And not once *after* January 6 did the government ever use this statute in this way. Consider that Steven Colbert lawfully sent in a crew to interview congressmen. But *after* their work was done, the crew was just "fooling around" in the hallways and they were arrested by Capitol police. What happened to them? Paperwork and dismissal.[8] Steven Colbert said, "My staff were just doing their job."

Consider that Democrat Congressman Jamaal Bowman illegally pulled a fire alarm on October 25, 2023, specifically to delay a House of Representatives vote on the budget. This is the exact criteria anticipated in 18 USC §1512(c)(2): "corruptly obstructing a federal proceeding." Bowman admitted he pulled the fire alarm to delay the House vote (which he did not want to occur), meaning he did obstruct a federal proceeding (House vote) for a personal gain (corrupt intent). Nonetheless, not only was he *not* charged with the twenty-year felony "obstruction of an official proceeding," prosecutors gave him the sweet deal of a misdemeanor of falsely pulling a fire alarm, *which will be stricken from his record* when he pays the $1,000 fine and serves three months' probation.[9]

In all of the history of the United States, there has *never* been an obstruction of justice charge without evidence tampering or interference. January 6, however, overturned that twenty-year precedent for hundreds of Americans.

Part I: "Elephants in Mouseholes"

The first legal issue for the Supreme Court in the Fischer case is whether a subset of a statue can be orphaned from its parent.

Chapter 73 of the federal criminal code is called "Obstruction of Justice." It is fifteen thousand words and more than thirty pages long. §1512(c)(2) is just one subsection among hundreds of subsections in this one chapter. Chapter 73 lists escalating penalties depending upon the facts of the case. For example, obstruction involving picketing and parading carries a maximum penalty of one year; obstruction with threatening force carries a penalty of five to ten years; and shredding or falsifying physical evidence comes with a heavier penalty of up to twenty years. It seems fairly obvious that each different variation of obstruction should be charged in connection with its specific penalty. However, in the Fischer case (and other J6 cases involving §1512(c)(2)), the government's interpretation of the law collapsed the variation of penalties for different types of obstruction, making *any* form of obstructing an official proceeding a twenty-year felony.

With a straight face, the government has been arguing that a subparagraph, nestled inside a subsection, found in the middle of nineteen otherwise narrow specifications, is actually a stand-alone "all-encompassing clause." This kind of absurd reasoning led to the best one-liner I've ever read in a judicial opinion (Judge Katsas quoting earlier precedent, page 36):

> *"Congress . . . does not alter the fundamental details of a regulatory scheme in vague terms or ancillary provisions—it does not, one might say, hide elephants in mouseholes." Whitman v. Am. Trucking Ass'ns, Inc. 531 U.S. 457, 468 (2001).*

No, it does not. The plain reading of Chapter 73 shows a logical scheme of penalties related to the seriousness and sophistication of the obstruction. Rudimentary forms of obstruction receive the lowest penalties, and the most sophisticated and nefarious receive the highest.

In his very lengthy dissent,[10] DC Appellate Court Judge Katsas noted that the government's interpretation would "swallow up all the immediately preceding subsections, entire statute, and the entire chapter" and says, "I am unaware of any case resolving ambiguity in favor of wholesale redundancy." He argues cogently that the plain text of §1512(c)(2) argues "against the government's all-encompassing interpretation." Here is some text from page 30:

> (1988). Here, the government's interpretation would make section 1512(c)(2) both improbably broad and unconstitutional in many of its applications.
>
> In the government's view, subsection (c)(2) reaches any act that obstructs, influences, or impedes an official proceeding—which means anything that affects or hinders the proceeding, *see Marinello*, 138 S. Ct. at 1106. Among other things, that construction would sweep in advocacy, lobbying, and protest—common mechanisms by which citizens attempt to influence official proceedings. Historically, these activities did not constitute obstruction unless they directly impinged on a proceeding's truth-seeking function through acts such as bribing a decisionmaker or falsifying evidence presented to it. And the Corporate Fraud Accountability Act of 2002, which created section 1512(c), seems an unlikely candidate to extend obstruction law into new realms of political speech, just as the Chemical Weapons Convention Implementation Act seemed an unlikely candidate to regulate the tortious use of commercially available chemicals to cause an "uncomfortable rash." *See Bond*, 572 U.S. at 851–52.
>
> Consider a few basic examples. An activist who successfully rails against bringing a bill to a vote on the Senate floor has obstructed or influenced an official proceeding. (For

The very title of the §1512(c)(2) statute must also be considered, along with congressional intent and history. The name of §1512(c)(2) is "Tampering with a witness, victim, or an informant" and it is part of a statute known by all to clearly refer to corporate fraud, not advocacy, protest, rioting, or assault. This law has been in effect for more than twenty years and has been used in thousands of cases, but not once had the government claimed it covered conduct that did not require interfering with evidence.

Part II: "Corruptly"

The second legal question for the Supreme Court in Fischer's case involves the first requirement of §1512(c)(2): that the defendant acted "corruptly." By plain reading of the statute and decades of precedent, the government must prove that the defendant acted with corrupt intent. For centuries, the common understanding of the English language has defined "acting corruptly" as acting "with an intent to procure an unlawful benefit for oneself." Even President Bush, upon signing this bill into law, specifically stated that:

> "*. . . the executive branch shall construe the term 'corruptly' in section 1512(c)(2) as requiring proof of a criminal state of mind on the part of the defendant.*"[11]

Law School 101 teaches that to break a law, a person must do two things. The person must do the specific *action* of breaking the law, and the person must have the *intention* to break the law. The act of doing the crime is called the *actus rea*, and the intent or mindset to do the crime is called the *mens rea*. Proof of both is required to charge someone with a crime because it is surprisingly common for people to accidentally break laws. For example, a blind man who bumps into another person is not charged with assault and battery, as he did not intend to bump into the person even though he actually *did* the associated action. Most statutes (including §1512(c)(2)) require the defendant to have a "criminal state of mind."

Almost All Crimes Require Criminal Intent

Having a criminal intent, or *mens rea*, is an essential element of most crimes. Many decades ago the Supreme Court held in a unanimous decision that even if a statute did not specifically require a *mens rea*, it is assumed that a *mens rea* is required.

> *The contention that an injury can amount to a crime only when inflicted by intention is no provincial or transient notion. It is as universal and persistent in mature systems of law as belief in freedom of the human will and a consequent ability and duty of the normal individual to choose between good and evil.*
>
> *A relation between some mental element and punishment for a harmful act is almost as instinctive as the child's familiar exculpatory "But I didn't mean to," . . .*
>
> *Crime, as a compound concept, generally constituted only from concurrence of an evil-meaning mind with an evil-doing hand, was congenial to an intense individualism and took deep and early root in American soil. As the state codified the common law of crimes, even if their enactments were silent on the subject, their courts assumed that the omission did not signify disapproval of the principle, but merely recognized that intent was so inherent in the idea of the offense that it required no statutory affirmation.*

In the case of §1512(c)(2), the language in the statute specifically requires a corrupt intent. It specifically starts with the phrase "whoever corruptly." This means proving that the defendant showed both corrupt action (*actus rea*) and corrupt intent (*mens rea*). In all of the January 6 cases involving §1512(c)(2), including that of Fischer (and me), the government evaporated the requirement for *mens rea* in its prosecution. Their argument was that the defendant must have had a corrupt intent (*mens rea*) in order to have been present as a protestor (*actus rea*), and so subsequently, a defendant's presence at the event (*actus rea*) proved their corrupt intent prior to the action (*mens rea*). This reasoning is so circular that it is meaningless. It erases the requirement to prove evidence of *mens rea* for any defendant.

The legal definition of acting corruptly means acting with an improper purpose, personally or by influencing another including for a personal benefit. In the original Arthur Andersen case, SCOTUS noted that the "natural meaning" of "corruptly" is "clear" and that the word is "normally associated with wrongful, immoral, depraved, or evil" conduct. To prove that a person had a corrupt intent, the person must have intended a personal gain for himself or another person. Otherwise, he would be charged with something that does not include corrupt *intent.* If the requirement for *mens rea* disappears, then criminal action becomes vague and hard to define, leaving common citizens susceptible to various felony charges at any time, in violation of their due process rights. It has never been argued that Fischer, or any other defendants in similar cases, gained any kind of individual benefits from their actions of January 6 that they *knew* to be unlawful. Nor has it been argued that they had any kind of corrupt intent, other than that which, apparently, automatically accompanies any person who decides to take action as a political protester.

Part III: Otherwise

The Supreme Court is also faced with an issue of language in the reading and interpretation of §1512 (c)(2) for *Fischer v. United States.* The presence of the word "otherwise" in the statute is key to recognizing the illegitimacy of the government's argument in the case. The language of the statute doesn't make sense the way the Department of Justice is asking the courts (and the rest of us) to read it. By skipping subsection (c)(1) and going straight to (c)(2), we are being asked to read as as if (c)(1) is not there:

> *Whoever corruptly—otherwise obstructs, influences, or impedes any official proceeding, or attempts to do so. . .*

This is not a correct use of English when asked to stand on its own. The presence of the word "otherwise" refers to something else that came before it. Without this caveat, the sentence doesn't make sense. Conveniently, that *something* is clarified right before in (c)(1):

> *Whoever corruptly alters, destroys, mutilates, or conceals a record, document, or other object, or attempts to do so, with the intent to impair the object's integrity or availability for use in an official proceeding; or . . .*

There is even an "or" at the end of (c)(1) to suggest that another part of the same idea is coming next. In an *amicus* brief for *Gonzalez v. Google* on §230, the authors argued that under standard canons of interpretation, the "otherwise" language refers specifically to material in the same genre as the terms preceding it. When a statute says "otherwise," it is a clear reference to something more specific that has been previously written in the law. With regard to §1512, the Department of Justice is asking the courts to totally ignore the presence of the word *otherwise.*

The consequence of skipping this word is to read (c)(2) as an expansive idea that can broadly mean anything the prosecution wants, rather than a clause based upon then limiting language included in (c)(1). This is not the way language is used in the law. If it were, it would also render the statute unconstitutionally vague.

By simply reading the statute (c)(2) alone, one has no way of knowing what conduct it (and its twenty-year penalty) applies to. For this reason, (c)(2) *must* be limited by the specific kind of conduct listed in (c)(1). This connection is clearly noted by the inclusion of the term "otherwise." The interpretation that comes from reading §1512 without either (c)(1) or the word "otherwise" is not a legitimate use of the statute, established statutory construction, or the English language.

Part IV: Overly Broad, Ambiguity

Finally, the DC Court of Appeals noted that historically the Supreme Court rejects "improbably broad interpretations of criminal statutes" and "disfavors interpretations that would make a statute unconstitutional." In addition, Supreme Court precedent also requires restraint and leniency: "Courts should not assign federal criminal statutes a 'breathtaking' scope when a narrower reading is reasonable." Finally, Supreme Court precedent is that ambiguity in how a statute is written always favors the defendant.

Three Felonies a Day

The book *Three Felonies a Day* describes how federal prosecutors today can charge almost any (white-collar) worker with a crime because federal statutes have become so disconnected from English common law. There are now hundreds of thousands of federal statutes from which prosecutors could select a vague or technical prohibition and charge nearly any person with a felony. This is exactly what happened to J6 defendants: Prosecutors picked an unrelated twenty-year felony because it carried such a lengthy prison sentence, and then *selectively* charged the people it wanted to charge. Consider that a law that was passed because of a financial securities scandal, involving the destruction of evidence, is now being used to incarcerate hundreds of noncorporate civilians whose actions had nothing to do with the destruction of evidence. This is shocking.

President Bush specifically warned us never to use this statute to charge civilian protestors,[12] but that is *exactly* what happened with J6: Hundreds of ordinary Americans were charged with a twenty-year felony *that has nothing to do with them.*

If the Supreme Court were to choose not to void the felony charge for Fischer, it would evaporate the concept of *mens rea* in law, eliminate the plain English meaning of the word "corruptly," and ignore congressional and executive intent. It will set precedent that any conduct that affects any kind of official proceeding, such as lobbying, will be deemed illegal. Finally, it will allow for infinite federal subsections of legislation to be read as vague, stand-alone clauses, and even allow for clarifying words to be excluded in the legal interpretation of legislation.

This decision will be felt far beyond this one statute, this one day, and this one cohort. If the Supreme Court sets aside decades of precedent, centuries of common law, and the plain meaning of the English language, then we will no longer be operating under the rule of law.

More than 350 defendants were charged with the felony §1512(c)(2), and on April 16, 2024, SCOTUS heard oral arguments on how this 2002-era corporate fraud statute was used to bludgeon ordinary civilian protestors for allegedly interrupting the counting of Electoral College votes. I say *allegedly* because, using myself as just one example, this exact statute was used against *me,* although I arrived at the Capitol building with absolutely no awareness of any political vote and long after the vote was already canceled. The government did not and could not dispute this in my case—the motorcade taking Vice President Pence away from the Capitol was videotaped leaving long before I arrived. It made no difference to them. But facts should matter.

Judicial Spanking

If any reader still has doubt about the bias of the DC judges, keep reading. After SCOTUS announced it would be hearing the Fischer appeal in December 2023, several DC District judges publicly whined that a SCOTUS reversal would increase their workload. Never mind managing appeals is part of their job! But in addition, for more than three years, dozens of criminal defense attorneys and hundreds of J6 defendants had repeatedly informed these same judges that what they were doing appeared to be illegal. For starters, it is indisputably unethical to treat some defendants differently than other defendants. For example, after reviewing his entire judicial record, I could not find any other misdemeanor defendant whom my judge ever sentenced to prison in his entire career. (In doing this research, I did find several examples of him giving absurdly low sentences to actual terrorists; see Chapter 12.)

It was not just Casey Cooper. It was nearly every single DC judge. Almost to a person, they displayed an incredible degree of antipathy towards J6 defendants. This dislike or hatred turned into obvious prejudice in sentencing. When you look at the defendants' actions and compare that to the overcharges filed, when you hear some of what the judges said in the courtroom, it cannot be denied.

The DC judges are rattled that SCOTUS (their boss, to the extent they have a boss) publicly disagreed with their prejudice. No matter what SCOTUS decides, merely by accepting the Fischer appeal, SCOTUS is spanking these wayward judges for their limited intellect and their prejudice. The DC judges were extraordinarily smug about there being no possibility that they were wrong.

In my codefendant's sentencing, his attorney requested that he be permitted to stay out of prison pending this very appeal. This is a common request which is granted more often than not if the defendant is not a flight risk and has a legitimate appeal. In my codefendant's case, Casey Cooper (I literally cannot write the honorific "Judge" as he is so clearly unworthy of this title) *scoffed* at the criminal defense attorney who made this motion. Casey Cooper simply could not believe that this was a legitimate issue for appeal. He mocked the very *notion* that the Supreme Court could possibly consider a J6 defendant questioning the government's vertical overcharging.

It is difficult to believe Casey Cooper was accepted to the same top law school I was. I know for certain I was accepted on merit. In addition to having already earned my medical degree by age twenty-three, my LSAT score was the 99.7 percent rank in the nation, placing me #3 out of every 1,000 law school applicants. I most definitely was accepted into Stanford Law School on merit. Casey appears to be a classic DEI acceptance.

Casey's intellect is inferior to what our nation deserves in a judge. He literally does not possess the intellectual capacity to imagine legal arguments outside his own prejudiced thoughts. Being able to overcome one's biases and think broadly intellectually is a hallmark of a superior judge. Those judges with more limited intellect (our nation has far too many of these) can train themselves to look past their own biases—but willingness to see past their own thoughts requires humility, which Casey lacks. Those two traits in combination—subpar intellect and arrogance—are why the DC judges, almost uniformly, are completely shocked that SCOTUS accepted Fischer's appeal. Essentially, we are all being victimized by arrogant dumb people who are too arrogant to know they are dumb.

. . . And Inappropriate Judicial Revenge

Here is the most shocking example of the bias of the DC judges. In April 2024, SCOTUS heard oral arguments on the Fischer appeal. The DC judges became nervous that their incompetence and bias would now be revealed to the world. So they appear to want to take revenge on the only people they can torment: the defendants. Several of the judges stated their intent to *change their own sentencing retrospectively—to order even longer prison sentences*, effectively nullifying SCOTUS. Here is how they plan to do this.

The American public would be surprised to know that our government typically engages in the illegal action of horizontal overcharging (see Chapters 7 and 10), whereby one act results in multiple charges. Highly unethical, but that is reality. For example, my trespass through public spaces resulted in the government charging me with *five* crimes: parading and picketing, entering and remaining, disorderly conduct in a restricted building, disorderly conduct in a Capitol building, and obstruction of an official proceeding. Apparently, I went from being a completely law-abiding citizen, working hard for decades earning two doctorate degrees, only to fall into a sordid life of deep criminality—*committing five crimes* within minutes (see DrGoldReferences Appendix 15).[13]

Judges sentence defendants on each charge. So a defendant might get two years on a felony, twelve months on a misdemeanor, twelve months on another misdemeanor, six months on another misdemeanor, six months on another misdemeanor. This would mean five years total incarceration—if the sentences are to run *consecutively*. But the judges (in a nod to what they realize is horizontal overcharging) almost always order the sentences to be served at the same time. If the sentences run *concurrently* in the above example, the defendant serves two years on the felony and simultaneously serves the twelve, twelve, six, and six months, for a total incarceration of two years.

At sentencing the judge will say something like this:

> *Pursuant to the Sentencing Reform Act of 1984 and in consideration of the provisions of 18 USC 3553 as well as the advisory Sentencing Guidelines, it is the judgment of the Court that you are hereby committed to the custody of the Bureau of Prisons for a term of 24 months as to Count 1, 12 months as to each of Counts 2 and 3, and six months as to each of Counts 4 and 5, with all counts to be served concurrently for a total of 24 months. You are further sentenced to serve a 24-month period of supervised release as to Count 1 and a 12-month period of supervised release as to Counts 2 and 3, with all counts to be served concurrently, for a total of 24 months.*

And this is indeed what happened in all (or virtually all) the J6 cases. *Concurrent* sentences. In other words, the judge, after carefully reviewing all the evidence, issues his/her ruling as to the defendant's punishment. Now some DC judges have indicated that if SCOTUS releases these defendants, these judges intend to go *backward in time and resentence these defendants.* This is unimaginable, unprecedented, despicable, and should be grounds for judicial impeachment.

It is impossible to overstate how shocking this is.

When higher judges (or justices) reverse a lower judge on appeal, there is nothing a lower judge can do. This is the way the system has always worked and the way it should work. Lower judges are always aware that they can be reversed on appeal. This is part of the reason they abide by certain guidelines and parameters—if they go outside these boundaries, they will be reversed. Lower judges being cognizant that a superior judge (or justice) might overrule them is virtually the only check on unlimited judicial power.

The DC judges already know when they issue their sentences that any defendant may appeal. But now they are saying that if *only* they had known the defendant would actually *win* his appeal, they would have sentenced him differently! Such a mindset—nullifying an upper court—is shocking and terribly dangerous.

Some DC judges have now said: If SCOTUS reverses us, we will find another way to additionally punish these defendants, even if we must create (another) new mechanism to do so. Rapists and murderers who must be released due to a successful appeal (for example, if the government fabricated evidence) do not face this judicial bias. This is blatant political bias—poison to an honest judiciary.

We all accept that the higher courts are the last word. But in J6 cases, the DC judges appear to be so biased and so aggrieved, that they are floundering about and searching for a way to nullify the Supreme Court's intentions.

Here is the proof. An ex-chief DC judge stated his intention to *resentence* a J6 defendant to a *longer* sentence should SCOTUS reverse Fischer. This judge had already sentenced this defendant, and if SCOTUS reverses this judge's assessment, this judge plans to nullify what SCOTUS has ruled by extending the defendant's original sentence. He is essentially saying: "Well, if I had *known* SCOTUS would say this felony was erroneously charged, I would have sentenced him more harshly at sentencing." Excuse me? *Every single case before a judge can be appealed. This is the entire system.* In addition, the vast majority of J6 defendants who were legally allowed to appeal have filed appeals. There is no surprise here.

We're naming names because people should be ashamed of themselves. Judge John Bates should be *humiliated*—read his words. He is saying if SCOTUS disagrees with him, he will nullify SCOTUS. The amount of arrogance a person has to have to believe this and to say this and to do this is breathtaking.

Harmeet Dhillon, one of our nation's most esteemed attorneys, tweeted: "This is so disgusting. If I had known 34 years ago when I went to law school that the courts would be led by judges like this, I might have chosen a different line of work. Sick, really."[14]

Even if Fischer requires vacatur of Brock's § 1512(c)(2) conviction, the Court would still likely resentence Brock to a sentence approaching 16 months. Without the § 1512(c)(2) conviction, Brock's Guidelines calculation would be driven by Counts Two and Three. These counts likely group and yield a base offense level of 10. See, e.g., United States v. Nassif, Crim. A. No. 21-421 (JDB), ECF No. 95 at 9–10, 42 (D.D.C. Apr. 27, 2023) (sentencing on same counts), aff'd, No. 23-3069, 2024 WL 1515004 (D.C. Cir. Apr. 9, 2024). Less two levels for § 4C1.1, that results in a base offense level of 8 and a Guidelines Range of 0 to 6 months. See U.S.S.G. Ch. 5, Pt. A. However, this Guidelines Range does not accurately reflect the seriousness of Brock's conduct. Brock's extremely violent rhetoric, his conduct on January 6, and his utter lack of

[1] This same analysis would likely apply to the extent that Brock files a petition for a writ of certiorari and then seeks release pending appeal under 18 U.S.C. § 3143(b)(1)(iv) based on his "likely reduced sentence."

[2] The Court expresses no view at this juncture on Brock's post-sentencing conduct and how it might affect the resentencing analysis. Should the government wish to rely on Brock's alleged threats against Bureau of Prisons employees, see Probation Mem. at 2, it must do more to substantiate this alleged activity.

5

Case 1:21-cr-00140-JDB Document 121 Filed 04/23/24 Page 6 of 6

remorse place him in a meaningfully different category than other January 6 misdemeanants sentenced by this Court. Accordingly, the Court would likely impose an above-Guidelines sentence approaching 16 months, whether by way of departure (whether based on U.S.S.G. § 5K2.7 or another provision) or variance. The Court would then run Brock's sentence on multiple counts consecutively so as to achieve this sentence. The upshot is that even if Fischer were to require vacatur of Brock's § 1512(c)(2) conviction, Brock's likely reduced sentence would still extend beyond the anticipated date of resentencing.

Hence, the Court will defer resentencing until after the Supreme Court decides Fischer so that resentencing can be conducted with any benefit of that decision in mind.

9:10 AM · Apr 26, 2024 · **789.9K** Views

It is very clear that the DC judges are so politically biased that they cannot administer justice. The juries they supervise, and the prosecutors who inform them, live in the same echo chamber. I am in favor of Congress passing a law that any person who is arrested in DC, who does not permanently live in DC, has the option to have an automatic change in venue due to this overwhelming political bias. There are thousands of people who temporarily work in DC but who hail from conservative areas, as well as millions who visit every year. With the demonstrated hatred toward conservatives now concretized throughout the District of Columbia judicial system, from judges to prosecutors to juries, it is not possible for conservatives to get a fair trial in DC. Defendants know this and won't go to trial there. I wouldn't. I wisely *didn't.* The conviction rate of J6 defendants has been 100 percent.

Unless we correct the weaponized Biden administration of the DOJ, this is the new fascist America. Just as Obama's DOJ was weaponized against politically conservative Americans in the form of markedly increased IRS audits of conservatives and conservative organizations (see Chapter 10), Biden's DOJ has been weaponized against politically conservative Americans in the form of criminal prosecutions. Both situations are designed to intimidate and bankrupt people who disagree with leftist elitists. There is no analogous targeting of leftists by conservatives.

Four years after J6, the DOJ has continued to aggressively, actively arrest more people. The largest proportion of these people come from Florida and Texas. Throughout 2024, the DOJ arrested people at the rate of one or two per day. Through January 2025, there have been over 1,500 people arrested. About half of these defendants were or are incarcerated, many for many years. Many defendants, like myself, were incarcerated for misdemeanors, something that simply did not and still does not happen in America—unless you are a J6er. Then, most shamefully, your own government does everything it can to destroy, maim, and kill you.

Still Living Under a Nation of Laws . . . For Now

On June 28, 2024, the last day of the term, SCOTUS[15] released its Fischer ruling. As the government overreach was so enormous, every legal scholar predicted Fischer would win. I believed we would win 7–2 because it was clear to me that if Fischer didn't win, we were no longer living under the rule of law. Either we indict and convict defendants based on the actual words written into a statute, or powerful people will be allowed to use fabricated theories to contort words into convicting a person who did not do the actions written in the statute.

In a 6–3 decision, Fischer prevailed. The majority justices were Roberts, Gorsuch, Kavanaugh, Thomas, Alito, and Jackson. Dissenting justices were Coney Barrett, Sotomayor, and Kagan. This was front-page news across the nation and across the world. What exactly did SCOTUS say?

The Court noted that 18 §1512(c)(2) or the Sarbanes-Oxley Act of 2002 (or "SOX") criminalizes company personnel shredding documents and tampering with witnesses in an official federal investigation. SCOTUS reduced Fischer's question to this:

Q: Does §1512(c)(2) criminalize only attempts to impair the availability or integrity of evidence, or does it include things like obstructing or protesting?

A: "To prove a violation of §1512(c)(2), the government must establish that the defendant impaired the availability or integrity of records, documents, objects or other things used in an official proceeding, or attempted to do so." The Court said that the DOJ incorrectly interpreted (the obstruction provisions of) §1512(c)(2). The Court said the DOJ may not charge someone for merely disrupting or delaying official proceedings; the disruption has to interfere with actual documents, evidence, or witnesses. Otherwise, the government could charge a peaceful protester or even a lobbyist for attempting to influence an official proceeding. The chief justice of the Supreme Court, in a 6–3 ruling said that the government misread the scope of the law and the government's interpretation would implicate normal activities such as lobbying.

The legal technicalities of SCOTUS's ruling include many pages of discussion on the meaning of the word "otherwise," similar to above Part III, and agreed with DC Appellate Judge Katsas that a subparagraph, nestled inside a subsection, found in the middle of nineteen otherwise narrow specifications, cannot actually be a stand-alone "all-encompassing clause." (That was the government's position.) Basically, SCOTUS confirmed that indeed

Judge Katsas is, by far, the brightest of the DC appellate judges and that Judge Pan is at the opposite end. I concur with journalist Julie Kelly who observed that Judge Pan should recuse herself from future J6 deliberations because SCOTUS revealed her muddled and mediocre intellect.

The terrible mediocrity of Florence Pan deserves more attention. Like Casey, Florence was also a classic DEI promotion. In the same June 2024 term as Fischer, Pan was deservedly humiliated twice. That's impressive. The second case was the *Loper Bright Enterprises* ruling.[16] SCOTUS held that Pan's judicial deference to executive agencies was unconstitutional. That is a *big* spanking.

It is critical that our judiciary is filled with extremely intelligent, dispassionate, and wise persons. When we fill these jobs with people who have an average intellect who follow their emotions, all of us pay the price. Judges who never deserved their jobs in the first place, and who have now proven their lack of judicial temperament and abilities, need to be removed.

This ruling affected every J6 defendant charged with §1512(c)(2), especially those still in prison for this charge. Several DC judges have delayed trials or released defendants pending this SCOTUS ruling. Based upon this SCOTUS ruling, the DOJ should simply have dismissed all the §1512(c)(2) charges. But instead, Mob Boss Attorney General Merrick Garland made each J6 defendant fight their way out of prison, one individual legal filing after another, or accept a garbage bargain that gave the wronged defendants virtually nothing. In the biased political world of 2024, defendants had the choice of waiting for the DC Appellate Court (Katsas, Walker, Pan) to opine again, post-Fischer, to accept Garland's bad faith offer that gave the defendants nothing in exchange or wait for President Trump's pardon. My codefendant John Strand, released by the United States Supreme Court Fischer ruling, had refused all of Mob Boss Garland's offers.

In January 2021, the Department of Injustice dismissed all charges and the tables have turned on the evil-doers at the DOJ. The Mob Boss Garland resigned on January 17, 2025, instead of waiting for the president to fire him three days later. Pam Bondi, who has committed to cleaning up the mob boss's misdeeds, has been sworn in as attorney general. Attorney

Harmeet Dhillon has been nominated to be the assistant attorney general of the United States. And the interim District of Columbia Attorney Ed Martin has opened an investigation into how this 18 §1512(c)(2) statute could possibly have been used in this illegitimate way.

Mr. Martin has said it was "a great failure of our office" that prosecutors during the Biden administration used this law to go after people. A senior administration official said: "The DOJ should never be in the business of filing hundreds of charges that end up being dismissed, clearly there was failure. This was inept . . . and we are going to find out why they did that."[17]

CHAPTER SIXTEEN

American Fascism

I hold it that a little rebellion now and then is a good thing, and as necessary in the political world as storms in the physical.

—Thomas Jefferson, January 30, 1787

Even before my arrest and imprisonment, friends and many others would ask if it was worth it to fight the system and risk everything, losing my career and many comforts, losing peaceful anonymity, and going from heartfelt thank-yous in the ER to a barrage of death threats and defamations in the media. For all such inquiries, the only answer is yes. Sooner or later, we're *all* going to have to fight. The only relevant question is how much you will have lost by the time you do.

The calculus of balancing risk and reward is different when you recognize the reality we now face. Despite the warnings of George Washington and many other founding fathers, and despite the protections against tyranny they implemented with the genius design of our Constitution, our institutions have been overtaken by men and women whose morals have been replaced by a desperate desire to acquire power. The usurpations prophesied by Washington are now being fulfilled with ominous effect, bearing down on citizens under the guise of "executive orders" and "public health," methodically eroding the Constitution—one line at a time.

The Equal Protection Clause

In particular, a key element of that Constitution, the Equal Protection clause, has been flagrantly trampled upon by a runaway Executive Branch. The Judicial Branch has been co-opted to enforce its will, weaponizing Selective Prosecution into *Selective Persecution*, a hallmark of despotic agencies such as the German Stasi. From my own painful experience, I believe that we are now witnessing the literal legalization of American Fascism. It begins in selective circles, but it will inevitably expand until it reaches #YouNext.

The Fourteenth Amendment to the Constitution guarantees all people "equal protection of the laws." While the entire Constitution is important, in many ways, our actual freedom depends entirely upon the Fourteenth Amendment to the Constitution. If people are not treated *equally* by the government, then it does not matter what is or isn't written into our laws. If a specific act meets the statutory definition of a crime, but the crime is only enforced against a subset of the population, then it is not a law—it is a weapon. If our federal government intends to enforce statutes against some people and not others, we are better off living with no laws at all. Anarchy is the absence of laws, and tyranny is too many laws. Humans live happier lives under anarchy than tyranny. Both are bad, but of the two, anarchy provides moments of freedom. With tyranny, there is no freedom at all.

Today's elitists are fond of saying that the Constitution is "right-wing." Such propaganda can only exist among people who have never read the Constitution. The Constitution is neither right nor left, but rather a short document that balances anarchy against tyranny.[1] FBI agents conducting raids against J6 defendants actually searched for Constitutions in our homes and on our persons. Possessing a Constitution was then submitted by the prosecution as evidence *against* many J6 defendants at their trials. These words should terribly frighten every reader. It was just a few decades ago that *learning* and *memorizing* the Constitution was *required* for all school children. In less than fifty years, our society went from advocating for the Constitution to using it as evidence of a crime.

Under tyrannical (fascist or communist) governments, any action by a targeted person can become evidence of a crime. In the United States, the existence of hundreds of thousands of federal statutes makes it easy to attack an undesirable group. Obama ordered the IRS to target conservatives. This is not a "conspiracy theory"—the IRS admitted it. Political conservatives were audited by the IRS far more frequently and aggressively than liberals, and it took years of fighting before the IRS was forced to admit it was doing this. In 2013, the Treasury Inspector General for Tax Administration released a report confirming that the IRS used inappropriate criteria to identify potential political cases. For example, it identified nonprofit organizations with the words "Tea Party" in their names. In 2017, the government settled a lawsuit on behalf of more than four hundred conservative nonprofit organizations, and the IRS also apologized, admitting that it had subjected conservatives to "heightened scrutiny and inordinate delays."

With so many "crimes" in the law, the paradigm shift is for all of us to realize that each person commits several crimes every day. Right now, the government *already has the choice to prosecute you.* Since even fascist governments cannot prosecute everyone, the Equal Protection Amendment is even more important. It is critical to stop the government from *selectively* prosecuting a specific disfavored individual.

Change in Venue

If a high-profile crime occurs in a town, the defendant can ask to be tried in another location to eliminate the emotional bias against the defendant that local jurors would naturally have. This is called "change in venue" and is enumerated in the Federal Rules of Criminal Procedure 21(a), which states: "the court must transfer the proceeding against that defendant to another district if the court is satisfied that so great a prejudice against the defendant exists in the transferring district that the defendant cannot obtain a fair and impartial trial there."

Certainly, if you lived in the District of Columbia, J6 was even more of an emotionally charged event. It was not only the hometown of these people, it was also their *company town.* A company town is where many people in the community depend on one employer. Close to half of DC residents—about three hundred thousand—work for the government. The next largest single employer is only 10 percent of that. It is expected that anyone would have a heightened emotional attachment to events that happen in their hometown, not to mention their employer or that of their family.

On top of that emotion was the negative media coverage about defendants, which continued for *years.* Specifically, the media engaged in *omission-bias.* Omission bias is the most dangerous type of bias because it is invisible. It is where something truthful is shown to sway your emotions or thoughts, but many essential truthful details are *left out,* rendering the statement highly misleading.

Omission bias happened on a grand scale in regard to January 6. For example, we all saw infinite loops of video showing people (who looked like Antifa) climbing scaffolding on the west side, whereas we saw almost *no* video of the more than one million peaceful people walking for hours in the city. We saw almost *no* video of the east side (where I was), which was peaceful, and we saw almost no cell phone videos that people shared with their friends on social media from that day.

The biggest and most obvious example was about President Trump. It was widely reported that the president encouraged violence, but what was *not* reported was the Big Tech censorship of President Trump's calls for calm *in real time.* At the Ellipse, I personally heard Trump say the following at approximately noon on January 6: *"I know that everyone here will soon be marching to the Capitol building to peacefully and patriotically make your voices heard."* Trump continued to speak until about 1:15 p.m. At 2:38 p.m., President Trump tweeted the following, but all his tweets were blocked and invisible to the public until Twitter released them in 2023.

Donald J. Trump · 1/6/21
I am asking for everyone at the U.S. Capitol to remain peaceful. No violence! Remember, WE are the Party of Law & Order – respect the Law and our great men and women in Blue. Thank you!
351K
232K
748K

The inability of people who live in a particular geographic area (jury pool) to be neutral due to heightened emotions about a local crime can be solved by moving the trial to a different geographic area. This is typically why "change in venue" is granted.

DC District judges, however, did *not* grant a change in venue to a single J6 defendant, although virtually all J6 defendants made this motion. They held that people who lived in DC were not really different from people who lived in other areas. DC judges were unimpressed by the argument that DC residents were likely more personally traumatized because it was their hometown, a company town, and by the nonstop omission bias media coverage for years.

It is true that judges rarely grant changes in venue even in other highly emotional cases, but J6 defendants were and are facing more than just a highly emotionally charged jury pool.

Change in Venue Should Be Granted on Equal Protection Grounds

However, I believe there is an entirely different reason why change of venue should be granted. I have not seen any case law on this subject, and I think defendants should be arguing this reason in their appeals, and it should be considered by the DC judges.

Imagine if a person was charged with public drunkenness. It is likely that a random group of twelve could be impartial. This is because *prior* to the crime, local jurors would have been a mixed bag, and thus in the aggregate, impartial. Our jury system is not "a jury of your peers"—that is a misquote. Rather, the system aims for an impartiality as a *group*: a dozen people with diverse life experiences and opinions is the safety valve in the system.

However, what if the entire town faithfully belonged to a church which forbade alcohol, and the defendant was a bar owner from the next town, who for years had been petitioning this town's City Hall for a liquor license to open his restaurant and bar in this town? The jury simply will not care if the defendant was actually publicly intoxicated or not—the opportunity to rid themselves of a perceived pest would be too delicious. In other words, the defendant is not able to get a *random* group. He is only able to get a group of teetotalers. There is no diversity of opinion or life experience among prospective jurors.

As of now, no one has successfully argued that change of venue must be granted because a jury pool was hopelessly biased *prior* to the crime. I could find no case law alleging that a group of people who live in a particular geographic area would all be so biased against a particular defendant for a reason other than heightened local emotions. But much as a tavern-owning defendant should not expect impartiality from a teetotaling town on a public drunkenness charge, neither should an unapologetic MAGA defendant expect impartiality in front of an anti-Trump town on a vertical overcharge for being present while protesting the election.

Change of venue for J6 defendants should be granted on equal protection grounds. The jury pool bias that has resulted in a 100 percent conviction rate was not due to heightened local emotions or media coverage of the crime, but to an *asymmetrical antecedent bias* that was so strong it was not possible to seat an impartial jury.

Biased Jurors = Show Trials

One of the most important safeguards against selectively prosecuting an unpopular person is the jury system. At the end of a trial, you are to be judged by a "jury" that our system goes to great pains to assure us is impartial. (It is obviously not a "jury of your peers" as, for example, typically a nurse or doctor is not seated on a medical malpractice trial.) There are myriad exclusions that prosecutors and defense attorneys use to try to shape a jury, but until 2020, there was at least a bipartisan agreement that the jury *should* be impartial. If it appears impossible to be impartial, a change in location is indicated.

The DC jury pool was 96 percent anti-Trump, and the content of the J6 trials were indisputably about Trump. My case was the least political of any J6 trial. I was *not* there to protest the election, I did *not* speak specifically about the election, and I was *not* wearing or carrying any political message. Despite this, the judge and the prosecutors *still* made my case about Trump! By definition, if 96 percent of people hold the same opinion, for example, who should be president, there can be no possibility of impartiality on the subject of the president. This reality turned all DC trials into show trials.

A show trial is a pretense. It looks like a real trial, since there is a judge and jury, prosecutors and defense attorneys. However, the role of each player is predetermined, like actors reading lines in a play. Just as the ending to the play is known before the performance, the verdict in a show trial is also known before the proceedings start. The possibility of an impartial jury has been the distinguishing factor of American trials, preventing them from becoming mere show trials. Without this possibility, the trial is nothing but a show.

The Epoch Times reported that 100 percent of January 6 defendants who chose a jury trial have been convicted and 100 percent of change-of-venue motions have been denied. The DOJ typically has a 65 percent conviction rate in the District of Columbia (much lower than elsewhere). How many trials and how high a conviction rate is necessary before the judges start to consider maybe it's not the evidence but the jurors?[2]

Justice Entertainment

The purpose of a show trial is to enable the community to *feel* as though justice has been served. The purpose of a real trial is to actually serve justice.

In our system of criminal justice, the prosecutor's job is to defend the *community*, not the victim. This is a critical distinction—and why criminal trials are not supposed to be win/lose events like sporting competitions. If the prosecutor's client is *justice* or the *community*, the prosecutor is focused on the total well-being of the community, meaning at all times he wants to see justice prevail for both the victim and the defendant. If, for example, the evidence shows that the wrong defendant is on trial, a prosecutor who is working for the community will want to dismiss charges as rapidly and eagerly as the defense attorney.

Our system is set up this way because Americans have always believed that it is better to let a hundred guilty men go than have one innocent man wrongly convicted. When it comes to punishment by a very powerful government against a single individual, we want to err on the side of caution.

For our system to result in justice rather than personal wins and losses, the prosecutor must work for the community. In today's reality, the system has devolved into a mere sporting competition, losing its goal of true justice. Prosecutors seem to have *entirely* lost touch with their noble purpose—they define their jobs as obtaining convictions, instead of achieving justice.

One very surprising fact I learned through my ordeal is that a large number of criminal defense attorneys used to be prosecutors. If you had asked me in law school which career direction I thought most attorneys might take, I would have guessed the opposite. I would have thought an idealistic young lawyer would start out in criminal defense, believing there are many wrongly convicted souls. As the lawyer became disillusioned with their guilty clients over the years, they would become frustrated and switch sides.

However, it is the exact opposite. In large numbers, federal prosecutors become disgusted with the lies they feel forced to tell, the exculpatory evidence they are forced to conceal, and the single-minded focus on "winning" (whether or not that was justice in any specific case) to advance their career. I had many conversations with different criminal defense attorneys, and personally observed so many prosecutors flat-out lying that I likely will never again vote for any prosecutor who later runs for office. I used to think having the credential of "former *federal* district attorney" or "former *federal* prosecutor" was a badge of honor. I now know it is a scarlet letter of shame. There may be a few exceptions—but in four years I have not seen a single one.

This book is about the fascist nature of the *federal* justice system—and that is because there are many differences between our federal and state criminal justice systems. State crimes are more typically acts we recognize as crimes, such as murder, assault, theft, public drunkenness. Relatedly, there is a more manageable amount of diversity and complexity of state criminal statutes. And there is a limit to the amount of resources the government will spend to prosecute a typical state crime.

In comparison, the federal justice system is estimated to have more than three hundred thousand statutes (no one knows for sure) filled with millions of typed words with hairsplitting intricate regulations and innumerable inchoate (incomplete or thought) crimes. The federal government can choose to divert nearly infinite resources in one specific direction at the request of a politician. And that is exactly what is happening. A FBI whistleblower documented that FBI agents were taken *off* child sex trafficking cases nationwide to do dragnets nationwide on peaceful J6 attendees. Four years post-J6 there were still one or two arrests per day on *misdemeanors.* This would be too expensive for any individual state to bother with.

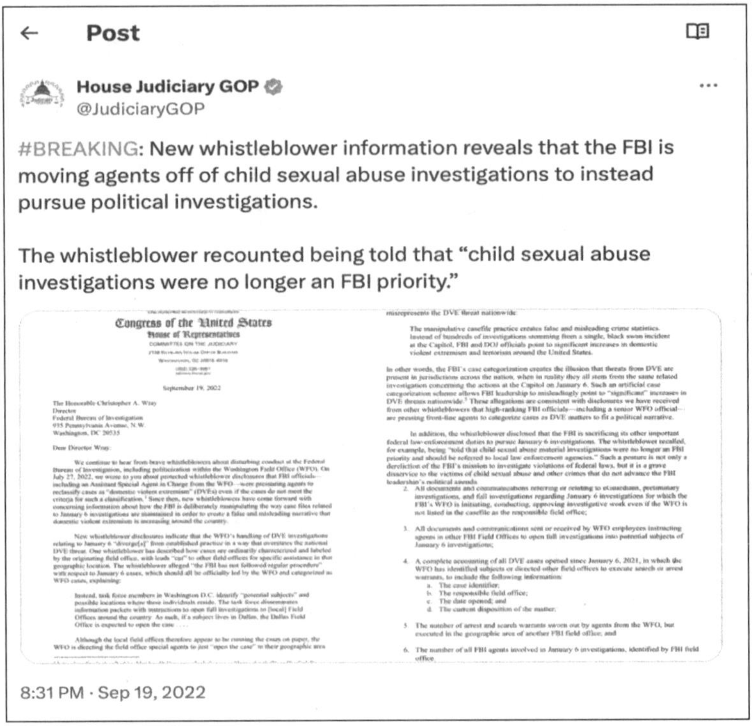
Post
House Judiciary GOP
@JudiciaryGOP
#BREAKING: New whistleblower information reveals that the FBI is moving agents off of child sexual abuse investigations to instead pursue political investigations.
The whistleblower recounted being told that "child sexual abuse investigations were no longer an FBI priority."
Congress of the United States
House of Representatives
September 19, 2022
8:31 PM · Sep 19, 2022

As most state crimes are *recognizable* as crimes, instinctively I would believe that the conviction rate for state crimes is closer to real justice. That is typically 75 percent. Jurors likely understand recognizable crimes (murder, assault, drunkenness . . .) but default to the "experts" (prosecutors and judges) when faced with unrecognizable crimes (conspiracy, obstruction, corruption . . .). This is also why these "experts" need to be honest.

The power to charge a specific crime is enormous. In our system, more than 90 percent of federal cases result in convictions. If you are a "law and order" type, as most of us think we are, we may think that sounds great. Isn't the goal to punish the guilty and release the innocent? The problem is that a 90 percent–plus conviction rate is only achieving justice if the police (local, county, state, sheriff, FBI, etc.) have a near or actual 100 percent correct arrest rate. That would imply the police always had all the relevant and none of the irrelevant evidence at the moment of arrest. That is simply not possible. As proof of the prevalence of wrongful convictions in our society, the Innocence Project has achieved 250 difficult exonerations to date of innocent people falsely convicted of serious crimes such as rape and murder. These innocent men and women collectively spent almost four thousand years wrongfully incarcerated.

This is why it is critical that prosecutors only bring charges that apply to the defendant. In a system where the prosecution *always* (well, more than 90 percent of the time) gets its pound of flesh, pretty much the only thing that matters is what the prosecution charges. That is why vertical overcharging is so dangerous. That is why having hundreds of thousands of statutes on the books is so dangerous. The jury (virtually) always convicts. They don't know what they are seeing.

If I challenged Serena Williams to a tennis match, would you be interested in watching? Who would want to watch a game where one team wins more than 90 percent of the time? I wouldn't be playing tennis against Williams as much as I would simply be happening to be holding a racquet while she served 6-0, 6-0, 6-0. No one would mistake that for a tennis match.

Now what if a *good* tennis player challenged Serena Williams? The players appear on the court: Each is athletic, nimble, dressed like a champion, and ready to go. A good player against an internationally ranked player, though, is the same 6-0, 6-0, 6-0 result. The difference is that an observer might mistake this for a real tennis match. But this is not a match; it is a show.

Our federal criminal justice system has become just this sort of show—the score is never in doubt, the prosecution always wins. The difference between our federal criminal justice system and sports entertainment is simply that the public doesn't know it is watching *justice entertainment*—we still think and hope it is real. WWE has been forced to truthfully market itself as sports entertainment, acknowledging they are not "legitimate contests but rather entertainment-based performance theater, featuring storyline-driven, scripted, and partially choreographed matches" (per Wikipedia[3]). Our federal criminal justice system, with a 90 percent–plus conviction rate, is equally predetermined—but the stakeholders, unlike WWE, have not been forced to admit it.

Considering yourself immune to prosecution, or more accurately, *persecution,* simply because it hasn't directly impacted you so far is a dangerous fantasy. Our government and its enablers are not going to stop waging this war against our freedoms, our health, and our property, until we have little if any remaining. By "*we,*" I certainly do not mean conservatives, freedom activists, patriots, or any such label. I mean everybody. Eventually, if we fail to think for ourselves, others will do the thinking *for* us, to the detriment (and eventual political and financial enslavement) of nearly every American. In fact, when despots succeed in concentrating power, they often first attack their own supporters specifically, fearing those supporters first attracted by a resistance to previous power structures will soon rebel against the inevitable totalitarian control of the state.

War of the Worlds

While Americans are growing less and less suspicious of the word *socialism* (four in ten now "embrace" some form of socialism), it is unknown if they really know what it means. The US remains somewhat resistant to a progression toward totalitarianism. This is a vestige of the high living standard created by centuries of free market capitalism, abundant resources, and, perhaps most importantly, the Second Amendment guarantee of the right to keep and bear arms.

Unable to take the nation by overt military force or to convince millions of people to give up their private property voluntarily, fear represents the best strategy for modern tyrants to reach their objective. What good is private property if a deadly new virus decimates the human race? What use is freedom if all life is wiped out by an imminent climate change "disaster"? Medical Marxism succeeded through harnessing human fear. Government agencies keep expanding, allegedly to protect the "public health," but are being used to indoctrinate the culture with a mindset of vulnerability and reliance on the government for safety and provision. Citizens who fear that a neighbor might kill them by simply breathing have far greater tolerance for a medical police state than for, for example, communism. But is there a difference?

Responsible citizens naturally feel that war requires sacrifice. *Frontline News* observed this in *German origins of militarized Public Health Service*, as Americans almost unanimously complied with a coronavirus approach that allowed "individual physical and mental health to be harmed for the 'greater good . . .'" More difficult to understand, however, is that public health officials have somehow managed to maintain any level of public support as their narrative has unraveled. How have they pulled off such a feat? Through domestic propaganda that has been institutionalized throughout the US.

As Mike Benz explained on a Tucker interview:

> The fundamental nature of war changed . . . NATO declared . . . we don't need to win military skirmishes . . . All we need to do is control the media and the social media ecosystem because that's what controls elections. And if you simply get the right administration into power, they control the military. . . . it's infinitely cheaper [than conducting a military war] to simply conduct an organized political influence operation over social media and legal media. . . . So NATO went from 70 years of tanks to this explicit capacity building for censoring tweets.[4]

Put plainly: The federal government engineers a propaganda campaign and Congress has been either unwilling or actually unable to provide the accountability they are entrusted with, having given up their oversight:

> While federal employees empowered with militaristic regulatory authority are obviously in need of heightened oversight, the US Congress abdicated its role in this oversight in a 2011 law which 'Eliminates the requirement of Senate approval of all appointments to and promotions for the Commissioned Officer Corps in the

> Public Health Service.' [This part of the] executive branch is thus left to police itself . . .[5]

The inevitable result of this abandoned oversight is an ever-expanding federal bulldozer that grinds away at constitutional protections. Public health professionals have become activists, claiming the moral high ground (and high budget) in furtherance of the goal of seeking to prevent disease. These activists are currently working toward gaining control over *everything:* food and water supplies, agriculture, mass immunizations, media (to push health campaign slogans), sexual and reproductive choices, and regulating or restricting access to items (cigarettes, meat, milk, ivermectin, etc.) per their judgment. And I was shocked to learn that leftist activists have literally deployed emergency physicians to engage their emergency patients in the political process. Arabella Advisors funds VOT-ER which they call "good for your health."[6] This is unthinkable and utterly despicable. Coercion anyone?

And just as our Congress seems to be abdicating responsibility for ensuring our inalienable rights to bureaucratic minions domestically, America's very sovereignty over its own public health is increasingly threatened by the Chinese Communist Party. This is happening in two ways—threats foreign and domestic. The World Health Organization is now firmly under the control of the Chinese Communist Party.[7] And the People's Republic of China (PCR) finances American universities to an astonishing degree. The FBI has warned our Congress that this money is ultimately beholden to the Chinese government. Note that the most influential school of public health in America is the Harvard T. H. Chan School of Public Health.

This communist-inspired public health posture—combined with a conscious weakening of the American commitment to God, family, and individual autonomy, achieved through the indoctrination by the government education and university systems—is a strategy that has succeeded in crippling the nation.

The attack will surely continue with the next wave of "climate change" or "overpopulation" or "discoveries" of new (man-made, gain-of-function) viral strains. Medical Marxism normalizes casual cruelty toward and by the individual, diluting the dignity of human lives.

When the next crisis is either created or exploited to erode our constitutional freedoms, we shouldn't expect help from our elected leaders. Far too often, their allegiance is not to the Constitution they swore to uphold. We only invite tyranny by failing to claim our own power as citizens. The American Republic was formed on the premise that each free person is sovereign and entitled to equal ownership in their nation.

But ownership necessitates responsibility, which is hard. The more we rely on government workers to solve our needs, the faster we fall into the black hole of totalitarianism. Every ounce of power that we relinquish in the pursuit of so-called safety and convenience will be seized by someone else. Henry David Thoreau is believed to have said: "Think for yourself, or others will think for you without thinking of you." And Benjamin Franklin understood this danger most presciently: "Those who would give up essential Liberty, to purchase a little temporary Safety, deserve neither Liberty nor Safety."

The path to real success is found in a return to the ideal of American sovereignty: each person is the hero of their own battle for freedom and prosperity. This is the famous "pursuit of happiness" enshrined in our great Declaration of Independence.

To do all these things, individuals need to push back on people and institutions who are dishonest. I taught people how to recognize propaganda in real time in my first (short!) book, *I Do Not Consent: My Fight Against Medical Cancel Culture*. And within your zone of authority, *push back*. Whether you're a mom, a teacher, a policeman; whether you're an officer worker or dog walker, don't ignore your intuition nor be silent in the face of lies. The truth will always be revealed—and there's a good chance *you* can speed it up. So many of our lawsuits paved the way for future legal victories: The State of Florida sat a grand jury to investigate vaccine manufacturers, and the Ninth Circuit ruled that these shots were not vaccines.

Pioneering a New World

I saw American Fascism in the citizen-policing-citizen during the COVID years. I saw American Fascism in the silenced staff at the ER. I see American Fascism in the immoral judiciary and DOJ. I see American Fascism in the callous people running the prison behemoth. And I see American Fascism in the indifferent doctors running the Medical Industrial Complex. Fascism in America is not going to look like defeated Naziism or modern China or the former USSR. It will be: cancel culture, de-banking, social credit scores ("show me your vaccine status" was a precursor), digital currency, government school indoctrination, and monolithic propaganda and censorship.

There are many forces leading us toward totalitarianism, from a bloated federal budget and weaponized bureaucracy, to an economy that doesn't allow for upward mobility, to an indoctrination government school system that keeps our young ignorant and dependent. But the final step that caused millions of Americans to really take a knee to the collectivist was medical fear. Medical fear could have been assuaged—but instead the public health system deployed maximum fear, maximum panic, to cause maximum mass delusion. If the average American had been able to access a physician who wasn't a widget in the socialized system we call "healthcare," so many would never have complied with what was so patently ridiculous. We have outsourced our medical thinking to such a degree that it's not realistic to expect Americans to make these decisions without guidance. But for decades, if not centuries, we trusted that our doctors would not lie to us.

Those days are over.

We Americans were caught unprepared: We never *considered* we couldn't trust our doctors. Now we know we cannot. Whether an individual doctor personally intended well or not, tragically as we saw during COVID, if the government tells your doctor *not* to prescribe you lifesaving medication and *yes* to prescribing you lethal medication, we now know ***for sure*** that the majority of doctors will hurt you. Yes—*your* doctor *will* sell you out. Believe me, I know. America's Frontline Doctors received close to one million inquiries from desperate Americans.

The reality is that over the past fifty years, the vast majority of doctors shifted from being self-employed to being employees, and like most Americans, they complied with their corporate or insurance paycheck. It's hard to keep the Hippocratic Oath when you have to work for an employer and you have graduated with more than $200,000 in debt.

The vast majority of doctors lied or misled—either inadvertently or purposefully—out of ignorance or fear or bias or malice—but misinform their patients they did.

You know which doctors lied the most? Pediatricians. Most earn half of their practice income from complying with government mandates and protocols.[8] Your grandmother didn't need to see the doctor every one to six months for a "well-baby visit" to tell her that her baby was well. She would have thought that was insane.

You know who lied the least? *Doctors who didn't take insurance*. Doctors who could make a living outside of government tentacles. Orthopedists, "concierge" doctors, chiropractors, and naturopathic doctors who don't rely on the state "permitting" them to share their knowledge.

Americans need better doctors for their own personal welfare. Doctors who are paid by the government or insurance companies are not good people to turn to for advice. In pursuit of woke-ism or their own paycheck, mainstream doctors now compete to say the stupidest things. One of the most hateful is an internal medicine doctor employed at one of our nation's most famous hospitals who posted on her TikTok video: "it's ok to be fat" and "it's ok to be unhealthy." That "you could be suffering from 'healthism' if you think being healthier is better." She of course is young and thin and healthy. Such arrogance, such hubris, and such overwhelming contempt for her patients. That is why I call her "hateful." If she actually *cared* for patients, she would try to help them, not virtue signal for her own self-interest.

People can avoid hiring this kind of contemptuous and stunted intellect when it is public, but there are infinite examples that are private. There are the hospital doctors who will be fired if they don't follow protocols, whether it is good for an individual patient or not. There are the pediatricians who can't afford their office rent if they don't comply with insurance companies' protocols regarding children's shots, whether it is good for an individual patient or not.

And did you know many questions your insurance doctor now asks you are not actually questions from your doctor? Of course there are the politicized gender questions—if your doctor doesn't ask you these, she or he cannot use the electronic medical chart. But it's not just woke gender questions. Your doctor is actually a data collector for the government. For example, two data points you may *not* want to respond to your insurance doctor: what shots you *choose* not to take,[9] and if you own a gun—the latter because you may be disinterested in your Second Amendment right someday becoming subordinate to your doctor's beliefs.

And it's not just for themselves. Americans also need better doctors for the welfare of our nation. The majority of Americans knew something was amiss within a few weeks of missing the "fifteen days to slow the spread" deadline. Many would never have complied with lockdowns, closing their businesses and schools, or followed mythical concepts such as "essential" businesses and six-feet social distancing, if only they had some trustworthy medical source of information.

As public health policy (or what I renamed the Religion of Public Health) is a key component of the machine moving us toward totalitarian control, many freedom doctors have joined together to create a replacement for the current unfixable system. I was an insider for more than twenty-five years. The incentive—to heal the patient, to help the patient be maximally well—is never going to be the goal of the current system. Of course you can have a good result within the broken system—but it is Russian roulette—and not only do you not know how many bullets there are, you don't even know who is holding the gun. You *can* use the system for your benefit, but only with the guidance of an honest and knowledgeable broker.

As the GoldCare® Health & Wellness website explains: "Because we don't allow government or insurance to control healthcare decisions, the physician-patient relationship can flourish."

The stark differences between these systems are laid out for easy comparison:

Current Healthcare Model	GoldCare™ PMA
Doctors are strongly encouraged and incentivized to practice medicine based on insurance, governmental, and office policies - frequently not in the best interest of the patient.	Members have access to ever-growing resources as our providers seek medical truth from a variety of evidence-based approaches that are not driven by profits.
Physicians are pressured to rush through appointments due to quotas and charting requirements justifying their recommendations.	Telemedicine and triage nurse services will be availabe to all members.
Insurance companies make patients jump through hoops and often require excessive and expensive interventions or specialty referrals.	Members will have access to pre-negotiated, cash-pay rates on labs, imaging, and specialty services.
Patients are told how to manage their health based on their physician's 'evidence' that is largely funded and distorted by Big Pharma entities.	Providers and specialist consultants are unshackled by the external pressures of traditional medicine to bring you unbiased, truthful healthcare recommendations.
Physicians are incentivized to recommend certain medicines, tests, and treatments that may cause harm to patients.	Clinicians will discuss all treatment options available to help members make health decisions. The risk-to-benefit ratio and member's goals remain at the center of all healthcare decisions.

GoldCare is a compelling example of how Americans can create new solutions by better addressing a current and ongoing human need. Using our own ingenuity, we can craft free-market decentralized solutions that will defeat American Fascism. We urgently need freedom solutions in five "M" areas: medicine, money (banking), mobile (telecommunications), minds (education), and media. Here are my suggestions.

For medicine: GoldCare.com. For freedom banking that will not politically de-bank customers: Old Glory Bank. In the telecommunications space (cellular): Patriot Mobile. For non-woke children's books there is Brave Books. For general purchases, consider Public Square and Mammoth Nation. For resources on education options: SorboStudios.com, MomsForAmerica, and AFLDS.org. For crowdfunding: GiveSendGo.

However, you may choose to join the fight for freedom, I'm with you. We must continue supporting health and wellness alternatives, freedom of speech, the right to bear arms, the right to homeschool or otherwise instill *your* values into *your* children, the right to live and speak without fear of political persecution, and many other efforts to protect individual rights.

The most vulnerable minorities are not women, homosexuals, blacks, whites, Christians, or Jews. The most vulnerable minority of all is the individual. The Bill of Rights ensures our individual rights, which not only allows us to pursue our own version of happiness but is also the prerequisite for building the best societal solutions. Enforcing the Bill of Rights is our vaccine against fascism.

Iron Sharpens Iron

Finally, to that question from so many, would I do it again, the answer is a resounding yes. The attacks didn't kill me so, as the adage goes, they made me stronger. I would do it all over again to help a human in need, to protect my children's future, and for love of country.

One of our founding states, New Hampshire, carries a favorite motto, "Live free or die." As you've happily reached the end of this story, you are clearly still graced with another day. So live . . . and live free.

We are not the land of the coward and the home of the slave.

We are the land of the free and home of the brave.

God bless America, land that I love
Stand beside her and guide her
Through the night with the light from above
From the mountains to the prairies
To the oceans white with foam
God bless America, my home sweet home

Afterword
by John C. Eastman, JD, PhD

On November 5, 2024, the once and future president, Donald Trump, won a resounding victory. The American people voted for a future "unburden by what has been" in the recent past—the lawfare; the weaponization of our institutions; the undermining of the constitutional rights protected by the First, Second, Fourth, Fifth, Sixth, and Eighth Amendments. But make no mistake, that recent past is only the next election away from being revived by the political enemies within. The authoritarian left, joined by the hysterical anti-Trump "right," has suffered a setback, but they are far from defeated. They still have immense power in their control of most of our nation's institutions, from the press, the deep state bureaucracy, the universities, Hollywood, the medical boards, bar disciplinary processes, etc. And they will use every bit of that power to thwart the president from implementing the constitutional agenda that the American people overwhelmingly chose.

That makes the stories of "what has been done" in the recent past so important. Shining a light on the truly evil, authoritarian tactics that were deployed over the past four years may be the most effective disinfectant. That is what makes this book by Dr. Simone Gold so critically important. As an outspoken critic of the government's COVID mandates, she was already on the government's radar when she attended the rally in Washington, DC, on January 6, 2021, and then, without knowledge that the Capitol grounds had been temporarily designated a restricted area and as an invited speaker at a lawfully permitted event, entered the Capitol building through doors that had been opened from the inside. She rightly describes what she experienced as resulting from an "infrastructure for fascism," as it indeed is.

But even more troubling is the compelling evidence of disparate treatment that she thoroughly documents. Protesters in Portland, Oregon, during the Summer of Rage, for example, who actually took over whole city blocks, closed and threatened to burn down courthouses, and viciously attacked police, were barely given slaps on the wrist. Protesters who occupied the Capitol Building and disrupted the confirmation hearings for Brett Kavanaugh were likewise given slaps on the wrist—a $50 "post and forfeit" fine. Protestors who tried to disrupt President Trump's first inauguration, some of whom attacked police and even set a limousine on fire, were not only not prosecuted—in most cases, even the misdemeanor charges were dropped—but they were paid more than $1.6 million in damages in settlement of their claims of false arrest and excessive force. Such selective application of the law undermines a critically important aspect of the rule of law—that of "equal justice under law," the phrase that is etched into the pediment atop the west entrance to the Supreme Court building itself.

Instead of "equal justice under law," what the nation has witnessed, and what Dr. Gold so eloquently exposes, is an abuse of prosecutorial power unparalleled in our nation's history. It gets traction because, in this hyper-partisan era, prosecutors are able to self-select their jury pools in jurisdictions, such as the District of Columbia, that have an overwhelmingly lopsided partisan balance—hardly the "jury of one's peers" that the Constitution requires. More troubling, however, is that the prosecutorial abuse is also a manifestation of the very sort that Franklin Roosevelt's Attorney General (and later Supreme Court justice and chief judge of the Nuremburg war crimes tribunal) Robert Jackson warned against.

In a famous speech he delivered in 1940 to the Conference of United States Attorneys, Jackson warned of the danger inherent in the prosecutor's authority not just to pick his cases but to pick his defendants. "Therein is the most dangerous power of the prosecutor," Jackson warned, "that he will pick people he thinks he should get, rather than pick cases that need to be prosecuted." Elaborating, he added:

> With the law books filled with a great assortment of crimes, a prosecutor stands a fair chance of finding at least a technical violation of some act on the part of almost anyone. In such a case, it is not a question of discovering the commission of a crime and then looking for the man who has committed it, it is a question of picking the man and then searching the law books, or putting investigators to work, to pin some offense on him. It is in this realm—in which the prosecutor picks some person whom he dislikes or desires to embarrass, or selects some group of unpopular persons and then looks for an offense, that the greatest danger of abuse of prosecuting power lies. It is here that law enforcement becomes personal, and the real crime becomes that of being unpopular with the predominant or governing group, being attached to the wrong political views, or being personally obnoxious to or in the way of the prosecutor himself.[1]

This is Soviet-style stuff. Recall that Lavrentiy Beria, the head of Josef Stalin's secret police, infamously said, "Show me the man, and I'll show you the crime." What Dr. Gold describes in the pages of this book is evidence that Jackson's warning and Beria's boast have instead become a playbook for our current Department of Justice.

No nation can long survive such an abuse of the justice system. What remains to be seen is whether the election of 2024 will result in the successful and permanent closing of the Pandora's box that had been opened by the "get Trump and his supporters at all costs" crowd, or whether it will be merely a temporary reprieve on the long march toward authoritarian despotism. If it is to be the former, books like this one will play a critical role in securing ultimate victory for freedom.

Dr. John Eastman is currently a senior fellow at the Claremont Institute and director of the institute's Center for Constitutional Jurisprudence. He has a PhD from the Claremont Graduate School in Government, focusing on the political philosophy of the American founding. He also earned a JD from the University of Chicago, following which he served as a law clerk to Supreme Court Justice Clarence Thomas. He was the Henry Salvatori Professor of Law & Community Service and former dean at Chapman University's Fowler School of Law before he was forced into early retirement in 2021 from that tenured position because he had the temerity to represent President Donald Trump in challenges to illegality in the conduct of the 2020 election.

EPILOGUE

The Road to Fascism Is Paved with Public Health

by Robert W. Malone, MD, MS

Public Health, Utilitarianism, and Socialism

"Public health" experts earn a "masters in public health" (MPH) degree that requires no prior medical or biological training but instead theorizes that imposing healthcare management decisions on the population at large will achieve statistically optimal minimized average disease for all people. Public health goals are distinct from, and often are in direct opposition to, the classic physician goal of working toward an individual patient's best outcome. While physicians classically work toward optimizing health on a case-by-case basis for each individual citizen, public health "experts" emphatically do not.

As the origins of public health are authoritarian and militarized, one consequence has been the rise of various public health "priesthoods," such as now exist in pediatrics, cardiology, infectious disease, and epidemiology. This is the direct consequence of the logic of centralized planning and socialist philosophy (ends justify the means) infiltrating the entire US national and global (WHO) healthcare enterprise. Central planning requires an anointed expert elite to guide and justify centralized decision-making. As history has repeatedly demonstrated, when centralized planning and decision-making imposed on populations errs in assumptions or interventions, the consequences are typically catastrophic due mainly to the scale of the imposed mistake. This is one of the key truths illustrated by the US COVID "public health" response—which massively worsened outcomes.

These interventions are promoted by various top-down mechanisms (governmental and corporate policies coupled with coercive judicial enforcement and propaganda). Often, these policies are enforced through mandates (notably vaccine mandates), insurance rate incentives, taxation (alcohol, cigarettes), financial compliance incentives to physicians, as well as other methods of theft, violence, and coercion, typically coupled to governmental, corporate, and social pressures.

Subsidiarity and Patient-Focused Medical Care

When those raised in the classical liberal Western tradition speak of "freedom," in many ways, they are referencing the principle of subsidiarity. Although not explicitly mentioned in the US Declaration of Independence, Constitution, or Bill of Rights, the principle of subsidiarity is a key subtext that runs through these founding documents. The ideas of freedom and subsidiarity underpin the assumption that, in a "free" society, individual adults are presumed to be competent to make their own personal daily decisions so long as they do not interfere with the rights of other citizens. Subsidiarity is the principle of social organization that holds that social and political issues should be dealt with at the most immediate or local level consistent with their resolution.

In the past, people saw authority first within themselves and their family and looked next to their local town, then to the county and after to the state and finally, last of all and least importantly, to the federal authority. In our very own Bill of Rights, the Tenth Amendment to the Constitution makes this belief clear. Namely, any power not expressly delegated in the Constitution to the federal government resides with the states or the people.

However, the deterioration of subsidiarity is evident in the United States today. The office of the presidency dominates modern political discussion while local politics is almost completely disregarded. The Supreme Court renders decisions (see *Roe v. Wade*, *Obergefell v. Hodges*) about all facets of life ranging from marriage to abortion. The default response to societal problems today is centralization. Physicians must combat this response in order to maintain the sacred relationship between them and their patients.

The Rise of Socialism in the US Public Health Enterprise

The Yellow Berets, also known as Public Health Service trainees, were a group of physicians who participated in the National Institutes of Health (NIH) Associate Training Program during the Vietnam War era. They were often derogatorily referred to as "Yellow Berets" by persons who viewed them as avoiding military service. Banding together, many later formed a network of influential scientists and medical leaders that continues to dominate the public health agencies to this day, particularly at NIH. They fostered a culture and mentored others who continue to enforce that culture and support the informal networks, alliances, and power relationships that dominate the USPHS and the overall US medical research enterprise.

The young adult male children of the wealthy and upper middle class, with parents who provided the best educational opportunities, facing the horrors of Vietnam and "The Draft" had a pathway to avoid the Selective Service sacrifices required of most of their age cohort. They did not need to debase themselves on an "Alice's Restaurant" group W bench strategy or even contrive claims of bone spurs to avoid the draft. They just had to apply to serve in the pseudo-military Public Health Service and receive a cushy job for the duration in DC or Atlanta. And so they did, with the consequence being that these "public health" agencies became captured by pseudo-hippies that viewed public service not as a responsibility and calling, but rather as yet another entitlement.

During the Vietnam War, physicians could serve their draft requirement by joining the USPHS, which allowed them to work at places like the CDC, NIH, and FDA. Their common experience, background, and cultural biases fostered natural affiliations that eventually developed into a loose network of influence that came to dominate both the NIH and the USPHS. Dr. Anthony Fauci is one example of a successful "Yellow Beret." It is no surprise that they jumped right into bed with corporate America and Big Pharma, for this was the caste from whence they whelped.

Today's NIH, CDC, and FDA Cultures Are Fundamentally Socialist and Pro-Corporatist

Given this background, it should surprise no one that the underlying cultures of NIH, CDC, and FDA are socialist/corporatist. Whether by intent or circumstance, these organizations are led by the children of privilege, typically graduates of elite East Coast "Ivy League" prep and finishing schools, and have been for decades. Federal policies have consequences, and those consequences often persist for a very long time. It will be extremely difficult to shift current USPHS culture and extremely difficult to shift the underlying cultures of NIH, CDC, and FDA. But without cultural change, any structural changes implemented by populist leadership will rapidly revert to current norms as soon as the focus shifts to other areas.

It is important to understand that these agencies see Congress rather than either the president or the voters as their customers. Congress has long viewed the USPHS, and in particular the NIH, as a pork barrel opportunity. The NIH director will find that the various NIH institute directors are focused on servicing their congressional benefactors (and in turn their client corporations) rather than responding to any direction coming from the overall NIH director.

Populist Pushback: MAGA and MAHA

The extreme encroachment on basic American freedoms by these socialist/corporatist public health officials during COVID strengthened and merged the populist political movements of MAGA and MAHA. Both MAHA (Make America Healthy Again) and MAGA (Make America Great Again) populism have now accomplished political milestones that are almost unprecedented in American history.

One has to reach back to Presidents Theodore Roosevelt (POTUS 26) and Andrew Jackson (POTUS 7) to find solid parallels to the presidency of Donald J. Trump (POTUS 45 and 47): Jackson for his battle with the Second US Bank and eliminating the US Federal Debt; and of course, "Teddy" Roosevelt was known for promoting a muscular expansionist US foreign policy and his commitment to health and exercise, in many ways foreshadowing a similar emphasis during the administration of John F. Kennedy (POTUS 35) and now JFK's nephew RFK Jr.

Not to be negative, but the history of US populist political movements is littered with stories of unmet high expectations and subversion of those movements by established political power centers. Typically, there is a failure to convert those bottom-up, decentralized politics into sustainable long-term policy changes.

MAHA has emerged mainly from the left and, out of frustration born of the Democrat Party corruption and rejection, has embraced the center-right. In turn, MAHA has been enthusiastically endorsed by MAGA and center-right populists, including many formerly associated with the Tea Party movement. Who does not want to be more healthy?

Pro-Regulation versus Deregulation

But there are fundamental fault lines between MAHA and MAGA, and there is a risk this resolves with pro-regulatory big government initiatives versus promotion of deregulation/small government. While there is a deregulatory aspect to the MAHA movement, at its core, MAHA is predominantly pro-regulation. MAHA logic favors using regulatory authority to improve transparency and eliminate that which leads to unhealthy outcomes.

Examples include drugs with side effects that, when considered in whole, do not have a strongly favorable risk/benefit ratio, and glyphosate (Roundup) contamination of our grain and soybeans. There is also an investigational research aspect, for example, what are the drivers behind the explosion of autism, obesity, and other childhood chronic diseases.

To date, the MAHA movement has primarily focused on things that big government can do to promote improved health of US citizens: removing known toxins from food, investigating autism causes, questioning the pediatric vaccine schedule, and revising the CDC Vaccine Adverse Event

Reporting System so truly informed decisions can be made concerning the safety and efficacy of vaccine products.

Pro-Regulation Can Lead to Nanny State Medical Fascism

But the MAHA initiative, if institutionalized and bureaucratized, can morph into another overbearing set of nanny state mandates. To make the point, I often use the example of the person who loves McDonald's hamburgers consumed with sugary Coca-Cola. You know who I am talking about. Should the state mandate that such a person not eat these things, despite the clear-cut health risks? Should the state outlaw cigars? And what about regulating foods? Where should MAHA draw the line? What principles should be applied to guide these decisions? What is the proper role of small government as it relates to food and drug regulation?

Consider seat belt mandates. Like many big government initiatives that stand at the top of slippery slopes, there is a general consensus that it is right and proper for government to mandate seat belts be installed in cars. But is it right to legally require their use when driving? Next comes motorcycle helmets. Same issues, but slightly less clear. Cigarette smoking? Experimental shots?

In all these cases, the argument is made that irresponsible health behaviors by individuals cost all of society due to increased health care and insurance costs (including publicly subsidized costs) and loss of person-years. The same logic then can be applied all the way down to whether the state should mandate your dietary choices, which is why I use the McDonald's hamburger example. Should we "allow" citizens to experiment with nutraceuticals and health supplements that are not officially endorsed by the FDA?

And there we go, straight to nanny state medical fascism. But seat belts save lives. Motorcycle helmets too. Maybe experimental shots work (to reduce fear). You get my point.

If we want a new, transformed, and sustainable set of public health enterprise policies without veering into medical fascism, we need to take some time to think about and define acceptable limits on the role of the state in promoting, advancing, and in some cases mandating limits on infringement of individual sovereignty and autonomy.

What are the boundaries between the proper role of a Constitutional Republic-based federal government, the constitutional role of individual states (which are responsible for regulating the practice of medicine), and both the sovereign rights of the individual and the global right to truly informed consent to medical interventions? What are the boundaries between individual sovereignty, libertarianism, anarcho-capitalism, and the utilitarian/socialist logic of modern "public health"?

Can the USPHS, NIH, CDC, and FDA Culture Be Changed?

The stated goal of our public health agencies is to seek to achieve collective health outcomes rather than individual outcomes. Our public health officials use top-down management via government, insurer, and health management organizations to require and deploy preapproved treatment protocols rather than consider individually optimized decisions. One size fits all, and do what you are told. The emphasis on the collective versus the individual increases the likelihood of a corrupted result, which we saw during COVID.

The bureaucracy is structurally biased toward a disease treatment model, and due to temperament, training, and financial incentives, constantly looking for opportunities to intervene to "stamp out disease" across the collective rather than a health promotion model for the individual. Is it possible to transform a deeply entrenched socialist/corporatist bureaucratic culture? This is a culture for which the idea of entrepreneurship is not only foreign but is seen as a threat. For which libertarian and conservative beliefs in the primacy of the individual and right to choose are alien. This is a culture that firmly believes in utilitarian outcomes-based socialism while fiercely defending their own privileges. For which risk-taking is a threat to be strictly avoided, suppressed, and never rewarded. Team players are promoted, and free thinkers are expunged.

The only way this can be changed will be to actively recruit, incentivize, and promote a new generation of leaders and help them to work up the ladder to replace the Yellow Berets and their bureaucratic offspring. If we don't make these changes, our public health officials will one day in the future, again, threaten our individual and national sovereignty.

Dr. Robert Malone is a renowned scientist, thought leader, and the author of several books, including *Lies My Government Told Me* and *PsyWar: Enforcing the New World Order*. He is known for his pioneering work in vaccine research and development, including inventing mRNA vaccines. Dr. Malone is an international speaker advocating for open scientific discourse and critical thinking in healthcare, with a focus on bioethics, restoring integrity in government, biological sciences, bioethics, and politics.

Endnotes

Chapter 1

1 America's Frontline Doctors, "SAVING LIVES: Real Stories of Frontline Interventions, Featuring Lidia" (video, September 22, 2021), https://americasfrontlinedoctors.org/videos/post/saving-lives-real-stories-of-frontline-interventions-featuring-lidia.

2 America's Frontline Doctors, "SAVING LIVES: Real Stories of Frontline Interventions, Featuring Chris Burgard" (video, November 3, 2021), https://americasfrontlinedoctors.org/videos/post/saving-lives-real-stories-of-frontline-interventions-featuring-chris-burgard.

3 America's Frontline Doctors, "SAVING LIVES: Real Stories of Frontline Interventions, Featuring The Halcomb Family" (video, October 20, 2021), https://americasfrontlinedoctors.org/videos/post/saving-lives-real-stories-of-frontline-interventions-featuring-the-halcomb-family.

4 For examples of these studies see: Roman Wölfel et al., "Virological Assessment of Hospitalized Patients with COVID-2019," *Nature* 581 (2020): 465-469, https://doi.org/10.1038/s41586-020-2196-x; Rita Jaafar et al., "Correlation Between 3790 Quantitative Polymerase Chain Reaction-Positives Samples and Positive Cell Cultures, Including 1941 Severe Acute Respiratory Syndrome Coronavirus 2 Isolates," *Clin. Infect. Dis.* 72 (2020): e921, https://doi.org/10.1093/cid/ciaa1491; Flora Marzia Liotti et al., "Assessment of SARS-CoV-2 RNA Test Results Among Patients Who Recovered From COVID-19 With Prior Negative Results." *JAMA Internal Medicine* 181 (2020): 702-704, https://doi.org/10.1001/jamainternmed.2020.7570; Jared Bullard et al., "Predicting Infectious Severe Acute Respiratory Syndrome Coronavirus 2 From Diagnostic Samples," *Clin. Infect. Dis.* 71 (2020): 2663-2666, https://doi.org/10.1093/cid/ciaa638.

5 Jim Dickerson and *Just the News*, "COVID tests may inflate numbers by picking up 'dead' virus," *KPGZ News*, November 9, 2020, https://1027kearneymo.com/kpgz-news/2020/11/9/covid-tests-may-inflate-numbers-by-picking-up-dead-virus.

6 America's Frontline Doctors, "The Uncensored Truth Tour: Albuquerque NM," (video, July 8, 2021), https://americasfrontlinedoctors.org/videos/post/the-uncensored-truth-tour-albuquerque-nm.

7 Apoorva Mandavilli, "Your Coronavirus Test is Positive. Maybe it Shouldn't Be," *The New York Times*, August 29, 2020 (updated July 3, 2021), https://www.nytimes.com/2020/08/29/health/coronavirus-testing.html.

8 The Nobel Prize, "The Nobel Prize in Physiology or Medicine 2015" (press release, October 5, 2015), https://www.nobelprize.org/prizes/medicine/2015/press-release/.

9 C19IVM.org and C19HCQ.org: over 500 studies. *All* ivermectin and the vast majority of hydroxychloroquine studies show improvement. These studies occurred worldwide >70 countries and >10,000 scientists and >750,000 patients.

10 Appendix 1, https://www.drsimonegold.com/book/resources.

11 America's Frontline Doctors, (website, accessed June 12, 2024), aflds.org.

12 America's Frontline Doctors, "White Coat Summit, SCOTUS Highlights" (video, 2020), https://fast.wistia.net/embed/iframe/6ndhhgyy3o.

13 America's Frontline Doctors, "White Coat Summit" (video, July 27, 2021), https://aflds.wistia.com/medias/3657il0bs7.

14 Dr. Simone Gold [@drsimonegold], *After our press conference, I was defamed by the media, censored by social media companies, terminated from employment, and viciously attacked, all for advocating for the right of physicians to prescribe what they believe is best for their patients* (video attached), X, August 2, 2020, https://x.com/drsimonegold/status/1290079600454729728.

15 Erik Ofgang, "How One Covid-19 Doctor Became a Ventilator Whistleblower," *Medium (Elemental)*, September 10, 2020, https://elemental.medium.com/how-one-covid-19-doctor-became-a-ventilator-whistleblower-a1c2dbdd1b06.

16 Cameron Kyle-Sidell, "From NYC ICU: Does COVID-19 really cause ARDS?" (YouTube video, 0:55, March 31, 2020), https://youtu.be/k9GYTc53r2o.

17 Ibid., 3:24.

18 Interview. *Tucker Carlson Tonight*. July 30, 2020. https://www.bitchute.com/video/JyOipakdQzK6.

19 Simone Gold, *I Do Not Consent: My Fight Against Medical Cancel Culture* (Bombardier Books, 2020).

20 Appendix 2, https://www.drsimonegold.com/book/resources.

Chapter 2

1 Marshal Cohen and Avery Lotz, "The January 6 insurrection: minute by minute," CNN, July 29, 2022, https://edition.cnn.com/2022/07/10/politics/jan-6-us-capitol-riot-timeline/index.html.

2 John Strand: Artist, Activist, American (website, accessed June 12, 2024), johnstrand.com.

3 Debra Heine, "Feds Quietly Dismiss Dozens of Cases Against Antifa Extremists Who Terrorized Downtown Portland Last Summer," *The Tennessee Star*, March 7, 2021, https://tennesseestar.com/2021/03/07/feds-quietly-dismiss-dozens-of-cases-against-antifa-extremists-who-terrorized-downtown-portland-last-summer/.

Chapter 3

1 Ryan J. Reilly, "Feds Say They'll Hunt Down Trump Mob That Violently Stormed The U.S. Capitol," *HuffPost*, January 7, 2021, https://www.huffpost.com/entry/trump-insurrectionists-capitol-building-fbi-doj_n_5ff74017c5b6fc79f463762.

2 Joseph M. Hanneman, “Prosecutor Admits DC Police Officers Acted As Provocateurs at US Capitol on Jan. 6,” *The Epoch Times*, March 24, 2023 (updated March 30, 2023), https://www.theepochtimes.com/prosecutor-admits-dc-police-officers-acted-as-provocateurs-at-us-capitol-on-jan-6_5148808.html.
3 Federal Bureau of Investigation, “Steven M. D’Anuono Named Assistant Director in Charge of the Washington Field Office” (press release, October 13, 2020), https://www.fbi.gov/news/press-releases/steven-m-dantuono-named-assistant-director-in-charge-of-the-washington-field-office.
4 BonginoReport, “‘FED!’—The Jan 6 Video They Don’t Want You to See,” (Rumble video, accessed June 7, 2024), https://rumble.com/vo1u5b-fed-the-jan-6-video-they-dont-want-you-to-see.html.
5 Tyler Durden, “‘I Also Orchestrated It’: Uncharged J6 Witness Ray Epps Transcript Released,” *Zero Hedge*, December 30, 2022, https://www.zerohedge.com/political/i-also-orchestrated-it-uncharged-j6-witness-ray-epps-transcript-released.
6 Andrew Kerr, “Ray Epps uncharged in Capitol riot, but feds engaged in similar conduct,” *The Washington Examiner*, January 13, 2022, https://www.washingtonexaminer.com/news/ray-epps-uncharged-in-capitol-riot-but-feds-arrested-woman-engaged-in-similar-conduct.
7 Thomas Massie (@RepThomas Massie), *I questioned Attorney General Garland about whether there were Federal Agents present on 1/16 and whether they agitated to go into the Capitol. Attorney General Garland refused to answer* (video attached), X, October 21, 2021, https://twitter.com/RepThomasMassie/status/1451310873604206597.
8 Patricia Tolson, “EXCLUSIVE: Capitol Police Use of Force Reports Expose Brutality of Unprovoked Attacks Against Jan. 5 Protesters,” *The Epoch Times*, July 27, 2022 (updated March 25, 2024), https://www.pennlive.com/nation-world/2022/04/first-person-acquitted-of-all-charges-in-jan-6-riot-said-police-let-him-enter-capitol.html.
9 “Meet Ray Epps: The Fed-Protected Provacateur Who Appears to Have Led the Very First 1/6 Attack on the US Capitol,” *Revolver*, January 3, 2023, https://www.revolver.news/2021/10/meet-ray-epps-the-fed-protected-provocateur-who-appears-to-have-led-the-very-first-1-6-attack-on-the-u-s-capitol/.
10 Associated Press, “First person acquitted of all charges in Jan. 6 riot said police let him enter Capitol,” *PennLive Patriot News*, April 7, 2022, https://www.pennlive.com/nation-world/2022/04/first-person-acquitted-of-all-charges-in-jan-6-riot-said-police-let-him-enter-capitol.html.
11 Office of Public Affairs, U.S. Department of Justice, “Statement of Acting Attorney General Jeffrey A. Rosen,” Thursday, January 7, 2021 (Press Release Number: 21-13), https://www.justice.gov/opa/pr/statement-acting-attorney-general-jeffrey-rosen#.
12 Ryan J. Reilly, “Feds Say They’ll Hunt Down Trump Mob That Violently Stormed the U.S. Capitol,” *HuffPost*, January 7, 2021, https://www.huffpost.com/entry/trump-insurrectionists-capitol-building-fbi-doj_n_5ff74017c5b6fc79f4637622.
13 Ibid.

14 This poster with my picture remained pinned to the *top of* the FBI Washington Field office X account for four years. @FBIWFO. On this account you can see that the FBI prioritized J6 arrests above everything else and continued to arrest people for alleged J6 *misdemeanors* until and including January 17, 2025, more than four years after the event.

15 FBI [@FBI], *Do you see anyone you recognize? The #FBI is still seeking information to help identify individuals who actively instigated violence on January 6 in Washington, D.C. Visit ow.ly/skY550D3JL1 to see images from current cases, and submit tips to fbi.gov/USCapitol,* (image attached), X, January 8, 2021, https://twitter.com/FBI/status/1347635668835577859.

16 Needa Satija, "'I do regret being there': Simone Gold, noted hydroxychloroquine advocate, was inside the Capitol during the riot," *The Washington Post*, January 12, 2021, https://www.washingtonpost.com/investigations/simone-gold-capitol-riot-coronavirus/2021/01/12/d1d39e84-545f-11eb-a817-e5e7f8a406d6_story.html.

17 Jacob Ryan, "Since Protests, LMPD Rarely Busts Down Doors For Drugs," *Leo Weekly*, August 20, 2021, https://www.leoweekly.com/2021/08/since-protests-lmpd-rarely-busts-down-doors-for-drugs/.

18 "Harvey Weinstein timeline: How the scandal has unfolded," *BBC*, February 24, 2023, https://www.bbc.com/news/entertainment-arts-41594672.

19 "Special Weapons and Tactics (SWAT): Concepts and Issues Paper," IACP National Law Enforcement Policy Center, March 2011, https://www.theiacp.org/sites/default/files/all/s/SWATPaper.pdf.

20 Ibid, p. 7.

21 Dinah Voyles Pulver, "Two months and nearly 300 Capitol riot arrests later, FBI is hunting hundreds more," *USA Today*, March 8, 2021, https://www.usatoday.com/story/news/2021/03/08/capitol-riot-insurrection-arrests-near-300-fbi-hunts-hundreds-more/6871403002/.

22 T.C. Sottek, "Why do online trolls call SWAT teams? Because the police hurt people: Police brutality is an on-demand service in the United States," *The Verge*, June 4, 2020, https://www.theverge.com/21280400/george-floyd-protests-swatting-police-violence-swat.

23 The first picture is an FBI training SWAT training team and somewhat resembles the team breaking into my home. The second picture is from the *Denver Post* and is similar to several (3–5) vehicles outside my home. The last picture resembles the officers on the street outside my home and is from Vox.com.

Chapter 4

1 America's Frontline Doctors (website, accessed June 12, 2024), aflds.org.

2 "First Amendment", *Constitution of the United States*, accessed June 4, 2024, https://constitution.congress.gov/constitution/.

3 "Sixth Amendment", *Constitution of the United States*, accessed June 4, 2024, https://constitution.congress.gov/constitution/.

4 Ibid.

5 Ibid.

6 Kim Christensen, Brittny Mejia, and Jack Dolan, "Times' sex abuse investigation triggers calls for reform of state Medical Board," *Los Angeles Times*, December 16, 2021, https://www.latimes.com/california/story/2021-12-16/medical-board-reaction-story.

7 Appendix 4, https://www.drsimonegold.com/book/resources. This accusation was a result of a mild-mannered physician (don't take my word for it; watch the video yourself, https://americasfrontlinedoctors.org/videos/post/doc-tracy-pi-s1-e1-lawsons-hunt) asking Ms. Lawson why she was being dishonest with Californians. Ms. Lawson was incensed that a member of the public would have the audacity to question her. The California physician investigator "Doc Tracy" talked to her in a well-lit public parking garage. She had coworkers with her, and he asked her a couple of questions. The whole interaction was about one minute long and videotaped. Ms. Lawson was *enraged* and called the police department (interesting that they were on speed dial on her phone) and then she promptly went to social media and TV shows complaining that I harassed and stalked her. Hardly. Not only was I not even present, Doc Tracy had two detectives with him and everything was done strictly by the book. Tyrants simply don't like to be questioned. Never mind she's serving as a *public servant.*

8 Appendix 5, https://www.drsimonegold.com/book/resources.

9 August 30, 2022, May 9, 2022 House hearings, page 4. The California House was so focused on stopping me and so afraid their attempts to revoke my physician license were illegitimate that they worked to pass a new law HB 2098 to stop *all* physicians' free speech. The bill became law on January 1, 2023, was immediately challenged, and was repealed later that year. https://leginfo.legislature.ca.gov/faces/billAnalysisClient.xhtml?bill_id=202120220AB2098.

10 America's Frontline Doctors, "PROFILES IN COURAGE: Tony Roman" (video, October 6, 2021), https://americasfrontlinedoctors.org/videos/post/profiles-in-courage-tony-roman.

11 "Supermarket owner in Florida defies face mask order in Collier County," *WPLG Local 10* (YouTube video, accessed June 4, 2024), https://www.youtube.com/watch?v=2U0dHhMLmnY.

12 Seed to Table, (website, accessed June 13, 2024), https://seedtotablemarket.com

13 America's Frontline Doctors, "The CMB and The Omnipresent Threat of Usurpation" (issues brief, accessed June 4, 2024), https://aflds.org/about-us/issue-briefs/the-cmb-and-the-omnipresent-threat-of-usurpation.

14 Also see Chapter 11 section "Double Jeopardy" for more on the California Medical Board.

15 In the novel *Catch-22*, by Joseph Heller, the captain did not want to fly dangerous missions, which meant he was sane enough to fly because he recognized it's dangerous. A Catch-22 is an impossible situation. "There was only one catch and that was Catch-22, which specified that a concern for one's safety in the face of dangers that were real and immediate was the process of a rational mind. Orr was crazy and could be grounded. All he had to do was ask; and as soon as he did, he

would no longer be crazy and would have to fly more missions. Orr would be crazy to fly more missions and sane if he didn't, but if he was sane he had to fly them. If he flew them he was crazy and didn't have to; but if he didn't want to he was sane and had to. Yossarian was moved very deeply by the absolute simplicity of this clause of Catch-22 and let out a respectful whistle. That's some catch, that catch-22" (Chapter 5).

16 Cambridge Dictionary, definition of "usurpation", https://dictionary.cambridge.org/us/dictionary/english/usurpation.

17 America's Frontline Doctors, "Dr. Gold Emerges Victorious in Landmark Free Speech Case" (issues brief, accessed June 4, 2024), https://aflds.org/about-us/issue-briefs/dr-gold-emerges-victorious-in-landmark-free-speech-case.

18 Appendix 6, https://www.drsimonegold.com/book/resources.

19 *ArtI.S10.C1.4 State Bills of Attainder*, Congress.gov (website, accessed June 4, 2024), https://constitution.congress.gov/browse/essay/artI-S10-C1-4/ALDE_00001100/.

20 Appendix 7, https://www.drsimonegold.com/book/resources.

21 Appendix 8, https://www.drsimonegold.com/book/resources.

22 *Missouri v. Biden*, 3:22-cv-01213, (W.D. La. Jul 04, 2023) ECF No. 293, p. 2, https://www.courtlistener.com/docket/63290154/293/missouri-v-biden/.

23 "Missouri Attorney General Andrew Bailey Obtains Court Order Blocking the Biden Administration from Violating First Amendment," Mo.gov (website, accessed June 4, 2024), https://ago.mo.gov/missouri-attorney-general-andrew-bailey-obtains-court-order-blocking-the-biden-administration-from-violating-first-amendment/.

24 *Missouri v. Biden*, 3:22-cv-01213-TAD-KDM, (W.D. La. Jul 04, 2023) ECF No. 293, https://www.courtlistener.com/docket/63290154/293/missouri-v-biden/.

25 Ibid., p. 4.

26 Ibid., pp. 85–86.

27 Ibid., p. 53.

28 Brief for America's Frontline Doctors and Dr. Simone Gold, M.D., J.D. as Amicus Curiae (23-411, February 9, 2024) for *Murthy v. Missouri*, 23-411(5th Cir. 2023), https://res.cloudinary.com/aflds/image/upload/v1707507071/aflds/Murthy_v_Missouri-Americas_Frontline_Doctors__Dr._Simone_Golds_Amici_Brief-file-stamped-2-9-2024_23-411-US2024_ki4q27.pdf.

29 *Missouri v. Biden*, 23-30455 (5th Cir. October 3, 2023), https://www.ca5.uscourts.gov/opinions/pub/23/23-30445-CV1.pdf.

30 Brief for America's Frontline Doctors and Dr. Simone Gold, M.D., J.D. as Amicus Curiae (23-411, February 9, 2024) for *Murthy v. Missouri*, 23-411(5th Cir. 2023), https://res.cloudinary.com/aflds/image/upload/v1707507071/aflds/Murthy_v_Missouri-Americas_Frontline_Doctors__Dr._Simone_Golds_Amici_Brief-file-stamped-2-9-2024_23-411-US2024_ki4q27.pdf.

31 *Missouri v. Biden*, 3:22-cv-01213, (W.D. La. Jul 04, 2023) ECF No. 293, p. 3, https://www.courtlistener.com/docket/63290154/293/missouri-v-biden/.

Chapter 5

1 Appendix A, https://www.drsimonegold.com/book/resources.

2 America's Frontline Doctors, "White Coat Summit" (video, July 27, 2021), https://aflds.wistia.com/medias/3657il0bs7.

3 Appendix 2, https://www.drsimonegold.com/book/resources.

4 Amy Baxter, "FDA says hydroxychloroquine unlikely to be effective in treating COVID-19," *HealthExec*, June 15, 2020, https://healthexec.com/topics/clinical/covid-19/fda-says-hydroxychloroquine-unlikely-be-effective-treating-covid-19.

5 "FDA cautions against use of hydroxychloroquine or chloroquine for COVID-19 outside of the hospital setting or a clinical trial due to risk of heart rhythm problems: Does not affect FDA-approved uses for malaria, lupus, and rheumatoid arthritis," *FDA U.S.Food & Drug Administration*, accessed June 5, 2024, https://www.fda.gov/drugs/drug-safety-and-availability/fda-cautions-against-use-hydroxychloroquine-or-chloroquine-covid-19-outside-hospital-setting-or.

6 Gail A. Van Norman, "Off-Label Use vs Off-Label Marketing of Drugs," *JACC Basic Transl Sci, 8*(2) (2023): 224–233, https://doi.org/10.1016/j.jacbts.2022.12.011; Retrieved from: https://www.ncbi.nlm.nih.gov/pmc/articles/PMC9998554/.

7 The Nobel Prize, "The Nobel Prize in Physiology or Medicine 2015" (press release, October 5, 2015), https://www.nobelprize.org/prizes/medicine/2015/press-release/.

8 America's Frontline Doctors, "Hydroxychloroquine" (website, accessed June 5, 2024), https://americasfrontlinedoctors.org/medical/hydroxychloroquine.

9 America's Frontline Doctors, "Early treatments—Hydroxychloroquine with Zinc" (online article, accessed June 5, 2024), https://aflds.org/covid-pedia/treatments-hydroxychloroquine-with-zinc.

10 The Medical Industrial Complex (MIC) refers to those institutional organizations and corporate business interests that control healthcare in the United States. Big Pharma (Pfizer, Moderna), but even bigger entities such as insurance companies (United Health Group, Kaiser, Anthem Blue Cross) and large hospital systems (HCA, Ascension, the VA, CommonSpirit, LifePoint, Tenet).

11 Sarah Boseley and Melissa Davey, "Covid-19: Lancet retracts paper that halted hydroxychloroquine trials," *The Guardian*, June 4, 2020, https://www.theguardian.com/world/2020/jun/04/covid-19-lancet-retracts-paper-that-halted-hydroxychloroquine-trials.

12 "WHO Model List of Essential Medicines," Wikipedia, accessed June 5, 2024, https://en.wikipedia.org/wiki/WHO_Model_List_of_Essential_Medicines

13 "Cancer Types," National Cancer Institute (website, accessed June 5, 2024), https://www.cancer.gov/types.

14 "Anxiety Disorders," National Cancer Institute, (website, accessed June 5, 2024), https://www.nimh.nih.gov/health/topics/anxiety-disorders#part_2225.

15 "The estimated number of human lives lost from incorrect HCQ advice . . ." (website, accessed June 5, 2024), https://web.archive.org/web/20201231042204/https://hcqlost.com/.

16 Geoff Mitchell and Sonya Naryshkin, "Profound and persistent disparity in COVID-19 mortality rates between USA/Western Europe and sub-Saharan Africa: A crossover effect of antimalarial drugs?" *Research Gate* (August 2021), http://dx.doi.org/10.13140/RG.2.2.24727.09122.

17 Harvey A. Risch, "The Key to Defeating COVID-19 Already Exists. We need to Start Using It—Opinion," *Newsweek*, July 23, 2020 (updated July 28, 2020), https://www.newsweek.com/key-defeating-covid-19-already-exists-we-need-start-using-it-opinion-1519535.

18 https://www.drsimonegold.com/book/resources.

19 Brian Tyson and George Fareed with Matthew Crawford, *Overcoming the COVID Darkness: How Two Doctors Successfully Treated 7000 Patients*, Self published, January 2, 2022, https://a.co/d/fprxJfi.

20 Law Offices of Matthew P. Tyson to CVS Pharmacy #16937, December 6, 2021, https://www.skirsch.com/covid/TysonIvermectin.pdf.

21 America's Frontline Doctors, "#ProtectTheChildren & EO" (website, accessed June 5, 2024), https://americasfrontlinedoctors.org/legal/lawsuits/protect-the-children.

22 America's Frontline Doctors, "#ProtectTheChildren: A Critical Lawsuit for Life" (video, July 2, 2021), https://americasfrontlinedoctors.org/videos/post/protectthechildren-a-critical-lawsuit-for-life.

23 America's Frontline Doctors, "#ProtectTheChildren & EO" (website, accessed June 5, 2024), https://americasfrontlinedoctors.org/legal/lawsuits/protect-the-children.

24 Ibid.

25 America's Frontline Doctors, "#ProtectTheChildren: The Story of Emma Burkey" (video, February, 2, 2022), https://americasfrontlinedoctors.org/videos/post/protectthechildren-the-story-of-emma-burkey.

26 Steve Kirsch, "The 'safe and effective' narrative is falling apart," *Steve Kirsch's Newsletter*, July 7, 2022, https://kirschsubstack.com/p/the-safe-and-effective-narrative.

27 America's Frontline Doctors, "#ProtectTheChildren & EO" (website, accessed June 5, 2024), https://americasfrontlinedoctors.org/legal/lawsuits/protect-the-children.

28 Steve Kirsch, "The 'safe and effective' narrative is falling apart," *Steve Kirsch's Newsletter*, July 7, 2022, https://kirschsubstack.com/p/the-safe-and-effective-narrative.

29 *America's Frontline Doctors, etc. v. Becerra*, 2:21-cv-00702 (N.D. Ala. March 10, 2023), https://www.courtlistener.com/docket/59929233/americas-frontline-doctors-etc-v-becerra/.

30 America's Frontline Doctors, "#ProtectTheChildren: A Critical Lawsuit for Life" (video, July 2, 2021), https://americasfrontlinedoctors.org/videos/post/protectthechildren-a-critical-lawsuit-for-life.

31 America's Frontline Doctors, "The EUA: Anthrax & Covid Vaccines by Colonel Tom Rempfer" (video, July 25, 2023), https://americasfrontlinedoctors.org/videos/post/the-eua-anthrax-and-covid-vaccines-by-colonel-tom-rempfer.

32 Colonel Thomas L. Rempfer, *Unyielding: Marathons Against Illegal Mandates* (Children's Health Defense, June 11, 2024).

33 The Climate Change and Public Health Law Site, "Court says military must get consent for anthrax vaccinations—*John Doe #1 v. Rumsfeld*, —F.Supp.2d—, 2003 WL 22994225 (D.D.C. Dec 22, 2003)" (website, accessed June 5, 2024), https://biotech.law.lsu.edu/cases/vaccines/Doe_v_Rumsfeld_I.htm.

34 *Robert v. Austin*, 1:21-cv-02228-STV (USDC Colorado, August 30, 2021), https://cms.aflds.dev/uploads/Verified_TRO_against_DOD_HHS_FDA_7224fe7ae8.pdf.

35 "Medical Services Immunizations and Chemoprophylaxis for the Prevention of Infectious Diseases," *Army Regulation 40–562 BUMEDINST 6230.15B AFI 48–110_IP CG COMDTINST M6230.4G*, p.6, https://www.health.mil/Military-Health-Topics/Health-Readiness/Immunization-Healthcare/Continuous-Quality-Immunization-Improvement-Process/Standards-for-Military-Immunization.

36 *Robert v. Austin*, 1:21-cv-02228-STV (USDC Colorado, January 11, 2022), https://storage.courtlistener.com/recap/gov.uscourts.cod.209086/gov.uscourts.cod.209086.48.0_1.pdf.

37 Associated Press, "Trump appointee blocks Biden federal worker vaccine mandate," *Federal Times*, January 21, 2022, https://www.federaltimes.com/management/2022/01/21/trump-appointee-blocks-biden-federal-worker-vaccine-mandate/.

38 Gilbert R. Cisneros Jr. to Senior Pentagon Leadership Commanders of the Combatant Commands Defense Agency and DOD Field Activity Directors (Memorandum, April 4, 2022), United States Department of Defense, https://media.defense.gov/2022/Apr/06/2002971407/-1/-1/1/CONSOLIDATED-DEPARTMENT-OF-DEFENSE-CORONAVIRUS-DISEASE-2019-FORCE-HEALTH-PROTECTION-GUIDANCE.PDF.

39 America's Frontline Doctors, "Kaiser Permanente" (website, accessed June 5, 2024), https://americasfrontlinedoctors.org/legal/lawsuits/kaiser-permanente.

40 America's Frontline Doctors, "America's Frontline Doctors Supports the Filing of a Petition for Preliminary Injunction to Prevent Kaiser Permanente From Enforcing Their Vaccine Mandate" (press release, November 2, 2021), https://americasfrontlinedoctors.org/about-us/press-releases/americas-frontline-doctors-supports-the-filing-of-a-petition-for-preliminary-injunction-to-prevent-kaiser-permanente-from-enforcing-their-vaccine-mandate.

41 America's Frontline Doctors, "Dr. Gold Explains the Preliminary Injunction Against Kaiser Permanente" (video, November 3, 2021), https://www.aflds.org/videos/post/dr-gold-explains-the-preliminary-injunction-against-kaiser-permanente.

42 United KP Freedom Alliance et al v. Kaiser Permanente, et al., 21-cv-07894-VC (USDC ND California, November 18, 2021), https://docs.justia.com/cases/federal/district-courts/california/candce/3:2021cv07894/386304/39.

43 The VSD function is to monitor vaccine safety.

44 S. V. Subramanian and Akhil Kumar, "Increases in COVID-19 are unrelated to levels of vaccination across 68 countries and 2947 counties in the United States," *European Journal of Epidemiology, 36* (2021): 1237–1240, p. 1237, https://doi.org/10.1007/s10654-021-00808-7.

45 District Judge Vince Chhabara San Francisco Courthouse, Courtroom 4 - 17th Floor 450 Golden Gate Avenue, San Francisco, CA 94102 (415) 522-2000 Case No.3:21-cv-07894-VC.https://cases.justia.com/federal/district-courts/california/candce/3:2021cv07894/386304/39/0.pdf?ts=1637311268.

46 America's Frontline Doctor's, "Dr. Gold Explains the Preliminary Injunction Against Kaiser Permanente" (video, November 3, 2021), https://www.aflds.org/videos/post/dr-gold-explains-the-preliminary-injunction-against-kaiser-permanente.

47 Aaron Kheriaty (@Aaron KheriatyMD), *I submitted this FOIA request to the FDA: they now claim it will take them 55 years to release the data on which Pfizer's vaccine approval was based, though it only took them 108 days to review this data for the approval process. New heights of absurdity* (picture attached), X, November 18, 2021, https://twitter.com/akheriaty/status/1461407823821037568.

48 America's Frontline Doctors, "Doctors with America's Frontline Doctors (AFLDS) Successfully Push Back on the FDA in Fight for Documents on the COVID Vaccine" (press release, February 4, 2022), https://aflds.org/about-us/press-releases/doctors-with-americas-frontline-doctors-aflds-successfully-push-back-on-the-fda-in-fight-for-documents-on-the-covid-vaccine.

49 Ibid.

50 *Public Health and Medical Professionals for Transparency v. Food and Drug Administration*, 4:21-cv-01058-P (USDC NWD Texas, January 6, 2022), https://res.cloudinary.com/aflds/image/upload/v1658477901/aflds/file_ivannh.pdf?updated_at=2022-02-09T00:20:55.000Z.

51 Aaron Siri, "Injecting Freedom by Aaron Siri," Substack, https://aaronsiri.substack.com/.

52 Brief for Betten Chevrolet, Inc. as Amicus Curiae (No. 21A259, November 5, 2021), p. 5, https://www.sirillp.com/wp-content/uploads/2022/01/Reply-8ee2b9e2c3199ed9ed5d15b9fa6c61fb.pdf.

53 *Jacobson v. Massachusetts*, 197 U.S. 11 (1905), https://supreme.justia.com/cases/federal/us/197/11/#:~:text=Massachusetts%2C%20197%20U.S.%2011%20(1905)&text=A%20state%20may%20enact%20a,smallpox%20and%20protect%20public%20health.

54 Ibid.

55 Ibid.

56 America's Frontline Doctors, "Dr. Gold Explains the Preliminary Injunction Against Kaiser Permanente" (video, November 3, 2021), https://www.aflds.org/videos/post/dr-gold-explains-the-preliminary-injunction-against-kaiser-permanente

57 Brief for America's Frontline Doctors as Amicus Curiae (21A243 et al., November 4, 2021), p. 3, https://www.supremecourt.gov/DocketPDF/21/21A244/207051/20211230162830733_AFLDS%20amicus%20brief%20in%20support%20of%20emergency%20applications%20re%20OSHA%20ETS%20cases.pdf.

58 Ibid., p. 10.
59 Ibid., p. 10.
60 *Cruzan v. Director, Missouri Dep't of Health*, 497 U.S. 261 (1990), https://supreme.justia.com/cases/federal/us/497/261/.
61 *National Federation of Independent Business et al. and Ohio et al. v. Department of Labor, Occupational Safety and Health Administration et al.*, (595 U.S. 2022), p. 5, https://www.supremecourt.gov/opinions/21pdf/21a244_hgci.pdf.
62 Appendix D, https://www.drsimonegold.com/book/resources.
63 Appendix E, https://www.drsimonegold.com/book/resources.
64 Katie Camero, "Why did CDC change its definition for 'vaccine'? Agency explains move as skeptics lurk," *The Miami Herald*, September 27, 2021, https://www.miamiherald.com/news/coronavirus/article254111268.html.
65 Thomas Massie (@RepThomasMassie), *Check out @CDCgov's evolving definition of "vaccination." They've been busy at the Ministry of Truth:* (picture attached), X, September 8, 2021, https://x.com/RepThomasMassie/status/1435606845926871041.
66 Ibid.
67 *Georgia v. Biden*, 1:21-cv-163 (USDC, S.D. Georgia, August Division, December 7, 2021), https://www.leagle.com/decision/infdco20211208b62.
68 Appeal (USDC 3:21-CV-356, February 9, 2022) for *Feds for Medical Freedom v. Biden*, 22-40043 (5th Cir. 2022), https://law.justia.com/cases/federal/appellate-courts/ca5/22-40043/22-40043-2022-02-09.html.
69 Brief for America's Frontline Doctors as Amicus Curiae (22-40043, June 1, 2022) for *Feds for Medical Freedom v. Biden*, 22-40043 (5th Cir. 2022), https://res.cloudinary.com/aflds/image/upload/v1658477011/aflds/file_ory2db.pdf.
70 The number of COVID "cases", at the time of this writing, can be tracked at: https://www.worldometers.info/coronavirus/country/us/.
71 Apoora Mandavilli, "Your Coronavirus Test is Positive. Maybe It Shouldn't Be," *The New York Times*, July 3, 2021, https://www.nytimes.com/2020/08/29/health/coronavirus-testing.html.
72 Korin Miller, "The CDC Is Reminding People That Face Masks Shouldn't Be Worn Below the Chin," *Prevention*, July 23, 2020, https://www.prevention.com/health/a33403481/wearing-face-mask-under-chin/.
73 America's Frontline Doctors, "The Uncensored Truth Tour: Albuquerque NM" (video, July 8, 2021), https://americasfrontlinedoctors.org/videos/post/the-uncensored-truth-tour-albuquerque-nm, minute 34, 36 on the Religion of Public Health and minute 17:45 about the faulty PCR testing.
74 Katherine Fung, "Fewer Americans Support Mask, Vaccine Mandates Ahead of Holiday Gatherings, Poll Finds," *Newsweek*, December 15, 2021, https://www.newsweek.com/fewer-americans-support-mask-vaccine-mandates-ahead-holiday-gatherings-poll-finds-1659833.
75 *Health Freedom Defense Fund v. Xavier Becerra*, 8:21-cv-01693-KKM-AEP (M.D. Fl. April 18, 2022), https://storage.courtlistener.com/recap/gov.uscourts.flmd.391798/gov.uscourts.flmd.391798.54.0_2.pdf.

76 Brief for U.S. Department of Justice as Appeal (USCA 11:22-11287, May 31, 2022) for *Health Freedom Defense Fund v. Biden*, 22-40043 (5th Cir. 2022), https://fingfx.thomsonreuters.com/gfx/legaldocs/xmvjoxyjypr/opening-brief-cdc-ca5-2022-05-31.pdf.

77 Transportation Security Administration, "DHS to Increase Civil Penalties for Violations of the Federal Face Mask Requirement" (National Press Release, September 9, 2021), https://www.tsa.gov/news/press/releases/2021/09/09/dhs-increase-civil-penalties-violations-federal-face-mask.

78 Bill Hutchinson, "Delta adds 460 people to no-fly list for refusing to wear masks," *ABC News*, October 25, 2020, https://abcnews.go.com/Business/delta-adds-460-people-fly-list-refusing-wear/story?id=73815553.

79 Steven Kirsch, "Silence: The story of COVID vaccine victims," *Rumble* (video, accessed June 6, 2024), https://rumble.com/vszi9y-silence-the-story-of-covid-vaccine-victims.html.

80 Paul E. Alexander, "Masking Children: Tragic, Unscientific, and Damaging," American Institute for Economic Research, March 10, 2021, https://www.aier.org/article/masking-children-tragic-unscientific-and-damaging/?gclid=Cj0KCQjwnf-kBhCnARIsAFlg493XAqcQc2R67n73zfpRLnN2HslfWNmtNKc9U0JZvYCn1RvQpkJfk7waAlR3EALw_wcB.

81 "USA Today Censors ER Doctor" (video, accessed June 6, 2024), https://aflds.wistia.com/medias/h80qbn0muz.

82 America's Frontline Doctors, "Masks Do Not Work-AFLDS Files Amicus Curiae Brief" (press releases, August 8, 2022), https://americasfrontlinedoctors.org/about-us/press-releases/masks-do-not-work-aflds-files-amicus-curiae-brief.

83 Brief for America's Frontline Doctors as Amicus Curiae (23-11287, August 8, 2022) for *Health Freedom Defense Fund v. Joseph R. Biden*, 22-11287 (USCA11, May 31, 2022), p. 1, https://res.cloudinary.com/aflds/image/upload/v1660068993/aflds/Health_Freedom_Defense_Fund_Inc_et_al_v_Biden_etc_et_al_Americas_Frontline_Doctors_Amicus_Motion_Brief_Stamped_8_8_2022_21_cv_1693_MDFL_22_11287_CA_11_759748977c.pdf.

84 "Medical misinformation policy," YouTubeHelp (website, accessed June 6, 2024, https://support.google.com/youtube/answer/13813322?hl=en&visit_id=638533166433554144-912589835&rd=1.

85 "COVID-19, medical misinformation policy," Internet Archive WayBackMachine (website, accessed June 6, 2024), https://web.archive.org/web/20220114225018/https://support.google.com/youtube/answer/9891785?hl=en&ref_topic=10833358.

86 America's Frontline Doctors (@AFLDSorg), *Are masks poisoning us? Earlier this year, a German team published an extensive review of masking during the COVID-19 pandemic that should put the final nail in the coffin of masking and mask mandates. Fresh air has a 0.04% carbon dioxide concentration. Wearing a mask increases that up to 3.5% which is an 8,800% increase! Acute and chronic carbon dioxide toxicity come with a laundry list of symptoms. The harms of masking are clear. Are you at all surprised?* (video attached), X, November 1, 2023, https://x.com/AFLDSorg/status/1719695775679033471.

87 America's Frontline Doctors, "Legal Freedom" (website, accessed June 7, 2024), https://americasfrontlinedoctors.org/legal.
88 America's Frontline Doctors, "Lawsuits" (website, accessed June 7, 2024), https://americasfrontlinedoctors.org/legal/lawsuits.
89 Patrick Whelan, "Testimony to the Select Subcommittee on the Coronavirus Pandemic: 'Assessing America's Vaccine Safety Systems, Part 2'" (Hearing, March 21, 2024), https://oversight.house.gov/wp-content/uploads/2024/03/Whelan-Testimony.pdf.

Chapter 6

1 Voltaire, *Questions sur les miracles* (1765).
2 National Citizens Inquiry (website, accessed June 8, 2024), https://nationalcitizensinquiry.ca.
3 Robert Malone, "Mass Formation Psychosis," *Who is Robert Malone* (Substack post, December 9, 2021), https://rwmalonemd.substack.com/p/mass-formation-psychosis.
4 Filipe Rafaeli, "The day I understood the 'good German'," *Pandemia*, (Substack post, February 24, 2022), https://filiperafaeli.substack.com/p/the-day-i-understood-the-good-german.
5 Ayla Ellison, "32 hospitals have filed for bankruptcy this year," *Becker's Hospital Review*, November 19, 2020, https://www.beckershospitalreview.com/finance/32-hospitals-have-filed-for-bankruptcy-this-year.html, https://www.aha.org/system/files/media/file/2020/06/aha-covid19-financial-impact-report.pdf.

This article includes a link to the American Hospital Association report mentioned: "Hospitals and Health Systems Continue to Face Unprecedented Financial Challenges due to COVID-19," American Hospital Association (online document,m June 2020), https://www.aha.org/system/files/media/file/2020/06/aha-covid19-financial-impact-report.pdf.
6 "HHS Provider Relief Fund," Centers for Disease Control and Prevention (website, accessed June 8, 2024), https://data.cdc.gov/Administrative/HHS-Provider-Relief-Fund/kh8y-3es6/data_preview.
7 For example, Dr. Peter Duesberg, infra, and Dr. Judy Mikovits.
8 Adam Andrzejewski, "NIH scientists made $710M in royalties from drug makers—a fact they tried to hide," *New York Post*, June 2, 2024, https://nypost.com/2024/06/02/opinion/nih-scientists-made-710m-in-royalties-from-drug-makers-a-fact-they-tried-to-hide/?utm_source=whatsapp&utm_campaign=android_nyp.
9 America's Frontline Doctors, "Flecca Talks: 'Brave Doctors, Threatened, Come Forth'" (video, accessed June 8, 2024), https://aflds.wistia.com/medias/z2cza5rqil.
10 "The Man Behind #LancetGate: A Breaking Science Scandal with Global Ramifications–James Todaro, MD" (YouTube video, accessed June 8, 2024), https://www.youtube.com/watch?v=4HYK5pL2Z_s.
11 James Heathers, "*The Lancet* has made one of the biggest retractions in modern history. How could this happen?" *The Guardian*, June 5, 2020, https://www

.theguardian.com/commentisfree/2020/jun/05/lancet-had-to-do-one-of-the-biggest-retractions-in-modern-historY-how-could-this-happen.
12 Catherine Offord, "The Surgisphere Scandal: What Went Wrong?" *The Scientist*, October 1, 2020, https://www.the-scientist.com/the-surgisphere-scandal-what-went-wrong—67955.
13 Virgile Faber, "(Eng Subs) Hydroxychloroquine Lancet Study: Former France Health Minister blows the whistle" (YouTube Video, May 24, 2020), https://www.youtube.com/watch?v=ZYgiCALEdpE.
14 Marcia Angell, *The Truth About the Drug Companies: How They Deceived Us and What to Do About It* (Random House New York, 2020).
15 Robert F. Kennedy Jr., *The Real Anthony Fauci: Bill Gates, Big Pharma, and the Global War on Democracy and Public Health* (Children's Health Defense, 2021).
16 Chief Nerd [@TheChiefNerd], *Dr. Joseph Ladapo Says Doctors Need Better Training on How to Examine Pharma Studies "Docs, medical students-they just don't get good training with data, interpretation . . . and learning how their interpretations ar potentially being manipulated*" (video attached), X, June 18, 2023, https://x.com/TheChiefNerd/status/1670449930752671746.
17 Dr. Judy Mikovits and Kent Heckenlively, JD, *Plague of Corruption: Restoring Faith in the Promise of Science* (Children's Defense Fund, 2020).
18 Anonymous, *Turtles All The Way Down: Vaccine Science and Myth* (Children's Defense Fund, 2022).
19 "Statement of William W. Thompson, Ph.D., Regarding the 2004 Article Examining the Possibility of a Relationship Between MMR Vaccine and Autism" (press release, August 27, 2014).
20 Kevin Barry, *Vaccine Whistleblower: Exposing Autism Research Fraud at the CDC* (Skyhorse Publishing, 2015).
21 Ron Johnson, U.S. senator for Wisconsin, "Sen. Johnson to DoD, FDA, CDC: Whistleblower Allegations about COVID-19 Vaccine Mislabeling and Unauthorized Manufacturing Must Be Fully Addressed" (press release, August 19, 2022), https://www.ronjohnson.senate.gov/2022/8/sen-johnson-to-dod-fda-cdc-whistleblower-allegations-about-covid-19-vaccine-mislabeling-and-unauthorized-manufacturing-must-be-fully-addressed.
22 Office of Public Affairs, U.S. Department of Justice, "Justice Department Announces Largest Health Care Fraud Settlement in Its History" (press release, September 2, 2009), https://www.justice.gov/opa/pr/justice-department-announces-largest-health-care-fraud-settlement-its-history.
23 Christina Jewett, "FDA's Drug Industry Fees Fuel Concerns Over Influence," *The New York Times*, September 15, 2022, https://www.nytimes.com/2022/09/15/health/fda-drug-industry-fees.html.
24 America's Frontline Doctors, "The Deadly Dozen/Disinformation" (video, 5:00, accessed June 9, 2024).
25 Alicia Ault, "Can a COVID-19 Vaccine Stop the Spread? Good Question," *Medscape*, June 9, 2024, https://www.medscape.com/viewarticle/941388.
26 Appendix B, https://www.drsimonegold.com/book/resources.

27 Frederik Plesner Lynsgse et al., "Household transmission of the SARS-CoV-2 Omicron variant in Denmark," *Nature Communications* 13, no. 5573 (2022): 5, https://doi.org/10.1038/s41467-022-33328-3.

28 Dr. Simon Goddek's publications and impact can be viewed in Google Scholar: https://scholar.google.is/citations?user=VnwhQloAAAAJ&hl=en.

29 Dr. Simon [@goddek], *Telegram*, September 23, 2022, https://t.me/goddek/2265.

30 For a lab, losing funding threatens prestige, future projects, and the ability to employ graduate and postdoctoral students. Even tenured professors with "safe" positions fear losing their labs over bureaucratic dissent, so predictably, researchers tread lightly. Even when presenting evidence that demonstrated the lack of effectiveness of the mRNA injection, for example, researchers still included a disclaimer of the terrible danger of the virus to protect themselves from criticism—a complete absurdity. This was a coronavirus 78 percent similar to SARS-CoV-1 from 17 years earlier, which we knew how to treat and which only threatened a tiny percentage of people with very advanced age or multiple comorbid conditions.

31 Serge Goldman et al., "Rapid Progression of Angioimmunoblastic T Cell Lymphoma Following BNT162b2 mRNA Vaccine Booster Shot: A Case Report," *Frontiers in Medicine* 8, no. 798095 (November 25, 2021), https://doi.org/10.3389/fmed.2021.798095.

32 National Citizens Inquiry Canada, "Dr. Jessica Rose" (Rumble video, May 30, 2024), https://rumble.com/v4yrp8e-dr.-jessica-rose-may-30-2024-regina-saskatchewan.html.

33 "Turbo cancer," Wikipedia, accessed June 16, 2024, https://en.wikipedia.org/wiki/Turbo_cancer.

34 Miki Gibo et al., "Increased Age-Adjusted Cancer Mortality After the Third mRNA-Lipid Nanoparticle Vaccine Dose During the COVID-19 Pandemic in Japan," *Cureus* 14: no. 4 (April 8, 2024), e57860, https://doi.org/10.7759/cureus.57860.

35 Ibid.

36 Also see Chapter 5 section "The Ministry of Truth" (changing definition of vaccine) and section "A Doctor & Lawyer Speaking Law To Power" (Ninth Circuit ruling that these shots are not vaccines, *Health Freedom Defense Fund*).

37 Appendix E, https://www.drsimonegold.com/book/resources.

38 Carolos Alegria, "Excess adjusted deaths from malignant neoplasms for ages 15 to 44, in England and Wales" in *UK—Death and Disability Trends for Malignant Neoplasms, Ages 15–44* (October 10, 2023), https://phinancetechnologies.com/HumanityProjects/UK%20Cause%20of%20Death/Report%20V-Damage%20Analysis%20-%20Malignant%20Cancers%2015-44%20-%20V2.pdf.

The tables within the chapter can be also be accessed here:

https://www.semanticscholar.org/paper/UK-Death-and-Disability-Trends-for-Malignant-Ages-Alegria/e5dedc69686e9350b1cd96fb1a22c93af859ec46.

39 https://www.sciencedirect.com/science/article/pii/S0379073824001968?via%3Dihub.

40 For a presentation on how medicine lost its way, watch America's Frontline Doctor's, "July 27th 2023, White Coat Summit: The Reckoning," (video, accessed June 9, 2024), https://www.whitecoatsummit.com/videos/2023.

41 Learn more at Gary Arndt, "A History of Scurvy," Everything Everywhere Daily (video, May 21, 2021), https://everything-everywhere.com/a-history-of-scurvy/.

42 Quoted in Jeremy Hugh Baron, "Sailors scurvy before and after James Lind—a reassessment," *Nutrition Reviews* 67, no. 6 (June 1, 2009): 317, https://doi.org/10.1111/j.1753-4887.2009.00205.x.

43 Saul Marcus, "History of scurvy, why does it matter today?" (online article, accessed June 9, 2024), https://saulmarcusnd.com/2021/01/15/history-of-scurvy-why-does-it-matter-today/.

44 Michael S. Gottlieb, "Pneumocystis Pneumonia—Los Angeles" (1981), *American Journal of Public Health* 96, no. 6 (June 2006): 980, https://doi.org/10.2105/ajph.96.6.980.

45 Stephen Israelstam et al., "Poppers, A New Recreational Drug Craze," *Canadian Psychiatric Association Journal* 23 (November 1978): 493, https://doi.org//10.1177/070674377802300711.

46 Ibid., p. 493.

47 Peter Duesberg, *Inventing the AIDS Virus* (Gateway Books, 1996), p. 271.

48 Eliyahu Tulshinski, "The real cause of AIDS, known to health officials since day one," *Frontline News*, March 28, 2022, https://frontline.news/post/the-real-cause-of-aids-known-to-health-officials-since-day-one.

49 "Dr Robert Willner Injects HIV Into Himself on TV" (video, December 7, 1994), https://archive.org/details/drrobertwillnerinjectshivintohimselfontv.

50 Nobel Prize, "The Nobel Prize in Physiology or Medicine 2008: Luc Montagnier Facts" (website, accessed June 10, 2024), https://www.nobelprize.org/prizes/medicine/2008/montagnier/facts/.

51 Ron Unz, "American Pravda: AIDS and the Revival of the Duesberg Hypothesis," *The Unz Review: An Alternative Media Selection*, December 29, 2021, https://www.unz.com/runz/aids-and-the-revival-of-the-duesberg-hypothesis/.

52 Eliyahu Tulshinski, "'I don't want to be a good German'—German-born researcher turns down NIH 'bribe,'" *Frontline News*, May 17, 2022, https://americasfrontlinenews.com/post/i-dont-want-to-be-a-good-german-german-born-researcher-turns-down-nih-bribe.

53 Eliyahu Tulshinski, "Fauci's deadly solution to a harmless virus . . . in 1987," *Frontline News*, May 25, 2022, https://americasfrontlinenews.com/post/faucis-deadly-solution-to-a-harmless-virus-in-1987.

54 "Selected top HIV/AIDS drugs worldwide based on revenue in 2023 (in million U.S. dollars)," Statista, (website, accessed June 10, 2024), https://www.statista.com/statistics/273434/revenue-of-the-worlds-most-important-aids-drugs/#:~:text=Top%20HIV%2FAIDS%20drugs%20worldwide%20

based%20on%20revenue%202023&text=In%202023%2C%20Genvoya%20generated%20some,billion%20U.S.%20dollars%20in%20revenue.

55 Celia Farber, "Interview Kary Mullins, AIDS: Words from the Front," *Spin*, July 1994, http://virusmyth.com/aids/hiv/cfmullis.htm.

56 America's Frontline Doctors, "The Deadly Dozen/Disinformation" (video, accessed June 10, 2024), https://fast.wistia.net/embed/iframe/kvajk1r8ro.

57 America's Frontline Doctors, "The Stand: Dr. Simone: Truth About the COVID-19 Vaccine" (Rumble video, accessed June 10, 2024), https://rumble.com/vgjynz-the-stand-dr.-simone-the-truth-about-the-covid-19-vaccine.html.

58 Please see Appendix A for >50 references. Also consider the India state of Uttar Pradesh (population: 250 million) where it was official government policy in 2021 to use early treatment (ivermectin) which rapidly eliminated COVID-19 (see: https://juanchamie.substack.com/p/ivermectin-in-uttar-pradesh). In Mexico, the state of Chiapas did not comply with banning early treatment but instead went door-to-door with ivermectin. Chiapas had almost no deaths, while the rest of Mexico had high death rates (see: https://juanchamie.substack.com/p/ivermectin-in-mexico).

59 Ian Miller, "Former CDC Director Makes Stunning Admission on COVID Vaccines," *OutKick*, May 21, 2024, https://www.outkick.com/analysis/former-cdc-director-makes-stunning-admission-on-covid-vaccines.

60 Dr. George Fareed [@GeorgeFareed2], *Criminal…* (video attached), X, June 8, 2024, https://x.com/GeorgeFareed2/status/1799491479246893300.

61 America's Frontline Doctors, "The Deadly Dozen/Disinformation" (video, first 1:30 minutes, accessed June 10, 2024), https://fast.wistia.net/embed/iframe/kvajk1r8ro.

62 Fauci has never been held accountable, and our children suffered. See Dr. Elli David [@DrEliDavid], Never forget what they did in the name of science (video attached), X, February 17, 2023, https://x.com/DrEliDavid/status/1626690499640803328.

63 Committee on the Coronavirus Pandemic Republican Staff to Committee on the Coronavirus Pandemic Republican Members (Memorandum, May 31, 2024), Congress of the United States House of Representatives: Select Subcommittee on the Coronavirus Pandemic, https://oversight.house.gov/wp-content/uploads/2024/05/FINAL_Fauci-Memo.pdf.

64 In 1980, the NIH budget was $3.4 billion ($13 billion current value). Today, the NIH budget is $47.7 billion. Under Fauci, the NIH budget exploded in size under his "AIDS research" and has kept exploding. You can see the data for yourself at: "Appropriations (Section 2)," The NIH Almanac, National Institutes of Health (website, accessed June 16, 2024), https://www.nih.gov/about-nih/what-we-do/nih-almanac/appropriations-section-2 In summary: After 20 years, Fauci had increased the agency's budget 206%, after 30 years by 344%, and after 40 years, by 387%.

1975–1980: additional 7% growth (pre-Fauci)
1980–1985: additional 15% growth (1981: AIDS identified)

1985–1990: additional 21% growth (1984: Fauci NIAID Director)
1990–1995: additional 28% growth
1995–2000: additional 40% growth
2000–2005: additional 40% growth
2005–2018: no additional growth
2018–2019: additional 3.5% growth (2019: SARS-2 identified)
2019–2023: additional 1.7% growth annually.

65 Dr. Mari [@drarce]. *Remember when Fauci told us about HIV and how it could jump to you if you were too close? This guy's advice was bull* then and you shoulda smelled the bull* in 2020.* X, June 20, 2024, 7:44 p.m. https://x.com/drarce/status/1803936984672489861.

66 Joseph Sonnabend, "The long road to PCP prophylaxis in AIDS. An early history," *POZ*, September 23, 2009, https://www.poz.com/blog/the-long-road-to-pcp.

67 Larry Kramer, "I CALL YOU MURDERERS: An open letter to an incompetent idiot, Dr. Anthony Fauci, of the National Institute of Allergy and Infectious Diseases," *The San Francisco Examiner*, June 26, 1988, https://www.newspapers.com/article/the-san-francisco-examiner/48237541/.

68 moviemaniacsDE, "The Normal Heart: official trailer (2014) HBO Mark Ruffalo Jim Parsons," (YouTube video, accessed June 10, 2024), https://www.youtube.com/watch?v=fZxR9XHS0H8.

69 Randy Shilts, *And the Band Played On: Politics, People, and the AIDS Epidemic* (St. Martin's Press, 1987).

70 "Anthony Fauci: The face of America's fight against coronavirus," *BBC*, July 13, 2020, https://www.bbc.com/news/world-us-canada-52027201.

71 Mary Talley Bowden [@MdBreathe], *Breaking: FDA loses its war on ivermectin and agrees to remove all social media posts and consumer directives regarding ivermectin and COVID, including its most popular tweet in FDA history. This landmark case sets an important precedent in limiting FDA overreach into the doctor-patient relationship …* (picture attached), X, March 21, 2024, https://x.com/mdbreathe/status/1771023714584273015?s=46.

72 Please see Appendix A (https://www.drsimonegold.com/book/resources) for > 50 references. You can also see: https://c19hcq.org.

73 The FDA database shows a total of 640 deaths attributable to HCQ over fifty years. To put this in context, "Each year the FDA receives over one million adverse event reports associated with the use of drug products." "This concerns the entirety of HCQ use over more than fifty years of data, likely millions of uses, and of longer-term use than the five days recommended for Covid-19 treatment." The 640 deaths represented 0.034% of all the deaths (1,910,212) attributable to medications. US Food & Drug Administration. FDA Adverse Events Reporting System (FAERS) Public Dashboard. https://fis.fda.gov/sense/app/d10be6bb-494e-4cd2-82e4-0135608ddc13/sheet/7a47a261-d58b-4203-a8aa-6d3021737452/state/analysis.

74 Alicia Ault, "Can a COVID-19 Vaccine Stop the Spread? Good Question," *Medscape*, November 20, 2020, https://www.medscape.com/viewarticle/941388.

75 Rochelle P. Walensky, "Statement from CDC Director Rochelle P. Walensky, MD, MPH on today's MMWR: media statement for immediate release: Friday, July 30, 2021," CDC (media release, July 27, 2021), https://stacks.cdc.gov/view/cdc/108440.

76 https://pubmed.ncbi.nlm.nih.gov/34351882/.

77 Ian Miller, "Former CDC Director Makes Stunning Admission On COVID Vaccines," *OutKick*, May 21, 2024, https://www.outkick.com/analysis/former-cdc-director-makes-stunning-admission-on-covid-vaccines.

78 While noteworthy that Cuomo went public, it's offensive to everyone that there is no apology. There has been no self-reflection. Cuomo blames "not being given real information." False. Many people told him the facts. He covered his ears. Dr. Simone Gold [@drsimonegold], *After pushing vaccine propaganda for years and saying that anyone who advocated for ivermectin should be shamed, Chris Cuomo now admits he himself is taking ivermectin* (video attached, May 18, 2024), X, https://x.com/drsimonegold/status/1791766125266563560.

79 https://www.sirillp.com/wp-content/uploads/2024/06/FDA-Reply-aP-Petition-4b2b5a444605c16234394e0517a23efd.pdf?utm_source=substack&utm_medium=email page 8.

80 Fleccas Talks, "Second Opinion: Doctors Discuss the Politicization of Hydroxychloroquine" (YouTube video, accessed June 11, 2024), https://www.youtube.com/watch?v=m_JIz780i5w&t=31s.

81 Ian Miller, "Former CDC Director Makes Stunning Admission On COVID Vaccines," *OutKick*, May 21, 2024, https://www.outkick.com/analysis/former-cdc-director-makes-stunning-admission-on-covid-vaccines.

82 The former CDC director is still in the Stone Age, because, as of 2024, we have had data for more than three years showing that the shots are bad for everyone. Appendix B, https://www.drsimonegold.com/book/resources.

83 Mary Talley Bowden MD [@MdBreathe], *If I had vaccinated the 6000 patients I treated for COVID, I would have made $1,500,000* (image attached), X, May 28, 2024, https://x.com/MdBreathe/status/1795597706385338531.

84 https://fast.wistia.net/embed/iframe/kvajk1r8ro.

85 https://www.arrestfauci.com/.

86 On August 5, 2021, she admitted on CNN that the shots did not stop transmission. This was known by December 2020 in the Pfizer and Moderna applications to the FDA in which they never claimed the shots stopped transmission. Pfizer application to the FDA: https://www.fda.gov/media/144245/download.

87 https://oversight.house.gov/release/wenstrup-releases-former-nih-director-francis-collinss-transcript-highlights-key-takeaways-in-new-memo/.

88 COVID-19 And The Global Predators: We Are The Prey, Chapter 14.

89 https://aflds.org/covid-pedia/effectiveness-of-lockdowns.

90 https://aflds.org/covid-pedia/damage-from-lockdowns and Appendix 1.

91 https://rumble.com/vgjynz-the-stand-dr.-simone-the-truth-about-the-covid-19-vaccine.html.

92 https://aflds.wistia.com/medias/h80qbn0muz, https://aflds.org/covid-pedia/masks.

93 https://aflds.org/covid-pedia/treatments-hydroxychloroquine-with-zinc, https://aflds.org/covid-pedia/treatments-ivermectin, Appendix A.

94 https://rumble.com/vgjynz-the-stand-dr.-simone-the-truth-about-the-covid-19-vaccine.html and Appendix B.

95 Appendix B https://www.drsimonegold.com/book/resources/.

96 Ibid.

97 Appendix C https://www.drsimonegold.com/book/resources/.

98 https://www.city-journal.org/article/lockdown-damage.

99 https://www.forbes.com/sites/gracemarieturner/2020/05/22/600-physicians-say-lockdowns-are-a-mass-casualty-incident/.

100 https://www.outkick.com/analysis/former-cdc-director-makes-stunning-admission-on-covid-vaccines and Chapter 6.

101 https://fast.wistia.net/embed/iframe/kvajk1r8ro.

102 https://c19hcq.org, https://c19ivm.org.

103 "The CDC (2021c) reports that COVID-19 was the only cause mentioned on death certificates in 5% of deaths, and 'for deaths with conditions or causes in addition to COVID-19, on average, there were 4.0 additional conditions or causes per death.'"

104 https://openvaers.com.

105 Pfizer application to the FDA: https://www.fda.gov/media/144245/download.

106 https://law.justia.com/cases/federal/appellate-courts/ca9/22-55908/22-55908-2024-06-07.html.

107 Mimi Nguyen Ly, "Luc Montagnier, Virologist Who Discovered HIV and Critic of COVID-19 Vaccine Mandates, Dies at 89," *The Epoch Times*, February 11, 2022, https://www.theepochtimes.com/world/luc-montagnier-virologist-who-discovered-hiv-and-critic-of-covid-19-vaccine-mandates-dies-at-89-4271110.

108 Renee Nal, "Bombshell: Nobel Prize Winner Reveals—Covid Vaccine is 'Creating Variants,'" RAIR Foundation USA, May 18, 2021, https://rairfoundation.com/bombshell-nobel-prize-winner-reveals-covid-vaccine-is-creating-variants/.

109 "Statements by Montagnier, Nobel prize winner, on the origins of the coronavirus" (Parliamentary question – E 002429/2020, European Parliament, April 22, 2020), https://www.europarl.europa.eu/doceo/document/E-9-2020-002429_EN.html.

110 "Didier Raoult" (Google Scholar, accessed June 11, 2024), https://scholar.google.com/citations?hl=en&user=n8EF_6kAAAAJ.

111 Jean-Christophe Lagier et al., "Outcomes of 3,737 COVID-19 patients treated with hydroxychloroquine/azithromycin and other regimens in Marseille, France: A retrospective analysis," *Travel Medicine and Infectious Disease* 36, no. 101791 (June 25, 2020), https://doi.org/10.1016/j.tmaid.2020.101791.

112 "He Was a Science Star. Then He Promoted A Questionable Cure for Covid-19," *The New York Times Magazine*, May 24, 2020, https://www.nytimes.com/2020/05/12/magazine/didier-raoult-hydroxychloroquine.html.

113 Cathleen O'Grady, "The Reckoning," *Science*, March 7, 2024, https://www.science.org/content/article/failure-every-level-how-science-sleuths-exposed-massive-ethics-violations-famed-french.

114 Robert Malone, "New Policy on Risks of Dodgy Biology Research Misses the Mark (again)," *Who is Robert Malone* (Substack post, May 13, 2024), https://rwmalonemd.substack.com/p/new-policy-on-risks-of-dodgy-biology?utm_source=profile&utm_medium=reader2.

115 "RNA Vaccine," *Wikipedia* (Internet Archive: WayBackMachine, accessed June 11, 2024), https://web.archive.org/web/20210614140319/https://en.wikipedia.org/wiki/RNA_vaccine.

116 Robert Malone, "A newsletter about Medicine, bioethics, analytics, politics and life," *Who is Robert Malone* (Substack post, accessed June 11, 2024), https://rwmalonemd.substack.com/about.

117 Robert Malone, "Letter to the U.K. Gov from 76 Doctors," *Who is Robert Malone* (Substack post, July 4, 2022), https://rwmalonemd.substack.com/p/letter-to-the-uk-gov-from-76-doctors.

118 Robert Malone, "FDA is using the COVID-19 Vaccines as a 'Platform Technology' for mRNA Vaccine Trials," *Who is Robert Malone* (Substack post, September 28, 2022), https://rwmalonemd.substack.com/p/fda-is-using-the-covid-19-vaccines.

119 "Michael Yeadon," Wikipedia, accessed June 11, 2024, https://en.wikipedia.org/wiki/Michael_Yeadon#COVID-19_misinformation.

120 "Ex-Pfizer VP Yeadon Warns: Children 50 Times More Likely to Die from Vaccine Than Virus" (Image on Internet Archive: WayBackMachine, accessed June 11, 2024), https://web.archive.org/web/20211112222831/https://thetruthaboutcovidvaccines.com/ex-pfizer-vp-yeadon-warns-children-50-times-more-likely-to-die-from-vaccine-than-virus/.

121 Brian Shilhavy, "CENSORED: Dr. Peter McCullough, MD testifies How Successful Home Treatments for COVID Make Experimental Vaccines Unnecessary," *Algora Blog*, April 4, 2021.

122 Flgov.com, "Governor DeSantis Hosts Discussion About COVID Boosters with State Surgeon General and Health Experts" (news release, September 13, 2023).

123 Floridahealth.gov, "Florida State Surgeon General Calls for Halt in the Use of COVID-19 mRNA Vaccines" (press release, January 3, 2024), https://www.floridahealth.gov/newsroom/2024/01/20240103-halt-use-covid19-mrna-vaccines.pr.html.

124 Mary Talley Bowden [@MdBreathe], *Breaking: FDA loses its war on ivermectin and agrees to remove all social media posts and consumer directives regarding ivermectin and COVID, including its most popular tweet in FDA history. This landmark case sets an important precedent in limiting FDA overreach into the doctor-patient relationship* . . . (picture attached), X, March 21, 2024, https://x.com/mdbreathe/status/1771023714584273015?s=46.

125 Aaron Siri [@Aaron SiriSG], *Transparency is essential for a true democracy because freedom dies behind closed doors* (video attached, May 17, 2024).

126 Aaron Siri Congressional Testimony June 2024. This is an outstanding piece of scholarship on the COVID shots, FDA complicity, and Pfizer/Moderna financial interest driving policy.

127 Mary Talley Bowden [@MdBreathe] "*We now have 186 elected officials, 103 candidates, 1 Surgeon General, 1 State Political Party, 1 State Congressional District, 17 County Political Committees and 7 physician organizations publicly stating the COVID shots must be pulled off the market and pledging not to take donations from Big Pharma. Over 17,000 physicians stand behind them* . . . (picture attached), X, April 26, 2024.

128 For a brilliant summary of the complex web of financial and international interests that led to COVID-19, see the video attached to this tweet: Kim Doctcom [@KimDotcom], *This is the most important video you will watch this year. Millions were killed with Covid-19 for profit* ... (video attached), X, May 25, 2023, https://x.com/KimDotcom/status/1661698114917646336.

129 Association of American Physicians and Surgeons (AAPS) (website, accessed June 11, 2024), https://aapsonline.org/.

130 FLCCC Alliance (website, accessed June 11, 2024), https://covid19criticalcare.com/.

131 Great Barrington Declaration (website, accessed June 11, 2024), https://gbdeclaration.org/.

132 Emily Oster, "Let's Declare a Pandemic Amnesty," *The Atlantic*, October 31, 2022, https://www.theatlantic.com/ideas/archive/2022/10/covid-response-forgiveness/671879/.

133 "Thousands Believe Covid Vaccines Harmed Them. Is Anyone Listening?" *The New York Times*, May 4, 2024, https://www.nytimes.com/2024/05/03/health/covid-vaccines-side-effects.html.

134 Governor Cuomo single-handedly caused the death of untold thousands of New Yorkers, mainly the frail elderly.

135 https://x.com/elonmusk/status/1657573239298588673.

136 Elon Musk [@elonmusk], *Until the Supreme Court struck down Biden's vaccination decree, he tried to demand that we fire all unvaccinated personnel—some of our finest people* (video attached), X, https://x.com/elonmusk/status/1657573239298588673.

137 If allowed to progress, segregating persons (whether the segregation is black and white, gay and straight, vaxxed and unvaxxed) inevitably leads to killing the disenfranchised group. The Ten Stages of Genocide starts with classification, a division of "us" and "them"; is followed by discrimination denying civil rights to certain groups; proceeds to dehumanization by treating others without personal dignity; leading to polarization by spreading propaganda; which leads to persecution including segregation, and worse. See "The Ten Stages of Genocide," *Holocaust Memorial Day Trust* (website, accessed June 12, 2024), https://www.hmd.org.uk/learn-about-the-holocaust-and-genocides/what-is-genocide/the-ten-stages-of-genocide/.

138 Classic Marxism posits that the individual's interest is always subordinate to the collective interest; if the individual would only just give way, everything will be good. In fact, it is the individual's obligation to be subordinate to the group. Karl Marx believed collectivism was a more positive form of social organization. See "Collectivism," *The Decision Lab* (website accessed June 12, 2024), https://thedecisionlab.com/reference-guide/psychology/collectivism.

139 CPSO [@cpso_ca], *CPSO Statement on Public Health Misinformation: https://bit.ly/3u9gNDw; Please continue to check our regularly updated COVID-19 resource pages and FAQs for members of the public and physicians: http://cpso.on.ca/covid-19* (image attached), X, April 30, 2021, https://x.com/cpso_ca/status/1388211577770348544.

140 Shahdin Farsi, "Compelled Speech Comes to B.C.'s Courts," *C2C Journal*, May 24, 2021, https://c2cjournal.ca/2021/05/compelled-speech-comes-to-b-c-s-courts/.

141 Peter Menzies, "Fists of Ham: Why the Liberals Keep Trying (and Failing) to Control the Internet," *C2C Journal*, April 2, 2024, https://c2cjournal.ca/2024/04/fists-of-ham-why-the-liberals-keep-trying-and-failing-to-control-the-internet/.

142 Ward v. Quebec (Commission des droits de la personne et des droits de la jeunesse), 2021 SCC 43 (CanLII), <https://canlii.ca/t/jk1tl>, retrieved on 2024-06-12.

143 Blake [@_BlakeHabyan], *Powerful Video: It's For The 'Greater Good': Will This Video Wake Up The Brainwashed? This video serves as [sic] wake up call to those who are 'just following orders'. While the clip may seem strange, it is the dystopian reality we are living through …* (video attached), X, September 11, 2023, https://x.com/_BlakeHabyan/status/1701359052247163017.

144 "Ethics of the Fathers: Chapter Two," *Talmud*, 16 (Chabad.org, accessed June 12, 2024), https://www.chabad.org/library/article_cdo/aid/2011/jewish/Chapter-Two.htm.

Chapter 7

1 Mark Hand, "DC Settles Trump Inauguration Day Protest Lawsuits For $1.6M," *Patch*, April 27, 2021, https://patch.com/district-columbia/washingtondc/dc-settles-trump-inauguration-day-protest-lawsuits-1-6m.

2 Gregory Krieg, "Police injured, more than 200 arrested at Trump inauguration protests in DC," CNN, January 21, 2017, https://edition.cnn.com/2017/01/19/politics/trump-inauguration-protests-womens-march/index.html.

3 Rick Massimo, "Charges dropped against last of Inauguration Day protest defendants, *Washington's Top News* (WTOP), July 6, 2018, https://wtop.com/dc/2018/07/charges-dropped-against-last-of-inauguration-day-protest-defendants/.

4 Mark Hand, "DC Settles Trump Inauguration Day Protest Lawsuits For $1.6M," *Patch*, April 27, 2021, https://patch.com/district-columbia/washingtondc/dc-settles-trump-inauguration-day-protest-lawsuits-1-6m.

5 Ibid.

6 Lia Eustachewich, "Portland protesters barricade courthouse with federal officers inside, then try to set it on fire," *New York Post*, July 22, 2022, https://nypost.com/2020/07/22/portland-protesters-barricade-courthouse-with-federal-officers-inside/.

7 Billy J. Williams, U.S. Attorney for the District of Oregon, "United States Attorney Statement Regarding Ongoing Violence in Portland" (press release, justice.gov, September 25, 2020), https://www.justice.gov/usao-or/pr/united-states-attorney-statement-regarding-ongoing-violence-portland.

8 Ibid.
9 Ibid.
10 Aruna Viswanatha and Sadie Gurman, "Almost Half of Federal Cases Against Portland Rioters Have Been Dismissed," *The Wall Street Journal*, updated April 15, 2021, https://www.wsj.com/articles/almost-half-of-federal-cases-against-portland-rioters-have-been-dismissed-11618501979.
11 Kyle Iboshi, "Feds quietly dismiss dozens of Portland protest cases," *KGW8*, March 2, 2021, https://www.kgw.com/article/news/investigations/portland-protest-cases-dismissed-feds/283-002f01d2-3217-4b12-8725-3fda2cad119f.
12 Aruna Viswanatha and Sadie Gurman, "Almost Half of Federal Cases Against Portland Rioters Have Been Dismissed," *The Wall Street Journal*, updated April 15, 2021, https://www.wsj.com/articles/almost-half-of-federal-cases-against-portland-rioters-have-been-dismissed-11618501979.
13 Ibid.
14 Karolina Rivas and Mariam Khan, "Nearly 600 protesters at Women's March arrested on Capitol Hill," *ABC News*, https://abcnews.go.com/Politics/womens-march-protesters-call-end-family-separation-capitol/story?id=56240419.
15 Jason Breslow, "The Resistance At The Kavanaugh Hearings: More Than 200 Arrests," NPR, September 8, 2018, https://www.npr.org/2018/09/08/645497667/the-resistance-at-the-kavanaugh-hearings-more-than-200-arrests.
16 Adam Rosenberg, "Brett Kavanaugh protesters ignore police barricades, occupy the U.S. Capitol," *Yahoo!News*, Updated October 6, 2018, https://www.yahoo.com/news/brett-kavanaugh-protesters-ignore-police-194043428.html.
17 Leslie McAdoo Gordon, "January 6 Cases Being Treated More Harshly by DOJ," RedState, June 29, 2021, https://redstate.com/leslie-mcadoo-gordon/2021/06/29/january-6-cases-being-treated-more-harshly-by-doj-n404096.
18 News This Second [@NewsThisSecond] (video attached), X, October 4, 2018, https://x.com/NewsThisSecond/status/1047936868988440576.
19 Cheyenne Haslett, "Kavanaugh protests escalate, over 120 arrested on Capitol Hill," *ABC News*, September 24, 2018, https://abcnews.go.com/Politics/kavanaugh-protests-escalate-120-arrested-capitol-hill/story?id=58048599.
20 ABC News Politics [@ABCPolitics], *"We believe the women!" Kavanaugh protesters take over the Russell rotunda on Capitol Hill and some arrests by U.S. Capitol Police are underway http://abcn.ws/2N1wJ4J*" (video attached), X, September 24, 2018, https://x.com/ABCPolitics/status/1044266100626788352.
21 Leslie McAdoo Gordon, "January 6 Cases Being Treated More Harshly by DOJ," RedState, June 29, 2021, https://redstate.com/leslie-mcadoo-gordon/2021/06/29/january-6-cases-being-treated-more-harshly-by-doj-n404096.
22 Ibid.
23 Jim Hoft, "INSURRECTION: Colbert's Staff Harassed GOP Lawmakers Inside US Capitol After It Closed—AND Also Mocked and Harassed Speakers at Rally for Families of J6 Defendants," *The Gateway Pundit*, June 20, 2022, https://www.thegatewaypundit.com/2022/06/comedy-criminals-colberts-staff-harassed-gop-lawmakers-inside-us-capitol-closed-also-mocked-harassed-speakers-rally-families-j6-defendants/.

24 Tom Fitton [@TomFitton], *New: Biden DOJ, which is prosecuting Trump supporters for "parading" in US Capitol, won't prosecute leftist Colbert staffers. . . .* (Tweet attached), X, July 18, 2022, https://x.com/TomFitton/status/1549156306946330624.

25 Jim Hoft, "INSURRECTION: Colbert's Staff Harassed GOP Lawmakers Inside US Capitol After It Closed—AND Also Mocked and Harassed Speakers at Rally for Families of J6 Defendants," *The Gateway Pundit*, June 20, 2022, https://www.thegatewaypundit.com/2022/06/comedy-criminals-colberts-staff-harassed-gop-lawmakers-inside-us-capitol-closed-also-mocked-harassed-speakers-rally-families-j6-defendants/.

26 Chad Pergram, "How Colbert show staffers got themselves hurled out of two House office buildings," *Fox News*, June 20, 2022, https://www.foxnews.com/politics/colbert-show-staffers-hurled-house-office-building.

27 Jim Hoft, "INSURRECTION: Colbert's Staff Harassed GOP Lawmakers Inside US Capitol After It Closed—AND Also Mocked and Harassed Speakers at Rally for Families of J6 Defendants," *The Gateway Pundit*, June 20, 2022, https://www.thegatewaypundit.com/2022/06/comedy-criminals-colberts-staff-harassed-gop-lawmakers-inside-us-capitol-closed-also-mocked-harassed-speakers-rally-families-j6-defendants/.

28 *United States v. Armstrong*, 517 U.S. 456 (1996), https://supreme.justia.com/cases/federal/us/517/456/.

29 *United States v. Rundo,* 24-2814 U.S. (2024), https://caselaw.findlaw.com/court/us-dis-crt-c-d-cal-sou-div/115856212.html.

30 Mary Lou Masters, "Trump Moves To Toss Florida Indictment Based On 'Vindictive Prosecution,'" *Daily Caller*, May 2, 2024, https://dailycaller.com/2024/05/02/trump-moves-dismiss-florida-indictment-based-vindictive-prosecution/.

31 *United States v. Donald J. Trump*, 23-80101 (SDFL, May 2, 2024), https://storage.courtlistener.com/recap/gov.uscourts.flsd.648652/gov.uscourts.flsd.648652.508.0_3.pdf.

32 Spencer S. Hsu and Tom Jackman, "Judge: Nonviolent J6 defendants shouldn't get 'serious jail time,'" *The Washington Post*, March 29, 2022, https://www.washingtonpost.com/dc-md-va/2022/03/29/mcfadden-jan6-jail-kavanaugh-sentences/.

33 *Staples v. United States*, 511 U.S. 600 (1994), https://supreme.justia.com/cases/federal/us/511/600/.

34 *Elonis v. United States*, 575 U.S. 723 (2015), https://www.law.cornell.edu/supremecourt/text/13-983#writing-13-983_OPINION_3.

35 Paul Rosenzweig, "Ignorance of the Law Is No Excuse, But It Is Reality," *The Heritage Foundation*, June 17, 2013, https://www.heritage.org/crime-and-justice/report/ignorance-the-law-no-excuse-it-reality.

36 Cindy Hill, J.D., "Laws for Posting No Trespassing Signs," *Legal Beagle*, June 7, 2017, https://legalbeagle.com/5456098-laws-posting-trespassing-signs.html.

37 *United States v. Matthew Martin*, 1:21-cr-00394-TNM (DOC, March 29, 2022), https://storage.courtlistener.com/recap/gov.uscourts.dcd.232204/gov.uscourts.dcd.232204.30.0_1.pdf.

38 18 U.S. Code §1752 - Restricted building or grounds, https://www.law.cornell.edu/uscode/text/18/1752.
39 Ibid.
40 John Strand [@JohnStrandUSA], THEY PUT ME IN PRISON FOR 32 MONTHS . . . FOR THIS?!? (video attached), X, June 2, 2023, https://x.com/JohnStrandUSA/status/1664660656899907585?s=20.

Chapter 8

1 *Brady v. Maryland*, 373 U.S. 83 (1963), https://supreme.justia.com/cases/federal/us/373/83/.
2 Jerry Dunleavy, "DOJ has images of police fist-bumping rioters but hasn't handed over evidence," *Washington Examiner*, August 13, 2021, https://www.washingtonexaminer.com/news/1786625/doj-has-images-of-police-fist-bumping-rioters-but-hasnt-handed-over-evidence/.
3 18 U.S.C. §1512(c)(2). Jacob Chansley was only convicted of the single §1512(c)(2) felony; please see Chapter 15.
4 Associated Press, "Judge issues the first outright acquittal of a defendant charged over the Jan. 6 riot," NPR, April 7, 2022, https://www.npr.org/2022/04/07/1091392445/jan-6-riot-acquittal.
5 *United States vs. Jenny Cudd*, 1:21-cr-00068-TNM (DOC, October 13, 2021), p. 6, https://www.justice.gov/usao-dc/case-multi-defendant/file/1442576/download.
6 40 U.S. Code § 5109 - Penalties, https://www.law.cornell.edu/uscode/text/40/5109.
7 Ibid.
8 Ibid.
9 Ibid.
10 18 U.S. Code §1512 - Tampering with a witness, victim, or an informant, https://www.law.cornell.edu/uscode/text/18/1512.
11 *Scott v. United States*, 419 F. 2d 264, https://scholar.google.com/scholar_case?case=4792425287924462607&q=Scott+v+United+States,+135+US+App+DC+377&hl=en&as_sdt=2003.
12 Albert Alschuler, "The Prosecutor's Role in the Plea Bargaining," *University of Chicago Law Review* 36 (1968): 50–112, https://chicagounbound.uchicago.edu/cgi/viewcontent.cgi?article=1901&context=journal_articles.
13 "Capitol Breach Cases," United States Attorney's Office: District of Columbia (website, accessed June 14, 2024), https://www.justice.gov/usao-dc/capitol-breach-cases.
14 Albert Alschuler, "The Prosecutor's Role in the Plea Bargaining," *University of Chicago Law Review* 36 (1968): 50–112, https://chicagounbound.uchicago.edu/cgi/viewcontent.cgi?article=1901&context=journal_articles.
15 18 U.S. Code §1512 - Tampering with a witness, victim, or an informant, https://www.law.cornell.edu/uscode/text/18/1512.
16 Sidney Powell, *Licensed to Lie: Exposing Corruption in the Department of Justice* (Brown Books Publishing Group, 2014), https://www.licensedtolie.com/.

17 18 U.S. Code §1512 - Tampering with a witness, victim, or an informant, https://www.law.cornell.edu/uscode/text/18/1512.

18 Daniel A. Shtob, "Corruption of a Term: The Problematic Nature of 18 U.S.C. §1512(c), the New Federal Obstruction of Justice Provision §1512(c)," *Vanderbilt Law Review* 57, no. 4 (2019): 1429–1464, https://scholarship.law.vanderbilt.edu/vlr/vol57/iss4/6/.

19 *Flynn: Deliver the Truth. Whatever the Cost*, produced by Scott Wiper (2024), https://www.flynnmovie.us.

20 18 U.S. Code §1505—Obstruction of proceedings before departments, agencies, and committees, https://www.law.cornell.edu/uscode/text/18/1505.

21 Kyle Graham, "Overcharging," *Santa Clara Law Digital Commons* (2013): 1–26, https://digitalcommons.law.scu.edu/cgi/viewcontent.cgi?httpsredir=1&article=1609&context=facpubs.

22 *Brady v. United States*, 397 US 742 (1970), https://scholar.google.com/scholar_case?case=15048134446978918971&q=coercing+plea+agreement&hl=en&as_sdt=4,60#[8].

23 *Lafler v. Cooper*, 132 S.Ct. 1376 (2012), https://www.leagle.com/decision/insco20120321e16.

24 American Bar Association, *Prosecution Function* (2017, 4th Ed.), (online standards manual, accessed June 14, 2024), https://www.americanbar.org/groups/criminal_justice/standards/ProsecutionFunctionFourthEdition/.

25 Paul Bennet, "Prosecutorial Overcharging," (1979), *NCJRS Virtual Library*, (online article, accessed June 14, 2024), https://www.ojp.gov/ncjrs/virtual-library/abstracts/prosecutorial-overcharging.

26 Channing D. Phillips, Acting United States Attorney to Carlos Vanegas (Letter, August 31, 2021 for Case 1:21-cr-000580-DLF), https://www.justice.gov/usao-dc/case-multi-defendant/file/1445271/download.

27 *United States v. Jenny Cudd*, 18 U.S.C. 1752 (2021), https://www.justice.gov/usao-dc/case-multi-defendant/file/1442576/download.

28 Jordan Fischer [@JordanOnRecord], *Prosecutors say Cudd, in her presentencing* [sic] *interview and her sentencing memo, claimed she didn't know it was illegal to enter the Capitol. That's a necessary element for the offense she pleaded guilty to. Her attorney says they're being "malicious" and should be sanctioned* (image attached), X, March 23, 2022, https://twitter.com/JordanOnRecord/status/1506641989747548165.

29 Ibid.

30 "Matthew Lawrence Perna Obituary," John Flynn Funeral Home & Crematory, Inc. (website, accessed June 14, 2024), https://www.tributearchive.com/obituaries/24489553/matthew-lawrence-perna/hermitage/pennsylvania/john-flynn-funeral-home-crematory-inc.

31 Anonymous FBI Special Agent, "Statement of Facts," Affidavit (January 18, 2021), https://www.justice.gov/opa/page/file/1356831/download.

32 *United States v. Perna*, 21-cr-156-2-JDB, (D.C. December 09, 2021), https://www.justice.gov/usao-dc/press-release/file/1457391/download.

33 Ibid.

34 United States Attorney's Office: District of Columbia, "Pennsylvania Man Pleads Guilty to Felony Charge For Obstructing Congress During Jan. 6 Capitol Breach" (press release, December 17, 2021), https://www.justice.gov/usao-dc/pr/pennsylvania-man-pleads-guilty-felony-charge-obstructing-congress-during-jan-6-capitol.

35 Constitutionally concerned fed up Floridian [@UpInTHeHills], *Jan. 6 Defendant Takes His Own Life, Died of 'Broken Heart,' Family Says … Perna learned that prosecutors would seek an even longer jail sentence based on "domestic terrorism deterrence." While BLM and Antifa were bailed out to terrorize some more* (Link to *The Epoch Times* article, see following note), X, February 28, 2022, https://x.com/UpInTheHills/status/1498397050894835715.

36 Joseph M. Hanneman, "Jan. 6 Defendant Takes His Own Life, Died of 'Broken Heart,' Family Says," *The Epoch Times*, February 27, 2022 (updated February 28, 2022), https://www.theepochtimes.com/us/jan-6-defendant-takes-his-own-life-died-of-broken-heart-family-says-4305919.

37 Brandon Straka [@BrandonStraka], "The True Stories of January 6th." X, March 8, 2023, https://x.com/BrandonStraka/status/1633584414293630976.

38 Geri Perna (Matthew Perna's aunt), personal communication with author, June 16, 2024.

39 Marjorie Taylor Greene, "Congresswoman Marjorie Taylor Greene Introduces the Matthew Lawrence Perna Act of 2024" (press release, March 1, 2024), https://greene.house.gov/news/documentsingle.aspx?DocumentID=683.

40 Ibid.

Chapter 9

1 Associated Press (website, accessed June 14, 2024), https://www.reportforamerica.org/newsrooms/associated-press-15/.

2 In 1945, the AP was accused of violating antitrust laws, promoting restraint of trade, and being anti-competition. *Associated Press v. United States*, 326 U.S. 1 (1945), https://supreme.justia.com/cases/federal/us/326/1/.

3 Simone Gold, *I Do Not Consent: My Fight Against Medical Cancel Culture* (Bombardier Books, 2020).

4 Sharon Lerner, "Doctor Who Joined Capital Attacks Leads a Far-Right Campaign Against COVID-19 Vaccine," *The Intercept*, January 14, 2021, https://theintercept.com/2021/01/14/capitol-riot-covid-vaccine-doctor/.

5 Carl Bernstein, "The CIA and the Media," *Rolling Stone*, October 20, 1977, https://www.carlbernstein.com/the-cia-and-the-media-rolling-stone-10-20-1977.

6 Kara Goldfarm, "Inside Operation Mockingbird—The CIA's Plan To Infiltrate The Media," *ATI*, December 4, 2021 (updated January 21, 2021), https://allthatsinteresting.com/operation-mockingbird.

7 "Afghan conflict: US and Taliban sign deal to end 18-year war," *BBC*, February 29, 2020, https://www.bbc.com/news/world-asia-51689443.

8 "Suspicions of Russian Bounties Were Bolstered by Data on Financial Transfers," *The New York Times*, July 29, 2020, https://www.nytimes.com/2020/06/30/us/politics/russian-bounties-afghanistan-intelligence.html.
9 Glenn Greenwald, "House Democrats, Working with Liz Cheney, Restrict Trump's Planned Withdrawal of Troops from Afghanistan and Germany," *The Intercept*, July 2, 2020, https://theintercept.com/2020/07/02/house-democrats-working-with-liz-cheney-restrict-trumps-planned-withdrawal-of-troops-from-afghanistan-and-germany/.
10 Courtney Kube and Ken Dilanian, "U.S. commander: Intel still hasn't established Russia paid Taliban 'bounties' to kill U.S. troops," *NBC News*, September 14, 2020, https://www.nbcnews.com/politics/national-security/u-s-commander-intel-still-hasn-t-established-russia-paid-n1240020.
11 Adam Rawnsley, Spencer Ackerman, and Asawin Suebsaeng, "It was a huge election-time story that prompted cries of treason. But according to a newly disclosed assessment, Donald Trump might have been right to call it a 'hoax,'" *The Daily Beast*, April 15, 2021, https://www.thedailybeast.com/us-intel-walks-back-claim-russians-put-bounties-on-american-troops.
12 Caitlin Johnstone, "White House Warns Russia on Bounties, but Stops Short of Sanctions," *The New York Times*, April 15, 2021, https://www.nytimes.com/2021/04/15/us/politics/biden-russian-bounties.html
13 AP reporter = Associated Press reporter, which is a reporter whose articles are printed in many publications, for example the *The New York Times*, *The Washington Post*, *USA Today*, *BBC*, etc. For me AP reporter = Associated Propaganda reporter.
14 Michael Biesecker and Jason Dearen, "GOP fronts 'pro-Trump' doctors to prescribe rapid reopening," Associated Press, May 20, 2020, https://apnews.com/article/health-us-news-ap-top-news-politics-virus-outbreak-4ee1a3a8d631b454f645b2a8d9597de7.
15 Ibid.
16 At the time of this writing, Robert Kennedy Jr. is a Democrat running as an Independent with millions of likely voters.
17 Nick Robins-Early, Hayley Miller, and Jesselyn Cook, "How Quack Doctors And Powerful GOP Operatives Spread Misinformation To Millions," *HuffPost*, July 28, 2020, https://www.huffpost.com/entry/how-quack-doctors-and-powerful-gop-operatives-spread-misinformation-to-millions_n_5f208048c5b66859f1f33148.
18 FrontlineFlash [@FrontlineFlash], *WHOA . . . when the dishonest media get a taste of their own medicine, it's never pretty—but its [sic] pretty revealing . . .* (video attached), X, February 11, 2022, https://x.com/FrontlineFlash/status/1492199904772427778?s=20.
19 Micah Lee, "Network of Right-Wing Health Care Providers is Making Millions off Hydroxychloroquine and Ivermectin, Hacked Data Reveals," *The Intercept*, September 28, 2021, https://theintercept.com/2021/09/28/covid-telehealth-hydroxychloroquine-ivermectin-hacked/.

20 Dr. Rich Swier, "CALIFORNIA: New Witch Hunt to Strip Honest Doctors of Their Licenses," May 5, 2022, https://drrichswier.com/2022/05/05/california-new-witch-hunt-to-strip-honest-doctors-of-their-licenses/.

21 "Chris Gilroy: Owner, Chief Marketing Strategist, Developer, Designer" (archived Linkedin profile, accessed June 14, 2024), https://archive.md/PbJUu.

22 "The Disinformation Dozen," Center for Countering Digital Hate (online document, March 24, 2021), https://252f2edd-1c8b-49f5-9bb2-cb57bb47e4ba.filesusr.com/ugd/f4d9b9_b7cedc0553604720b7137f8663366ee5.pdf.

23 Dr. Rich Swier, "CALIFORNIA: New Witch Hunt to Strip Honest Doctors of Their Licenses," May 5, 2022, https://drrichswier.com/2022/05/05/california-new-witch-hunt-to-strip-honest-doctors-of-their-licenses/.

24 Mary Talley Bowden MD [@mdBreathe], *Should I organize a class-action lawsuit against No License for Disinformation, a non-profit worth at least $17MM who launched media attacks and encouraged the public to report me and other doctors to the medical boards?* (image attached), X, March 8, 2023, https://x.com/MdBreathe/status/1633535659297103901.

25 America's Frontline Doctors, "The Deadly Dozen/Disinformation" (video, accessed June 14, 2024), https://fast.wistia.net/embed/iframe/kvajk1r8ro.

26 Elon Musk [@Elon Musk], *Yikes* (video attached), X, May 27, 2023, https://x.com/elonmusk/status/1662667558539886592.

27 Sharon Lerner, "Doctor Who Joined Capital Attacks Leads a Far-Right Campaign Against COVID-19 Vaccine," *The Intercept*, January 14, 2021, https://theintercept.com/2021/01/14/capitol-riot-covid-vaccine-doctor/.

28 Micah Lee, "Network of Right-Wing Health Care Providers is Making Millions off Hydroxychloroquine and Ivermectin, Hacked Data Reveals," *The Intercept*, September 28, 2021, https://theintercept.com/2021/09/28/covid-telehealth-hydroxychloroquine-ivermectin-hacked/.

29 Vera Bergengruen, "How 'America's Frontline Doctors' Sold Access to Bogus COVID-19 Treatments—and Left Patients in the Lurch," *Time*, August 26, 2021, https://time.com/6092368/americas-frontline-doctors-covid-19-misinformation/.

30 The FDA has a pathway for medications to change categories, but the drug manufacturer usually initiates the change. The list of drugs that have switched is very long, including Motrin, Aleve, Antivert, Nasonex, Voltaren, Plan B, Nicotrol, Mucinex, Claritin, Narcan, and Flonase. Occasionally, the drug manufacturer will not pursue this switch, typically when there is too much controversy or no profit potential. Plan B was the former, and hydroxychloroquine was in the latter. Plan B did become over-the-counter following citizens filing a "Citizen's Petition" to the FDA in 2001. **So I filed the same paperwork for hydroxychloroquine (HCQ), as it is a completely safe drug and should already have been over-the-counter** (see Appendix 2 at https://www.drsimonegold.com/book/resources). The only reason HCQ is not over-the-counter in America is it would not sell well due to minimal demand. Also, see minute 5:35 of the following video where I state, "I'm in favor of making it over-the-counter. Give it to the people. Give it to the people" during the original White Coat Summit in 2020:

America's Frontline Doctors, "White Coat Summit" (video, 2023), https://fast.wistia.net/embed/iframe/6ndhhgyy3o.

31 America's Frontline Doctors (website, accessed June 15, 2024), AFLDS.org. If a donor chooses to support AFLDS with donations, that does not affect my salary, which is both a flat rate well within the range for nonprofit salaries for physician leaders, and a small portion of the AFLDS budget to fund public service activities, ranging from medical freedom litigation to compiling an online library of scientific resources. In fact, throughout most of 2020 I took no salary at all, and eventually I took a salary that was a fraction of my prior earnings as a physician. Even the proceeds of my first book were donated to AFLDS.

32 Appendix 6, https://www.drsimonegold.com/book/resources.

33 Stephanie Mencimer, "Doctor, Lawyer, Insurrectionist: The Radicalization of Simone Gold," *Mother Jones*, May 6, 2021, https://www.motherjones.com/politics/2021/05/doctor-lawyer-insurrectionist-the-radicalization-of-simone-gold/.

34 Ben Mathis-Lilley, "New Florida Surgeon General Appeared at Demon-Sperm COVID Conspiracy Summit With Future Capitol Rioter," *Slate*, September 22, 2021, https://slate.com/news-and-politics/2021/09/florida-surgeon-general-demon-sperm-capitol-rioter-connections.html.

35 Dr. Stella Immanuel MD [@stell_immanuel], X, accessed June 15, 2024, https://x.com/stella_immanuel?ref_src=twsrc%5Egoogle%7Ctwcamp%5Eserp%7Ctwgr%5Eauthor.

36 Dr. Joseph Mercola, "Big Pharma Hunts Down Dissenting Doctors," Mercola.com (online article, November 29, 2021), https://articles.mercola.com/sites/articles/archive/2021/11/29/big-pharma-hunts-down-dissenting-doctors.aspx?merintrev=1.

37 "Forward" by Robert F. Kennedy Jr. in Dr. Joseph Mercola and Ronnie Cummins, *The Truth About COVID-19: Exposing The Great Reset, Lockdowns, Vaccine Passports, and the New Normal* (Chelsea Green Publishing, 2021).

38 Emmarie Huetterman, "The top 3 House Democrat leaders have pocketed millions from pharma," *Kaiser Health News*, November 29, 2018 (accessed from FiercePharma website, June 15, 2024), https://www.fiercepharma.com/pharma/top-3-house-democrat-leaders-have-pocketed-millions-from-pharma.

39 "Pfizer Inc PAC Contributions to Federal Candidates," OpenSecrets.com (website accessed June 15, 2024), https://www.opensecrets.org/political-action-committees-pacs/pfizer-inc/C00016683/candidate-recipients/2020.

40 "Crony capitalism," Merriam-webster.com (website accessed June 15, 2024), https://www.merriam-webster.com/dictionary/crony%20capitalism.

41 H.R.5546 - National Childhood Vaccine Injury Act of 1986, https://www.congress.gov/bill/99th-congress/house-bill/5546.

42 "National Vaccine Injury Compensation Program," Health Resources & Services Administration, (website accessed June 15, 2024), https://www.hrsa.gov/vaccine-compensation. An article published in 2007 (17 years from the time of this writing) noted that taxpayers had paid over $4 billion to compensate vaccine injury victims. Imagine what that number is now: Richard F.

Edlich MD, PHD et al., "Update on the National Vaccine Injury Compensation Program," *The Journal of Emergency Medicine* 33, no. 2 (2007): 199–211, https://doi.org/10.1016/j.jemermed.2007.01.001.

43 Lauren Gardner, "Vaccine injury compensation programs overwhelmed as congressional reform languishes," *Politico*, June 1, 2022, https://www.politico.com/news/2022/06/01/vaccine-injury-compensation-programs-overwhelmed-as-congressional-reform-languishes-00033064.

44 "Operation Warp Speed," U.S. Government Accountability Office (Report GAO-21-319), February 11, 2021, https://www.gao.gov/products/gao-21-319.

45 Noah Higgins-Dunn, "The U.S. has already invested billions in potential coronavirus vaccines. Here's where the deals stand," CNBC, August 14, 2020, https://www.cnbc.com/2020/08/14/the-us-has-already-invested-billions-on-potential-coronavirus-vaccines-heres-where-the-deals-stand.html.

46 Chris Isidore, "Pfizer revenue and profits soar on its Covid vaccine business," CNN, November 2, 2021, https://www.cnn.com/2021/11/02/business/pfizer-earnings/index.html.

47 Micah Lee, "Network of Right-Wing Health Care Providers is Making Millions off Hydroxychloroquine and Ivermectin, Hacked Data Reveals," *The Intercept*, September 28, 2021, https://theintercept.com/2021/09/28/covid-telehealth-hydroxychloroquine-ivermectin-hacked/.

48 "1 in every 246 Vaccinated People has died within 60 days of Covid-19 Vaccination in England according to UK Government," *The Expose*, August 9, 2022, https://expose-news.com/2022/08/09/1-in-246-people-die-shortly-after-covid-vaccination/.

49 Appendix A, https://www.drsimonegold.com/book/resources.

50 Alex Brenson, "More people died in the key clinical trial for Pfizer's Covid vaccine than the company publicly reported," *The Burning Platform*, November 17, 2021, https://www.theburningplatform.com/2021/11/17/more-people-died-in-the-key-clinical-trial-for-pfizers-covid-vaccine-than-the-company-publicly-reported/.

51 "Improving Detection of and Response to Adverse Events," National Library of Medicine (website, accessed June 15, 2024), https://www.ncbi.nlm.nih.gov/books/NBK232983/.

52 Carolos Alegria, "Excess adjusted deaths from malignant neoplasms for ages 15 to 44, in England and Wales" in *UK—Death and Disability Trends for Malignant Neoplasms, Ages 15–44* (October 10, 2023), https://phinancetechnologies.com/HumanityProjects/UK%20Cause%20of%20Death/Report%20V-Damage%20Analysis%20-%20Malignant%20Cancers%2015-44%20-%20V2.pdf Some of the tables within the chapter can be also be accessed here: https://www.semanticscholar.org/paper/UK-Death-and-Disability-Trends-for-Malignant-Ages-Alegria/e5dedc69686e9350b1cd96fb1a22c93af859ec46.

53 "Maddie de Garay: Ohio 13-year-old cannot and did not 'consent' to vaccine clinical trials," *The COVID Blog*, July 8, 2021, https://thecovidblog.com/2021/07/08/maddie-de-garay-ohio-13-year-old-cannot-and-did-not-consent-to-vaccine-clinical-trials/.

54 Leigh [@Leigh76777], *PHIZER TRIAL...MADDIE DE GARAY. This one injury should have stopped these. She's still paralyzed,* (picture attached), X, August 27, 2022, https://twitter.com/Leigh76777/status/1563471492696121344.
55 Sunfellow On COVID-19, "Rigged: Maddie de Garay's Story (*The Highwire*)," (Rumble video, accessed June 15, 2024), https://rumble.com/v1fpa69-rigged-maddie-de-garays-story-the-highwire.html.

Chapter 10

1 *New York Times Co. v. Sullivan*, 376 U.S. 254 (1964), https://supreme.justia.com/cases/federal/us/376/254/. Overall, this case has been terrible precedent because it has been interpreted to all but eliminate the ability to bring winning defamation lawsuits. Its original intent was to protect the First Amendment.
2 John Strand [@JohnStrandUSA], *"a D.C. judge's fury at my public criticism of the government's behavior has landed me years in prison; that is the textbook definition of fascism." I testified for @RepMattGaetz: J6 is a severe abuse of power against the people* (video attached), X, June 26, 2023, https://x.com/JohnStrandUSA/status/1673334266002915329?s=20*.
3 *Curtis Publishing Co. v. Butts*, 388 U.S. 130 (1967), https://supreme.justia.com/cases/federal/us/388/130/.
4 Dan McLaughlin, "Justice Thomas, Alone, Wants to Revisit *New York Times v. Sullivan*." *National Review*, June 27, 2022, https://www.nationalreview.com/corner/justice-thomas-alone-wants-to-revisit-new-york-times-v-sullivan/.
5 Shoshannah Brombacher, "A Pillow Full of Feathers," Chabad.org (online article, accessed June 16, 2024), https://www.chabad.org/library/article_cdo/aid/812861/jewish/A-Pillow-Full-of-Feathers.htm.
6 Proverbs 18:8, from The Message Bible Translation.
7 The Matt Walsh Show [@MattWalshShow], *As I was feeling slightly discouraged last night, @jordanbpeterson said something that put things in perspective: "When you speak the truth, whatever happens is the best possible thing that could have happened." In other words, there's no use lamenting the consequences of speaking the truth, because if you remain silent, the results will always be worse anyway* (video attached), X, https://x.com/MattWalshShow/status/1664707553241059348.
8 "Confidence in U.S. Institutions Down; Average at New Low," Gallup (online article, July 5, 2022), https://news.gallup.com/poll/394283/confidence-institutions-down-average-new-low.aspx.
9 John Sands, "Americans are losing faith in an objective media. A new Gallup/Knight study explores why," Knight Foundation (online article, August 4, 2020), https://knightfoundation.org/articles/americans-are-losing-faith-in-an-objective-media-a-new-gallup-knight-study-explores-why/.
10 To read about financial troubles in traditional news organizations see David Bauder, Associated Press, "2 news chains to end use of The Associated Press," *Arkansas Democrat Gazette*, March 21, 2024, https://www.arkansasonline.com/news/2024/mar/21/2-news-chains-to-end-use-of-the-associated-press/.

11 "Media and tech firms join forces to tackle harmful Covid vaccine myths," BBC, December 10, 2020, https://www.bbc.com/news/entertainment-arts-55257814.
12 Leo Hohmann, "Highly Cited COVID Doctor Comes To Stunning Conclusion: Gov't 'Scrubbing Unprecedented Numbers' Of Injection-Related Deaths," LewRockwell.com (online article, May 4, 2021), https://www.lewrockwell.com/2021/05/no_author/highly-cited-covid-doctor-comes-to-stunning-conclusion-govt-scrubbing-unprecedented-numbers-of-injection-related-deaths/.
13 European Broadcasting Union, "Trusted News Initiative announces plans to tackle harmful coronavirus disinformation" (press release, March 27, 2020), https://www.ebu.ch/news/2020/03/trusted-news-initiative-announces-plans-to-tackle-harmful-coronavirus-disinformation.
14 Dr. Simone Gold [@drsimonegold], *Just remember… The government did more to stop the distribution of Ivermectin and Hydroxycloroquine [sic] than it did to stop the distribution of Fentanyl*, X, February 12, 2024, https://x.com/drsimonegold/status/1757205905697824849.
15 Katelyn Beaty, "QAnon: The alternative religion that's coming to your church," Religion News Service, August 17, 2020, https://religionnews.com/2020/08/17/qanon-the-alternative-religion-thats-coming-to-your-church/.
16 Ramon Tomey, "Dr. Vladimir Zelenko urges people to stand up against government tyranny," *Medical Martial Law*, December 10, 2021, https://medicalmartiallaw.com/index.html.
17 America's Frontline Doctors, "The Uncensored Truth Tour: Albuquerque NM" (video, July 8, 2021), https://americasfrontlinedoctors.org/videos/post/the-uncensored-truth-tour-albuquerque-nm.
18 America's Frontline Doctors, "Dr. Gold Speaks at ReAwaken American Tour" (video, July 19, 2021), https://americasfrontlinedoctors.org/videos/post/dr-gold-speaks-at-reawaken-america-tour.
19 "Next Conferences," ThriveTimeShow (website, accessed June 16, 2024), https://www.thrivetimeshow.com/reawaken-america-tour/.
20 "Learn How to Grow Your Business," ThriveTimeShow (website, accessed June 16, 2024), https://www.thrivetimeshow.com/.
21 Bill Sherman, "Blind son who gained sight makes Mrs. Oklahoma contestant believe in miracles," *Tulsa World*, March 19, 2016, https://tulsaworld.com/life-entertainment/blind-son-who-gained-sight-makes-mrs-oklahoma-contestant-believe-in-miracles/article_1268b6ca-8ffe-57d2-8246-b5f21dae52f3.html.
22 *Flynn: Deliver the Truth. Whatever the Cost*, produced by Scott Wiper (2024), https://www.flynnmovie.us.
23 "Dr. Simone Gold, Dr. Peter McCullough, Dr. Richard Bartlett," Day Star TV (video, March 3, 2022), https://daystar.tv/player/37118/444945.
24 Kennedy/Shanahan, (website, accessed June 16, 2024), https://www.kennedy24.com/.
25 "Dr. Peter McCullough The Most Cited MD on COVID-19 Treatments," People's World War (online article, May 24, 2021), https://peoplesworldwar.com/dr-peter-mccullough-the-most-cited-md-on-covid-19-treatments/.

26 "Jim Meehan MD," MeehanMD (website, accessed June 16, 2024), https://www.meehanmd.com/jim-meehan-md.
27 "Meet the Benjamins," Remnant Church (website, accessed June 16, 2024), https://therealremnantchurch.com/meet-the-benjamins/.
28 Thrivetime Show, "The ReAwaken America Tour" (Rumble video, accessed June 16, 2024), https://rumble.com/vhxyy9-pastor-bill-cook-if-pastors-will-stand-up-we-can-this-battle.html.
29 "America's Frontline Doctors presents, 'The Uncensored Truth Tour', live from New Orleans. Doctor Simone Gold and guests present vital information about Covid19," The HighWire (video, accessed June 16, 2024), https://thehighwire.com/videos/live-from-the-uncensored-truth-tour/.
30 *Flynn: Deliver the Truth. Whatever the Cost*, produced by Scott Wiper (2024), https://www.flynnmovie.us.
31 "Robert Tyler," Advocates for Faith and Freedom (website, accessed June 16, 2024), https://faith-freedom.com/our-team/robert-tyler.
32 Nina Martin, "This Alabama Judge Has Figured Out How to Dismantle Roe v. Wade," Propublica.org, online article, October 10, 2014, https://www.propublica.org/article/this-alabama-judge-has-figured-out-how-to-dismantle-roe-v-wade.
33 "Kelly Shackelford," First Liberty (website, accessed June 16, 2024), https://firstliberty.org/team/kelly-shackelford/.
34 America's Frontline Doctors, "AFLDS.org presents, 'We Are The World'" (video, August 3, 2021), https://americasfrontlinedoctors.org/videos/post/afldsorg-presents-we-are-the-world.
35 America's Frontline Doctors, "The Normal Symbol" (video, July 15, 2021), https://americasfrontlinedoctors.org/videos/post/the-normal-symbol.
36 https://americasfrontlinedoctors.org/videos/post/the-uncensored-truth-tour-albuquerque-nm minute 34, 36. Minute 17:45 is about the faulty PCR testing.

Chapter 11

1 Exodus 2:11, Chabad.org (accessed, July 1, 2024), https://www.chabad.org/parshah/torahreading.asp?aid=2492603&p=3.
2 "Shemot Rabbah 1, The Sefaria Midrash Rabbah (2022)," Sefaria.org, (accessed, July 1, 2024), https://www.sefaria.org/Shemot_Rabbah.1.28?lang=bi&with=Translations&lang2=en.
3 *United States v. Armstrong*, 517 U.S. 456 (1996), pp. 456–7, https://supreme.justia.com/cases/federal/us/517/456/.
4 Peter Overby, "IRS Apologizes For Aggressive Scrutiny Of Conservative Groups," NPR, October 27, 2017, https://www.npr.org/2017/10/27/560308997/irs-apologizes-for-aggressive-scrutiny-of-conservative-groups.
5 Judicial Watch, "The IRS Abuse Scandal" (website article, accessed July 1, 2024), https://www.judicialwatch.org/irs/.
6 Sari Horwitz, "No criminal charges will be filed against ex-IRS official Lois Lerner," *The Washington Post*, October 23, 2015, https://www.washingtonpost.com/world/national-security/no-criminal-charges-will-be-filed-against-ex-irs

-official-lois-lerner/2015/10/23/d9fab80a-79bc-11e5-a958-d889faf561dc_story.html.

7 Debra Heine, "Feds Quietly Dismiss Dozens of Cases Against Antifa Extremists Who Terrorized Downtown Portland Last Summer," *The Tennessee Star*, March 7, 2021, https://tennesseestar.com/news/feds-quietly-dismiss-dozens-of-cases-against-antifa-extremists-who-terrorized-downtown-portland-last-summer/admin/2021/03/07/.

8 Ibid. In addition, see the embedded links from the *Tennessee Star* article: Catherine Smith, "Portland Riots Caused at Least $2.3 Million in Damage to Federal Buildings," *American Greatness*, February 4, 2021, https://amgreatness.com/2021/02/04/portland-riots-caused-at-least-2-3m-in-damage-to-federal-buildings/; Steven Nelson, "Federal officers in Portland suffered 113 eye injuries from lasers, DHS official says," *New York Post*, August 4, 2020, https://nypost.com/2020/08/04/federal-officers-in-portland-suffered-113-eye-injuries-from-lasers-dhs/; Debra Heine, "DHS Agent: Portland Rioters 'Mentally Ill,' 'Drug Abusers,' 'Catatonic With Hate,'" *American Greatness*, July 27, 2020, https://amgreatness.com/2020/07/27/dhs-agent-portland-rioters-mentally-ill-drug-abusers-catatonic-with-hate/.

9 William F. Jasper, "NEWS FLASH TO MEDIA: Antifa Is COMMUNIST!" *The New American*, October 9, 2017, https://thenewamerican.com/us/crime/news-flash-to-media-antifa-is-communist/. In addition, see the embedded link from the article: Eric Owens, "EXCLUSIVE: The Antifa Professor Who Celebrated Dead Cops Has A COMMUNIST Grading Policy," *Daily Caller*, September 25, 2017, https://dailycaller.com/2017/09/25/exclusive-the-antifa-professor-who-celebrates-dead-cops-has-a-communist-grading-policy/.

10 Debra Heine, "Feds Quietly Dismiss Dozens of Cases Against Antifa Extremists Who Terrorized Downtown Portland Last Summer," *The Tennessee Star*, March 7, 2021, https://tennesseestar.com/news/feds-quietly-dismiss-dozens-of-cases-against-antifa-extremists-who-terrorized-downtown-portland-last-summer/admin/2021/03/07/. In addition, see the embedded links from the *Tennessee Star* article: Debra Heine, "Portland's 'Do Nothing' DA and Mayor Denounce BLM Assault After Distrubing Video Goes Viral," *American Greatness*, August 18, 2020, https://amgreatness.com/2020/08/18/portlands-do-nothing-da-and-mayer-denounce-blm-assault-after-disturbing-video-goes-viral/; Debra Heine, "Seven Antifa Agitators Face Federal Charges After Portland Riots," *American Greatness*, July 8, 2020, https://amgreatness.com/2020/07/08/seven-antifa-agitators-face-federal-charges-after-portland-riots/.

11 *The New York Times* [@nytimes], *The House committee investigating the assault on the Capitol and what led to it is employing the aggressive tactics prosecutors use on mobsters and terrorists* (picture attached), X, February 5, 2022, https://x.com/nytimes/status/1490065213902757890.

12 Save for a solitary protester with a remote concealed gun, not on his person, and which he never held, none of the protesters were carrying firearms inside the building.

13 Conn Caroll, "FBI confirms there was no insurrection on Jan. 6," *Washington Examiner*, August 20, 2021, https://www.washingtonexaminer.com/opinion/51440/fbi-confirms-there-was-no-insurrection-on-jan-6/. See also links from article: Cambridge Dictionary, "insurrection" (definition from dictionary.cambridge.org), https://dictionary.cambridge.org/us/dictionary/english/insurrection; Mark Hosenball and Sarah N. Lynch, "Exclusive: FBI finds scant evidence U.S. Capitol attack was coordinated—sources," Reuters, August 20, 2021, https://www.reuters.com/world/us/exclusive-fbi-finds-scant-evidence-us-capitol-attack-was-coordinated-sources-2021-08-20/.

14 Ibid.

15 Jordan Boyd, "Investigators: Pelosi Responsible For Jan. 6 Security Breakdown At U.S. Capitol," *The Federalist*, June 23, 2022, https://thefederalist.com/2022/06/23/investigators-pelosi-responsible-for-jan-6-security-breakdown-at-u-s-capitol/.

16 Oversight Committee [@OversightAdmn], *Since January 6, 2021, Nancy Pelosi spent 3+ years and nearly $20 million creating a narrative to blame Donald Trump. NEW FOOTAGE shows on January 6, Pelosi ADMITTED: "I take responsibility." WATCH:*, (video attached), X, June 10, 2024, https://x.com/OversightAdmn/status/1800207258514575730.

17 NOVA Campaigns [@NoVA_Campaigns], *@CapitolPolice @ChiefSund asked to resign by @SpeakerPelosi right after Jan 6; Sund requested @NationalGuard before Jan 6 (denied by @MayorBowser & House SGT at arms/Pelosi) & for 71 mins after 1st breach on Jan 6; House SGT & DoD too worried about optics; Sund deserves apology*, (video attached; see minute 3), June 14, 2024, https://x.com/NoVA_Campaigns/status/1801596114698727865.

18 Committee on House Administration, Chairman Bryan Steil, "Chairman Loudermilk Releases Timeline of D.C. National Guard Deployment on January 6, 2021" (press release, June 14, 2024), https://cha.house.gov/press-releases?id=4E4C35BF-F697-4706-B22C-1631F0FC51CE.

19 William F. Jasper, "January 6 Melee: Insurrection or Fedsurrection?" *The New American*, January 7, 2022, https://thenewamerican.com/us/crime/january-6-melee-insurrection-or-fedsurrection/.

20 Joseph M. Hannemann, "Prosecutor Admits DC Police Officers Acted as Provocateurs at US Capitol on Jan. 6," *The Epoch Times*, March 24, 2023, https://www.theepochtimes.com/us/prosecutor-admits-dc-police-officers-acted-as-provocateurs-at-us-capitol-on-jan-6-5148808.

21 Julie Kelly [@julie_kelly2], *J6 conspiracy theorist, insurrection denier. Former food blogger. Real Clear https://realclearinvestigations.com/authors/julie_kelly/*, X, profile accessed July 2, 2024, https://x.com/julie_kelly2.

22 Julie Kelly [@julie_kelly2], *I'll say again-as evidence continues to emerge about massive numbers of uniformed, undercover, and CHSs from multiple agencies were on the ground on Jan 6–why did they not stop the "insurrection?" In any other situation, they'd be called to task. Not the case here. Why?*, X, April 12, 2023, https://x.com/julie_kelly2/status/1646319707459313664?s=20.

23 John Solomon, "Jan. 6 commission chairman once sympathized with black secessionist group that killed cops," *Just the News*, October 4, 2021, https://justthenews.com/government/congress/jan-6-commission-chairman-once-sympathized-black-secessionist-group-killed-cops.

24 Ibid. Also, see referenced embedded in text: Chuck McFadden, "Armed Black Panthers in the Capitol, 50 years on," *Capitol Weekly*, April 26, 2017, https://capitolweekly.net/black-panthers-armed-capitol/.

25 Chapter 7 fn 28: The US Supreme Court has held citizens to be constitutionally protected from selective prosecution under the equal protection component of the Fifth Amendment's Due Process Clause. *United States v. Armstrong*, 517 U.S. 456 (1996), https://supreme.justia.com/cases/federal/us/517/456/.

26 Joseph M. Hanneman, "After a Pause, Jan. 6 Arrests Are Now Sharply Increasing," *The Epoch Times*, March 6, 2024, https://www.theepochtimes.com/article/after-a-pause-doj-is-now-sharply-increasing-jan-6-arrests-5600972.

27 *United States v. Armstrong*, 517 U.S. 456 (1996), p. 457, https://supreme.justia.com/cases/federal/us/517/456/.

28 Ibid., p. 463.

29 Ibid., p. 464.

30 Melissa L. Jampol, "Goodbye to the Defence of Selective Prosecution," *Journal of Criminal Law and Criminology* 87 (1997): 932–966, https://scholarlycommons.law.northwestern.edu/jclc/vol87/iss3/10/.

31 America's Frontline Doctors, "The Gold Report: Ep. 24 '*Fischer v. United States*' with Mat Staver (Rumble video, accessed July 2, 2024), https://rumble.com/v4s97lo-the-gold-report-ep.-24-fischer-v.-united-states-with-mat-staver.html.

32 Realpac, "Dr. Simone Gold Speaks at CPAC 2024" (Rumble video, accessed July 2, 2024), https://rumble.com/v4fgjr5-dr.-simone-gold-speaks-at-cpac-2024.html.

33 I had to walk this very tightrope in my trial with the California Medical Board. That sworn testimony is Appendix 9, https://www.drsimonegold.com/book/resources.

34 Appendix 10, https://www.drsimonegold.com/book/resources.

35 I experienced a prosecutor trying to frame me for perjury before. As previously noted, that testimony is in Appendix 9, https://www.drsimonegold.com/book/resources.

36 John Strand [@JohnStrandUSA], THEY PUT ME IN PRISON FOR 32 MONTHS . . . FOR THIS?!? (video attached), X, June 2, 2023, https://x.com/JohnStrandUSA/status/1664660656899907585?s=20.

37 "Cal. Code Regs. Tit. 16, §1360 - Substantial Relationship Criteria," Cornell Law School: Legal Information Institute, accessed July 2, 2024, https://www.law.cornell.edu/regulations/california/16-CCR-1360#:~:text=(a)%20For%20the%20purposes%20of,holding%20a%20license%20if%20to.

38 *Bryce v. Board of Medical Quality Assurance* (1986), p. 1476.

39 Appendix 9, https://www.drsimonegold.com/book/resources.

40 John Strand [@JohnStrandUSA], THEY PUT ME IN PRISON FOR 32 MONTHS . . . FOR THIS?!? (video attached), X, June 2, 2023, https://x.com/JohnStrandUSA/status/1664660656899907585?s=20.

41 "Twenty-Eight Teachings from Rabbi Schneur Zalman of Liadi," Chabad.org (website, accessed July 2, 2024), https://www.chabad.org/library/article_cdo/aid/3074/jewish/28-Teachings.htm.

42 Goldcare Health and Wellness (website, accessed July 2, 2024), https://www.goldcare.com/. This is the freedom solution for all people who want access to physicians who follow their Hippocratic Oath.

43 Allison Royal, "Dr. Simone Gold tells all before heading to prison for January 6th" (Rumble video, accessed July 2, 2024), https://rumble.com/v1daadd-dr.-simone-gold-tells-all-before-heading-to-prison-for-january-6th.html.

44 I urge everyone to watch this four-minute video explaining what Americans are enduring. Brandon Straka [@BrandonStraka], *The True Stories of January 6th (Parts 1 and 2)* . . . (video attached), X, March 8, 2023, https://x.com/BrandonStraka/status/1633584414293630976.

Chapter 12

1 "29 CFR §2200.68 – Recusal of the Judge," Cornell Law School: Legal Information Institute, accessed July 3, 2024, https://www.law.cornell.edu/cfr/text/29/2200.68.

2 "Code of Conduct for United States Judges," United States Courts, accessed July 3, 2024, https://www.uscourts.gov/judges-judgeships/code-conduct-united-states-judges.

3 Ibid.

4 "Washington, D.C. presidential results," *Politico*, January 6, 2021, https://www.politico.com/2020-election/results/washington-dc/.

5 Amy Jeffress and Alyssa T. Gerstner, "Garland Vows to Make Domestic Terrorism a Top Priority but Is More Cautious About Promoting Statutory Changes," Arnold & Porter (online article, March 4, 2021), https://www.arnoldporter.com/en/perspectives/blogs/enforcement-edge/2021/03/garland-to-make-domestic-terrorism-top-priority.

6 Dr. Rich Swier, "Judge in Case of Anti-Trump Clinton Lawyer Who Fabricated Russia Hoax Is Married to Attorney for Ex-FBI lawyer Lisa Page (Who Was Having Affair With Deputy Director Andrew McCabe)," Dr. Rich Swier, September 27, 2021, https://drrichswier.com/2021/09/27/judge-in-case-of-anti-trump-clinton-lawyer-who-fabricated-russia-hoax-is-married-to-attorney-for-ex-fbi-lawyer-lisa-page-who-was-having-affair-with-deputy-director-andrew-mccabe/.

7 Ibid.

8 Chuck Ross, "'We Can't Take That Risk'—FBI Officials Discussed 'Insurance Policy' Against Trump Presidency," *Daily Caller*, December 13, 2017, https://dailycaller.com/2017/12/13/fbi-officials-discussed-insurance-policy-against-trump-presidency/.

9 Lisa Page [@NatSecLisa], *National security and tech lawyer. Former federal prosecutor. Not always lovely. Views my own,* (picture attached), X, profile accessed July 3, 2024, https://x.com/NatSecLisa.

10 "REMINDER: Judge in Sussmann Trial is Married to Lisa Page's Lawyer," The Conservative Treehouse, May 13, 2022, https://theconservativetreehouse.com/blog/2022/05/13/reminder-judge-in-sussmann-trial-is-married-to-lisa-pages-lawyer/.

11 To learn more about this case, see Dr. Rich Swier, "Judge in Case of Anti-Trump Clinton Lawyer Who Fabricated Russia Hoax Is Married to Attorney for Ex-FBI lawyer Lisa Page (Who Was Having Affair With Deputy Director Andrew McCabe)," Dr. Rich Swier, September 27, 2021,https://drrichswier.com/2021/09/27/judge-in-case-of-anti-trump-clinton-lawyer-who-fabricated-russia-hoax-is-married-to-attorney-for-ex-fbi-lawyer-lisa-page-who-was-having-affair-with-deputy-director-andrew-mccabe/; David Bossie, "Does the judge in the Sussmann case have a conflict of interest?" *The Washington Times*, March 27, 2022, https://www.washingtontimes.com/news/2022/mar/27/does-the-judge-in-the-sussmann-case-have-a-conflic/.

12 Benny Johnson [@bennyjohnson], *TURLEY: "I mean, he is facing a jury that has three Clinton donors, an AOC donor, and a woman whose daughter is on the same sports team with Sussmann's daughter. With the exception of randomly selecting people out of the DNC headquarters, you could not come up with a worse jury"* (video attached), X, May 26, 2022, https://x.com/bennyjohnson/status/1529958022822432773.

13 Elizabeth Stauffer, "Was the Trial Rigged from the Start? Sussmann Jury, Judge Accused of Having Conflicts of Interest," *The Western Journal*, June 1, 2022, https://www.westernjournal.com/trial-rigged-start-sussmann-jury-judge-accused-conflicts-interest/.

14 See footnote 11. https://www.foxnews.com/us/judge-sussman-case-recusal-wife-lisa-page-lucas.

15 Fred Lucas, "Will judge in Sussmann case consider recusal after wife represented Lisa Page?," *Fox News Channel*, September 23, 2021, https://www.foxnews.com/us/judge-sussman-case-recusal-wife-lisa-page-lucas.

16 "Code of Conduct for United States Judges," United States Courts, accessed July 3, 2024, https://www.uscourts.gov/judges-judgeships/code-conduct-united-states-judges.

17 Zoe Tillman, "Five Protesters Who Disrupted The Supreme Court Will Spend A Few Days in Jail," *BuzzFeed News*, July 24, 2017, https://www.buzzfeednews.com/article/zoetillman/five-protesters-who-disrupted-the-supreme-court-are-going.

18 *Citizens United v. Federal Election Commission*, 558 U.S. 310 (2010), https://supreme.justia.com/cases/federal/us/558/310/.

19 99Rise is a progressive social movement founded by socialist Kai Newkirk. In the words of Occupy San Francisco, 99Rise "was born . . . in the "wake of . . . Occupy," a communist, Marxist aligned movement. For more information on this movement, see "The 10 Principles of 99Rise" (website archive accessed July 5, 2024), https://web.archive.org/web/20180526225715/http://www.99rise.org/our_principles; Kai Newkirk and Rev. Stephen A. Green, "Why Kingian democratic socialism is the best path forward for the progressive left," *Nation*

of Change, (online article, April 5, 2021), https://www.nationofchange.org/2021/04/05/why-kingian-democratic-socialism-is-the-best-path-forward-for-the-progressive-left/; 99Rise, "Democracy Spring 2017" (website article, July 20, 2017), https://occupysf.net/index.php/democracy-spring-2/; William F. Jasper, "Occupy Wall Street: Meet the Professors Behind It," *New American*, November 30, 2011, https://thenewamerican.com/us/politics/occupy-wall-street-meet-the-professors-behind-it/

20 Zoe Tillman, "Five Protesters Who Disrupted The Supreme Court Will Spend A Few Days in Jail," *BuzzFeed News*, July 24, 2017, https://www.buzzfeednews.com/article/zoetillman/five-protesters-who-disrupted-the-supreme-court-are-going.

21 Ibid.

22 https://www.politico.com/news/2022/07/26/benghazi-22-year-sentence-appeal-00047954.

23 Kelly Hooper and Josh Gerstein, "Appeals court rules Benghazi plotter's 22-year sentence isn't enough," *Politico*, July 26, 2022, https://www.politico.com/news/2022/07/26/benghazi-22-year-sentence-appeal-00047954.

24 Christopher R. Cooper to Hon. Patrick J. Leahy (Letter, January 6, 2014), https://www.judiciary.senate.gov/imo/media/doc/Christopher-Cooper-Senate-Questionnaire-Final.pdf.

25 Eliyahu Tulshinski, "Breaking: Judge who handed Dr. Gold harsh prison sentence propositioned her in law school," *Frontline News*, July 28, 2022, https://frontline.news/post/breaking-judge-who-handed-dr-gold-harsh-prison-sentence-propositioned-her-in-law-school.

26 Cleveland Clinic, "What is Gaslighting?" July 8, 2022, https://health.clevelandclinic.org/gaslighting. Gaslighting gets its name from the 1938 British play *Gas Light* and its 1944 film adaptation *Gaslight*. Both focus on an abusive husband and his efforts to convince his wife she's lost her mind.

27 Ryan J. Reilly, "Jan. 6 Defendant Who Said She's 'Definitely Not Going To Jail' Sentenced to Prison," *The Huffington Post*, November 5, 2021, https://www.huffpost.com/entry/jenna-ryan-sentenced-capitol-attack-trump_n_6182bb4fe4b0c8666bd6f913?wmi.

28 Patrick Lakamp, "Judge sentences Amherst woman to probation for her role in Capitol riot," *Buffalo News*, February 24, 2022 (archived article, retrieved from WayBackMachine), https://web.archive.org/web/20220624103239/https://buffalonews.com/news/local/judge-sentences-amherst-woman-to-probation-for-her-role-in-capitol-riot/article_b4ba3906-9591-11ec-aeb4-ffd80f22e739.html.

29 Eliyahu Tulshinski, "Judge in Dr Gold case applauded anti-free speech socialists disrupting SCOTUS," *Frontline News*, June 22, 2022, https://frontline.news/post/judge-in-dr-gold-case-applauded-anti-free-speech-socialists-disrupting-scotus.

30 Kipp Jones, "Judge Rips Former City Councilor During Sentencing For Jan. 6 Actions: 'Too Old' For 'Nonsense Like This'," *Media-Ite*, June 14, 2022, https://www.mediaite.com/politics/judge-rips-former-city-councilor-during-sentencing-for-jan-6-actions-too-old-for-nonsense-like-this/.

31 Ibid.

32 Ibid.

33 Ibid. Also see embedded link in quote: United States Attorney Office, District of Columbia, "Texas Man Sentenced to 21 Days in Prison on Federal Charge Stemming from Disturbance at U.S. Supreme Court" (press release, December 10, 2015), https://www.justice.gov/usao-dc/pr/texas-man-sentenced-21-days-prison-federal-charge-stemming-disturbance-us-supreme-court.

34 Spencer S. Hsu, "Anti-vaccine doctor sentenced to prison for Jan. 6 trespassing," *The Washington Post*, January 16, 2022, https://www.washingtonpost.com/national-security/2022/06/16/simone-gold-sentenced/.

35 I am not claiming to have had a permit to be *inside* the Capitol. I am saying that I was an invited guest speaker with a permit, who was inexplicably canceled, which led to my last-minute and unplanned presence in the Capitol (See Chapter 2).

36 It's nearly impossible for me to write the honorific "Judge" as Casey Cooper does not have a judicial temperament or intellect. In fairness though, it is clear that he is not even close to being the worst of the District of Columbia judges. But that is not high praise. Most of the J6 judges have been downright despicable, displaying shocking bias and often hatred.

37 Warner Todd Huston, "Fact-Check: Biden Falsely Claims 5 Cops Were Killed by Trump Supporters on Jan. 6," *The Western Journal*, March 3, 2022, https://www.westernjournal.com/fact-check-biden-falsely-claims-5-cops-killed-trump-supporters-jan-6/. In addition, see articles linked to the article quote: Andy Nguyen, "No, Joe Biden never said 'dozens of police were killed' during the U.S. Capitol attack," *PolitiFact*, January 19, 2022, https://www.politifact.com/factchecks/2022/jan/19/facebook-posts/no-joe-biden-never-said-dozens-police-were-killed-/; Grant Atkinson, "Biden Falsely Claims 'Criminal' Trump Supporters Killed Cop Brian Sicknick During Jan. 6 Unrest," *The Western Journal*, June 16, 2021, https://www.westernjournal.com/biden-falsely-claims-criminal-trump-supporters-killed-cop-brian-sicknick-jan-6-unrest/.

38 Cara Castronuova, "BREAKING EXCLUSIVE: Jan. 6 Committee Hearing Liars EDITED OUT FOOTAGE Last Night of Ashli Babbitt and Rosanne Boyland's Death from FROM KEY WITNESS TESTIMONY! See LEAKED VIDEO HERE!!" *The Gateway Pundit*, June 10, 2024, https://www.thegatewaypundit.com/2022/06/breaking-exclusive-jan-6-committee-liars-edited-footage-ashli-babbitt-rosanne-boylands-death-key-witness-testimony-footage/.

39 Jack Cashill, *ASHLI: The Untold Story of the Women of January 6* (Bombardier Books, May 14, 2024).

40 Zoe Tillman, "Five Protesters Who Disrupted The Supreme Court Will Spend A Few Days in Jail," *BuzzFeed News*, July 24, 2017, https://www.buzzfeednews.com/article/zoetillman/five-protesters-who-disrupted-the-supreme-court-are-going.

41 Hannah Rabinowitz, "Doctor known for spreading Covid misinformation is sentenced to prison for role in US Capitol attack," CNN, June 16, 2022, https://edition.cnn.com/2022/06/16/politics/simone-gold-january-6-covid-us-capitol/index.html.

42 Spencer S. Hsu, "Anti-vaccine doctor sentenced to prison for Jan. 6 trespassing," *The Washington Post*, January 16, 2022, https://www.washingtonpost.com/national-security/2022/06/16/simone-gold-sentenced/.

43 "Kai Newkirk," Netroots Nation (website, accessed July 5, 2024), https://www.netrootsnation.org/profile/kai-newkirk./

44 Kai Newkirk and Rev. Stephen A. Green, "Why Kingian democratic socialism is the best path forward for the progressive left," *Nation of Change* (online article, April 5, 2021), https://www.nationofchange.org/2021/04/05/why-kingian-democratic-socialism-is-the-best-path-forward-for-the-progressive-left/.

45 See, for example: John Strand [@JohnStrandUSA], THEY PUT ME IN PRISON FOR 32 MONTHS … FOR THIS?!? (video attached), X, June 2, 2023, https://x.com/JohnStrandUSA/status/1664660656899907585?s=20.

46 Bridge Initiative Team, "FACTSHEET: LEGAL CHALLENGES TO GUANTÁNAMO BAY DETENTION CAMP" The Bridge Initiative, June 19, 2020, https://bridge.georgetown.edu/research/factsheet-legal-challenges-to-guantanamo-bay-detention-camp/.

47 *The Washington Times* Opinion [@WashTimesOpEd], *The fact that these tapes have not been released, I think, is just a huge blot on the Department of Justice. It's just outrageous to the American justice system that they're not being required to make the videos available." - @replouiegohmert* (article attached), August 3, 2022, X, https://x.com/WashTimesOpEd/status/1554921310794416128.

48 Associated Press, "Mike Johnson to publicly release 44,000 hours of sensitive January 6 footage," *The Guardian*, November 17, 2023, https://www.theguardian.com/us-news/2023/nov/17/mike-johnson-january-6-video-footage.

49 Lauren Moye, "Republicans demand release of illegally withheld Jan. 6 surveillance," *FISM News*, August 9, 2022, https://fism.tv/republicans-demand-release-of-illegally-withheld-jan-6-surveillance-footage/.

50 Attorney Sidney Powell's book, *License to Lie* (https://www.licensedtolie.com) provides many detailed examples of the DOJ lying to the public. See also Chapter 8.

51 Appendix 11, https://www.drsimonegold.com/book/resources.

52 Marisa Sarnoff, "Judge Sends Jan. 6 Rioter and 'America's Frontline Doctors' Founder to Jail," *Law and Crime*, June 16, 2022, https://lawandcrime.com/u-s-capitol-breach/judge-sends-jan-6-rioter-and-americas-frontline-doctors-founder-to-jail/.

53 Mitch Rylals, "More Than Two-Thirds of the People Arrested in D.C. Are Never Charged," *Washington City Paper*, March 15, 2023, https://washingtoncitypaper.com/article/595163/more-than-two-thirds-of-the-people-arrested-in-d-c-are-never-charged/.

54 Katie Daviscourt, "Rioter who punched female Capitol Police officer during 'ceasefire' protest at DNC sentenced to 48 hours community service: report," *The Post Millennial*, May 19, 2024, https://thepostmillennial.com/rioter-who-punched-female-capitol-police-officer-during-ceasefire-protest-at-dnc-sentenced-to-48-hours-community-service-report.

55 Currently, you can input your name and be alerted when the book is available for purchase. JohnStrand.com.
56 Appendix 12, https://www.drsimonegold.com/book/resources.
57 Eliyahu Tulshinski, "Feds coerce Jan 6 defendants into waiving right to appeal jail time," *Frontline News*, June 30, 2022, https://frontline.news/post/feds-coerce-jan-6-defendants-to-waive-right-to-appeal-jail-time.
58 Jonathan Turley, "Antifa Member Who Took Axe to Senate Office Given Probation and his Axe Back," Jonathanturley.org (online article, November 26, 2021), https://jonathanturley.org/2021/11/26/antifa-member-who-took-axe-to-senate-office-given-probation-and-his-axe-back/comment-page-2/.
59 Eliyahu Tulshinski, "Politicizing medicine: FBI/DOJ/Court jail Dr Simone Gold for trespass," *Frontline News*, June 16, 2022, https://frontline.news/post/fbidojcourt-jail-dr-simone-gold-for-trespass-politicizing-medicine.
60 "Ohio man who assaulted flight attendants gets 60-day prison sentence," Reuters, May 4, 2022, https://www.reuters.com/world/us/ohio-man-who-assaulted-flight-attendants-gets-60-day-prison-sentence-2022-05-04/.
61 Midwest Safety, "Here's Why You Don't Punch a Cop" (YouTube video, April 20, 2024), https://www.youtube.com/watch?v=5FMtL7saNKE.
62 (Repeat from Chapter 6) If allowed to progress, segregating persons (whether the segregation is black and white, gay and straight, vaxxed and unvaxxed) inevitably leads to killing the disenfranchised group. The Ten Stages of Genocide starts with classification, a division of "us" and "them"; is followed by discrimination denying civil rights to certain groups; proceeds to dehumanization by treating others without personal dignity; leading to polarization by spreading propaganda; which leads to persecution including segregation, and worse. See "The Ten Stages of Genocide," *Holocaust Memorial Day Trust*, (website, accessed June 12, 2024), https://www.hmd.org.uk/learn-about-the-holocaust-and-genocides/what-is-genocide/the-ten-stages-of-genocide/.
63 Joseph M. Hanneman, "Judge Ordered Jan. 6 Defendant's Computer Monitored for 'Disinformation'—Appeals Court Overturns," *The Epoch Times*, April 6, 2024 (updated April 7, 2024), https://archive.ph/eH45H.
64 Julie Kelly [@julie_kelly2], (three smiley faces + text image attached), X, https://x.com/julie_kelly2/status/1801319228152369582.

Chapter 13

1 Federal Bureau of Prisons: FDC Miami (website, accessed July 6, 2024), https://www.bop.gov/locations/institutions/mim/.
2 U.S. Department of Justice: Federal Bureau of Prisons, "Inmate Security Designation and Custody Classification" (online document, September 4, 2019), https://www.bop.gov/policy/progstat/5100_008cn.pdf.
3 Eliyahu Tulshinski, "Deep State jails Dr Gold with violent felons; moves Ghislaine Maxwell to 'Club Fed,'" *Frontline News*, July 27, 2022, https://americasfrontlinenews.com/post/deep-state-jails-dr-gold-with-violent-felons-moves-ghislaine-maxwell-to-club-fed.

4 For readers who wish to know more about this remarkable man of faith and his story, read Genesis 37-50. "What you intended for evil, God intended for good," when he encounters his brothers later in the story (once he's been exalted to second in command over all of Egypt).

5 Dr. Simone Gold [@drsimonegold], *You may have heard they put me in prison to silence me. You may have heard sordid attacks on my credibility & integrity. But I am here because I spoke the truth, and I am still standing on truth. The lies WILL be exposed. Don't be fooled by propaganda. Stand with me* (video attached), X, November 12, 2022, https://x.com/drsimonegold/status/1591476721995640833.

6 Mr. Beast, "$10,000 Every Day You Survive In A Grocery Store" (YouTube video, December 2, 2023), https://www.youtube.com/watch?v=tnTPaLOaHz8.

7 The Correctional Leaders Association & The Arthur Liman Center for Public Interest Law at Yale Law School, "Time-in-Cell: A 2021 Snapshot of Restrictive Housing: Based on a Nationwide Survey of U.S. Prison Systems," August 2022, https://law.yale.edu/sites/default/files/area/center/liman/document/time_in_cell_2021.pdf.

8 Editorial board, "Solitary confinement is torture. U.S. prisons should stop using it," *The Washington Post*, September 6, 2022, https://www.washingtonpost.com/opinions/2022/09/06/solitary-confinement-torture-prison/.

9 National Religious Campaign Against Torture (website, accessed July 6, 2024), https://www.nrcat.org/.

10 Erik Ortiz, "Biden pledged to end solitary confinement. Federal prisons are increasing its use," *NBC News*, September 30, 2022, https://www.nbcnews.com/politics/justice-department/biden-pledged-end-solitary-confinement-federal-prisons-are-increasing-rcna49980.

11 To learn more, see "Anti-Kickback Statute and Stark Law" (online article, accessed July 6, 2024), https://constantinecannon.com/practice/whistleblower/whistleblower-types/healthcare-fraud/anti-kickback-stark/.

12 The Anti-Kickback Statute, 42 U.S.C. §1320a-7b(b), https://www.govinfo.gov/content/pkg/USCODE-2010-title42/html/USCODE-2010-title42-chap7-subchapXI-partA-sec1320a-7b.htm.

13 Paul Rosenzweig, "Ignorance of the Law Is No Excuse, But It Is Reality," The Heritage Foundation, June 17, 2013, https://www.heritage.org/crime-and-justice/report/ignorance-the-law-no-excuse-it-reality.

14 Harvey A. Silverglate, *Three Felonies a Day: How the Feds Target the Innocent* (Encounter Books, 2011).

15 Ibid.

16 Keith Griffith, "'I thought this was a free country': Canadian woman slams cop for hounding her at home when she posted on Facebook that she might attend Freedom Convoy protest," DailyMail.com, February 16, 2022, https://www.dailymail.co.uk/news/article-10520533/Canadian-woman-slams-cop-hounding-home-Facebook-post.html.

17 Brandon Showalter, "Police Interrogate Stay-at-Home Mom for Tweets Critical of Teen's Sex Change Surgery," *The Christian Post*, March 13, 2018, https:

//www.christianpost.com/news/police-interrogate-stay-at-home-mom-for-tweets-critical-of-teens-sex-change-surgery.html.

18 Rachel del Guidice, "Police Question UK Journalist for 'Misgendering' a Transgender Woman," *The Daily Signal*, March 19, 2019, https://www.dailysignal.com/2019/03/19/police-question-uk-journalist-for-misgendering-a-transgender-woman/.

19 Eliyahu Tulshinski, "FBI—No time to interview rape victims; plenty for Jan 6 trespass," *Frontline News*, June 12, 2022, https://frontline.news/post/fbi-no-time-to-interview-rape-victims-plenty-for-jan-6-trespass.

20 House Judiciary GOP [@JudiciaryGOP], *#BREAKING: New whistleblower information reveals that the FBI is moving agents off of child sexual abuse investigations to instead pursue political investigations. The whistleblower recounted being told that "child sexual abuse investigations were no longer an FBI priority"* (image attached), X, September 19, 2022, https://x.com/JudiciaryGOP/status/1572020677087236096.

21 Jim Hoft, "Whistleblower Identified: FBI Special Agent Steve Friend Goes Public—Exposed Disgusting FBI Lies and Unprecedented Attacks on Conservative Americans—ARREST CHRIS WRAY! (VIDEO)," *The Gateway Pundit*, September 21, 2022, https://www.thegatewaypundit.com/2022/09/whistleblower-identified-fbi-special-agent-steve-friend-goes-public-exposed-disgusting-fbi-lies-unprecedented-attacks-conservative-americans-jail-chris-wray-video/.

Chapter 14

1 We grew up thinking a person is "innocent until proven guilty" in America. Those days are over. In Chapter 8, I show how prosecutors virtually always win based on allegations alone. I use the example of a wife and husband, because it is a classic example where the prosecution (lazily) does not prove the wife actually knew, but the mere allegation becomes the proof, and the jury will only acquit if the wife proves her innocence. Although this is *not* the way our system is supposed to work, this is actually how it *does* work, for now. The presumption of innocence must be restored.

2 There are times a person *can* be legally criminally charged and punished twice for the same crime in the US. For example, one crime can be punished by both the state and federal government. But in general, it is not common.

3 Michele Dargan, "For Palm Beach sex offender Jeffrey Epstein, house arrest in home stretch," *Palm Beach Daily News*, April 1, 2012, https://www.palmbeachdailynews.com/story/news/2012/04/01/for-palm-beach-sex-offender/9659806007/.

4 Jane Musgrave, "Billionaire sex offender Jeffrey Epstein's year-long probation to end next week," *The Palm Beach Post*, April 1, 2012, https://www.palmbeachpost.com/story/news/2012/04/01/billionaire-sex-offender-jeffrey-epstein/7684584007/.

5 Andrew Kwan, "Judicial Profile: Hon. Kennet A. Mara, Senor U.S. District Judge, South District of Florida," *The Federal Lawyer*, July/August 2021, https://www.fedbar.org/wp-content/uploads/2021/08/JudicialProfile_Marra_TFL_July-Aug20216.pdf.

6 In West Palm Beach in 2010, Epstein was sentenced to thirteen months in a county jail and was granted an exception to "work" six days/week including the right to keep flying all over the country on his private plane. It is estimated that Epstein trafficked more than five hundred girls over the years, many of them minors.

7 Chabad.org, "Prison and Reform: A Torah View."

8 Ashley Nellis, PhD, and Liz Komar, "The First Step Act: Ending Mass Incarceration in Federal Prisons," The Sentencing Project, August 22, 2023, https://www.sentencingproject.org/policy-brief/the-first-step-act-ending-mass-incarceration-in-federal-prisons/.

9 To learn more, see Walter Pavlo, "Tzedek Association Worked The Halls Of Congress To Push First Step Act Into Law," *Forbes*, December 21, 2022, https://www.forbes.com/sites/walterpavlo/2022/12/21/tzedek-association-worked-the-halls-of-congress-to-push-first-step-act-into-law/ and this document from the Aleph Insitutue: https://aleph-institute.org/wp-content/uploads/2023/12/Aleph_AnnualReport-2023-low-2.pdf.

Chapter 15

1 https://scholarship.law.vanderbilt.edu/cgi/viewcontent.cgi?article=1686&context=vlr footnote 7, 148 CONG. REC. H5464 (daily ed. July 25, 2002) (statement of Representative Sensenbrenner).

2 Law-abiding citizens instinctively cringe from hearing of such a charge. We all must learn to resist the instinct to automatically think negatively about any charge against any J6 defendant. The overcharge "assaulting a police officer" has been used against many J6 defendants for actions that would *never* have been charged thusly on any other day/location. In my own case, during the plea deal process, our federal government very aggressively threatened to charge ***me*** with this!

3 Appendix 16. See the Congressional Record from July 10, 2002 debating §1512(c)(2), *Statement by the President (Text Only)* and Vanderbilt Law Review page 1432.

4 *Statement by the President (Text Only)* (ibid).

5 Kalhan Rosenblatt, "Protesters pound the doors of the Supreme Court following Kavanaugh confirmation," NBC News, October 6, 2018, https://www.nbcnews.com/politics/supreme-court/protests-build-capitol-hill-ahead-brett-kavanaugh-vote-n917351.

6 Paul Kane and Ed O'Keefe, "Republicans vote to rebuke Elizabeth Warren, saying she impugned Sessions's character," *Washington Post*, February 8, 2017, https://www.washingtonpost.com/news/powerpost/wp/2017/02/07/republicans-vote-to-rebuke-elizabeth-warren-for-impugning-sessionss-character/.

7 Associated Press, "Government drops charges against all inauguration protesters," NBC News, 2025, https://www.nbcnews.com/news/us-news/government-drops-charges-against-all-inauguration-protesters-n889531.

8 Michael Balsamo, "No charges for 'Late Show' crew arrested on Capitol Hill," AP News, July 19, 2022, https://apnews.com/article/entertainment-arrests-stephen-colbert-government-and-politics-84ebcc654735f619655d264944da0227.
9 Justin Papp, "House censures Rep. Jamaal Bowman for pulling fire alarm," *Roll Call*, December 7, 2023, https://rollcall.com/2023/12/07/house-censures-rep-jamaal-bowman-for-pulling-fire-alarm/#:~:text=Bowman%20has%20maintained%20the%20alarm,to%20further%20investigate%20the%20incident.
10 https://www.cadc.uscourts.gov/internet/opinions.nsf/F435A13F03207AF28525898A004F9D45/$file/22-3038-1993753.pdf.
11 Daniel A. Shtob, Corruption of a Term: The Problematic Nature of 18 U.S.C. §1512(c), the New Federal Obstruction of Justice Provision, 57 *Vanderbilt Law Review* 1429 (2019), https://scholarship.law.vanderbilt.edu/cgi/viewcontent.cgi?article=1686&context=vlr page 1432.
12 *Statement by the President (Text Only).*
13 https://drgold.vercel.app/book/resources/.
14 https://x.com/pnjaban/status/1784043529591030160.
15 https://www.supremecourt.gov/opinions/23pdf/23-5572_l6hn.pdf.
16 https://www.supremecourt.gov/opinions/23pdf/22-451_7m58.pdf.
17 Alex Swoyer and Stephen Dinan, "D.C.'s new U.S. attorney launches review of Jan. 6 obstruction charge shot down by Supreme Court," *Washington Times*, January 27, 2025, https://www.washingtontimes.com/news/2025/jan/27/edward-martin-launches-review-jan-6-obstruction-ch/.

Chapter 16

1 The Constitution is 4,500 words, about ten pages. The original Bill of Rights is about 10% of that length.
2 Joseph M. Hanneman, "After a Pause, Jan. 6 Arrests Are Now Sharply Increasing," *The Epoch Times*, March 06, 2024, https://www.theepochtimes.com/article/after-a-pause-doj-is-now-sharply-increasing-jan-6-arrests-5600972.
3 https://en.wikipedia.org/wiki/WWE.
4 Eliyahu Tulshinski, German Origins of Militarized Public Health, Frontline News, May 2, 2022, https://frontline.news/post/german-origins-of-militarized-public-health-service.
5 Ibid.
6 Maura Kelly, "Voting is good for your health. These doctors want to help," *Harvard Public Health,* October 9, 2024, https://harvardpublichealth.org/policy-practice/vot-er-helps-patients-register-to-vote-for-better-health/.
7 WhoControlsWho.com.
8 https://x.com/DrSyedHaider/status/1831229436278063424.
9 The latest ICD-10-CM guidelines contain code Z28. 310 "(Voluntary as opposed to medical reason) unvaccinated for COVID-19," when the patient has *chosen* not to receive a dose of any COVID-19 vaccine. https://www.aafp.org/pubs/fpm/blogs/gettingpaid/entry/covid_immunization_codes.html

#:~:text=According%20to%20ICD%2D10%2DCM,of%20any%20COVID%2D19%20vaccine.

Afterword

1 https://thejacksonlist.com/2024/04/01/the-federal-prosecutor-1940/

About the Author

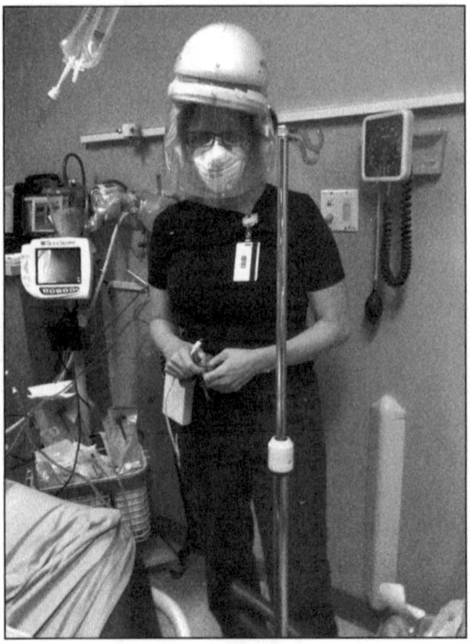

Dr. Gold preparing to intubate a
COVID-19 patient, May 2020.

In the early days of COVID, on July 27, 2020, Dr. Simone Gold organized doctors and social media influencers to hold a White Coat Summit in Washington, DC. This was an entire day of physicians combating the propaganda of masks, lockdowns, school closures, early treatment, and fear mongering. In the middle of the day, the doctors held a press conference in front of the Supreme Court, which reached twenty million views in just eight hours, becoming the most rapidly viral video of all time. They were on track to have one hundred million views by the next morning—but all Big Tech coordinated to simultaneously deplatform them.

Instantly, Dr. Gold became famous—or infamous depending on your perspective. Suddenly, this board-certified emergency physician and attorney was fired from her job. She pivoted to speaking the truth about the government's deadly COVID policies and appeared frequently on news and social media. On January 5, 2021, she was invited to speak on medical freedom at Freedom Plaza in Washington, DC, and on January 6, 2021, she was among twenty scheduled speakers who were granted a permit to speak on the Capitol grounds. That is where this story begins.

Selective Persecution: The Legalization of American Fascism explains how the infrastructure of fascism has already taken hold in the United States. Weaving a narrative from her personal experience as a COVID whistleblower and her forty-eight minutes around and inside the US Capitol Building on January 6, Dr. Gold walks readers through the array of COVID lies and corruption, the course of January 6 itself, her arrest, and her prison experience and that of other women in prison. She endured a militarized FBI SWAT team arrest, was victimized by the Department of Justice and the Federal Bureau of Prisons, and witnessed massive corruption of the judiciary. She was persecuted by the California Medical Board, the New York Bar, Congress, TSA, and FBI, and defamed by the press.

Selective Persecution is Dr. Gold's chilling story about how a weaponized federal government can be turned against any citizen. This is Dr. Gold's third book. Her first, *I Do Not Consent: My Fight Against Medical Cancel Culture*, describes how her work as an emergency physician led to her organizing frontline doctors to be the first physicians to stand against government and media propaganda. Her second, *The Plot Against the Kids*, is a children's book that explains the flawed COVID policies to children and adults.

Because the inviolate trust between doctor and patient was broken, and because the legacy healthcare system is unsalvageable, Dr. Gold launched GoldCare.com, the medical freedom platform that returns control to the individual and restores trust to the doctor-patient relationship. This platform provides complete access to the full spectrum of allopathic and naturopathic care, along with world-class education and early treatment access. GoldCare also hosts monthly medical townhalls for the general public.

During COVID, Dr. Gold fled the tyranny of California for the free state of Florida with her partner in crime, John Strand, who tells his half of the story in Patriot Plea. She has two magnificent sons, who have also endured persecution as a result of COVID policies and a weaponized government.

Index

P

R

S

T